Elegant Glassware
of the
Depression Era

IDENTIFICATION AND VALUE GUIDE

TENTH EDITION

Gene Florence

Cambridge
Fostoria
Heisey
& Others

COLLECTOR BOOKS
A Division of Schroeder Publishing Co., Inc.

On the front cover: Rosepoint cream soup and liner, $225.00; Caprice 7½" vase #346, $295.00; Deerwood iced tea, $55.00; Dancing Nymph 8" bowl, $275.00.
On the back cover: Trojan (Fostoria), see pages 214 – 215.

Cover design by Beth Summers
Book design by Beth Ray

COLLECTOR BOOKS
P.O. Box 3009
Paducah, Kentucky 42002-3009

www.collectorbooks.com

Gene Florence

P.O. Box 22186   P.O. Box 64
Lexington, KY 40522   Astutula, FL 34705

Copyright © 2003 Gene Florence

The current values in this book should be used only as a guide. They are not intended to set prices, which vary from one section of the country to another. Auction prices as well as dealer prices vary greatly and are affected by condition as well as demand. Neither the author nor the publisher assumes responsibility for any losses that might be incurred as a result of consulting this guide.

Searching For A Publisher?

We are always looking for people knowledgeable within their fields. If you feel that there is a real need for a book on your collectible subject and have a large comprehensive collection, contact Collector Books.

ABOUT THE AUTHOR

Gene M. Florence, Jr., a native Kentuckian, graduated from the University of Kentucky in 1967. He held a double major in mathematics and English that he immediately put to use in industry and subsequently, in teaching junior and senior high school. He taught one year at the Lincoln Institute for gifted, but disadvantaged, students — a wonderful teaching experience, but a 160 mile daily commute!

A collector since childhood, Mr. Florence progressed from baseball cards, comic books, coins, and bottles to glassware. His buying and selling glassware "hobby" began to override his nine-year teaching career. During a teaching hiatus in the summer of 1972, he wrote a book on Depression glassware that was well received by collectors in the field, persuading him to leave teaching in 1976 and pursue the antique glass business full time. This allowed time to travel to glass shows throughout the country, where he assiduously studied the prices of glass being sold... and of that remaining unsold. This change, also, permitted him to dedicate more time to research on glass, a time-consuming process.

Books written by Mr. Florence include the following titles: *The Collector's Encyclopedia of Depression Glass, Stemware Identification, The Collector's Encyclopedia of Akro Agate, The Pocket Guide to Depression Glass, Kitchen Glassware of the Depression Years, Collectible Glassware from the 40s, 50s, and 60s..., Glass Candlesticks of the Depression Era, Anchor Hocking's Fire-King and More, Glassware Pattern Identification Guide, Standard Baseball Card Price Guide*, and six editions of *Very Rare Glassware of the Depression Years*. He has also written six volumes of *The Collector's Encyclopedia of Occupied Japan* and a book on Degenhart glassware for that museum. His most recent book is *Florence's Big Book of Salt and Pepper Shakers*. Mr. Florence has now authored 70 books on collectibles.

PRICING

All prices in this book are retail for mint condition glassware. This book is intended only as a guide to prices. There continue to be regional price disparities that cannot be adequately dealt with herein.

You may expect dealers to pay approximately 30 to 60 percent less than the prices listed. My personal knowledge of prices comes from buying and selling glass for 34 years and from traveling to and selling at shows in various parts of the United States. Strangely, I am working even harder at markets and shows, today, to remain current with the ever-fluctuating prices. You can find me on the Internet at www.geneflorence.com. I readily admit that I solicit price information from persons known to be authorities in certain wares in order to provide you with the latest, most accurate pricing information. However, final pricing judgments are always mine!

MEASUREMENTS AND TERMS

All measurements and terminology in this book are from factory catalogs and advertisements or actual measurements from the piece. It has been my experience that actual measurements vary slightly from those listed in most factory catalogs; so, do not get unduly concerned over slight variations. For example, Fostoria always seems to have measured plates to the nearest inch, but I have found that most Fostoria plates are never exact inches in measurement.

PREFACE

"Elegant" glassware, as defined in this book, refers mostly to the hand-worked, acid-etched glassware that was sold by better department and jewelry stores during the Depression era through the 1950s, differentiating it from the dime store and give-away glass that is widely known as Depression glass.

The rise in collecting Elegant glassware has been incredible the past few years. Many dealers who would dare not stock that crystal glass a few years ago are buying as much or more Elegant than basic Depression glass, today. Glass shows used to display 15% to 20% Elegant glass; now, there are many shows where more than 50% of the stock is Elegant. Many collectors who have completed sets of Depression glassware have now shifted to acquiring sets of Elegant.

I hope you enjoy this book, and will feel my years of working to furnish you the best books possible on glassware were well spent.

ACKNOWLEDGMENTS

Photography sessions for this book were spread over a two-year period with one session lasting almost two weeks. We never photograph for only one book anymore. We photograph for six or seven each time. Accolades are due Dick and Pat Spencer for loaning their glass, borrowing other glassware to bring to our session, helping at the photography sessions, and lending their expertise on pricing Heisey and Duncan patterns in this book. Now that Dick has "retired," he has helped us even more in acquiring glassware. Exceptional people behind the scenes make this book what it is. Some loaned glass, some gave their time, others used their expertise and furnished information. These wonderful people have continued to be friends even after exhausting hours of packing, unpacking, arranging, sorting, and repacking glass! Some traveled hundreds of miles to bring their priceless glass to share with you. Some spent hours cussing and discussing or listing their prices, often late at night after long show hours. Without these marvelous "giving" folks, this book would not be what it is. Some of those remarkable people include Charles and Maxine Larson, Paul and Margaret Arras, Dr. Phillip Edwards, Violet Moore, Joe and Florence Solito, Geri and Dan Tucker, Lottie Porter, Quinten Keech, Barbara Adt Namon, Jane White, Beth Ray, Zibby Walker, and numerous anonymous readers from throughout the U.S. and Canada who shared pictures and information about their collections and findings. Richard Walker and Charles R. Lynch did the photography for this book. Richard and Zibby journey from New York each October. They work ten to twelve hour days for over a week helping us picture the wide range of patterns in this book. It really is an impressive task that is performed every autumn. Thanks, too, to Cathy's parents, Charles and Sibyl, who tirelessly helped sort, list, and pack glass for photography and shows! Chad, my eldest son, took time from lateral drilling to help Cathy move, load, and unload boxes of glass; Marc, my youngest son, teaching in the world of computer technology, tries to keep my web page available when you look for it at www.geneflorence.com.

Some health problems are causing us to try to readjust our lives to a less frenetic pace. This year has been rather difficult up until now. An out-patient kidney stone removal turned into a hospital stay. A wreck in January from trying to avoid someone head-on (on my side of the road) totaled my van, broke my coccyx (tail bone), tore up all kinds of cartilage in my side from the seat belt, and broke over $17,000 worth of glass. I am lucky to be here. There must be some additional purpose for me yet to complete. Recovery from that ordeal is still painful. Concentration has been difficult at best. The stress of all my problems has not helped Cathy's blood pressure. We are reducing our inventory as fast as we can through my website www.geneflorence.com and cutting back our shows. I will continue to sell books and teach seminars at shows, but I even plan to cut back on that. Over thirty years of our lives has been involved in this business and we need some time to smell the roses — or fish. I have only been fishing in my boat four times this year. That's being way too busy!

Cathy has taken on an additional position of chauffeur this year, as, for me driving has been difficult trying to sit in that one position. She has always worked extensive hours as chief editor, sounding board, research assistant, and proofreader. No one could have taken my rambling thoughts and worked them into coherent paragraphs as well as Cathy. The deadline on this book, finishing the *Pocket Guide to Depression Glass* and the third volume of *Pattern Identification* have not been conducive to the peaceful atmosphere she really needs.

With apologies, another thing I will be slowing down is answering letters. In the past, I have asked that questions be limited to patterns that I have researched in my books. I will try to continue answering requests that follow those guidelines. I will no longer even try to identify every picture of glassware sent me. In that regard, I have accurately tried to show and identify much of what I have received letters about in my three *Pattern Identification* books. You should look there first to find unknown glassware items. These *Pattern Identification* books should save you research time and writing letters. The likelihood of your having a known Depression era pattern not in one of these books will be slim. You are getting years of knowledge in these three books!

I want to say thank you to readers whose generous responses to my books have made this career possible. Know, too, that many pieces have been added to lists over the years via your efforts, and collectors as a whole have benefitted.

CONTENTS

CONTENTS BY COMPANY

Color: crystal

Alexis was an early Fostoria pattern that was ending its production run about the time that many of the patterns in this book were just beginning to be made. It is a plainer pattern that has always sold well at shows. It is not an expensive pattern to collect as many items can be bought for around $20.00; but there are difficult items that will set you back more, i.e. pitchers, water bottles, and syrups or cruets. This pressed ware is gathering momentum in the collectibles market, particularly now, that it's nearly 100 years old and a long-lived product of a major company now out of business. Too, it is one of those patterns that bridges the gap from pattern glass to Depression glass.

Besides glass shows, antique malls, and antique shows, you will find a few pieces of Alexis on Internet auctions. One of the best sources on the Internet for all glass shopping is www.glassshow.com. I recommend few sites, but this one I will.

Item	Price	Item	Price
Bowl, 4½", nappy	12.50	Salt, table, flat	15.00
Bowl, 5", nappy	15.00	Spooner	30.00
Bowl, 7", nappy	20.00	Stem, claret, 5 oz.	15.00
Bowl, 8", nappy	22.50	Stem, cocktail, 3 oz.	12.50
Bowl, 9", nappy	25.00	Stem, cordial, 1 oz.	15.00
Bowl, crushed ice	25.00	Stem, crème de menthe, 2½ oz.	15.00
Bowl, finger (flat edge)	15.00	Stem, egg cup	12.50
Butter dish w/cover	75.00	Stem, ice cream, high foot	15.00
Catsup bottle	65.00	Stem, pousse café, ¾ oz.	15.00
Celery, tall	32.50	Stem, sherbet, high	15.00
Comport, 4½" high	22.50	Stem, sherbet, low	12.50
Cream, short, hotel	25.00	Stem, water, 10 oz.	15.00
Cream, tall	22.50	Stem, wine, 2 oz.	20.00
Cup, hdld. custard	10.00	Stem, wine, 3 oz.	20.00
Decanter w/stopper	100.00	Sugar shaker	55.00
Horseradish jar w/spoon	60.00	Sugar, hdld., hotel	25.00
Molasses can ewer, drip cut	65.00	Sugar, no handles w/lid	40.00
Mustard w/slotted cover	35.00	Toothpick	30.00
Nut bowl	15.00	Tray, celery	25.00
Oil, 2 oz.	30.00	Tray, olive	20.00
Oil, 4 oz.	35.00	Tray, pickle	22.50
Oil, 6 oz.	40.00	Tumbler, ice tea	17.50
Oil, 9 oz.	45.00	Tumbler, ice tea, ftd., 10 oz.	20.00
Pitcher, 16 oz.	45.00	Tumbler, water	15.00
Pitcher, 32 oz.	75.00	Tumbler, water, ftd., 8½ oz.	20.00
Pitcher, 64 oz., ice	85.00	Tumbler, whiskey	15.00
Pitcher, 64 oz., tall	100.00	Tumbler, wine	15.00
Plate, crushed ice liner	10.00	Vase, 7", sweet pea, ftd.	50.00
Salt shaker, pr. (2 styles)	35.00	Vase, 9" ftd.	65.00
Salt, individual, flat	12.50	Vase, Nasturtium (sic)	37.50
Salt, individual, ftd.	15.00	Water bottle	85.00

Colors: crystal; some amber, blue, green, yellow, pink tinting to purple in late 1920s; white, red in 1980s; and being newly made in crystal for Lancaster Colony

American was Fostoria's most prolific pattern having been made from 1915 until Fostoria's demise in 1986. Even then, American continued to be made under the auspices of the new owner, Lancaster Colony. Many items were contracted to Viking (later Dalzell-Viking) and sold as Fostoria American by Lancaster Colony. Don't be confused by a newly designed Whitehall pattern that was created by Indiana Glass Company and is similar to American. Whitehall's quality is less than that of American and shapes and sizes are different as well. Still, novices often confuse the two patterns.

America, though adored by collectors, is beginning to be spurned by some dealers because it is, presently, a slow selling pattern due to its availability. Rarely found items still sell well if priced within reason, but many of the expensively priced items are also slowing in sales due to the economy and collectors deciding to do without every piece made. Too, the continuing manufacture of commonly found pieces by Lancaster Colony keeps adding to the supply. None of the current American or look-alike American pieces are marked in any way. American pieces that have been produced in recent years are marked with an asterisk (*) in the price listing below. A profusion of Whitehall is found in colors of pink, avocado green, and several shades of blue. The glassware section of your local discount store is a good place to peruse new colors and items recently made. Numerous specialty catalogs suggest new colored glassware to be Depression glass in an effort to enhance its value. Whitehall's pink colored ware is also frequently confused with Jeannette's Depression era Cube pattern judging by the letters I receive. There is no footed pitcher or tumbler in Cube.

Many auction advertisements announce Fostoria is being sold when they mean only American pieces. These were the "good" dishes used by Mom or Grandma. When Fostoria was no longer available in the department or jewelry stores then the secondary market (glass shows, flea markets, local antique or thrift shops) became the centers to replace broken wares. Today, an abundance of available American keeps most of the prices within the range of the average collector. Harder to find pieces are almost out of the realm of the general collector. The Internet has added to the adventure of finding American, but the risk there is that many sellers are inexperienced or unscrupulous regarding glass condition. Try to buy only from those who guarantee their merchandise.

Notice there are visible price adjustments for American items being found in England. The Internet has balanced that playing field. European antique dealers have become watchful of our glass collecting proclivities. Those formerly hard-to-find English Fostoria American pieces are now not as hard to find here, since so many have been imported! Dealers who own wash bowl and pitcher sets, for example, have been gradually setting their sights lower. Once any collectible glass item reaches a price in the four-digit area, typical collectors do without. Reissued cookie jars continue to pose a problem. A majority of the new issues have wavy lines in the pattern itself and crooked knobs on the top. Old cookie jars do not. (A telling point that works about 80% of the time is to try to turn the lid around while it rests inside the cookie jar. The new lids seem to hang up and stop somewhere along the inside making the whole cookie jar turn. The old jars will allow you to turn the lid completely around without catching on the sides.)

If you enjoy the timeless beauty American pattern exudes, then by all means purchase it. Collecting what you like has always been a major reason to do so. Little pleasures in life should be indulged when possible.

	*Crystal		*Crystal
Appetizer, tray, 10½", w/6 inserts	32.50	Bottle, cologne, w/stopper, 6 oz., 5¾"	72.50
Appetizer, insert, 3¼"	32.50	Bottle, cologne, w/stopper, 7¼", 8 oz.	80.00
Ashtray, 2⅞", sq.	7.50	Bottle, cordial, w/stopper, 7¼", 9 oz.	90.00
Ashtray, 3⅞", oval	9.00	Bottle, water, 44 oz., 9¼"	625.00
Ashtray, 5", sq.	45.00	Bowl, banana split, 9" x 3½"	550.00
Ashtray, 5½", oval	20.00	Bowl, finger, 4½" diam., smooth edge	40.00
Basket, w/reed handle, 7" x 9"	95.00	Bowl, 3½", rose	20.00
Basket, 10", new in 1988	40.00	Bowl, 3¾", almond, oval	18.00
Bell	450.00	Bowl, 4¼", jelly, 4¼" h.	15.00
Bottle, bitters, w/tube, 5¾", 4½ oz.	72.50	* Bowl, 4½", 1 hdld.	10.00
Bottle, condiment/ketchup w/stopper	145.00	Bowl, 4½", 1 hdld., sq.	11.00

*See note in second paragraph above.

	*Crystal			*Crystal
Bowl, 4½", jelly, w/cover, 6¾" h.	28.00		Bowl, 5½", lemon, w/cover	55.00
* Bowl, 4½", nappy	13.00		Bowl, 5½", preserve, 2 hdld., w/cover	100.00
Bowl, 4½", oval	15.00		Bowl, 6", bonbon, 3 ftd.	15.00
Bowl, 4¾", fruit, flared	15.00		* Bowl, 6", nappy	15.00
Bowl, 5", cream soup, 2 hdld.	45.00		Bowl, 6", olive, oblong	12.00
Bowl, 5", 1 hdld., tri-corner	12.00		Bowl, 6½", wedding,	
* Bowl, 5", nappy	10.00		w/cover, sq., ped. ft., 8" h.	110.00
Bowl, 5", nappy, w/cover	30.00		Bowl, 6½", wedding, sq., ped. ft., 5¼" h.	75.00
Bowl, 5", rose	30.00		Bowl, 7", bonbon, 3 ftd.	12.50

	*Crystal		*Crystal
Bowl, 7", cupped, 4½" h.	55.00	Candlestick, 2", chamber with finger-	
* Bowl, 7", nappy	25.00	hold	47.50
Bowl, 8", bonbon, 3 ftd.	17.50	**Candlestick, 3", rnd. ft.	15.00
Bowl, 8", deep	60.00	Candlestick, 4⅜", 2-lite, rnd. ft.	40.00
Bowl, 8", ftd.	90.00	Candlestick, 6", octagon ft.	25.00
Bowl, 8", ftd., 2 hdld., "trophy" cup	125.00	Candlestick, 6½", 2-lite, bell base	130.00
* Bowl, 8", nappy	25.00	Candlestick, 6¼", round ft.	195.00
* Bowl, 8", pickle, oblong	15.00	* Candlestick, 7", sq. column	115.00
Bowl, 8½", 2 hdld.	50.00	Candlestick, 7¼", "Eiffel" tower	150.00
* Bowl, 8½", boat	16.00	Candy box, w/cover, 3 pt., triangular	90.00
Bowl, 9", boat, 2 pt.	12.50	Candy, w/cover, ped. ft.	37.50
* Bowl, 9", oval veg.	30.00	Cheese (5¾" compote) & cracker	
Bowl, 9½", centerpiece	50.00	(11½" plate)	65.00
Bowl, 9½", 3 pt., 6" w.	37.50	Cigarette box, w/cover, 4¾"	40.00
Bowl, 10", celery, oblong	20.00	Coaster, 3¾"	9.00
* Bowl, 10", deep	35.00	Comport, 4½", jelly	15.00
Bowl, 10", float	45.00	* Comport, 5", jelly, flared	15.00
Bowl, 10", oval, float	32.50	* Comport, 6¾", jelly, w/cover	35.00
Bowl, 10", oval, veg., 2 pt.	35.00	Comport, 8½", 4" high	45.00
Bowl, 10½", fruit, 3 ftd.	40.00	Comport, 9½", 5¼" high	85.00
Bowl, 11", centerpiece	45.00	Comport, w/cover, 5"	25.00
Bowl, 11", centerpiece, tri-corner	45.00	**Cookie jar, w/cover, 8⅞" h.	295.00
Bowl, 11", relish/celery, 3 pt.	30.00	Creamer, tea, 3 oz., 2⅜" (#2056½)	9.00
Bowl, 11½", float	65.00	Creamer, individual, 4¾ oz.	9.00
Bowl, 11½", fruit, rolled edge, 2¾" h.	42.50	Creamer, 9½ oz.	12.50
Bowl, 11½", oval, float	45.00	Crushed fruit, w/cover & spoon, 10"	2,000.00
Bowl, 11½", rolled edge	50.00	Cup, flat	7.50
Bowl, 11¾", oval, deep	42.50	Cup, ftd., 7 oz.	8.00
Bowl, 12", boat	17.50	Cup, punch, flared rim	11.00
* Bowl, 12", fruit/sm. punch, ped. ft.,		Cup, punch, straight edge	10.00
(Tom & Jerry)	225.00	Decanter, w/stopper, 24 oz., 9¼" h.	85.00
Bowl, 12", lily pond	65.00	Dresser set: powder boxes w/covers	
Bowl, 12", relish "boat," 2 pt.	20.00	& tray	475.00
Bowl, 13", fruit, shallow	75.00	Flower pot, w/perforated cover, 9½"	
Bowl, 14", punch, w/high ft. base (2 gal.)	395.00	diam., 5½" h.	1,850.00
Bowl, 14", punch, w/low ft. base	350.00	Goblet, #2056, 2½ oz., wine, hex ft.,	
Bowl, 15", centerpiece, "hat" shape	200.00	4⅜" h.	12.00
Bowl, 16", flat, fruit, ped. ft.	210.00	Goblet, #2056, 4½ oz., oyster cocktail,	
Bowl, 18", punch, w/low ft. base (3¾ gal.)	400.00	3½" h.	17.50
Box, pomade, 2" square	325.00	Goblet, #2056, 4½ oz., sherbet, flared,	
* Box, w/cover, puff, 3⅛" x 2¾"	225.00	4⅜" h.	9.00
Box, w/cover, 4½" x 4½"	225.00	Goblet, #2056, 4½ oz., fruit, hex ft.,	
Box, w/cover, handkerchief, 5⅝" x 4⅝"	295.00	4¾" h.	9.00
Box, w/cover, hairpin, 3½" x 1¾"	325.00	Goblet, #2056, 5 oz., low ft., sherbet,	
Box, w/cover, jewel, 5¼" x 2¼"	375.00	flared, 3¼" h.	9.00
Box, w/cover, jewel, 2 drawer, 4¼" x 3¼"	5,000.00	Goblet, #2056, 6 oz., low ft., sundae,	
* Box, w/cover, glove, 9½" x 3½"	295.00	3⅛" h.	9.00
* Butter, w/cover, rnd. plate, 7¼"	125.00	Goblet, #2056, 7 oz., claret, 4⅞" h.	55.00
* Butter, w/cover, ¼ lb.	25.00	* Goblet, #2056, 9 oz., low ft., 4⅜" h.	11.00
Cake stand (see salver)		Goblet, #2056, 10 oz., hex ft., water,	
Candelabrum, 6½", 2-lite, bell base		6⅞" h.	14.00
w/bobeche & prisms	145.00	Goblet, #2056, 12 oz., low ft., tea, 5¾" h.	15.00
Candle lamp, 8½", w/chimney, candle		Goblet, #2056½, 4½ oz., sherbet, 4½" h.	10.00
part, 3½"	145.00	Goblet, #2056½, 5 oz., low sherbet,	
Candlestick, twin, 4⅛" h., 8½" spread	60.00	3½" h.	10.00

**Amber, May 2000

AMERICAN

	*Crystal
Goblet, #5056, 1 oz., cordial, 3⅛", w/plain bowl	40.00
Goblet, #5056, 3½ oz., claret, 4⅝", w/plain bowl	18.00
Goblet, #5056, 3½ oz., cocktail, 4", w/plain bowl	15.00
Goblet, #5056, 4 oz., oyster cocktail, 3½", w/plain bowl	15.00
Goblet, #5056, 5½ oz., sherbet, 4⅛", w/plain bowl	12.00
Goblet, #5056, 10 oz., water, 6⅛", w/plain bowl	18.00
Hair receiver, 3" x 3"	395.00
Hat, 2⅛" (sm. ashtray)	16.00
Hat, 3" tall	27.50
Hat, 4" tall	65.00
Hat, western style	295.00
Hotel washbowl and pitcher	3,500.00
Hurricane lamp, 12" complete	195.00
Hurricane lamp base	55.00
Ice bucket, w/tongs	60.00
Ice cream saucer (2 styles)	50.00
Ice dish for 4 oz. crab or 5 oz. tomato liner	35.00
Ice dish insert	10.00
Ice tub, w/liner, 5⅝"	90.00
Ice tub, w/liner, 6½"	95.00
Jam pot, w/cover	65.00
Jar, pickle, w/pointed cover, 6" h.	325.00
Marmalade, w/cover & chrome spoon	50.00
* Mayonnaise, div.	17.50
Mayonnaise, w/ladle, ped. ft.	55.00
Mayonnaise, w/liner & ladle	35.00
Molasses can, 11 oz., 6¾" h., 1 hdld.	425.00
* Mug, 5½ oz., Tom & Jerry, 3¼" h.	40.00
* Mug, 12 oz., beer, 4½" h.	70.00
Mustard, w/cover	35.00
Napkin ring	12.50
Oil, 5 oz.	35.00
Oil, 7 oz.	35.00
Picture frame	15.00
Pitcher, ½ gal. w/ice lip, 8¼", flat bottom	85.00
Pitcher, ½ gal., w/o ice lip	295.00
Pitcher, ½ gal., 8", ftd.	70.00
Pitcher, 1 pt., 5⅜", flat	27.50
Pitcher, 2 pt., 7¼", ftd.	65.00
Pitcher, 3 pt., 8", ftd.	70.00
Pitcher, 3 pt., w/ice lip, 6½", ftd., "fat"	60.00
* Pitcher, 1 qt., flat	30.00
Plate, cream soup liner	12.00
Plate, 6", bread & butter	12.00
Plate, 7", salad	10.00
Plate, 7½" x 4⅜", crescent salad	50.00
Plate, 8", sauce liner, oval	27.50
Plate, 8½", salad	12.00

	*Crystal
Plate, 9", sandwich (sm. center)	14.00
Plate, 9½", dinner	24.00
Plate, 10", cake, 2 hdld.	27.50
Plate, 10½", sandwich (sm. center)	20.00
Plate, 11½", sandwich (sm. center)	20.00
Plate, 12", cake, 3 ftd.	25.00
Plate, 13½", oval torte	50.00
Plate, 14", torte	80.00
Plate, 18", torte	145.00
Plate, 20", torte	225.00
Plate 24", torte	250.00
* Platter, 10½", oval	40.00
Platter, 12", oval	55.00
Ring holder	200.00
Salad set: 10" bowl, 14" torte, wood fork & spoon	135.00
Salt, individual	9.00
Salver, 10", sq., ped. ft. (cake stand)	265.00
Salver, 10", rnd., ped. ft. (cake stand)	135.00
* Salver, 11", rnd., ped. ft. (cake stand)	30.00
Sauce boat & liner	55.00
Saucer	3.00
Set: 2 jam pots w/tray	150.00
Set: decanter, 6 – 2 oz. whiskeys on 10½" tray	245.00
Set: toddler, w/baby tumbler & bowl	100.00
Set: youth, w/bowl, hdld. mug, 6" plate	100.00
Set: condiment, 2 oils, 2 shakers, mustard w/cover & spoon w/tray	350.00
Shaker, 3", ea.	10.00
* Shaker, 3½", ea.	7.00
Shaker, 3¼", ea.	10.00
Shakers w/tray, individual, 2"	22.00
Sherbet, handled, 3½" high, 4½ oz.	115.00
Shrimp bowl, 12¼"	395.00
Soap dish	975.00
Spooner, 3¾"	35.00
**Strawholder, 10", w/cover	275.00
Sugar, tea, 2¼" (#2056½)	13.00
Sugar, hdld., 3¼" h.	12.00
Sugar shaker	65.00
Sugar, w/o cover	10.00
Sugar, w/cover, no hdl., 6¼" (cover fits strawholder)	65.00
Sugar, w/cover, 2 hdld.	20.00
Syrup, 6½ oz., #2056½, Sani-cut server	80.00
Syrup, 6 oz., non pour screw top, 5¼" h.	225.00
Syrup, 10 oz., w/glass cover & 6" liner plate	235.00
Syrup, w/drip proof top	35.00
Toothpick	25.00
Tray, cloverleaf for condiment set	165.00
Tray, tid bit, w/question mark metal handle	40.00
Tray, 5" x 2½", rect.	80.00

	*Crystal
Tumbler, #2056½, 8 oz., straight side, water, 3⅞" h.	13.00
Tumbler, #2056½, 12 oz., straight side, tea, 5" h.	18.00
Tumbler, #5056, 5 oz., ftd., juice, 4⅛" w/plain bowl	12.00
Tumbler, #5056, 12 oz., ftd., tea, 5½" w/plain bowl	12.00
Urn, 6", sq., ped. ft	30.00
Urn, 7½", sq. ped. ft.	37.50
Vase, 4½", sweet pea	80.00
Vase, 6", bud, ftd.	18.00
* Vase, 6", bud, flared	18.00
Vase, 6", straight side	35.00
Vase, 6½", flared rim	15.00
Vase, 7", flared	80.00
* Vase, 8", straight side	40.00
* Vase, 8", flared	80.00
Vase, 8", porch, 5" diam.	450.00
Vase, 8½", bud, flared	25.00
Vase, 8½", bud, cupped	25.00
Vase, 9", w/sq. ped. ft.	45.00
Vase, 9½", flared	150.00
Vase, 10", cupped in top	295.00
Vase, 10", porch, 8" diam.	750.00
* Vase, 10", straight side	90.00
Vase, 10", swung	225.00
Vase, 10", flared	90.00
Vase, 12", straight side	250.00
Vase, 12", swung	250.00
Vase, 14", swung	250.00
Vase, 20", swung	395.00

	*Crystal
Tray, 6" oval, hdld.	35.00
Tray, pin, oval, 5½" x 4½"	210.00
Tray, 6½" x 9" relish, 4 part	45.00
Tray, 9½", service, 2 hdld.	35.00
Tray, 10", muffin (2 upturned sides)	30.00
Tray, 10", square, 4 part	75.00
Tray, 10", square	165.00
Tray, 10½", cake, w/question mark metal hdl.	32.00
Tray, 10½" x 7½", rect.	70.00
Tray, 10½" x 5", oval hdld.	45.00
Tray, 10¾", square, 4 part	155.00
Tray, 12", sand. w/ctr. handle	35.00
Tray, 12", round	175.00
Tray, 13½", oval, ice cream	185.00
Tray for sugar & creamer, tab. hdld., 6¾"	12.00
Tumbler, hdld. iced tea	375.00
Tumbler, #2056, 2 oz., whiskey, 2½" h.	11.00
Tumbler, #2056, 3 oz., ftd. cone, cocktail, 2⅞" h.	14.00
Tumbler, #2056, 5 oz., ftd., juice, 4¾"	13.00
Tumbler, #2056, 6 oz., flat, old-fashion, 3⅜" h.	15.00
Tumbler, #2056, 8 oz. flat, water, flared, 4⅛" h.	15.00
* Tumbler, #2056, 9 oz. ftd., water, 4⅞" h.	15.00
Tumbler, #2056, 12 oz., flat, tea, flared, 5¼" h.	17.00
Tumbler, #2056½, 5 oz., straight side, juice	13.00

Colors: amber, amethyst, crystal, crystal w/ebony stem, light and dark Emerald, Gold Krystol, Heatherbloom, Peach Blo, Royal blue, Willow blue

Cambridge's Apple Blossom continues to attract new collectors particularly in the yellow called Gold Krystol by Cambridge. It is the most abundantly found color of Apple Blossom and also the most reasonably priced except for crystal. You can still collect a small set, but harder to find items and serving pieces are beginning to be pricey. Beverage items can still be obtained in most colors. Buy serving pieces and dinner plates whenever you have the chance.

Colors other than yellow and crystal can be found with time (and funds); however, availability of pink, green, blue, and Heatherbloom is quite limited in comparison to yellow or crystal. Very little dark Emerald Green, amethyst, or amber is found. Groupings of blue when displayed at a show, produce a lot of "ooh and ahs," but usually the price makes viewers pause at buying. Note the Royal blue, gold encrusted pitcher used as a pattern shot. This was found in Florida and now belongs in a New York collection. The abundance of wonderful ice buckets pictured throughout this book is due to a serious collector from Georgia who brought many of his prized pieces to our photography session last October. Apple Blossom is found on several Cambridge stemware lines, but the #3130 line is most often seen and collected. Some collectors even mix stem lines, but the bowl shapes differ and many will not mix them. I once asked a collector why she was mixing different stem lines together and was told she liked the pattern and bought whatever she could find. I think that collecting practice may become more and more prevalent in the future, particularly in patterns like this one.

	Crystal	Yellow Amber	Pink *Green
Ashtray, 6", heavy	50.00	125.00	150.00
Bowl, #3025, ftd., finger, w/plate	45.00	65.00	75.00
Bowl, #3130, finger, w/plate	40.00	60.00	70.00
Bowl, 3", indiv. nut, 4 ftd.	55.00	75.00	80.00
Bowl, 5¼", 2 hdld., bonbon	25.00	40.00	45.00
Bowl, 5½", 2 hdld., bonbon	25.00	40.00	40.00
Bowl, 5½", fruit "saucer"	20.00	28.00	30.00
Bowl, 6", 2 hdld., "basket" (sides up)	30.00	48.00	50.00
Bowl, 6", cereal	35.00	50.00	55.00
Bowl, 9", pickle	30.00	55.00	60.00
Bowl, 10", 2 hdld.	55.00	95.00	110.00
Bowl, 10", baker	60.00	100.00	110.00
Bowl, 11", fruit, tab hdld.	65.00	110.00	125.00
Bowl, 11", low ftd.	60.00	100.00	120.00
Bowl, 12", relish, 4 pt.	45.00	70.00	75.00
Bowl, 12", 4 ftd.	60.00	100.00	110.00
Bowl, 12", flat	55.00	90.00	95.00
Bowl, 12", oval, 4 ftd.	65.00	95.00	110.00
Bowl, 12½", console	55.00	75.00	80.00
Bowl, 13"	55.00	90.00	100.00
Bowl, cream soup, w/liner plate	35.00	55.00	60.00
Butter w/cover, 5½"	195.00	350.00	475.00
Candelabrum, 3-lite, keyhole	35.00	50.00	70.00
Candlestick, 1-lite, keyhole	24.00	35.00	40.00
Candlestick, 2-lite, keyhole	30.00	45.00	50.00
Candy box w/cover, 4 ftd. "bowl"	85.00	125.00	165.00
Cheese (compote) & cracker (11½" plate)	45.00	75.00	100.00
Comport, 4", fruit cocktail	20.00	28.00	30.00

* Blue prices 25% to 30% more.

	Crystal	Yellow Amber	Pink *Green
Comport, 7", tall	45.00	70.00	95.00
Creamer, ftd.	20.00	26.00	30.00
Creamer, tall, ftd.	22.00	30.00	35.00
Cup	16.00	28.00	35.00
Cup, A.D.	50.00	75.00	110.00
Ice bucket	95.00	145.00	225.00
Fruit/oyster cocktail, #3025, 4½ oz.	20.00	25.00	30.00
Mayonnaise, w/liner & ladle (4 ftd. bowl)	45.00	65.00	80.00
Pitcher, 50 oz., ftd., flattened sides	195.00	275.00	350.00
Pitcher, 64 oz., #3130	215.00	295.00	350.00
Pitcher, 64 oz., #3025	215.00	295.00	350.00
Pitcher, 67 oz., squeezed middle, loop hdld.	225.00	325.00	395.00
Pitcher, 76 oz.	125.00	315.00	395.00
Pitcher, 80 oz., ball	225.00	395.00	550.00
Pitcher w/cover, 76 oz., ftd., #3135	250.00	375.00	550.00
Plate, 6", bread/butter	8.00	10.00	12.00
Plate, 6", sq., 2 hdld.	10.00	20.00	22.00
Plate, 7½", tea	12.00	22.00	25.00
Plate, 8½"	20.00	25.00	30.00
Plate, 9½", dinner	55.00	90.00	115.00
Plate, 10", grill	35.00	55.00	65.00

* Blue prices 25% to 30% more.

	Crystal	Yellow Amber	Pink *Green
Plate, sandwich, 11½", tab hdld.	30.00	45.00	50.00
Plate, sandwich, 12½", 2 hdld.	32.00	50.00	60.00
Plate, sq., bread/butter	8.00	10.00	12.00
Plate, sq., dinner	55.00	90.00	115.00
Plate, sq., salad	12.00	22.00	25.00
Plate, sq., servce	30.00	45.00	50.00
Platter, 11½	55.00	95.00	120.00
Platter, 13½" rect., w/tab handle	65.00	125.00	195.00
Salt & pepper, pr.	50.00	95.00	125.00
Saucer	5.00	7.00	8.00
Saucer, A.D.	20.00	30.00	35.00
Stem, #1066, parfait	25.00	110.00	150.00
Stem, #3025, 7 oz., low fancy ft., sherbet	17.00	25.00	28.00
Stem, #3025, 7 oz., high sherbet	18.00	30.00	33.00
Stem, #3025, 10 oz.	24.00	35.00	45.00
Stem, #3130, 1 oz., cordial	65.00	110.00	175.00
Stem, #3130, 3 oz., cocktail	18.00	32.00	35.00
Stem, #3130, 6 oz., low sherbet	16.00	24.00	28.00
Stem, #3130, 6 oz., tall sherbet	18.00	30.00	33.00
Stem, #3130, 8 oz., water	22.00	30.00	45.00
Stem, #3135, 3 oz., cocktail	18.00	32.00	35.00
Stem, #3135, 6 oz., low sherbet	16.00	24.00	28.00
Stem, #3135, 6 oz., tall sherbet	18.00	30.00	33.00
Stem, #3135, 8 oz., water	22.00	30.00	33.00
Stem, #3400, 6 oz., ftd., sherbet	15.00	22.00	26.00
Stem, #3400, 9 oz., water	22.00	30.00	45.00
Sugar, ftd.	20.00	26.00	30.00
Sugar, tall ftd.	20.00	30.00	35.00
Tray, 7", hdld. relish	25.00	40.00	45.00
Tray, 11", ctr. hdld. sand.	35.00	50.00	60.00
Tumbler, #3025, 4 oz.	16.00	24.00	28.00
Tumbler, #3025, 10 oz.	20.00	30.00	35.00
Tumbler, #3025, 12 oz.	25.00	40.00	45.00
Tumbler, #3130, 5 oz., ftd.	16.00	28.00	33.00
Tumbler, #3130, 8 oz., ftd.	22.00	30.00	35.00
Tumbler, #3130, 10 oz., ftd.	25.00	35.00	40.00
Tumbler, #3130, 12 oz., ftd.	30.00	40.00	50.00
Tumbler, #3135, 5 oz., ftd.	16.00	30.00	35.00
Tumbler, #3135, 8 oz., ftd.	22.00	35.00	40.00
Tumbler, #3135, 10 oz., ftd.	25.00	35.00	45.00
Tumbler, #3135, 12 oz., ftd.	30.00	40.00	50.00
Tumbler, #3400, 2½ oz., ftd.	35.00	75.00	85.00
Tumbler, #3400, 9 oz., ftd.	22.00	30.00	35.00
Tumbler, #3400, 12 oz., ftd.	30.00	40.00	50.00
Tumbler, 12 oz., flat (2 styles) – 1 mid indent to match 67 oz. pitcher	25.00	50.00	60.00
Tumbler, 6"	25.00	45.00	50.00
Vase, 5"	65.00	110.00	145.00
Vase, 6", rippled sides	75.00	125.00	150.00
Vase, 8", 2 styles	85.00	135.00	175.00
Vase, 12", keyhole base w/neck indent	95.00	175.00	250.00

* Blue prices 25% to 30% more.

Note: See pages 236 – 237 for stem identification.

Colors: Amber, Amethyst, green, pink

We know "Balda" to be a Central Glass Works pattern that was designed by Joseph Balda who was better known for his Heisey designs. As yet, no one has unearthed an "authentic" name from the factory except Etch #410; hence its designer's designation thus far. Stemware is the most seen item, as is the case with most Elegant glassware from this time. Amethyst (lilac) is the most often found color and therefore the most collected. I have added the pieces to my listing that I have been able to document since the last book. New items continue to turn up especially for a pattern where no official factory listing has been forthcoming. There are most likely additional pieces and/or colors other than those I have listed. You are unlikely to find large batches of "Balda," except for stemware, but it does happen sporadically, as people become aware of its existence. I am hoping this presentation of "Balda" will result in even more discoveries for the next book. Fellow dealers and collectors have supplied the information listed. Another Central Glass pattern, Morgan (page 136) is also found on the same stem line shown here in Amethyst. Morgan is etched on two additional stems, but I have only seen "Balda" etched on this one.

	Amethyst	Pink Green Amber
Candy and lid, cone shaped, 7⅝" tall	195.00	135.00
Cup	25.00	20.00
Decanter and stopper	495.00	395.00
Ice bucket	295.00	195.00
Pitcher		695.00
Plate, 6"	12.50	10.00
Plate, lunch	20.00	14.00
Platter	85.00	55.00
Saucer	6.00	4.00

	Amethyst	Pink Green Amber
Shaker, pr		150.00
Stem, champagne/sherbet	25.00	20.00
Stem, claret	75.00	40.00
Stem, cordial	75.00	45.00
Stem, water	45.00	25.00
Stem, wine	45.00	30.00
Tumbler, ftd. juice	25.00	15.00
Tumbler, ftd. tea	35.00	25.00
Tumbler, ftd. water	30.00	20.00
Tumbler, ftd. whiskey	40.00	25.00

Colors: crystal, Azure blue, Topaz yellow, amber, green, pink, red, cobalt blue, black amethyst

I keep getting letters and e-mails about Wisteria Baroque vases, bowls, and candlesticks being discovered. Lancaster Colony produced a few pieces of Baroque in a color similar to Wisteria for Tiara. I have seen the bowl and vase, but not the candle. My old Tiara catalog does not show the candle. These items have a purple/pink tint; do not pay an "antique" price for Baroque pieces in this color. Baroque was never originally made in this color, which, by the way, does not change tints in natural or artificial light, as does the original Fostoria Wisteria.

Candlesticks are one item that new collectors are currently seeking regardless of the pattern. I have a book out addressing this collecting fancy. It's called *Glass Candlesticks of the Depression Era* and the second volume will be out in 2003. It had been almost 20 years since a candlestick book had been released and now there have been at least three I know of since mine.

Fostoria's Baroque pattern enjoys several different varieties of candlesticks. You will find both 4" and 5½" single light candles and a 4½" double candle. The 6" three-light (triple) candlesticks are called candelabra with prisms attached. Many collectors desire these elusive candelabra with older prism wires attached. Some collectors are substituting modern wires for the old, rusty ones. Once prisms are clamped on properly, they rarely come off, even if moved. New prisms are available at lamp and hardware stores.

Triple candlesticks without the prisms have been located in all the colors listed above, but matching console bowls have yet to be found in red, cobalt blue, or amethyst. Some pieces of Azure Baroque seem to be light green (bad batches of blue that were released anyhow). That light green color is not as prized as Azure. Fewer collectors pursue color variances; you probably could not find enough pieces of light green to complete a set, but it would be challenging to try.

Baroque cream soups and individual shakers are elusive in colors, or even crystal. They have always been expensive. Speaking of shakers, the regular size came with both metal and glass tops. Today, most collectors fancy glass lids. Glass lids were easily broken by over tightening them; and Fostoria changed to metal lids before Baroque was discontinued. Replacement lids were always metal. Metal tops are generally found on the later crystal patterns of Navarre, Chintz, Lido, and Meadow Rose that used Baroque blanks. Pitchers and punch bowls are not plenteous; but blue ones are nearly impossible to find. Straight tumblers are more arduous to find than footed ones, but are favored over cone-shaped, footed pieces even though they are more costly. The photo above illustrates the larger sweetmeats as compared to the smaller covered jelly.

	Crystal	Blue	Yellow
Ashtray	10.00	22.00	15.00
Bowl, cream soup	35.00	95.00	77.50
Bowl, ftd., punch	400.00	1,300.00	
Bowl, 3¾", rose	30.00	110.00	70.00
Bowl, 4", hdld. (4 styles)	12.50	30.00	22.50
Bowl, 5", fruit	15.00	35.00	27.50
Bowl, 6", cereal	22.00	50.00	40.00
Bowl, 6", sq.	12.00	28.00	25.00
Bowl, 6½", 2 pt.	15.00	35.00	23.00
Bowl, 7", 3 ftd.	12.50	25.00	25.00
Bowl, 7½", jelly, w/cover	45.00	150.00	95.00
Bowl, 8", pickle	15.00	32.50	25.00
Bowl, 8½", hdld.	30.00	75.00	50.00
Bowl, 9½", veg., oval	40.00	95.00	65.00
Bowl, 10", hdld.	35.00	110.00	75.00
Bowl, 10½", hdld., 4 ftd.	35.00	85.00	65.00
Bowl, 10" x 7½", hdld.	30.00		
Bowl, 10", relish, 3 pt.	22.00	45.00	30.00
Bowl, 11", celery	28.00	45.00	35.00

	Crystal	Blue	Yellow
Bowl, 11", rolled edge	30.00	80.00	60.00
* Bowl, 12", flared	30.00	45.00	35.00
Candelabrum, 8¼", 2-lite, 16 lustre	100.00	165.00	110.00
Candelabrum, 9½", 3-lite, 24 lustre	150.00	225.00	165.00
Candle, 7¾", 8 lustre	50.00	90.00	80.00
Candlestick, 4"	15.00	52.50	35.00
Candlestick, 4½", 2-lite	20.00	60.00	50.00

*Pink just discovered.

	Crystal	Blue	Yellow
Candlestick, 5½"	30.00	65.00	45.00
* Candlestick, 6", 3-lite	32.50	100.00	75.00
Candy, 3 part w/cover	55.00	140.00	95.00
Comport, 4¾"	20.00	50.00	33.00
Comport, 6½"	22.00	55.00	40.00
Creamer, 3¼", indiv.	10.00	30.00	25.00
Creamer, 3¾", ftd.	12.00	30.00	20.00
Cup	10.00	33.00	24.00
Cup, 6 oz., punch	15.00	30.00	
Ice bucket	60.00	135.00	85.00
Mayonnaise, 5½", w/liner	30.00	95.00	70.00
Mustard, w/cover	50.00	110.00	85.00
Oil, w/stopper, 5½"	85.00	400.00	225.00
Pitcher, 6½"	100.00	800.00	450.00
Pitcher, 7", ice lip	100.00	750.00	550.00
Plate, 6"	5.00	12.00	10.00
Plate, 7½"	8.00	17.00	11.00
Plate, 8½"	9.00	22.50	18.00
Plate, 9½"	20.00	67.50	47.50
Plate, 10", cake	30.00	45.00	35.00
Plate, 11", ctr. hdld., sandwich	30.00		
Plate, 14", torte	28.00	65.00	40.00
Platter, 12", oval	40.00	85.00	52.50
Salt & pepper, pr.	60.00	165.00	120.00
Salt & pepper, indiv., pr.	60.00	250.00	200.00
Sauce dish	30.00	85.00	70.00
Sauce dish, divided	25.00	75.00	65.00
Saucer	2.00	7.00	6.00
Sherbet, 3¾", 5 oz.	12.00	27.50	20.00
Stem, 6¾", 9 oz., water	18.00	40.00	28.00
Sugar, 3", indiv.	10.00	30.00	25.00
Sugar, 3½", ftd.	12.00	30.00	20.00
Sweetmeat, covered, 9"	90.00	210.00	165.00
Tray, 12½", oval	40.00	85.00	52.50
Tray, 6¼" for indiv. cream/sugar	15.00	25.00	20.00
Tumbler, 3½", 6½ oz., old-fashion	22.50	95.00	60.00
Tumbler, 3", 3½ oz., ftd., cocktail	12.00	28.00	20.00
Tumbler, 6", 12 oz., ftd., tea	20.00	40.00	30.00
Tumbler, 3¾", 5 oz., juice	15.00	48.00	30.00
Tumbler, 5½", 9 oz., ftd., water	12.00	30.00	25.00
Tumbler, 4¼", 9 oz., water	25.00	55.00	37.50
Tumbler, 5¾", 14 oz., tea	35.00	90.00	60.00
Vase, 6½"	50.00	145.00	110.00
Vase, 7"	60.00	175.00	135.00

* Red $150.00
  Green $120.00
  Black Amethyst $140.00
  Cobalt Blue $140.00
  Amber $75.00

Colors: amber, black, ice blue, crystal, green, pink, red, cobalt

Collectors on the Internet have discovered Black Forest. Prices for many pieces have jumped to previously unknown heights, yet you need to realize there are only a few collectors who pay high prices for a rarely seen item! Perhaps the next time that item appears, no one will bid the price up to that level. A small collecting cadre of Black Forest enthusiasts used to keep the pricing of this very limited pattern under wraps. Internet auctions have blown the previously standard prices out of the water. Black items and those with gold encrusting are especially pricey the last few years. A throng of new collectors has caused a noticeable deficiency of pieces for collectors; many former collectors have disposed of their sets due to the high prices being obtained.

Internet activity has also inspired sales in Deerwood, a pattern often confused with Black Forest. Black Forest pattern depicts moose and trees, while deer and trees are on Deerwood. Some pieces of etched Deerwood (made at the Tiffin plant of U. S. Glass) have been found on Paden City blanks, which adds to the confusion.

I am repeatedly asked about those Black Forest etched, heavy goblets that were made in the 1970s in amber, amberina, dark green, blue, crystal, and ruby by L. G. Wright, a glass company dedicated to remaking glass from older moulds or from newly made moulds of older designs. These are selling in the $20.00 to $35.00 range with red and blue on the upper side of that price. These newer goblets have a heavy, predominant "Daisy and Button" cubed stem and are not considered to be Black Forest by some long-time collectors. However, newer collectors have no such reservations.

	Amber	*Black	Crystal	Green	Pink	Red
Batter jug			250.00			
Bowl, 4½", finger				40.00		
Bowl, 9¼", center hdld.				125.00	125.00	
Bowl, 11", console	95.00	150.00	65.00	125.00	125.00	
Bowl, 11", fruit		150.00		125.00	125.00	
Bowl, 13", console		195.00				
Bowl, 3 ftd.			100.00			
Cake plate, 2" pedestal	95.00	150.00		125.00	125.00	
Candlestick, mushroom style	50.00	95.00	50.00	85.00	85.00	
Candlestick double			100.00			
Candy dish, w/cover, several styles	155.00	250.00		225.00	225.00	
Creamer, 2 styles	50.00	75.00	35.00	65.00	65.00	
Comport, 4", low ftd.				75.00	75.00	
Comport, 5½", high ftd.		125.00		100.00	100.00	
Cup and saucer, 3 styles		150.00		125.00	125.00	175.00
Decanter, w/stopper, 8½", 28 oz., bulbous				350.00	350.00	
Decanter w/stopper, 8¾", 24 oz., straight			195.00	350.00	350.00	
Egg cup				150.00		
Ice bucket		225.00		125.00	125.00	
Ice pail, 6", 3" high	150.00					
Ice tub, 2 styles (ice blue $750.00)	160.00	250.00		195.00	195.00	
Mayonnaise, with liner		175.00		125.00	125.00	
Night set: pitcher, 6½", 42 oz. & tumbler				595.00	595.00	
Pitcher, 8", 40 oz. (cobalt $1,250.00)						
Pitcher, 8", 62 oz.			250.00			
Pitcher, 9", 80 oz.					500.00	
Pitcher, 10½", 72 oz.				600.00	600.00	
Plate, 6½", bread/butter		35.00		30.00	30.00	
Plate, 8", luncheon		50.00		40.00	40.00	
Plate, 10", dinner		225.00				
Plate, 11", 2 hdld.		125.00		65.00	65.00	
Plate, 13¾", 2 hdld.				100.00	100.00	
Relish, 10½", 5 pt. covered				500.00	500.00	
Salt and pepper, pr.			125.00		175.00	
Server, center hdld.	50.00	40.00	35.00	50.00	35.00	
Shot glass, 2 oz., 2½"	40.00					
Stem, 2 oz., wine, 4¼"			17.50	50.00		
Stem, 6 oz., champagne, 4¾"			17.50		30.00	
Stem, 9 oz., water, 6"			22.50			
Sugar, 2 styles	50.00	75.00	35.00	65.00	65.00	
Tumbler, 3 oz., juice, flat or footed, 3½"			50.00	95.00	95.00	
Tumbler, 8 oz., old fashion, 3⅞"					95.00	
Tumbler, 9 oz., ftd., 5½"	50.00					
Tumbler, 12 oz., tea, 5½"				125.00	125.00	
Vase, 6½" (cobalt $300.00)		195.00	100.00	175.00	175.00	
Vase, 10", 2 styles in black		250.00		195.00	195.00	
Whipped cream pail	95.00					

*Add 20% for gold decorated.

Colors: pink, pink & green w/crystal, green, all w/Optic

Bo Peep is credited by another author as being made by Monongah; the shapes are very similar to those we recognize as Tiffin. Cathy found a green footed juice tumbler years ago and asked me to look for other pieces in the pattern. Bo Peep is not plentiful, but I was proudly carrying three pieces in my inventory when I totaled my van. Unfortunately, I totaled them too! (Forgive me. I was trying to avoid the driver using my side of the road. I have seen one large set of Bo Peep in an antique mall. Prices were more than I was willing to pay for stems. I coerced myself into buying the expensive cracked pitcher and the more expensive vase shown here since I had never seen them previously. The pitcher has an unetched lid, as Tiffin pitchers do. Another collector was happy I turned down the set; he ultimately bought it. One of the hardest lessons to learn as a dealer comes from wanting to buy pieces you like. Most times you have a tendency to pay too much. I have made more money from things I do not like because I always buy them cheap enough to sell profitably!

	Pink Green			Pink Green
Finger bowl, ftd.	95.00		Stem, water	125.00
Jug w/cover	695.00		Stem, wine	125.00
Jug w/o cover	595.00		Tumbler, 5 oz., ftd., juice	75.00
Plate, 7½", salad	40.00		Tumbler, 9 oz., ftd., water	75.00
Stem, cocktail	75.00		Tumbler, 12 oz., ftd., iced tea	95.00
Stem, high sherbet	75.00		Tumbler, ftd., seltzer	95.00
Stem, low sherbet	70.00		Vase, 9", ruffled edge	495.00
Stem, parfait	100.00			

Colors: Azure blue, crystal, Ebony, green, Orchid, Rose

Grape

Pictured again are several Fostoria Brocades, showing you can easily blend the different designs rather than buy only one. Designs are shown separately on page 27. Hopefully, the labeled small group shots will make identification easier. You should know that Oak Leaf pattern with iridescence is correctly referred to as Oak Wood, and Paradise with iridescence is called Victoria, Decoration #71.

	Crystal	#290 Oakleaf Green/Rose	Ebony	#72 Oakwood Orchid/Azure	#289 Paradise Green/Orchid	#73 Palm Leaf Rose/Green	Blue	#287 Grape Green	Orchid
Bonbon, #2375	30.00	40.00		50.00		50.00		40.00	
Bowl, finger, #869	60.00	70.00		75.00					
Bowl, 4½", mint, #2394	30.00	40.00							
Bowl, 7½", "D," cupped rose, #2339							85.00	60.00	110.00
Bowl, 10", scroll hdld, #2395	90.00	145.00	125.00			200.00			
Bowl, 10", 2 hdld, dessert, #2375	80.00	110.00		165.00		165.00			
Bowl, 10½", "A," 3 ftd., #2297					95.00		95.00	70.00	120.00
Bowl, 10½", "C," sm roll rim, deep, #2297							95.00	70.00	120.00
Bowl, 10½", "C," pedestal ftd., #2315					95.00				
Bowl, 11", roll edge ctrpiece, #2329					100.00		155.00	135.00	175.00
Bowl, 11", ctrpiece, #2375				185.00		155.00			
Bowl, 11", cornucopia hdld, #2398	100.00	135.00							
Bowl, 12", 3 toe, flair rim, #2394	100.00	125.00		185.00		150.00			
Bowl, 12", console, #2375	85.00	115.00							
Bowl, 12" low, "saturn rings," #2362					85.00		115.00	90.00	135.00
Bowl, 12", hexagonal, 3 tab toe, #2342	110.00	135.00		195.00	100.00				
Bowl, 12", "A," 3 tab toe, #2297					115.00		125.00	110.00	135.00
Bowl, 12½", "E," flat, shallow, #2297							125.00	100.00	135.00
Bowl, 13", ctrpiece rnd., #2329					140.00		225.00	195.00	235.00

BROCADE

	Crystal	#290 Oakleaf Green/Rose	Ebony	#72 Oakwood Orchid/Azure	#289 Paradise Green/Orchid	#73 Palm Leaf Rose/Green	#287 Blue	#287 Grape Green	#287 Orchid
Bowl, ctrpiece oval, #2375½		125.00		165.00		295.00			
Bowl, 13", oval, roll edge w/grid frog, #2371					175.00		225.00	185.00	250.00
Bowl, #2415 comb, candle hdld.	120.00	165.00	175.00	250.00		250.00			
Candlestick, 2", mushroom, #2372					25.00		35.00	30.00	35.00
Candlestick, 2", 3 toe, #2394	40.00	55.00				70.00			
Candlestick, 3", scroll, #2395	50.00	65.00	75.00						
Candlestick, 3", #2375	45.00	60.00		65.00		75.00			
Candlestick, 3", stack disc, #2362					40.00		35.00	30.00	35.00
Candlestick, 4", #2324					35.00		35.00	30.00	35.00
Candlestick, hex mushroom, #2375½	45.00	55.00		75.00					
Candlestick, trindle, #2383 ea.						145.00			
Candy box, cov., 3 pt, #2331	100.00	150.00	200.00	250.00			185.00	145.00	200.00
Candy, box, cone lid, #2380	100.00	145.00			115.00				
Candy, cov., oval, #2395		135.00		200.00					
Cheese & cracker, #2368	65.00	75.00							
Cigarette & cov. (small), #2391	65.00	135.00	120.00	175.00					
Cigarette & cov. (large), #2391	85.00	135.00	125.00	185.00					
Comport, 6", #2400						125.00			
Comport, 7" tall, twist stem, #2327					75.00		75.00	55.00	75.00
Comport, 8", short, ftd. #2350					65.00				
Comport, 8", pulled stem, #2400				115.00					
Comport, 11", stack disc stem, ftd., #2362					100.00		125.00	100.00	120.00
Ice bucket, #2378	100.00	145.00		225.00		155.00	100.00	90.00	95.00
Ice bucket, w/drainer, handle & tongs #2378				150.00		140.00	125.00	130.00	
Jug, #5000	395.00	595.00		995.00	695.00				
Lemon, "bow" hdld., #2375	30.00	45.00		65.00	60.00	40.00		40.00	
Mayonnaise, #2315	55.00	70.00		225.00					
Plate, mayonnaise, #2332	20.00	30.00		35.00					
Plate, 6", #2283	15.00	20.00							
Plate, 7", #2283	20.00	25.00		35.00					
Plate, 8", sq., #2419						35.00			
Plate, 8", #2283	22.00	30.00		45.00					
Plate, 10", cake, #2375	65.00	90.00		125.00		155.00			
Plate, 12", salver, #2315	100.00	125.00		160.00					
Plate, 13", lettuce, #2315	60.00	90.00		145.00					
Stem, ¾ oz., cordial, #877	65.00			150.00					
Stem, 2¾ oz., wine, #877	35.00			85.00					
Stem, 3½ oz., cocktail, #877	25.00			55.00					
Stem, 4 oz., claret, #877	35.00			85.00					
Stem, 6 oz., hi sherbet, #877	32.50			65.00					
Stem, 6 oz., low sherbet, #877	22.50			55.00					
Stem, 10 oz., water, #877	45.00			85.00					
Sugar Pail, #2378	105.00	150.00		195.00		250.00			
Sweetmeat, hex 2 hdld bowl, #2375	35.00	45.00		60.00		60.00		40.00	
Tray, rnd, fleur de lis hdld., #2387							95.00	90.00	95.00
Tray, ctr. hdld., #2342	65.00	95.00		160.00	75.00	140.00	95.00	90.00	95.00
Tumbler, 2½ oz., ftd. whiskey, #877	30.00	75.00							
Tumbler, 4½ oz., ftd. oyster cocktail	22.50								
Tumbler, 5 oz., ftd. juice, #877	30.00								
Tumbler, 5½ oz., parfait, #877	40.00	65.00							
Tumbler, 9 oz., ftd., #877				75.00	60.00				
Tumbler, 12 oz., ftd. tea, #877				95.00	65.00				
Urn & cover, #2413		200.00		395.00		495.00			
Vase, 3", 4", #4103, bulbous	50.00	60.00	75.00		70.00		85.00	70.00	80.00
Vase, 5", 6", #4103, optic					75.00		105.00	90.00	100.00
Vase, 6", #4100, flat straight side optic					85.00		105.00	90.00	100.00
Vase, 6", #4105, scallop rim	65.00	85.00		140.00	85.00				

	Crystal	#290 Oakleaf Green/Rose	Ebony	#72 Oakwood Orchid/Azure	#289 Paradise Green/Orchid	#73 Palm Leaf Rose/Green	Blue	#287 Grape Green	Orchid
Vase, 7", 9", ftd. urn, #2369		85.00		100.00		135.00		120.00	150.00
Vase, 8", cupped melon, #2408						255.00			
Vase, 8", #2292, ftd. flair flat, straight side	85.00	100.00	125.00						
Vase, 8", #4100					95.00		125.00	115.00	135.00
Vase, 8", #4105	70.00	95.00		250.00		250.00			
Vase, 8", melon, #2387	90.00	115.00		185.00					
Vase, 8½" fan, #2385	150.00	200.00		375.00		285.00			
Vase, 10½" ftd., #2421						295.00			
Vase, sm. or lg. window & cov., #2373	150.00	200.00	350.00	350.00		350.00			
Whip cream, scallop 2 hdld bowl #2375	35.00	50.00		55.00		40.00			
Whip cream pail, #2378	90.00	135.00		195.00				40.00	

Oak Leaf

Paradise

Palm Leaf

BROCADE, McKee, 1930s

Colors: pink and green

McKee's Brocade only came in the one pattern unlike Fostoria's many. I have heard it referred to many times by collectors as "Poinsettia" and even "Palm Tree" though I have no official reference for either name. Help me find a few more pieces to portray!

	Pink/Green
Bowl, 12", flared edge	55.00
Bowl, center, hdld. nut	45.00
Bowl, 12", console, rolled edge	55.00
Candlestick, rolled edge, octagonal	25.00
Candy box/cover	75.00
Candy jar, ftd., w/cover	65.00
Cheese and cracker	55.00
Compote, 10", flared edge	65.00
Compote, cone shape, octagonal	65.00
Mayonnaise, 3 pc.	50.00
Salver, ftd. (cake stand)	45.00
Server, center hdld.	40.00

Colors: crystal, yellow; some pink

Cadena stemware is a collectors' plague, but finding any serving pieces is an infrequent occurrence even if you are willing to pay the price for them! They are rarely available! I have never been able to buy a bowl of any size in 25 years of looking. Oh, I have seen one, but it has always been more highly prized by its owner even with a thumb sized piece missing. Never pass a piece you discover at a reasonable price. Someone wants it, even if you don't.

Tiffin pitchers were sold either with or without a lid. The top edge of pitchers without lids were often curved in or "cupped" so much that a lid will not fit inside the lip. Thus, buying a lid separately may be a bit speculative. Remember that the pitcher cover does not have an etching, even though the Cadena pitcher itself will.

	Crystal	Pink Yellow		Crystal	Pink Yellow
Bowl, cream soup	25.00	45.00	Plate, 7¾"	10.00	20.00
Bowl, finger, ftd.	25.00	45.00	Plate, 9¼"	45.00	75.00
Bowl, grapefruit, ftd.	50.00	100.00	Saucer	15.00	25.00
Bowl, 6", hdld.	20.00	30.00	Stem, 4¾", sherbet	18.00	25.00
Bowl, 10", pickle	30.00	45.00	Stem, 5¼", cocktail	22.00	30.00
Bowl, 12", console	35.00	65.00	Stem, 5¼", ¾ oz., cordial	75.00	135.00
Candlestick	30.00	55.00	Stem, 6", wine	35.00	65.00
Creamer	20.00	30.00	Stem, 6⁵⁄₁₆", 8 oz., parfait	35.00	65.00
Cup	45.00	100.00	Stem, 6½", champagne	25.00	32.00
Mayonnaise, ftd., w/liner	50.00	85.00	Stem, 7½", water	35.00	38.00
Oyster cocktail	20.00	30.00	Sugar	20.00	30.00
Pitcher, ftd.	225.00	295.00	Tumbler, 4¼", ftd., juice	22.00	30.00
Pitcher, ftd., w/cover	295.00	395.00	Tumbler, 5¼", ftd., water	25.00	33.00
Plate, 6"	8.00	12.00	Vase, 9"	115.00	150.00

Colors: crystal, crystal and Crown Tuscan with gold decoration

We are trying to include some pamphlets identifying each piece as space permits. Shown is a 1951 Candlelight brochure of the type usually given to people who were registering a pattern for bridal gifts. We have opened it to show you the typical stems found in Candlelight. Hopefully, this will help you identify them. Too, terminology has undergone subtle changes over the years. For instance, today, when people ask for wine goblets, you need to find out if they want water goblets. Originally, wine goblets held 2½ to 4 ounces; but, now, many people think of wine goblets as holding 8 or 9 ounces. The brochure shows #3776 stems while the photo below shows mostly #3114 stemware. Candlelight is not as plentiful as some other Cambridge patterns. Candlelight was made in two ways. The pattern was cut into some pieces, but was acid etched on others. The cut items are scarcer, but there are fewer collectors for cut pieces. To illustrate the difference, there are two icers and liners in the photograph, one etched, the other cut. The pattern is harder to see on the cut one at the right! Etching was accomplished by covering the glass except where the design was desired and then dipping the glass into acid.

With so many new collectors beginning to search for this pattern the dearth of supply for shakers, butter dishes, basic serving pieces, candlesticks, and even cups and saucers is apparent. Don't pass any of those items if you have a chance to buy them. Again, even if you don't want them, someone does.

	Crystal		Crystal
Bonbon, 7", ftd., 2 hdld., #3900/130	40.00	Bowl, 11½", ftd., 2 hdld., #3900/28	85.00
Bowl, 10", 4 toed, flared, #3900/54	75.00	Bowl, 12", 4 ftd., flared, #3400/4	85.00
Bowl, 11", 2 hdld., #3900/34	90.00	Bowl, 12", 4 ftd., oblong, #3400/160	90.00
Bowl, 11", 4 ftd., fancy edge, #3400/48	100.00	Bowl, 12", 4 toed, flared, #3900/62	90.00

	Crystal
Bowl, 12", 4 toed, oval, hdld., #3900/65	110.00
Butter dish, 5", #3400/52	325.00
Candle, 5", #3900/67	60.00
Candle, 6", 2-lite, #3900/72	75.00
Candle, 6", 3-lite, #3900/74	95.00
Candlestick, 5", #646	65.00
Candlestick, 6", 2-lite, #647	75.00
Candlestick, 6", 3-lite, #1338	95.00
Candy box and cover, 3-part, #3500/57	150.00
Candy w/lid, rnd. #3900/165	160.00
Cocktail shaker, 36 oz., #P101	245.00
Comport, 5", cheese, #3900/135	45.00
Comport, 5⅜", blown, #3121	80.00
Comport, 5½", #3900/136	70.00
Creamer, #3900/41	25.00
Creamer, indiv., #3900/40	25.00
Cruet, 6 oz., w/stopper, #3900/100	150.00
Cup, #3900/17	33.00
Decanter, 28 oz., ftd., #1321	265.00
Ice bucket, #3900/671	165.00
Icer, 2 pc., cocktail, #968	120.00
Lamp, hurricane, #1617	225.00
Lamp, hurricane, keyhole, w/bobeche, #1603	275.00
Lamp, hurricane, w/bobeche, #1613	325.00
Mayonnaise, 3 pc., #3900/129	75.00
Mayonnaise, div., 4 pc., #3900/111	85.00
Mayonnaise, ftd., 2 pc., #3900/19	75.00
Nut cup, 3", 4 ftd., #3400/71	70.00
Oil, 6 oz., #3900/100	125.00
Pitcher, Doulton, #3400/141	435.00
Plate, 6½", #3900/20	14.00
Plate, 8", 2 hdld., #3900/131	30.00
Plate, 8", salad, #3900/22	22.00
Plate, 10½", dinner, #3900/24	85.00
Plate, 12", 4 toed, #3900/26	75.00
Plate, 13", torte, 4 toed, #3900/33	85.00
Plate, 13½", cake, 2 hdld., #3900/35	85.00
Plate, 13½", cracker, #3900/135	75.00
Plate, 14", rolled edge, #3900/166	85.00
Relish, 7", 2 hdld., #3900/123	45.00
Relish, 7", div., 2 hdld., #3900/124	50.00
Relish, 8", 3 part, #3400/91	65.00
Relish, 9", 3 pt., #3900/125	65.00
Relish, 12", 3 pt., #3900/126	75.00
Relish, 12", 5 pt., #3900/120	85.00
Salt & pepper, pr., #3900/1177	135.00
Saucer, #3900/17	7.00
Stem, 1 oz., cordial, #3776	85.00
Stem, 2 oz., sherry, #7966	85.00
Stem, 2½ oz., wine, #3111	75.00
Stem, 3 oz., cocktail, #3111	40.00
Stem, 3 oz., cocktail, #3776	40.00
Stem, 3½ oz., wine, #3776	65.00
Stem, 4 oz., cocktail, #7801	35.00

	Crystal
Stem, 4½ oz., claret, #3776	85.00
Stem, 4½ oz., oyster cocktail, #3111	40.00
Stem, 4½ oz., oyster cocktail, #3776	40.00
Stem, 7 oz., low sherbet, #3111	23.00
Stem, 7 oz., low sherbet, #3776	24.00
Stem, 7 oz., tall sherbet, #3111	30.00
Stem, 7 oz., tall sherbet, #3776	28.00
Stem, 9 oz., water, #3776	45.00
Stem, 10 oz., water, #3111	45.00
Sugar, #3900/41	25.00
Sugar, indiv., #3900/40	35.00
Tumbler, 5 oz., ftd., juice, #3111	30.00
Tumbler, 5 oz., juice, #3776	30.00
Tumbler, 12 oz., ftd., iced tea, #3111	40.00
Tumbler, 12 oz., iced tea, #3776	40.00
Tumbler, 13 oz., #3900/115	45.00
Vase, 5", ftd., bud, #6004	95.00
Vase, 5", globe, #1309	85.00
Vase, 6", ftd., #6004	100.00
Vase, 8", ftd., #6004	120.00
Vase, 9", ftd., keyhole, #1237	125.00
Vase, 10", bud, #274	95.00
Vase, 11", ftd., pedestal, #1299	175.00
Vase, 11", ftd., #278	125.00
Vase, 12", ftd., keyhole, #1238	150.00
Vase, 13", ftd, #279	175.00

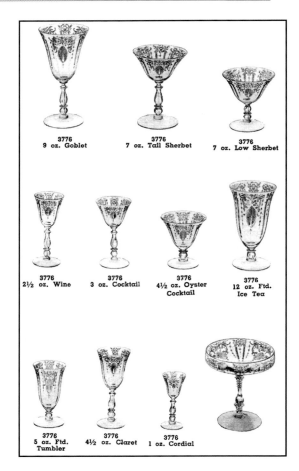

3776 9 oz. Goblet

3776 7 oz. Tall Sherbet

3776 7 oz. Low Sherbet

3776 2½ oz. Wine

3776 3 oz. Cocktail

3776 4½ oz. Oyster Cocktail

3776 12 oz. Ftd. Ice Tea

3776 5 oz. Ftd. Tumbler

3776 4½ oz. Claret

3776 1 oz. Cordial

Colors: crystal, blue, pink, yellow, black, red, cobalt blue, green, caramel slag

Not all Candlewick has a ball in its stem. Note the blue oyster cocktail shown on page 34. I found a dozen of these at a monthly antique show last fall. They were reasonably priced and had been there for three months according to the dealer. I got back from Florida in time to go to the last show of the year and was able to buy them because no one recognized them as Candlewick. See the bottom of page 33 to note differences in stemware lines #3400 and #3800. The red stems with slightly cupped tops are #3800 while the flared top stems are #3400 stemware. If your red or cobalt stemware has some other shape, then it is not Candlewick and might be Bryce. Tumbler and stemware identification is a primary concern of new collectors of Candlewick. Stemware line 400/190 comes with a hollow stem. These are not pictured this time, but should be self-explanatory. The tumblers designated 400/19 have flat bases with knobs around that base as opposed to 400/18 that has a domed foot. The 400/... was Imperial's factory listing for each piece. If you can find a copy of my first *Elegant Glassware of the Depression Era* book, there is a 15 page reprint of Imperial's Catalog B showing Candlewick listings as given by the factory.

Viennese blue Candlewick (shown on page 35) continues to sell, but higher priced red and black items have presently leveled off. One of the problems has been the many reproductions of Candlewick coming into the market. Candlewick was never made by Imperial in Jadite. Dalzell Viking made red and cobalt blue pieces before they went bankrupt and many people rushed to their outlet store to buy these pieces.

For now, prices have stalled as a result of those colored reproductions. Ruby and black fancy bowls sell in the ballpark of $225.00 – $250.00 with the Viennese blue pieces bringing 50 to 60 percent of that. Ruby stems continue to be found in the 3400 and 3800 lines with most of these selling in the $85.00 to $120.00 range. However, cordials are selling in Ruby and Ritz blue (cobalt) from $125.00 to $175.00. Other Ritz blue stems are fetching $125.00 to $175.00. All of these original colored pieces of Candlewick, except black, were made before 1940.

Be sure to notice the hanging lamp on page 32. It was interesting watching the photographers figure how to support it for a photo. It was heftier than it looked. It now hangs in the home of a Texas collector.

	Crystal
Ashtray, eagle, 6½", 1776/1	55.00
Ashtray, heart, 4½", 400/172	10.00
Ashtray, heart, 5½", 400/173	12.00
Ashtray, heart, 6½", 400/174	15.00
Ashtray, indiv., 400/64.	8.00
Ashtray, oblong, 4½", 400/134/1	6.00
Ashtray, round, 2¾", 400/19	9.00
Ashtray, round, 4", 400/33	11.00
Ashtray, round, 5", 400/133	8.00
Ashtray, square, 3¼", 400/651	40.00
Ashtray, square, 4½", 400/652	40.00
Ashtray, square, 5¾", 400/653	50.00
Ashtray, 6", matchbook holder center, 400/60	150.00
Ashtray set, 3 pc. rnd. nesting (crys. or colors), 400/550	35.00
Ashtray set, 3 pc. sq. nesting, 400/650	130.00
Ashtray set, 4 pc. bridge (cigarette holder at side), 400/118	50.00
Basket, 5", beaded hdld., 400/273	295.00
Basket, 6½", hdld., 400/40/0	40.00
Basket, 11", hdld., 400/73/0	275.00
Bell, 4", 400/179	85.00
Bell, 5", 400/108	95.00
Bottle, bitters, w/tube, 4 oz., 400/117	75.00
Bowl, bouillon, 2 hdld., 400/126	50.00
Bowl, #3400, finger, ftd.	35.00
Bowl, #3800, finger	35.00
Bowl, 4½", nappy, 3 ftd., 400/206	80.00
Bowl, 4¾", round, 2 hdld., 400/42B	12.50
Bowl, 5", cream soup, 400/50	45.00
Bowl, 5", fruit, 400/1F	12.00
Bowl, 5", heart w/hand., 400/49H	22.00

	Crystal
Bowl, 5", square, 400/231	100.00
Bowl, 5½", heart, 400/53H	22.00
Bowl, 5½", jelly, w/cover, 400/59	75.00
Bowl, 5½", sauce, deep, 400/243	40.00
Bowl, 6", baked apple, rolled edge, 400/53X	30.00
Bowl, 6", cottage cheese, 400/85	25.00
Bowl, 6", fruit, 400/3F	12.00
Bowl, 6", heart w/hand., 400/51H	30.00
Bowl, 6", mint w/hand., 400/51F	23.00
Bowl, 6", round, div., 2 hdld., 400/52	25.00
Bowl, 6", 2 hdld., 400/52B	15.00
Bowl, 6", 3 ftd., 400/183	60.00
Bowl, 6", sq., 400/232	135.00
Bowl, 6½", relish, 2 pt., 400/84	25.00
Bowl, 6½", 2 hdld., 400/181	30.00
Bowl, 7", round, 400/5F	25.00
Bowl, 7", round, 2 hdld., 400/62B	17.50
Bowl, 7", relish, sq., div., 400/234	165.00
Bowl, 7", ivy, high, bead ft., 400/188	225.00
Bowl, 7", lily, 4 ft., 400/74J	75.00
Bowl, 7", relish, 400/60	25.00
Bowl, 7", sq., 400/233	175.00
Bowl, 7¼", rose, ftd. w/crimp edge, 400/132C	550.00
Bowl, 7½", pickle/celery, 400/57	27.50
Bowl, 7½", lily, bead rim, ftd., 400/75N	295.00
Bowl, 7½", belled (console base), 400/127B	85.00
Bowl, 8", round, 400/7F	37.50
Bowl, 8", relish, 2 pt., 400/268	20.00
Bowl, 8", cov. veg., 400/65/1	325.00
Bowl, 8½", rnd., 400/69B	35.00
Bowl, 8½", nappy, 4 ftd., 400/74B	75.00
Bowl, 8½", 3 ftd., 400/182	135.00
Bowl, 8½", 2 hdld., 400/72B	22.00
Bowl, 8½", pickle/celery, 400/58	20.00
Bowl, 8½", relish, 4 pt., 400/55	22.00
Bowl, 9", round, 400/10F	50.00
Bowl, 9", crimp, ftd., 400/67C	165.00
Bowl, 9", sq., fancy crimp edge, 4 ft., 400/74SC	85.00
Bowl, 9", heart, 400/49H	135.00
Bowl, 9", heart w/hand., 400/73H	175.00
Bowl, 10", 400/13F	45.00
Bowl, 10", banana, 400/103E	1,795.00
Bowl, 10", 3 toed, 400/205	175.00
Bowl, 10", belled (punch base), 400/128B	95.00
Bowl, 10", cupped edge, 400/75F	45.00
Bowl, 10", deep, 2 hdld., 400/113A	155.00
Bowl, 10", divided, deep, 2 hdld., 400/114A	195.00
Bowl, 10", fruit, bead stem (like compote), 400/103F	225.00
Bowl, 10", relish, oval, 2 hdld., 400/217	40.00
Bowl, 10", relish, 3 pt., 3 ft., 400/208	110.00
Bowl, 10", 3 pt., w/cover, 400/216	495.00
Bowl, 10½", belled, 400/63B	60.00
Bowl, 10½", butter/jam, 3 pt., 400/262	195.00
Bowl, 10½", salad, 400/75B	40.00

CANDLEWICK

	Crystal
Bowl, 10½", relish, 3 section, 400/256	30.00
Bowl, 11", celery boat, oval, 400/46	65.00
Bowl, 11", centerpiece, flared, 400/13B	55.00
Bowl, 11", float, inward rim, ftd., 400/75F	40.00
Bowl, 11", oval, 400/124A	275.00
Bowl, 11", oval w/partition, 400/125A	325.00
Bowl, 12", round, 400/92B	45.00
Bowl, 12", belled, 400/106B	100.00
Bowl, 12", float, 400/92F	40.00
Bowl, 12", hdld., 400/113B	165.00
Bowl, 12", shallow, 400/17F	47.50
Bowl, 12", relish, oblong, 4 sect., 400/215	135.00
Bowl, 13", centerpiece, mushroom, 400/92L	60.00
Bowl, 13", float, 1½" deep, 400/101	65.00
Bowl, 13½", relish, 5 pt., 400/209	82.50
Bowl, 14", belled, 400/104B	110.00
Bowl, 14", oval, flared, 400/131B	275.00
Butter and jam set, 5 piece, 400/204	450.00
Butter, w/ cover, rnd., 5½", 400/144	35.00
Butter, w/ cover, no beads, California, 400/276	150.00
Butter, w/ bead top, ¼ lb., 400/161	30.00
Cake stand, 10", low foot, 400/67D	60.00
Cake stand, 11", high foot, 400/103D	75.00
Calendar, 1947, desk	250.00
Candleholder, 3 way, beaded base, 400/115	125.00
Candleholder, 2-lite, 400/100	24.00
Candleholder, flat, 3½", 400/280	40.00
Candleholder, 3½", rolled edge, 400/79R	17.50
Candleholder, 3½", w/fingerhold, 400/81	60.00
Candleholder, flower, 4", 2 bead stem, 400/66F	65.00
Candleholder, flower, 4½", 2 bead stem, 400/66C	65.00
Candleholder, 4½", 3 toed, 400/207	100.00
Candleholder, 3-lite on cir. bead. ctr., 400/147	40.00
Candleholder, 5", hdld./bowled up base, 400/90	65.00
Candleholder, 5", heart shape, 400/40HC	110.00
Candleholder, 5½", 3 bead stems, 400/224	150.00
Candleholder, flower, 5" (epergne inset), 400/40CV	195.00
Candleholder, 5", flower, 400/40C	35.00
Candleholder, 6½", tall, 3 bead stems, 400/175	175.00
Candleholder, flower, 6", round, 400/40F	40.00
Candleholder, urn, 6", holders on cir. ctr. bead, 400/129R	175.00
Candleholder, flower, 6½", square, 400/40S	75.00
Candleholder, mushroom, 400/86	40.00
Candleholder, flower, 9", centerpiece, 400/196FC	225.00
Candy box, round, 5½", 400/59	50.00
Candy box, sq., 6½", rnd. lid, 400/245	295.00
Candy box, w/ cover, 7", 400/259	165.00
Candy box, w/ cover, 7" partitioned, 400/110	125.00
Candy box, w/ cover, round, 7", 3 sect., 400/158	250.00
Candy box, w/ cover, beaded, ft., 400/140	395.00
Cigarette box w/cover, 400/134	35.00

	Crystal
Cigarette holder, 3", bead ft., 400/44	40.00
Cigarette set: 6 pc. (cigarette box & 4 rect. ashtrays), 400/134/6	67.50
Clock, 4", round	295.00
Coaster, 4", 400/78	10.00
Coaster, w/spoon rest, 400/226	18.00
Cocktail, seafood w/bead ft., 400/190	90.00
Cocktail set: 2 pc., plate w/indent; cocktail, 400/97	40.00
Compote, 4½", 400/63B	40.00
Compote, 5", 3 bead stems, 400/220	85.00
Compote, 5½", 4 bead stem, 400/45	30.00
Compote, 5½, low, plain stem, 400/66B	22.00
Compote, 5½", 2 bead stem, 400/66B	22.00
Compote, 8", bead stem, 400/48F	100.00
Compote, 10", ftd. fruit, crimped, 40/103C	200.00
Compote, ft. oval, 400/137	1,400.00
Creamer, domed foot, 400/18	140.00
Creamer, 6 oz., bead handle, 400/30	8.00
Creamer, indiv. bridge, 400/122	9.00
Creamer, plain ft., 400/31	9.00
Creamer, flat, bead handle, 400/126	32.50
Cup, after dinner, 400/77	20.00
Cup, coffee, 400/37	7.50
Cup, punch, 400/211	8.00
Cup, tea, 400/35	8.00
Decanter, w/stopper, 15 oz. cordial, 400/82/2	495.00
Decanter, w/stopper, 18 oz., 400/18	350.00
Decanter, w/stopper, 26 oz., 400/163	400.00
Deviled egg server, 12", ctr. hdld., 400/154	125.00
Egg cup, bead. ft., 400/19	55.00
Fork & spoon, set, 400/75	40.00

	Crystal
Hurricane lamp, 2 pc. candle base, 400/79	135.00
Hurricane lamp, 2 pc., hdld. candle base, 400/76	195.00
Hurricane lamp, 3 pc. flared & crimped edge globe, 400/152	195.00
Ice tub, 5½" deep, 8" diam., 400/63	125.00
Ice tub, 7", 2 hdld., 400/168	250.00
Icer, 2 pc., seafood/fruit cocktail, 400/53/3	100.00
Icer, 2 pc., seafood/fruit cocktail #3800 line, one bead stem	75.00
Jam set, 5 pc., oval tray w/2 marmalade jars w/ladles, 400/1589	115.00
Jar tower, 3 sect., 400/655	495.00
Knife, butter, 4000	500.00
Ladle, marmalade, 3 bead stem, 400/130	12.00
Ladle, mayonnaise, 6¼", 400/135	12.00
Marmalade set, 3 pc., beaded ft. w/cover & spoon, 400/1989	45.00
Marmalade set, 3 pc. tall jar, domed bead ft., lid, spoon, 400/8918	100.00
Marmalade set, 4 pc., liner saucer, jar, lid, spoon, 400/89	55.00
Mayonnaise set, 2 pc. scoop side bowl, spoon, 400/23	40.00
Mayonnaise set, 3 pc. hdld. tray/hdld. bowl/ladle, 400/52/3	55.00

	Crystal
Mayonnaise set, 3 pc. plate, heart bowl, spoon, 400/49	40.00
Mayonnaise set, 3 pc. scoop side bowl, spoon, tray, 400/496	125.00
Mayonnaise 4 pc., plate, divided bowl, 2 ladles, 400/84	45.00
Mirror, 4½", rnd., standing	135.00
Mustard jar, w/spoon, 400/156	40.00
Oil, 4 oz., bead base, 400/164	55.00
Oil, 6 oz., bead base, 400/166	75.00
Oil, 4 oz., bulbous bottom, 400/274	55.00
Oil, 4 oz., hdld., bulbous bottom, 400/278	75.00
Oil, 6 oz., hdld., bulbous bottom, 400/279	90.00
Oil, 6 oz., bulbous bottom, 400/275	65.00
Oil, w/stopper, etched "Oil," 400/121	70.00
Oil, w/stopper, etched "Vinegar," 400/121	70.00
Party set, 2 pc., oval plate w/indent for cup, 400/98	27.50
Pitcher, 14 oz., short rnd., 400/330	210.00
Pitcher, 16 oz., low ft., 400/19	250.00
Pitcher, 16 oz., no ft., 400/16	200.00
Pitcher, 20 oz., plain, 400/416	40.00
Pitcher, 40 oz., juice/cocktail, 400/19	210.00
Pitcher, 40 oz., manhattan, 400/18	250.00
Pitcher, 40 oz., plain, 400/419	50.00

	Crystal
Pitcher, 64 oz., plain, 400/424	60.00
Pitcher, 80 oz., plain, 400/424	70.00
Pitcher, 80 oz., 400/24	165.00
Pitcher, 80 oz., beaded ft., 400/18	250.00
Plate, 4½", 400/34	8.00
Plate, 5½", 2 hdld., 400/42D	12.00
Plate, 6", bread/butter, 400/1D	8.00
Plate, 6", canape w/off ctr. indent, 400/36	18.00
Plate, 6¾", 2 hdld. crimped, 400/52C	30.00
Plate, 7", salad, 400/3D	9.00
Plate, 7½", 2 hdld., 400/52D	15.00
Plate, 7½", triangular, 400/266	95.00
Plate, 8", oval, 400/169	25.00
Plate, 8", salad, 400/5D	10.00
Plate, 8", w/indent, 400/50	12.00
Plate, 8¼", crescent salad, 400/120	65.00
Plate, 8½", 2 hdld., crimped, 400/62C	30.00
Plate, 8½", 2 hdld., 400/62D	13.00
Plate, 8½", salad, 400/5D	12.00
Plate, 8½", 2 hdld. (sides upturned), 400/62E	28.00
Plate, 9", luncheon, 400/7D	15.00
Plate, 9", oval, salad, 400/38	45.00
Plate, 9", w/indent, oval, 400/98	24.00
Plate, 10", 2 hdld., sides upturned, 400/72E	40.00
Plate, 10", 2 hdld. crimped, 400/72C	42.00
Plate, 10", 2 hdld., 400/72D	35.00
Plate, 10½", dinner, 400/10D	45.00
Plate, 12", 2 hdld., 400/145D	45.00

	Crystal
Plate, 12", 2 hdld. crimp., 400/145C	55.00
Plate, 12", service, 400/13D	35.00
Plate, 12½", cupped edge, torte, 400/75V	33.00
Plate, 12½", oval, 400/124	90.00
Plate, 13½", cupped edge, serving, 400/92V	47.00
Plate, 14" birthday cake (holes for 72 candles), 400/160	550.00
Plate, 14", 2 hdld., sides upturned, 400/113E	50.00
Plate, 14", 2 hdld., torte, 400/113D	50.00
Plate, 14", service, 400/92D	50.00
Plate, 14", torte, 400/17D	50.00
Plate, 17", cupped edge, 400/20V	95.00
Plate, 17", torte, 400/20D	95.00
Platter, 13", 400/124D	110.00
Platter, 16", 400/131D	235.00
Punch ladle, 400/91	30.00
Punch set, family, 8 demi cups, ladle, lid, 400/139/77	750.00
Punch set, 15 pc. bowl on base, 12 cups, ladle, 400/20	300.00
Relish & dressing set, 4 pc. (10½" 4 pt. relish w/marmalade), 400/1112	115.00
Salad set, 4 pc. (buffet; lg. rnd. tray, div. bowl, 2 spoons), 400/17	135.00
Salad set, 4 pc. (rnd. plate, flared bowl, fork, spoon), 400/75B	110.00
Salt & pepper pr., bead ft., straight side, chrome top, 400/247	20.00

	Crystal
Salt & pepper pr., bead ft., bulbous, chrome top, 400/96	18.00
Salt & pepper pr., bulbous w/bead stem, plastic top, 400/116	110.00
Salt & pepper, pr., indiv., 400/109	14.00
Salt & pepper, pr., ftd. bead base, 400/190	60.00
Salt dip, 2", 400/61	11.00
Salt dip, 2¼", 400/19	10.00
Salt spoon, 3, 400/616	11.00
Salt spoon, w/ribbed bowl, 4000	11.00
Sauce boat, 400/169	125.00
Sauce boat liner, 400/169	50.00
Saucer, after dinner, 400/77AD	5.00
Saucer, tea or coffee, 400/35 or 400/37	3.00
Set: 2 pc. hdld. cracker w/cheese compote, 400/88	65.00
Set: 2 pc. rnd. cracker plate w/indent; cheese compote, 400/145	65.00
Snack jar w/cover, bead ft., 400/139/1	625.00
Stem, 1 oz., cordial, 400/190	90.00
Stem, 4 oz., cocktail, 400/190	22.00
Stem, 5 oz., tall sherbet, 400/190	15.00
Stem, 5 oz., wine, 400/190	25.00
Stem, 6 oz., sherbet, 400/190	16.00
Stem, 10 oz., water 400/190	22.00
Stem, #3400, 1 oz., cordial	42.00
Stem, #3400, 4 oz., cocktail	20.00
Stem, #3400, 4 oz., oyster cocktail	16.00
Stem, #3400, 4 oz., wine	26.00
Stem, #3400, 5 oz., claret	58.00
Stem, #3400, 5 oz., low sherbet	11.00
Stem, #3400, 6 oz., parfait	58.00
Stem, #3400, 6 oz., sherbet/saucer champagne	18.00
Stem, #3400, 9 oz., goblet, water	22.00
Stem, #3800, low sherbet	28.00
Stem, #3800, brandy	60.00
Stem, #3800, 1 oz., cordial	50.00
Stem, #3800, 4 oz., cocktail	25.00
Stem, #3800, 4 oz., wine	30.00
Stem, #3800, 6 oz., champagne/sherbet	30.00
Stem, #3800, 5 oz. claret	75.00
Stem, #3800, 9 oz., water goblet	40.00
Stem, #4000, 1¼ oz., cordial	40.00
Stem, #4000, 4 oz., cocktail	25.00
Stem, #4000, 5 oz., wine	32.00
Stem, #4000, 6 oz., tall sherbet	25.00
Stem, #4000, 11 oz., goblet	35.00
Stem, #4000, 12 oz., tea	35.00
Strawberry set, 2 pc. (7" plate/sugar dip bowl), 400/83	50.00
Sugar, domed foot, 400/18	135.00
Sugar, 6 oz., bead hdld., 400/30	8.00
Sugar, flat, bead handle, 400/126	42.00
Sugar, indiv. bridge, 400/122	9.00
Sugar, plain ft., 400/31	7.00
Tete-a-tete 3 pc. brandy, a.d. cup, 6½" oval tray, 400/111	125.00
Tidbit server, 2 tier, cupped, 400/2701	60.00
Tidbit set, 3 pc., 400/18TB	225.00
Toast, w/cover, set, 7¾", 400/123	350.00

	Crystal
Tray, 5½", hdld., upturned handles, 400/42E	25.00
Tray, 5½", lemon, ctr. hdld., 400/221	37.50
Tray, 5¼" x 9¼", condiment, 400/148	45.00
Tray, 6½", 400/29	18.00
Tray, 6", wafer, handle bent to ctr. of dish, 400/51T	25.00
Tray, 10½", ctr. hdld. fruit, 400/68F	150.00
Tray, 11½", ctr. hdld. party, 400/68D	40.00
Tray, 13½", 2 hdld. celery, oval, 400/105	35.00
Tray, 13", relish, 5 sections, 400/102	77.50
Tray, 14", hdld., 400/113E	95.00
Tumbler, 3½ oz., cocktail, 400/18	55.00
Tumbler, 5 oz., juice, 400/18	60.00
Tumbler, 6 oz., sherbet, 400/18	60.00
Tumbler, 7 oz., old-fashion, 400/18	70.00
Tumbler, 7 oz., parfait, 400/18	85.00
Tumbler, 9 oz., water, 400/18	75.00
Tumbler, 12 oz., tea, 400/18	80.00
Tumbler, 3 oz., ftd., cocktail, 400/19	18.00
Tumbler, 3 oz., ftd., wine, 400/19	25.00
Tumbler, 5 oz., low sherbet, 400/19	16.00
Tumbler, 5 oz., juice, 400/19	12.50
Tumbler, 7 oz., old-fashion, 400/19	38.00
Tumbler, 10 oz., 400/19	14.00
Tumbler, 12 oz., 400/19	25.00
Tumbler, 14 oz., 400/19, tea	25.00
Tumbler, #3400, 5 oz., ft., juice	18.00
Tumbler, #3400, 6 oz., parfait	70.00
Tumbler, #3400, 9 oz., ftd.	20.00
Tumbler, #3400, 10 oz., ftd.	20.00
Tumbler, #3400, 12 oz., ftd.	20.00
Tumbler, #3800, 5 oz., juice	30.00
Tumbler, #3800, 9 oz.	30.00
Tumbler, #3800, 12 oz.	37.50
Vase, 4", bead ft., sm. neck, ball, 400/25	65.00
Vase, 5¾", bead ft., bud, 400/107	65.00
Vase, 5¾", bead ft., mini bud, 400/107	65.00
Vase, 6", flat, crimped edge, 400/287C	50.00
Vase, 6", ftd., flared rim, 400/138B	175.00
Vase, 6" diam., 400/198	350.00
Vase, 6", fan, 400/287 F	40.00
Vase, 7", ftd., bud, 400/186	295.00
Vase, 7", ftd., bud, 400/187	310.00
Vase, 7", ivy bowl, 400/74J	150.00
Vase, 7", rolled rim w/bead hdld., 400/87 R	45.00
Vase, 7", rose bowl, 400/142 K	275.00
Vase, 7¼", ftd., rose bowl, crimped top, 400/132C	495.00
Vase, 7½", ftd., rose bowl, 400/132	450.00
Vase, 8", fan, w/bead hdld., 400/87F	35.00
Vase, 8", flat, crimped edge, 400/143C	95.00
Vase, 8", fluted rim w/bead hdlds., 400/87C	40.00
Vase, 8½", bead ft., bud, 400/28C	110.00
Vase, 8½", bead ft., flared rim, 400/21	295.00
Vase, 8½", bead ft., inward rim, 400/27	295.00
Vase, 8½", hdld. (pitcher shape), 400/227	495.00
Vase, 10", bead ft., straight side, 400/22	250.00
Vase, 10", ftd., 400/193	250.00

Color: crystal, Sapphire blue, Cape Cod blue, Chartreuse, Ruby, Cranberry pink, Jasmine yellow

Canterbury, or line No. 115, was the mould blank Duncan used for several of their etched patterns, First Love is the most recognized. You can find First Love in my *Collectible Glassware of the 40s, 50s, and 60s* book if that pattern interests you. In order to have space for the new patterns in this book I've removed most of the copies of original catalog pages that were included in previous editions. If you are a new collector and wish to see Canterbury as listed by Duncan, you will have to track down an earlier edition. I will warn you that older editions have become collectible themselves and sell at a premium price!

First introduced in 1937, Canterbury had its biggest production runs through the 1940s and early 1950s. Later, moulds were transferred to Tiffin where most of the colored Canterbury was made. I see the yellow-green colored Canterbury (called Chartreuse) more than any other color in my travels. Many of the items being found in this color are Tiffin pieces manufactured from Duncan's moulds sometime after 1955.

Moderately priced when compared to patterns made by Cambridge, Heisey, or Fostoria, Canterbury is beginning to creep up in price with new collectors seeking it. Pieces are heavier than most patterns, which bothers some collectors, but that has also meant greater survival over the years. Canterbury exudes that 50s love of fluid shapes.

I have only shown crystal ware except for the ice buckets pictured on page 40. Note that silver decorated beauty! I have not found enough Canterbury in other colors to get a feel for those prices. Opalescent items seem to be priced three to four times those for crystal, but I rarely see them sell. Duncan's light blue was called Sapphire and the opalescent blue was dubbed Cape Cod blue. The red was Ruby. You may find opalescent pieces of Canterbury in pink, called Cranberry, or yellow, called Jasmine. I keep running into Ruby pieces that are priced either very high or rather low. There does not seem to be any consensus. Time will determine whether this color is rare. In Florida, Canterbury pieces are often cloudy or stained, which probably indicates the hard water from wells here leaves residue that will not remove easily. Be aware of this problem when buying early in the morning by flashlight when dew is on the glass! Water hides the cloudiness until it dries out later and you see your buying error. If you know of additional pieces not listed or wish to relate prices on colored wares, just drop me a postcard. The 64 ounce water pitcher and candlesticks seem to be the items that sell fastest.

	Crystal
Ashtray, 3"	6.00
Ashtray, 3", club	8.00
Ashtray, 4½", club	10.00
Ashtray, 5"	12.00
Ashtray, 5½", club	15.00
Basket, 3" x 3" x 3¼", oval, hdld.	20.00
Basket, 3" x 4", crimped, hdld.	27.50
Basket, 3½", crimped, hdld.	35.00
Basket, 3½", oval, hdld.	25.00
Basket, 4½" x 4¾" x 4¾", oval, hdld.	40.00
Basket, 4½" x 5" x 5", crimped, hdld.	45.00
Basket, 9¼" x 10" x 7¼"	55.00
Basket, 10" x 4¼" x 7", oval, hdld.	70.00
Basket, 10" x 4½" x 8", oval, hdld.	75.00
Basket, 11½", oval, hdld.	75.00
Bowl, 4¼" x 2", finger	12.00
Bowl, 5" x 3¼", 2 part, salad dressing	12.50
Bowl, 5" x 3¼", salad dressing	12.50
Bowl, 5½" x 1¾", one hdld., heart	9.00
Bowl, 5½" x 1¾", one hdld., square	9.00
Bowl, 5½" x 1¾", one hdld., star	10.00
Bowl, 5½" x 1¾", one hdld., fruit	7.00
Bowl, 5½" x 1¾", one hdld., round	7.00
Bowl, 5", fruit nappy	8.00
Bowl, 6" x 2", 2 hdld., round	10.00
Bowl, 6" x 2", 2 hdld., sweetmeat, star	15.00
Bowl, 6" x 3¼", 2 part, salad dressing	14.00
Bowl, 6" x 3¼", salad dressing	14.00
Bowl, 6" x 5¼" x 2¼", oval olive	10.00
Bowl, 7½" x 2¼", crimped	15.00
Bowl, 7½" x 2¼", gardenia	17.50
Bowl, 8" x 2¾", crimped	22.50

	Crystal
Bowl, 8" x 2½", flared	17.50
Bowl, 8½" x 4"	22.00
Bowl, 9" x 2", gardenia	27.50
Bowl, 9" x 4¼", crimped	27.50
Bowl, 9" x 6" x 3", oval	30.00
Bowl, 10" x 5", salad	30.00
Bowl, 10" x 8½" x 5", oval	27.50
Bowl, 10¾" x 4¾"	27.50
Bowl, 10½" x 5", crimped	32.50
Bowl, 11½" x 8¼", oval	32.50
Bowl, 12" x 2¾", gardenia	30.00
Bowl, 12" x 3½", flared	30.00
Bowl, 12" x 3¾", crimped	32.50
Bowl, 13" x 8½" x 3¼", oval, flared	35.00
Bowl, 13" x 10" x 5", crimped, oval	40.00
Bowl, 15" x 2¾", shallow salad	42.00
Candle, 3", low	12.50
Candle, 3½"	15.00
Candlestick, 6", 3-lite	37.50
Candlestick, 6"	25.00
Candlestick, 7", w/U prisms	75.00
Candy and cover, 8" x 3½", 3 hdld., 3 part	35.00
Candy, 6½", w/5" lid	32.50
Celery and relish, 10½" x 6¾" x 1¼", 2 hdld., 2 part	32.50
Celery and relish, 10½" x 6¾" x 1¼", 2 hdld., 3 part	32.50
Celery, 9" x 4" x 1¼", 2 hdld.	22.50
Cheese stand, 5½" x 3½" high	15.00
Cigarette box w/cover, 3½" x 4½"	22.50
Cigarette jar w/cover, 4"	30.00
Comport, high, 6" x 5½" high	20.00

	Crystal
Comport, low, 6" x 4½" high	18.00
Creamer, 2¾", 3 oz., individual	9.00
Creamer, 3¾", 7 oz.	9.00
Cup	8.00
Decanter w/stopper, 12", 32 oz.	75.00
Ice bucket or vase, 6"	32.50
Ice bucket or vase, 7"	35.00
Lamp, hurricane, w/prisms, 15"	100.00
Marmalade, 4½" x 2¾", crimped	20.00
Mayonnaise, 5" x 3¼"	20.00
Mayonnaise, 5½" x 3¼", crimped	22.00
Mayonnaise, 6" x 3¼"	24.00
Pitcher, 9¼", 32 oz., hdld., martini	85.00
Pitcher, 9¼", 32 oz., martini	75.00
Pitcher, 64 oz.	250.00
Plate, 6½", one hdld., fruit	6.00
Plate, 6", finger bowl liner	6.00
Plate, 7½"	9.00
Plate, 7½", 2 hdld., mayonnaise	12.00
Plate, 8½"	12.00
Plate, 11¼", dinner	27.50
Plate, 11", 2 hdld. w/ring, cracker	20.00
Plate, 11", 2 hdld., sandwich	22.00
Plate, 13½", cake, hdld.	35.00
Plate, 14", cake	25.00
Relish, 6" x 2", 2 hdld., 2 part, round	14.00
Relish, 6" x 2", 2 hdld., 2 part, star	14.00
Relish, 7" x 5¼" x 2¼", 2 hdld., 2 part, oval	16.00
Relish, 8" x 1¾", 3 hdld., 3 part	17.50
Relish, 9" x 1½", 3 hdld., 3 part	22.00
Rose bowl, 5"	20.00
Rose bowl, 6"	25.00
Salt and pepper	22.50
Sandwich tray, 12" x 5¼", center handle	47.50
Saucer	3.00
Sherbet, crimped, 4½", 2¾" high	10.00
Sherbet, crimped, 5½", 2¾" high	11.00
Stem, 3¾", 6 oz., ice cream	6.00
Stem, 4", 4½ oz., oyster cocktail	12.50
Stem, 4¼", 1 oz., cordial, #5115	28.00
Stem, 4¼", 3½ oz., cocktail	12.00
Stem, 4½", 6 oz., saucer champagne	12.00
Stem, 5", 4 oz., claret or wine	20.00
Stem, 5¼", 3 oz., cocktail, #5115	14.00
Stem, 5½", 5 oz., saucer champagne, #5115	12.00
Stem, 6", 3½ oz., wine, #5115	27.50
Stem, 6", 9 oz., water	15.00
Stem, 6¾", 5 oz., claret, #5115	27.00
Stem, 7¼", 10 oz., water, #5115	20.00

	Crystal
Sugar, 2½", 3 oz., individual	9.00
Sugar, 3", 7 oz.	9.00
Top hat, 3"	18.00
Tray, 9", individual cr/sug	10.00
Tray, 9" x 4" x 1¼", 2 part, pickle and olive	17.50
Tumbler, 2½", 1½ oz., whiskey	12.50
Tumbler, 2½", 5 oz., ftd., ice cream, #5115	10.00
Tumbler, 3¼", 4 oz., ftd., oyster cocktail, #5115	12.50
Tumbler, 3¾", 5 oz., flat, juice	8.00
Tumbler, 4¼", 5 oz., ftd., juice	10.00
Tumbler, 4¼", 5 oz., ftd., juice, #5115	12.00
Tumbler, 4½", 9 oz., flat, table, straight	14.00
Tumbler, 4½", 10 oz., ftd., water, #5115	14.00
Tumbler, 5½", 9 oz., ftd., luncheon goblet	14.00
Tumbler, 5¾", 12 oz., ftd., ice tea, #5115	17.50
Tumbler, 6¼", 13 oz., flat, ice tea	18.00
Tumbler, 6¼", 13 oz., ftd., ice tea	20.00
Urn, 4½" x 4½"	15.00
Vase, 3", crimped violet	15.00
Vase, 3½", clover leaf	15.00
Vase, 3½", crimped	15.00
Vase, 3½", crimped violet	15.00
Vase, 3½", oval	15.00
Vase, 4", clover leaf	17.50
Vase, 4", crimped	17.50
Vase, 4", flared rim	17.50
Vase, 4", oval	17.50
Vase, 4½" x 4¾"	15.00
Vase, 4½", clover leaf	20.00
Vase, 4½", crimped violet	17.50
Vase, 4½", oval	17.50
Vase, 5" x 5", crimped	17.50
Vase, 5", clover leaf	25.00
Vase, 5", crimped	17.50
Vase, 5½", crimped	20.00
Vase, 5½", flower arranger	27.50
Vase, 6½", clover leaf	35.00
Vase, 7", crimped	32.00
Vase, 7", flower arranger	40.00
Vase, 8½" x 6"	50.00
Vase, 12", flared	75.00

Colors: amber, Antique blue, Azalea, black, crystal, Evergreen, milk glass, Ritz blue, Ruby, Verde

Crystal is most collected Cape Cod, because it is available whereas colored wares are difficult to accumulate. There are several hundred different pieces in crystal giving collectors a wide range of choices as to how much to gather. Colored items were mostly made in the late 1960s and 1970s. You can see examples of most Cape Cod colors pictured here. Below on top and second row is Verde (green) and the dark green goblet is Emerald. The pitcher and tumbler on end of top row were made for Tiara and not considered true Imperial Cape Cod by knowledgeable collectors. Rounding out the second row are pieces in milk glass, ebony, and crystal trimmed in red. Those latter two items were made very early in Cape Cod's production and pieces trimmed in red are difficult to find with that red flashing intact. The top row on page 42 is all Azalea with Ruby, amber and Antique blue filling in the bottom row. As can be seen by those photos, stems and tumblers are what turn up regularly in color.

Actually stems and tumblers are what is found most often in crystal, a fact which is causing them to sell at lower prices than several years ago. Now might be the time to stock some for the future. Rarely found items continue to escalate in price, but commonly found items have stagnated of late. Probably, the easiest color to acquire a small set of would be the Ruby. It won't come cheaply, but there was enough made to find it. Recently, Ruby old fashions have been selling for $75.00 rather quickly. I was offered a 52-piece Ruby set early this year and the only way I could afford to buy it was for the old fashion in the group which I knew to be sought by collectors. You can still buy most of the basic pieces of Cape Cod reasonably, but for how long is anybody's guess. Buy it now if you like it.

	Crystal		Crystal
Ashtray, 4", 160/134/1	14.00	Bowl, 4", finger, 1602	12.00
Ashtray, 5½", 160/150	17.50	Bowl, 4½", finger, 1604½A	12.00
Basket, 9", handled, crimped, 160/221/0	225.00	Bowl, 4½", handled spider, 160/180	22.50
Basket, 11" tall, handled, 160/40	150.00	Bowl, 4½", dessert, tab handled, 160/197	24.00
Bottle, bitters, 4 oz., 160/235	60.00	Bowl, 5", dessert, heart shape, 160/49H	22.00
Bottle, cologne, w/stopper, 1601	60.00	Bowl, 5", flower, 1605N	25.00
Bottle, condiment, 6 oz., 160/224	65.00	Bowl, 5½", fruit, 160/23B	10.00
Bottle, cordial, 18 oz., 160/256	115.00	Bowl, 5½", handled spider, 160/181	25.00
Bottle, decanter, 26 oz., 160/244	150.00	Bowl, 5½", tab handled, soup, 160/198	22.50
Bottle, ketchup, 14 oz., 160/237	225.00	Bowl, 6", fruit, 160/3F	10.00
Bowl, 3", handled mint, 160/183	20.00	Bowl, 6", baked apple, 160/53X	11.00
Bowl, 3", jelly, 160/33	12.00	Bowl, 6", handled, round mint, 160/51F	22.00

	Crystal
Bowl, 6", handled heart, 160/40H	22.00
Bowl, 6", handled mint, 160/51H	22.00
Bowl, 6", handled tray, 160/51T	30.00
Bowl, 6½", handled portioned spider, 160/187	27.50
Bowl, 6½", handled spider, 160/182	32.50
Bowl, 6½", tab handled, 160/199	30.00
Bowl, 7", nappy, 160/5F	22.00
Bowl, 7½", 160/7F	22.00
Bowl, 7½", 2-handled, 160/62B	27.50
Bowl, 8¾", 160/10F	30.00
Bowl, 9", footed fruit, 160/67F	62.50
Bowl, 9½", 2 handled, 160/145B	40.00
Bowl, 9½", crimped, 160/221C	95.00
Bowl, 9½", float, 160/221F	65.00
Bowl, 10", footed, 160/137B	75.00
Bowl, 10", oval, 160/221	75.00
Bowl, 11", flanged edge, 1608X	150.00
Bowl, 11", oval, 160/124	80.00
Bowl, 11", oval divided, 160/125	85.00
Bowl, 11", round, 1608A	95.00
Bowl, 11", salad, 1608D	60.00
Bowl, 11¼", oval, 1602	75.00
Bowl, 12", 160/75B	40.00
Bowl, 12", oval, 160/131B	90.00
Bowl, 12", oval crimped, 160/131C	150.00
Bowl, 12", punch, 160/20B	65.00
Bowl, 13", console, 160/75L	42.50
Bowl, 15", console, 1601/0L	75.00
Butter, 5", w/cover, handled, 160/144	30.00
Butter, w/cover, ¼ lb., 160/161	45.00
Cake plate, 10", 4 toed, 160/220	100.00
Cake stand, 10½", footed, 160/67D	50.00
Cake stand, 11", 160/103D	85.00
Candleholder, twin, 160/100	95.00
Candleholder, 3", single, 160/170	17.50
Candleholder, 4", 160/81	27.50
Candleholder, 4", Aladdin style, 160/90	150.00

	Crystal
Candleholder, 4½", saucer, 160/175	30.00
Candleholder, 5", 160/80	20.00
Candleholder, 5", flower, 160/45B	60.00
Candleholder, 5½", flower, 160/45N	110.00
Candleholder, 6", centerpiece, 160/48BC	95.00
Candy, w/cover, 160/110	85.00
Carafe, wine, 26 oz., 160/185	195.00
Celery, 8", 160/105	30.00
Celery, 10½", 160/189	55.00
Cigarette box, 4½", 160/134	45.00
Cigarette holder, ftd., 1602	12.50
Cigarette holder, Tom & Jerry mug, 160/200	32.50
Cigarette lighter, 1602	30.00
Coaster, w/spoon rest, 160/76	12.00
Coaster, 3", square, 160/85	20.00
Coaster, 4", round, 160/78	15.00
Coaster, 4½", flat, 160/1R	9.00
Comport, 5¼", 160F	27.50
Comport, 5¾", 160X	30.00
Comport, 6", 160/45	25.00
Comport, 6", w/cover, ftd., 160/140	80.00
Comport, 7", 160/48B	37.50
Comport, 11¼", oval, 1602, 6½" tall	195.00
Creamer, 160/190	30.00
Creamer, 160/30	8.00
Creamer, ftd., 160/31	15.00
Cruet, w/stopper, 4 oz., 160/119	25.00
Cruet, w/stopper, 5 oz., 160/70	30.00
Cruet, w/stopper, 6 oz., 160/241	40.00
Cup, tea, 160/35	7.00
Cup, coffee, 160/37	7.00
Cup, bouillon, 160/250	30.00
Decanter, bourbon, 160/260	110.00
Decanter, rye, 160/260	110.00
Decanter w/stopper, 30 oz., 160/163	70.00
Decanter w/stopper, 24 oz., 160/212	75.00
Egg cup, 160/225	32.50

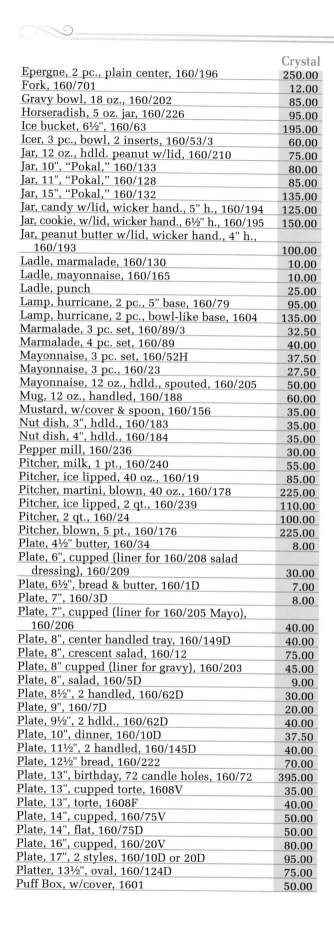

	Crystal
Epergne, 2 pc., plain center, 160/196	250.00
Fork, 160/701	12.00
Gravy bowl, 18 oz., 160/202	85.00
Horseradish, 5 oz. jar, 160/226	95.00
Ice bucket, 6½", 160/63	195.00
Icer, 3 pc., bowl, 2 inserts, 160/53/3	60.00
Jar, 12 oz., hdld. peanut w/lid, 160/210	75.00
Jar, 10", "Pokal," 160/133	80.00
Jar, 11", "Pokal," 160/128	85.00
Jar, 15", "Pokal," 160/132	135.00
Jar, candy w/lid, wicker hand., 5" h., 160/194	125.00
Jar, cookie, w/lid, wicker hand., 6½" h., 160/195	150.00
Jar, peanut butter w/lid, wicker hand., 4" h., 160/193	100.00
Ladle, marmalade, 160/130	10.00
Ladle, mayonnaise, 160/165	10.00
Ladle, punch	25.00
Lamp, hurricane, 2 pc., 5" base, 160/79	95.00
Lamp, hurricane, 2 pc., bowl-like base, 1604	135.00
Marmalade, 3 pc. set, 160/89/3	32.50
Marmalade, 4 pc. set, 160/89	40.00
Mayonnaise, 3 pc. set, 160/52H	37.50
Mayonnaise, 3 pc., 160/23	27.50
Mayonnaise, 12 oz., hdld., spouted, 160/205	50.00
Mug, 12 oz., handled, 160/188	60.00
Mustard, w/cover & spoon, 160/156	35.00
Nut dish, 3", hdld., 160/183	35.00
Nut dish, 4", hdld., 160/184	35.00
Pepper mill, 160/236	30.00
Pitcher, milk, 1 pt., 160/240	55.00
Pitcher, ice lipped, 40 oz., 160/19	85.00
Pitcher, martini, blown, 40 oz., 160/178	225.00
Pitcher, ice lipped, 2 qt., 160/239	110.00
Pitcher, 2 qt., 160/24	100.00
Pitcher, blown, 5 pt., 160/176	225.00
Plate, 4½" butter, 160/34	8.00
Plate, 6", cupped (liner for 160/208 salad dressing), 160/209	30.00
Plate, 6½", bread & butter, 160/1D	7.00
Plate, 7", 160/3D	8.00
Plate, 7", cupped (liner for 160/205 Mayo), 160/206	40.00
Plate, 8", center handled tray, 160/149D	40.00
Plate, 8", crescent salad, 160/12	75.00
Plate, 8" cupped (liner for gravy), 160/203	45.00
Plate, 8", salad, 160/5D	9.00
Plate, 8½", 2 handled, 160/62D	30.00
Plate, 9", 160/7D	20.00
Plate, 9½", 2 hdld., 160/62D	40.00
Plate, 10", dinner, 160/10D	37.50
Plate, 11½", 2 handled, 160/145D	40.00
Plate, 12½" bread, 160/222	70.00
Plate, 13", birthday, 72 candle holes, 160/72	395.00
Plate, 13", cupped torte, 1608V	35.00
Plate, 13", torte, 1608F	40.00
Plate, 14", cupped, 160/75V	50.00
Plate, 14", flat, 160/75D	50.00
Plate, 16", cupped, 160/20V	80.00
Plate, 17", 2 styles, 160/10D or 20D	95.00
Platter, 13½", oval, 160/124D	75.00
Puff Box, w/cover, 1601	50.00

	Crystal
Relish, 8", hdld., 2 part, 160/223	37.50
Relish, 9½", 4 pt., 160/56	35.00
Relish, 9½", oval, 3 part, 160/55	25.00
Relish, 11", 5 part, 160/102	55.00
Relish, 11¼", 3 part, oval, 1602	75.00
Salad dressing, 6 oz., hdld., spouted, 160/208	60.00
Salad set, 14" plate, 12" bowl, fork & spoon, 160/75	95.00
Salt & pepper, individual, 160/251	20.00
Salt & pepper, pr., ftd., 160/116	20.00
Salt & pepper, pr., ftd., stemmed, 160/243	40.00
Salt & pepper, pr., 160/96	18.00
Salt & pepper, pr. square, 160/109	27.50
Salt dip, 160/61	20.00
Salt spoon, 1600	8.00
Saucer, tea, 160/35	2.00
Saucer, coffee, 160/37	2.00
Server, 12", ftd. or turned over, 160/93	85.00
Spoon, 160/701	12.00
Stem, 1½ oz., cordial, 1602	8.00
Stem, 3 oz., wine, 1602	6.00
Stem, 3½ oz., cocktail, 1602	6.00
Stem, 5 oz., claret, 1602	8.00
Stem, 6 oz., low sundae, 1602	4.00
Stem, 6 oz., parfait, 1602	8.00
Stem, 6 oz., sherbet, 1600	14.00
Stem, 6 oz., tall sherbet, 1602	9.00
Stem, 9 oz., water, 1602	7.50
Stem, 10 oz., water, 1600	18.00
Stem, 11 oz., dinner goblet, 1602	8.00
Stem, 14 oz., goblet, magnum, 160	40.00
Stem, oyster cocktail, 1602	8.00
Sugar, 160/190	30.00
Sugar, 160/30	7.00
Sugar, ftd., 160/31	15.00
Toast, w/cover, 160/123	225.00
Tom & Jerry footed punch bowl, 160/200	350.00
Tray, sq. cov. sugar & creamer, 160/25/26	150.00
Tray, 7", for creamer/sugar, 160/29	15.00
Tray, 11", pastry, center hdld., 160/68D	70.00
Tumbler, 2½ oz., whiskey, 160	10.00
Tumbler, 6 oz., ftd., juice, 1602	6.00
Tumbler, 6 oz., juice, 1600	6.00
Tumbler, 7 oz., old-fashion, 160	10.00
Tumbler, 10 oz., ftd., water, 1602	8.00
Tumbler, 10 oz., water, 160	8.00
Tumbler, 12 oz., ftd., ice tea, 1602	10.00
Tumbler, 12 oz., ftd., tea, 160	15.00
Tumbler, 12 oz., ice tea, 160	14.00
Tumbler, 14 oz., double old-fashion, 160	30.00
Tumbler, 16 oz., 160	35.00
Vase, 6¼", ftd., 160/22	35.00
Vase, 6½", ftd., 160/110B	70.00
Vase, 7½", ftd., 160/22	40.00
Vase, 8", fan, 160/87F	225.00
Vase, 8½", flip, 160/143	60.00
Vase, 8½", ftd., 160/28	45.00
Vase, 10", cylinder, 160/192	80.00
Vase, 10½", hdld., urn, 160/186	195.00
Vase, 11", flip, 1603	175.00
Vase, 11½", ftd., 160/21	70.00

Colors: crystal, Moonlight Blue, amber, amethyst, La Rosa, Emerald green dark, Pistachio, Ritz blue, milk glass

Caprice is widely collected in Moonlight Blue and crystal. Many pieces made in crystal and blue were never made in (La Rosa) pink which affects people's choice of collecting that color. Caprice can be collected in a variety of colors; most are illustrated on the next page. Only luncheon sets, a few stems, vases, bowls, and candles can be amassed in any color besides crystal, Moonlight Blue, and pink.

Pink is the most difficult color to find; nevertheless, some collectors are trying to put large sets together. Pink is not as expensive as buying blue. Let me qualify that by saying if you found a large set of pink at one time, it would be quite expensive; but you probably will only locate a piece or two at a time. Prices for seldom seen colors of Caprice follow closely those of blue. Collectors searching for amber or amethyst, should know those particular colors are priced closer to their crystal counterparts. One of the largest collections of blue Caprice in the country came on the market recently, sadly, due to the death of the owner. The buyer offered many scarce pieces, at some "scarce item" prices. Some major collectors balked. Many rare items sold, but others are still being offered — if that interests you.

Some blue Caprice items have become difficult to sell at the level of prices that they were bringing a few years ago. Some items turned out to be more common than previously thought and others were bought up by the four or five collectors willing to pay the price being asked. Once those collectors filled their needs, others turned down the asked prices. Now, clarets, moulded, straight side, nine and twelve-ounce tumblers, footed whiskeys, and finger bowls are sitting in dealers' inventories instead of collections. Things will probably change, but more collectors recently are willing to settle on not owning every piece in a pattern than in the past.

Blue bitters bottles and covered cracker jars have once again been on the market and most major collections now have a Doulton pitcher. The small supply of those has drastically diminished; and the price shocks all but the rich.

Once shunned Alpine Caprice items are being collected by many beginners. Alpine pieces have satinized panels or bases and are found on both crystal and blue items. You should be aware that collecting tastes change as more people come into our collecting society. It is now possible to attain this finish with equipment from a craft shop. The satinized decoration on newly embellished pieces is not as smoothly done as it was originally — but it can be done.

Crystal Caprice candle reflectors and punch bowls are seldom found; but there is serious money waiting for those that do find them. Should you desire, you could put a fairly large set of crystal together for a reasonable figure when compared to other patterns of this quality — if you avoid buying those rarely found items.

Be aware that the non-designed centers on all flat pieces had a tendency to be damaged with use. Do not pay mint condition prices for items found that way.

	Crystal	Blue / Pink
Ashtray, 2¾", 3 ftd., shell, #213	8.00	15.00
* Ashtray, 3", #214	6.00	12.00
* Ashtray, 4", #215	8.00	16.00
* Ashtray, 5", #216	10.00	25.00
Bonbon, 6", oval, ftd., #155	22.00	50.00
Bonbon, 6", sq., 2 hdld., #154	18.00	45.00
Bonbon, 6", sq., ftd., #133	20.00	50.00
Bottle, 7 oz., bitters, #186	225.00	595.00
Bowl, 2", 4 ftd., almond, #95	25.00	65.00
* Bowl, 5", 2 hdld., jelly, #151	15.00	35.00
Bowl, 5", fruit, #18	30.00	80.00
Bowl, 5", fruit, crimped, #19	30.00	95.00
Bowl, 8", 4 ftd., #49	45.00	120.00
Bowl, 8", sq., 4 ftd., #50	55.00	130.00
* Bowl, 8", 3 pt., relish, #124	20.00	45.00
Bowl, 9½", crimped, 4 ftd., #52	45.00	120.00
Bowl, 9", pickle, #102	25.00	60.00
Bowl, 10", salad, 4 ftd., #57	45.00	135.00
Bowl, 10", sq., 4 ftd., #58	50.00	135.00
Bowl, 10½", belled, 4 ftd., #54	40.00	85.00
Bowl, 10½", crimped, 4 ftd., #53	40.00	115.00
Bowl, 11", crimped, 4 ftd., #60	45.00	120.00
* Bowl, 11", 2 hdld., oval, 4 ftd., #65	45.00	120.00
Bowl, 11½", shallow, 4 ftd., #81	40.00	120.00
* Bowl, 12", 4 pt. relish, oval, #126	90.00	250.00
* Bowl, 12", relish, 3 pt., rect., #125	50.00	150.00
Bowl, 12½", belled, 4 ftd., #62	40.00	110.00
Bowl, 12½", crimped, 4 ftd., #61	40.00	110.00

	Crystal	Blue / Pink
Bowl, 13", cupped, salad, #80	75.00	195.00
Bowl, 13", crimped, 4 ftd., #66	45.00	135.00
Bowl, 13½", 4 ftd., shallow cupped, #82	50.00	140.00
Bowl, 15", salad, shallow, #84	60.00	195.00
Bridge set:		
* Cloverleaf, 6½", #173	32.00	115.00
* Club, 6½", #170	32.00	115.00
Diamond, 6½", #171	32.00	115.00
* Heart, 6½", #169	38.00	130.00
* Spade, 6½", #172	32.00	115.00
* Butterdish, ¼ lb., #52	235.00	
Cake plate, 13", ftd., #36	150.00	395.00
Candle reflector, #73	350.00	
Candlestick, 2½", ea., #67	15.00	32.50
Candlestick, 2-lite, keyhole, 5", #647	20.00	65.00
Candlestick, 3-lite, #74	50.00	125.00
Candlestick, 3-lite, keyhole, #638	25.00	75.00
Candlestick, 3-lite, #1338	45.00	100.00
Candlestick, 5-lite, #1577	165.00	
Candlestick, 5", ea., keyhole, #646	20.00	35.00
Candlestick, 6", 2-lite, ea., #72	40.00	95.00
Candlestick, 7", ea., w/prism, #70	25.00	75.00
Candlestick, 7½", dbl., ea., #69	195.00	650.00
Candy, 6", 3 ftd., w/cover, #165	42.50	120.00
Candy, 6", w/cover (divided), #168	90.00	195.00
Celery & relish, 8½", 3 pt., #124	20.00	45.00
Cigarette box, w/cover, 3½" x 2¼", #207	20.00	50.00

	Crystal	Blue Pink
Cigarette box, w/cover, 4½" x 3½", #208	25.00	75.00
Cigarette holder, 2" x 2¼", triangular, #205	20.00	72.50
Cigarette holder, 3" x 3", triangular, #204	22.00	55.00
Coaster, 3½", #13	15.00	35.00
Comport, 6", low ftd., #130	22.00	50.00
Comport, 7", low ftd., #130	35.00	75.00
Comport, 7", tall, #136	40.00	100.00
Cracker jar & cover, #202	495.00	1,500.00
* Creamer, large, #41	13.00	30.00
* Creamer, medium, #38	11.00	22.00
* Creamer, ind., #40	12.00	27.50
Cup, #17	14.00	35.00
Decanter, w/stopper, 35 oz., #187	195.00	495.00
Finger bowl & liner, #16	45.00	90.00
Finger bowl and liner, blown, #300	50.00	100.00
Ice bucket, #201	75.00	200.00
Marmalade, w/cover, 6 oz., #89	75.00	225.00
* Mayonnaise, 6½", 3 pc. set, #129	42.00	115.00
* Mayonnaise, 8", 3 pc. set, #106	55.00	135.00
Mustard, w/cover, 2 oz., #87	60.00	175.00
Nut Dish, 2½", #93	22.00	55.00
Nut Dish, 2½", divided, #94	25.00	60.00
* Oil, 3 oz., w/stopper, #101	35.00	90.00
* Oil, 5 oz., w/stopper, #100	70.00	250.00
Pitcher, 32 oz., ball shape, #179	135.00	350.00
Pitcher, 80 oz., ball shape, #183	125.00	365.00
Pitcher, 90 oz., tall Doulton style, #178	750.00	3,995.00
Plate, 5½", bread & butter, #20	12.00	27.50
Plate, 6½", bread & butter, #21	11.00	24.00
Plate, 6½", hdld., lemon, #152	15.00	30.00
Plate, 7½", salad, #23	15.00	30.00
Plate, 8½", luncheon, #22	15.00	35.00
* Plate, 9½", dinner, #24	50.00	175.00
Plate, 11", cabaret, 4 ftd., #32	30.00	75.00
Plate, 11½", cabaret, #26	30.00	75.00
Plate, 14", cabaret, 4 ftd., #33	40.00	95.00
Plate, 14", 4 ftd., #28	35.00	95.00
Plate, 16", #30	45.00	135.00
Punch bowl, ftd., #498	2,750.00	
* Salad dressing, 3 pc., ftd. & hdld., 2 spoons, #112	195.00	525.00
Salt & pepper, pr., ball, #91	45.00	135.00
* Salt & pepper, pr., flat, #96	35.00	90.00
Salt & pepper, indiv., ball, pr., #90	50.00	160.00
Salt & pepper, indiv., flat, pr., #92	40.00	135.00
Salver, 13", 2 pc. (cake atop pedestal), #31	165.00	600.00
Saucer, #17	2.50	5.50
Stem, #300, blown, 1 oz., cordial	52.50	150.00
Stem, #300, blown, 2½ oz., wine	25.00	70.00
Stem, #300, blown, 3 oz., cocktail	25.00	50.00
Stem, #300, blown, 4½ oz., claret	80.00	195.00
Stem, #300, blown, 4½ oz., low oyster cocktail	20.00	50.00
Stem, #300, blown, 5 oz., parfait	95.00	225.00
Stem, #300, blown, 6 oz., low sherbet	14.00	25.00
Stem, #300, blown, 6 oz., tall sherbet	14.00	35.00
Stem, #300, blown, 9 oz., water	20.00	50.00
Stem, #301, blown, 1 oz., cordial	40.00	
Stem, #301, blown, 2½ oz., wine	20.00	
Stem, #301, blown, 3 oz., cocktail	22.00	
Stem, #301, blown, 4½ oz., claret	40.00	

	Crystal	Blue Pink
Stem, #301, blown, 6 oz., sherbet	15.00	
Stem, #301, blown, 9 oz., water	20.00	
* Stem, 3 oz., wine, #6	40.00	110.00
* Stem, 3½ oz., cocktail, #3	25.00	60.00
* Stem, 4½ oz., claret, #5	80.00	175.00
Stem, 4½ oz., fruit cocktail, #7	30.00	85.00
Stem, 5 oz., low sherbet, #4	25.00	50.00
* Stem, 7 oz., tall sherbet, #2	17.50	36.00
Stem, 10 oz., water, #1	27.50	50.00
* Sugar, large, #41	12.50	25.00
* Sugar, medium, #38	10.00	22.50
* Sugar, indiv., #40	12.00	25.00
* Tray, for sugar & creamer, #37	17.50	40.00
Tray, 9" oval, #42	22.00	50.00
* Tumbler, 2 oz., flat, #188	25.00	70.00
Tumbler, 3 oz., ftd., #12	27.50	75.00
Tumbler, 5 oz., ftd., #11	22.00	55.00
Tumbler, 5 oz., flat, #180	22.00	55.00
Tumbler, #300, 2½ oz., whiskey	55.00	225.00
Tumbler, #300, 5 oz., ftd., juice	20.00	40.00
Tumbler, #300, 10 oz., ftd. water	20.00	50.00
Tumbler, #300, 12 oz., ftd. tea	20.00	50.00
Tumbler, #301, blown, 4½ oz., low oyster cocktail	17.50	
Tumbler, #301, blown, 5 oz., juice	15.00	
Tumbler, #301, blown, 12 oz., tea	20.00	
* Tumbler, 9 oz., straight side, #14	40.00	125.00
* Tumbler, 10 oz., ftd., #10	20.00	45.00
Tumbler, 12 oz., flat., #184	53.00	53.00
Tumbler, 12 oz., ftd., #9	22.50	50.00
* Tumbler, 12 oz., straight side, #15	37.50	95.00
Tumbler, #310, 5 oz., flat, juice	25.00	75.00
Tumbler, #310, 7 oz., flat, old-fashion	45.00	145.00
Tumbler, #310, 10 oz., flat, table	25.00	70.00
Tumbler, #310, 11 oz., flat, tall, 4¹³⁄₁₆"	25.00	90.00
Tumbler, #310, 12 oz., flat, tea	30.00	135.00
Vase, 3½", #249	70.00	195.00
Vase, 4", blown, #251, blown	70.00	195.00
Vase, 4¼", #241, ball	60.00	115.00
Vase, 4½", #237, ball	75.00	175.00
Vase, 4½", #252, blown	55.00	160.00
Vase, 4½", #337, crimped top	55.00	130.00
Vase, 4½", #344, crimped top	85.00	185.00
Vase, 4½", #244	60.00	150.00
Vase, 5", ivy bowl, #232	90.00	225.00
Vase, 5½", #245	65.00	165.00
Vase, 5½", #345, crimped top	90.00	210.00
Vase, 6", #242, ftd.	80.00	195.00
Vase, 6", blown, #254	185.00	395.00
Vase, 6", #342, crimped top	95.00	200.00
Vase, 6", #235, ftd., rose bowl	75.00	150.00
Vase, 6½", #238, ball	65.00	165.00
Vase, 6½", #338, crimped top	100.00	250.00
Vase, 7½", #246	65.00	195.00
Vase, 7½", #346, crimped top	115.00	295.00
Vase, 8", #236, ftd., rose bowl	100.00	225.00
Vase, 8½", #243	110.00	225.00
Vase, 8½", #239, ball	125.00	295.00
Vase, 8½", #339, crimped top	125.00	300.00
Vase, 8½", #343, crimped top	150.00	300.00
Vase, 9¼" #240, ball	140.00	310.00
Vase, 9½" #340, crimped top	175.00	425.00

Colors: Amber. blue, cobalt blue, crystal, red

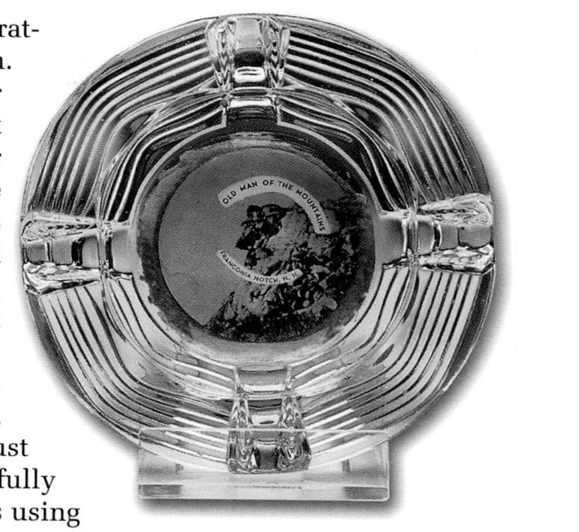

Blue Caribbean dinner plates are difficult to find, but even more frustrating is finding them worn and scratched with mint condition prices on them. Collectors shopping for fundamental Caribbean dinnerware items (dinner plates, cups, and saucers) are not finding many. When basic items are not found in any quantity, new collectors tend to shun the pattern. Prices for blue have remained rather steady as so little is being offered for sale. I see fewer pieces of crystal on the market than I once did. Of course, dealers have a tendency to avoid procuring patterns that few collectors seek, and therein is the second hex for crystal Caribbean. The blue punch bowl, pitchers, and some of the stemware, particularly cordials, will all cost you plenty — if you can find them to buy.

A combination of blue and crystal makes a pleasing array. Collectors started mixing colors due to a decorating trend featured in magazines. Now, mixing glass colors has come about from necessity (due to lack of finding just one color) as much as anything. However, it's producing some wonderfully artistic collections! I've seen pictures of truly visionary table arrangements using this wonderful older glassware.

Amber Caribbean is rarely seen except for the cigarette jar and ashtrays. Other pieces are unusual; keep that in mind. I have been unable to garner a mate for my amber three-footed candle. How about finding one in blue?

Crystal punch sets can be found with all crystal cups or with crystal cups with colored handles of red, cobalt blue, or amber. With the colored handled punch cup and ladle, these sets sell for about $75.00 more than the plain crystal set priced in the listings. Red and cobalt blue handled pieces appear to be more desirable than amber. Many collectors mix the colored punch cups so that they have four of each handle with their set. I have seen so many with four of each cup that I'm wondering if that was the way they were marketed in some areas.

	Crystal	Blue
Ashtray, 6", 4 indent	15.00	32.50
Bowl, 3¾" x 5", folded side, hdld.	16.00	35.00
Bowl, 4½", finger	16.00	32.00
Bowl, 5", fruit nappy (takes liner), hdld.	12.50	27.50
Bowl, 5" x 7", folded side, hdld.	20.00	40.00
Bowl, 6½", soup (takes liner)	16.00	37.50
Bowl, 7", hdld.	25.00	45.00
Bowl, 7¼", ftd., hdld., grapefruit	20.00	45.00
Bowl, 8½"	30.00	75.00
Bowl, 9", salad	30.00	75.00
Bowl, 9¼", veg., flared edge	32.50	75.00
Bowl, 9¼", veg., hdld.	40.00	85.00
Bowl, 9½", epergne, flared edge	37.50	95.00
Bowl, 10", 6¼ qt., punch	90.00	475.00
Bowl, 10", 6¼ qt., punch, flared top (catalog lists as salad)	90.00	425.00
Bowl, 10¾", oval, flower, hdld.	40.00	95.00
Bowl, 12", console, flared edge	50.00	115.00
Candelabrum, 4¾", 2-lite	40.00	90.00
Candlestick, 7¼", 1-lite, w/blue prisms	65.00	185.00
Candy dish w/cover, 4" x 7"	50.00	110.00
Cheese/cracker crumbs, 3½" h., plate 11", hdld.	50.00	100.00
Cigarette holder (stack ashtray top)	35.00	80.00
Cocktail shaker, 9", 33 oz.	100.00	250.00
Creamer	14.00	25.00
Cruet	45.00	95.00
Cup, tea	15.00	60.00
Cup, punch	10.00	22.50
Epergne, 4 pt., flower (12" bowl, 9½" bowl, 7¾" vase, 14" plate)	225.00	450.00
Ice bucket, 6½", hdld.	75.00	195.00

	Crystal	Blue
Ladle, punch	35.00	100.00
Mayonnaise, w/liner, 5¾", 2 pt., 2 spoons, hdld.	42.50	100.00
Mayonnaise, w/liner, 5¾", hdld., 1 spoon	35.00	80.00
Mustard, 4", w/slotted cover	35.00	65.00
Pitcher, 4¾" 16 oz., milk	95.00	275.00
Pitcher, w/ice lip, 9", 72 oz., water	225.00	650.00
Plate, 6", hdld., fruit nappy liner	4.00	12.00
Plate 6¼", bread/butter	5.00	12.00
Plate, 7¼", rolled edge, soup liner	5.00	12.50
Plate, 7½", salad	10.00	20.00
Plate, 8", hdld., mayonnaise liner	6.00	14.00
Plate, 8½", luncheon	15.00	35.00
Plate, 10½", dinner	65.00	150.00
Plate, 11", hdld., cheese/cracker liner	20.00	42.50
Plate, 12", salad liner, rolled edge	22.00	55.00
Plate, 14"	25.00	75.00
Plate, 16", torte	35.00	110.00
Plate, 18", punch underliner	40.00	110.00
Relish, 6", round, 2 pt.	12.00	25.00
Relish, 9½", 4 pt., oblong	30.00	65.00
Relish, 9½", oblong	27.50	60.00
Relish, 12¾", 5 pt., rnd.	40.00	95.00
Relish, 12¾", 7 pt., rnd.	40.00	95.00
Salt dip, 2½"	11.00	25.00
Salt & pepper, 3", metal tops	32.00	95.00
Salt & pepper, 5", metal tops	37.50	125.00
Saucer	4.00	8.00
Server, 5¾", ctr. hdld.	13.00	45.00
Server, 6½", ctr. hdld.	22.00	50.00
Stem, 3", 1 oz., cordial	75.00	265.00
Stem, 3½", 3½ oz., ftd., ball stem, wine	20.00	45.00
Stem, 3⅝", 2½ oz., wine (egg cup shape)	22.50	40.00
Stem, 4", 6 oz., ftd., ball stem, champagne	14.00	27.50
Stem, 4¼", ftd., sherbet	10.00	24.00
Stem, 4¾", 3 oz., ftd., ball stem, wine	22.00	55.00
Stem, 5¾", 8 oz., ftd., ball stem	20.00	45.00
Sugar	11.00	25.00
Syrup, metal cutoff top	100.00	250.00
Tray, 6¼", hand., mint, div.	14.00	30.00
Tray, 12¾", rnd.	25.00	50.00
Tumbler, 2¼", 2 oz., shot glass	25.00	60.00
Tumbler, 3½", 5 oz., flat	20.00	45.00
Tumbler, 5¼", 11½ oz., flat	20.00	45.00
Tumbler, 5½", 8½ oz., ftd.	22.00	50.00
Tumbler, 6½", 11 oz., ftd., ice tea	27.50	60.00
Vase, 5¾", ftd., ruffled edge	22.00	55.00
Vase, 7¼", ftd., flared edge, ball	27.50	60.00
Vase, 7½", ftd., flared edge, bulbous	32.50	70.00
Vase, 7¾", flared edge, epergne	40.00	125.00
Vase, 8", ftd., straight side	40.00	85.00
Vase, 9", ftd., ruffled top	50.00	195.00
Vase, 10", ftd.	55.00	145.00

Colors: crystal, Ebony (gold encrusted)

Although Chantilly was made and sold along with the popular Rose Point, it never caught on with customers then or now as did Rose Point. I have included a couple of fold out pages from a pamphlet showing the readily available #3625 Chantilly stems and an array of vases at the top of page 51. It is nearly impossible to put numbers by each piece in the actual photographs, but maybe this will help those having trouble distinguishing stems or line numbers. There are two pages to help identify Cambridge stems in the back of this book (236 – 237).

There is a more comprehensive inventory for Cambridge pieces under Rose Point later in this book. Many Chantilly pieces are not listed here as I am only attempting to familiarize you to the pattern itself. When pricing missing Chantilly items by using the Rose Point list, do remember that Rose Point items are presently a minimum of 30% to 50% higher due to collector demand.

	Crystal
Bowl, 7", bonbon, 2 hdld., ftd.	25.00
Bowl, 7", relish/pickle, 2 pt.	30.00
Bowl, 7", relish/pickle	32.00
Bowl, 9", celery/relish, 3 pt.	38.00
Bowl, 10", 4 ftd., flared	50.00
Bowl, 11", tab hdld.	50.00
Bowl, 11½", tab hdld. ftd.	55.00
Bowl, 12", celery/relish, 3 pt.	50.00
Bowl, 12", 4 ftd., flared	55.00
Bowl, 12", 4 ftd., oval	60.00
Bowl, 12", celery/relish, 5 pt.	55.00
Butter, w/cover, round	235.00
Butter, ¼ lb.	295.00
Candlestick, 5"	28.00
Candlestick, 6", 2-lite, "keyhole"	40.00
Candlestick, 6", 3-lite	50.00
Candy box, w/cover, ftd.	165.00
Candy box, w/cover, rnd.	95.00
Cocktail icer, 2 pc.	65.00
Comport, 5½"	35.00
Comport, 5⅜", blown	40.00
Creamer	18.00
Creamer, indiv., #3900, scalloped edge	15.00
Cup	17.50
Decanter, ftd.	210.00
Decanter, ball	250.00
Hat, small	210.00
Hat, large	295.00
Hurricane lamp, candlestick base	160.00
Hurricane lamp, keyhole base w/prisms	250.00
Ice bucket, w/chrome handle	125.00
Marmalade & cover	60.00
Mayonnaise (sherbet type bowl w/ladle)	40.00
Mayonnaise, div. w/liner & 2 ladles	65.00
Mayonnaise, w/liner & ladle	50.00
Mustard & cover	95.00
Oil, 6 oz., hdld., w/stopper	125.00
Pitcher, ball	225.00
Pitcher, Doulton	395.00
Pitcher, upright	250.00
Plate, crescent, salad	150.00
Plate, 6½", bread/butter	8.00
Plate, 8", salad	12.50
Plate, 8", tab hdld., ftd., bonbon	20.00
Plate, 10½", dinner	75.00
Plate, 12", 4 ftd., service	50.00
Plate, 13", 4 ftd.	60.00
Plate, 13½", tab hdld., cake	65.00
Plate, 14", torte	45.00
Salad dressing bottle	150.00
Salt & pepper, pr., flat	35.00
Salt & pepper, footed	40.00
Salt & pepper, handled	40.00
Saucer	4.00

	Crystal
Stem, #3600, 1 oz., cordial	60.00
Stem, #3600, 2½ oz., cocktail	26.00
Stem, #3600, 2½ oz., wine	35.00
Stem, #3600, 4½ oz., claret	45.00
Stem, #3600, 4½ oz., low oyster cocktail	18.00
Stem, #3600, 7 oz., tall sherbet	20.00
Stem, #3600, 7 oz., low sherbet	18.00
Stem, #3600, 10 oz., water	28.00
Stem, #3625, 1 oz., cordial	60.00
Stem, #3625, 3 oz., cocktail	30.00
Stem, #3625, 4½ oz., claret	45.00
Stem, #3625, 4½ oz., low oyster cocktail	20.00
Stem, #3625, 7 oz., low sherbet	18.00
Stem, #3625, 7 oz., tall sherbet	20.00
Stem, #3625, 10 oz., water	28.00
Stem, #3775, 1 oz., cordial	60.00
Stem, #3775, 2½ oz., wine	35.00
Stem, #3775, 3 oz., cocktail	28.00
Stem, #3775, 4½ oz., claret	45.00
Stem, #3775, 4½ oz., oyster cocktail	18.00
Stem, #3775, 6 oz., low sherbet	18.00
Stem, #3775, 6 oz., tall sherbet	20.00
Stem, #3779, 1 oz., cordial	75.00
Stem, #3779, 2½ oz., wine	35.00
Stem, #3779, 3 oz., cocktail	28.00
Stem, #3779, 4½ oz., claret	45.00
Stem, #3779, 4½ oz., low oyster cocktail	18.00
Stem, #3779, 6 oz., tall sherbet	20.00
Stem, #3779, 6 oz., low sherbet	18.00
Stem, #3779, 9 oz., water	28.00
Sugar	18.00
Sugar, indiv., #3900, scalloped edge	15.00
Syrup	225.00
Tumbler, #3600, 5 oz., ftd., juice	18.00
Tumbler, #3600, 12 oz., ftd., tea	25.00
Tumbler, #3625, 5 oz., ftd., juice	18.00
Tumbler, #3625, 10 oz., ftd., water	20.00
Tumbler, #3625, 12 oz., ftd., tea	26.00
Tumbler, #3775, 5 oz., ftd., juice	18.00
Tumbler, #3775, 10 oz., ftd., water	20.00
Tumbler, #3775, 12 oz., ftd., tea	24.00
Tumbler, #3779, 5 oz., ftd., juice	20.00
Tumbler, #3779, 12 oz., ftd., tea	25.00
Tumbler, 13 oz.	26.00
Vase, 5", globe	75.00
Vase, 6", high ftd., flower	50.00
Vase, 8", high ftd., flower	55.00
Vase, 9", keyhole base	60.00
Vase, 10", bud	95.00
Vase, 11", ftd., flower	95.00
Vase, 11", ped. ftd., flower	100.00
Vase, 12", keyhole base	95.00
Vase, 13", ftd., flower	150.00

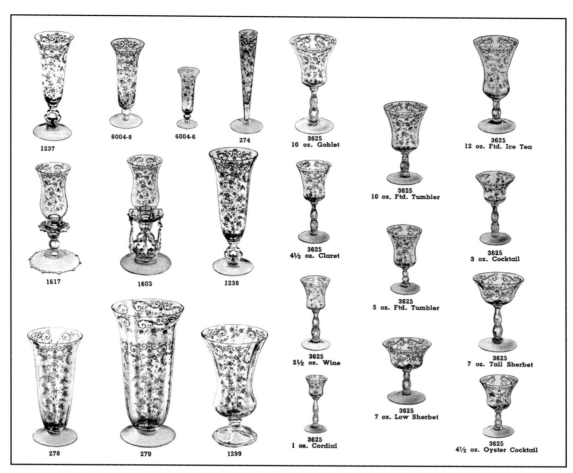

1237

6004-8

6004-6

274

3625
10 oz. Goblet

3625
12 oz. Ftd. Ice Tea

3625
10 oz. Ftd. Tumbler

1617

1603

1238

3625
4½ oz. Claret

3625
3 oz. Cocktail

3625
5 oz. Ftd. Tumbler

278

279

1299

3625
2½ oz. Wine

3625
7 oz. Tall Sherbet

3625
7 oz. Low Sherbet

3625
1 oz. Cordial

3625
4½ oz. Oyster Cocktail

Colors: Crystal, Flamingo, Moongleam, Hawthorne, Marigold

Charter Oak is being recognized more now since including it in my book. I used to be able to find a piece or two priced as pretty, pink Depression glass, but now it seems to always be identified and priced by "book" or higher. Flamingo Charter Oak pieces are available occasionally, but I seldom see other colors. Stemware appears to turn up in small batches rather than a piece or two. Prices have remained stable over the last few years. That frequently means there has been ample supply for collector demand. Price increases often signal not enough being found to supply all who want it. Many pieces of Charter Oak are unmarked, however, and bargains can still be uncovered. Those acorns are the hallmark of this pattern. Plantation with its pineapple stems and Charter Oak with acorn stems are hard to miss if you pay attention.

Unfortunately, I did not find that clever "Acorn" #130, one lite candleholder to photograph for my *Glass Candlesticks of the Depression Era* book. However, I did find one for the *Pattern Identification II* book. The base is an oak leaf with stem curled up and an acorn for the candle cup. Strictly speaking, this is not considered to be Charter Oak pattern, but a number of Charter Oak collectors try to obtain these to go with their sets. Heisey designed a number of candles to "blend" (their words) with numerous patterns. This candle was made in the same time frame of Charter Oak and mostly in the same colors. In that vein Yeoman cups and saucers are often used with this set since there were no cups and saucers made. A Yeoman set is pictured here, but not priced in the Charter Oak listing. I mention that since several readers have wanted to know why I did not price the cup and saucer in my listings. These are priced under Yeoman.

I have only pictured Flamingo (pink) over the years since that is what I have been able to borrow from collectors, but there are several other colors of Charter Oak that can be collected. Moongleam is striking. It's worth a visit to a Heisey show to see these patterns displayed. One is held annually in Newark, Ohio, in June.

	Crystal	Flamingo	Moongleam	Hawthorne	Marigold
Bowl, 11", floral, #116 (oak leaf)	50.00	50.00	70.00	85.00	
Bowl, finger, #3362	10.00	17.50	20.00		
Candleholder, 1-lite, #130, "Acorn"	100.00	125.00	135.00		
Candlestick, 3", #116 (oak leaf)	25.00	35.00	45.00	125.00	
Candlestick, 5", 3-lite, #129, "Tricorn"		90.00	110.00	140.00	150.00
Comport, 6", low ft., #3362	45.00	55.00	60.00	80.00	100.00

	Crystal	Flamingo	Moongleam	Hawthorne	Marigold
Comport, 7", ftd., #3362	50.00	65.00	70.00	160.00	175.00
Lamp, #4262 (blown comport/water filled to magnify design & stabilize lamp)	400.00	700.00	850.00		
Pitcher, flat, #3362		160.00	180.00		
Plate, 6", salad, #1246 (Acorn & Leaves)	5.00	10.00	12.50	20.00	
Plate, 7", luncheon/salad, #1246 (Acorn & Leaves)	8.00	12.00	17.50	22.50	
Plate, 8", luncheon, #1246 (Acorn & Leaves)	10.00	15.00	20.00	25.00	
Plate, 10½", dinner, #1246 (Acorn & Leaves)	30.00	45.00	55.00	70.00	
Stem, 3 oz., cocktail, #3362	10.00	25.00	25.00	45.00	40.00
Stem, 3½ oz., low ft., oyster cocktail, #3362	8.00	20.00	20.00	40.00	35.00
Stem, 4½ oz., parfait, #3362	15.00	25.00	35.00	60.00	50.00
Stem, 6 oz., saucer champagne, #3362	10.00	15.00	20.00	50.00	40.00
Stem, 6 oz., sherbet, low ft., #3362	10.00	15.00	22.00	50.00	40.00
Stem, 8 oz., goblet, high ft., #3362	20.00	35.00	35.00	95.00	60.00
Stem, 8 oz., luncheon goblet, low ft., #3362	20.00	40.00	40.00	95.00	60.00
Tumbler, 10 oz., flat, #3362	10.00	20.00	25.00	35.00	30.00
Tumbler, 12 oz., flat, #3362	12.50	20.00	25.00	40.00	35.00

Colors: crystal

Cherokee Rose stemware line #17399 is the tear drop style in the back of the photo, while the #17403 stem is represented by the cordial in the front row. Should you find a Cherokee Rose cup or saucer, please let me know.

	Crystal
Bowl, 5", finger	30.00
Bowl, 6", fruit or nut	30.00
Bowl, 7", salad	45.00
Bowl, 10", deep salad	75.00
Bowl, 10½", celery, oblong	50.00
Bowl, 12", crimped	65.00
Bowl, 12½", centerpiece, flared	65.00
Bowl, 13", centerpiece	75.00
Cake plate, 12½", center hdld.	55.00
Candlesticks, pr., double branch	110.00
Comport, 6"	52.50
Creamer	22.00
Icer w/liner	110.00
Mayonnaise, liner and ladle	65.00
Pitcher	595.00
Plate, 6", sherbet	8.00
Plate, 8", luncheon	15.00
Plate, 13½", turned-up edge, lily	50.00
Plate, 14", sandwich	55.00
Relish, 6½", 3 pt.	32.50
Relish, 12½", 3 pt.	55.00
Shaker, pr.	85.00
Stem, 1 oz., cordial	55.00
Stem, 2 oz., sherry	35.00

	Crystal
Stem, 3½ oz., cocktail	20.00
Stem, 3½ oz., wine	35.00
Stem, 4 oz., claret	50.00
Stem, 4½ oz., parfait	50.00
Stem, 5½ oz., sherbet/champagne	20.00
Stem, 9 oz., water	25.00
Sugar	22.00
Table bell	75.00
Tumbler, 4½ oz., oyster cocktail	24.00
Tumbler, 5 oz., ftd., juice	24.00
Tumbler, 8 oz., ftd., water	25.00
Tumbler, 10½ oz., ftd., ice tea	38.00
Vase, 6", bud	25.00
Vase, 8", bud	35.00
Vase, 8½", tear drop	85.00
Vase, 9¼", tub	95.00
Vase, 10", bud	45.00
Vase, 11", bud	50.00
Vase, 11", urn	110.00
Vase, 12", flared	135.00

Colors: crystal, Sahara yellow (Chintz only), Moongleam green, Flamingo pink, and Alexandrite orchid (all colors made in Formal Chintz)

Heisey Chintz pattern is found in two different motifs and on various Heisey line blanks. Pieces pictured below are known as Chintz. Pieces with encompassing circles are pictured at the bottom of page 56 and are termed Formal Chintz. These patterns are comparably priced. I have never been fortunate enough to find any tumblers or stemware in Formal Chintz though they were made on the #3390 Carcassone stem line. I like the definitive design of Formal Chintz better than the delicate Chintz, but that is only a personal choice.

Several long-time collectors have reported chintz salt and pepper shakers in #1401 Empress line. Some items slip by my listings until someone writes. If you have pieces that are not in any pattern's listing, please let me know. Sahara is the color most desired, but a few collectors search for crystal. Alexandrite Chintz is quite rare and was only made in Formal Chintz. It is very striking when displayed in quantity. There is so little of Alexandrite that putting a set together would be an extreme challenge. However, someone did run into a large set a few years ago.

Do not confuse this pattern with Fostoria's or Tiffin's Chintz; and recognize that you must also specify the company name when you ask for any pattern named Chintz. It was a popular appellation that was used by many glass companies for their wares.

	Crystal	Sahara
Bowl, cream soup	18.00	35.00
Bowl, finger, #4107	10.00	20.00
Bowl, 5½", ftd., preserve, hdld.	15.00	30.00
Bowl, 6", ftd., mint	20.00	32.00
Bowl, 6", ftd., 2 hdld., jelly	17.00	35.00
Bowl, 7", triplex relish	20.00	40.00
Bowl, 7½", Nasturtium	20.00	40.00
Bowl, 8½", ftd., 2 hdld., floral	35.00	70.00
Bowl, 11", dolphin ft., floral	45.00	110.00
Bowl, 13", 2 pt., pickle & olive	15.00	35.00
Comport, 7", oval	40.00	85.00
Creamer, 3 dolphin ft.	20.00	45.00
Creamer, individual	12.00	30.00
Cup	15.00	25.00
Grapefruit, ftd., #3389, Duquesne	30.00	60.00
Ice bucket, ftd.	85.00	135.00
Mayonnaise, 5½", dolphin ft.	35.00	65.00

	Crystal	Sahara
Oil, 4 oz.	60.00	135.00
Pitcher, 3 pint, dolphin ft.	200.00	300.00
Plate, 6", sq., bread	6.00	15.00
Plate, 7", sq., salad	8.00	18.00
Plate, 8", sq., luncheon	10.00	22.00
Plate, 10½", sq., dinner	40.00	85.00
Plate, 12", two hdld.	25.00	47.50
Plate, 13", hors d' oeuvre, two hdld.	30.00	65.00
Platter, 14", oval	35.00	85.00
Salt and pepper, pr.	40.00	85.00
Saucer	3.00	5.00
Stem, #3389, Duquesne, 1 oz., cordial	115.00	250.00
Stem, #3389, 2½ oz., wine	25.00	50.00
Stem, #3389, 3 oz., cocktail	17.50	35.00
Stem, #3389, 4 oz., claret	25.00	50.00
Stem, #3389, 4 oz., oyster cocktail	12.50	25.00
Stem, #3389, 5 oz., parfait	17.50	35.00
Stem, #3389, 5 oz., saucer champagne	12.50	25.00
Stem, #3389, 5 oz., sherbet	10.00	17.50
Stem, #3389, 9 oz., water	17.50	35.00
Sugar, 3 dolphin ft.	20.00	45.00
Sugar, individual	12.00	30.00
Tray, 10", celery	15.00	30.00
Tray, 12", sq., ctr. hdld., sandwich	35.00	65.00
Tray, 13", celery	18.00	45.00
Tumbler, #3389, 5 oz., ftd., juice	12.00	22.00
Tumbler, #3389, 8 oz., soda	13.00	24.00
Tumbler, #3389, 10 oz., ftd., water	14.00	27.50
Tumbler, #3389, 12 oz., iced tea	16.00	33.00
Vase, 9", dolphin ft.	95.00	185.00

Colors: crystal, pink

Classic is one of those patterns where I have enjoyed finding new pieces over the years. When complete catalog listings are found, then there are few surprises that turn up. When you do not have very good listings, you can find a lot of suprises in your travels. Dinner plates shocked me several years ago, as did a pink cup. Alas, I have never found a saucer to go with it, but it will turn up. Each book adds new pieces to the listings.

I prefer the pink, but only stemmed beverage items are surfacing in that color. Tiffin pitchers (one pictured in pink) came with and without a lid. The one here has the top curved in so it will not take a lid. Remember that Tiffin pitcher lids have no pattern etched on them.

Note the crystal pitcher at the bottom of page 58, which is a different style, but holds approximately 60 ounces. I have priced both styles in the same listing. As with all glass dinner plates with no pattern in the center, you need to check for marring and scratching from use. Of course, finding any mint condition dinner plate 70 or 80 years after its manufacture is nearly impossible. I, personally, have found few serving pieces save for that two-handled bowl and a mayonnaise. As one lady in her nineties explained to me recently, "Everybody bought stems to go with their china. No one wanted to drink coffee or serve on glass back then!"

Pink Classic stems are found on the #17024 line that is also found with Tiffin's Flanders pattern. Crystal stemmed items seem to surface on the #14185 line. There are some size discrepancies within these two stemware lines. We have measured both colors and noted them in my price listings.

	Crystal	Pink
Bowl, 2 hdld., 8" x 9¼"	135.00	
Cheese & cracker set	100.00	
Comport, 6" wide, 3¼" tall	75.00	
Creamer, flat	40.00	85.00
Creamer, ftd.	35.00	
Cup	65.00	
Finger bowl, ftd.	20.00	45.00
Mayonnaise, ftd.	65.00	

	Crystal	Pink
Pitcher, 61 oz.	275.00	495.00
Pitcher, 61 oz., w/cover	350.00	595.00
Plate, 6⅜", champagne liner	10.00	
Plate, 8"	12.50	25.00
Plate, 10", dinner	110.00	
Saucer	10.00	
Sherbet, 3⅛", 6½ oz., short	17.50	35.00
Stem, 3⅞", 1 oz., cordial	55.00	
Stem, 4¹⁵⁄₁₆", 3 oz., wine	32.50	60.00
Stem, 4⅞", 3¾ oz., cocktail	40.00	
Stem, 4⅞", 4 oz., cocktail	27.50	
Stem, 6½", 5 oz., parfait	35.00	70.00
Stem, 6", 7½ oz., saucer champagne	22.50	45.00
Stem, 7¼", 9 oz., water	30.00	60.00
Sugar, flat	35.00	85.00
Sugar, ftd.	35.00	
Tumbler, 3½", 5 oz., ftd., juice	17.50	
Tumbler, 4½", 8½ oz., ftd., water	20.00	50.00
Tumbler, 4⅛", 10½ oz., flat, water	25.00	
Tumbler, 5⁹⁄₁₆", 14 oz., ftd., tea	30.00	
Tumbler, 6", 13 oz., ftd., iced tea		60.00
Tumbler, 6¹⁄₁₆", 14 oz., ftd., iced tea	30.00	
Tumbler, 6¼", 6½ oz., ftd., Pilsner	32.50	
Vase, bud, 6½"	27.50	

Colors: amber, Willow blue, crystal, Ebony, Emerald green light, Gold Krystol, Peach Blo

Be sure to see the seven ice pails and tubs pictured on page 61. Not often will you see that many at one time. Prices for Willow blue Cleo continue upward, but at a slower pace than in the past. Most blue is found on Cambridge's Decagon blank. There are more collectors looking for blue than supplies turning up. I know of some collectors of blue recently who have broken up their sets and made a substantial profit.

Cleo Peach Blo (pink) and Emerald have remained steady and supplies of those colors continue to be found. Green Cleo has seen little activity of late. It appears to be sitting in dealer inventories; why is a mystery. Cleo can be collected in large sets of pink or green, but not all pieces were made in the other colors.

I have had a talent for spotting rare pieces of Cleo in the past but they always seem to be in amber rather than colors that captivate collectors. This pattern will continue to attract new collectors as long as the supply lasts. You might consider mixing colors or even collecting one particular item such as the ice buckets and pails like those pictured. Hopefully, you will run into a large set for a reasonable price; but those chances are not as frequent as in the past.

	Blue	Pink Green Yellow Amber
Almond, 2½", individual	110.00	75.00
Basket, 7", 2 hdld. (upturned sides), Decagon	70.00	30.00
Basket, 11", 2 hdld. (upturned sides), Decagon	95.00	50.00
Bouillon cup, w/saucer, 2 hdld., Decagon	95.00	55.00
Bowl, 2 pt., relish	40.00	22.00
Bowl, 3½", cranberry	65.00	40.00
Bowl, 5½", fruit	40.00	25.00
Bowl, 5½" 2 hdld., bonbon, Decagon	60.00	22.00
Bowl, 6", 4 ft., comport	60.00	35.00

	Blue	Pink Green Yellow Amber
Bowl, 6", cereal, Decagon	60.00	35.00
Bowl, 6½", 2 hdld., bonbon, Decagon	40.00	22.00
Bowl, 7½", tab hdld., soup	75.00	35.00
Bowl, 8", miniature console		175.00
Bowl, 8½"	90.00	40.00
Bowl, 8½" 2 hdld., Decagon	100.00	40.00
Bowl, 9", covered vegetable		250.00
Bowl, 9½", oval veg., Decagon	145.00	60.00
Bowl, 9", pickle, Decagon	75.00	45.00
Bowl, 10", 2 hdld., Decagon	125.00	75.00
Bowl, 11", oval	125.00	75.00
Bowl, 11½", oval	125.00	75.00

	Blue	Pink Green Yellow Amber
Bowl, 12", console	140.00	60.00
Bowl, 15½", oval, Decagon		225.00
Bowl, cream soup w/saucer, 2 hdld., Decagon	85.00	45.00
Bowl, finger w/liner, #3077	75.00	45.00
Bowl, finger w/liner, #3115	75.00	45.00
Candlestick, 1-lite, 2 styles	40.00	30.00
Candlestick, 2-lite	110.00	65.00
Candlestick, 3-lite	150.00	85.00
Candy box w/lid	275.00	185.00
Candy & cover, tall	295.00	195.00
Comport, 7", tall, #3115	110.00	75.00
Creamer, Decagon	35.00	25.00
Creamer, ewer style, 6"	195.00	150.00
Creamer, ftd.	40.00	22.00
Cup, Decagon	30.00	15.00
Decanter, w/stopper		295.00
Gravy boat, w/liner plate, Decagon	495.00	300.00
Ice pail	250.00	125.00
Ice tub	175.00	125.00
Mayonnaise, w/liner and ladle, Decagon	145.00	90.00
Mayonnaise, ftd.	75.00	45.00
Oil, 6 oz., w/stopper, Decagon	750.00	175.00
Pitcher, 3½ pt., #38		225.00
Pitcher, w/cover, 22 oz.		250.00
Pitcher, w/cover, 60 oz., #804		395.00
Pitcher, w/cover, 62 oz., #955	500.00	395.00
Pitcher, w/cover, 63 oz., #3077	995.00	425.00
Pitcher, w/cover, 68 oz., #937		395.00
Plate, 7"	28.00	18.00
Plate, 7", 2 hdld., Decagon	30.00	20.00
Plate, 8½", luncheon, Decagon	40.00	20.00
Plate, 9½", dinner, Decagon	175.00	40.00
Plate, 9½", grill		100.00
Plate, 11", 2 hdld., Decagon	120.00	40.00

	Blue	Pink Green Yellow Amber
Platter, 12"	195.00	125.00
Platter, 15"	325.00	225.00
Platter, w/cover, oval (toast)		400.00
Platter, asparagus, indented, w/sauce & spoon		395.00
Salt dip, 1½"	145.00	95.00
Saucer, Decagon	8.00	5.00
Server, 12", ctr. hand.	65.00	45.00
Stem, #3077, 1 oz., cordial	225.00	195.00
Stem, #3077, 2½ oz., cocktail		35.00
Stem, #3077, 3½ oz., wine	95.00	70.00
Stem, #3077, 6 oz., low sherbet	35.00	20.00
Stem, #3077, 6 oz., tall sherbet	45.00	25.00
Stem, #3115, 9 oz.		30.00
Stem, #3115, 3½ oz., cocktail		25.00
Stem, #3115, 6 oz., fruit		16.00
Stem, #3115, 6 oz., low sherbet		16.00
Stem, #3115, 6 oz., tall sherbet		18.00
Stem, #3115, 9 oz., water		27.50
Sugar cube tray		185.00
Sugar, Decagon	35.00	25.00
Sugar, ftd.	40.00	22.00
Sugar sifter, ftd., 6¾"	850.00	325.00
Syrup pitcher, drip cut		195.00
Syrup pitcher, glass lid		250.00
Toast & cover, round		500.00
Tobacco humidor		500.00
Tray, 12", handled serving		155.00
Tray, 12", oval service, Decagon	225.00	145.00
Tray, creamer & sugar, oval		50.00
Tumbler, #3077, 2½ oz., ftd.	125.00	65.00
Tumbler, #3077, 5 oz., ftd.	60.00	20.00
Tumbler, #3077, 8 oz., ftd.	60.00	25.00
Tumbler, #3077, 10 oz., ftd.	65.00	27.50
Tumbler, #3022, 12 oz., ftd.	95.00	35.00
Tumbler, #3115, 2½ oz., ftd.		55.00
Tumbler, #3115, 5 oz., ftd.		25.00
Tumbler, #3115, 8 oz., ftd.		25.00
Tumbler, #3115, 10 oz., ftd.		37.50
Tumbler, #3115, 12 oz., ftd.		35.00
Tumbler, 12 oz., flat		65.00
Vase, 5½"		95.00
Vase, 9½"		155.00
Vase, 11"		195.00
Wafer tray		250.00

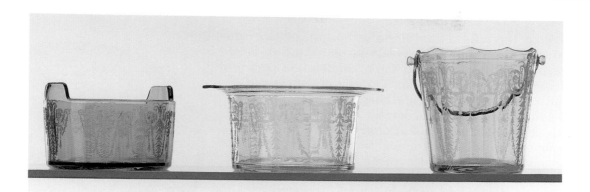

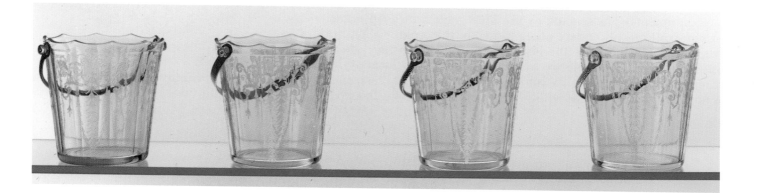

Colors: crystal; some yellow, opaque blue, green, white, amber, red in 1980s as Maypole

Fostoria's Colony was refined from an earlier Fostoria pattern called Queen Ann. A few Colony pieces were made as late as 1983. Fostoria called colored pieces Maypole in the 1980s. Red vases, candlesticks, and bowls being found were produced by Viking for Fostoria in the early 1980s. Note the red bud vase pictured. Dalzell Viking made red for Lancaster Colony who now owns the Fostoria name.

Goblets with a thin, plain bowl and a Colony patterned foot (sold to go with this pattern) were called Colonial Dame. You might even find these stems with colored bowls particularly dark emerald green.

I found the round stacking set of three ashtrays containing a 3", 4½" and 6" last year. I had never seen round ones, though the square ones appear regularly.

Experimental pieces such as the blue goblets turn up occasionally, but you could never collect many pieces in that color. Colony prices have been steadily rising since the last edition, indicating there are new collectors searching for it. Some pieces you may have trouble locating include finger bowls, cream soups, punch bowl, ice tub with flat rim, flat tumblers, and cigarette boxes. The supply of pitchers is adequate for now. All the flat pieces with plain centers need to be checked closely for wear, but that is true for any pattern.

	Crystal		Crystal
Ashtray, 2⅞", sq.	12.00	Bowl, 10½", oval, 2 part	55.00
Ashtray, 3", round	15.00	Bowl, 11", oval, ftd.	75.00
Ashtray, 3½", sq.	16.00	Bowl, 11", flared	40.00
Ashtray, 4½", round	20.00	Bowl, 11½", celery	30.00
Ashtray, 6", round	25.00	Bowl, 13", console	40.00
Bowl, 2¾" ftd., almond	20.00	Bowl, 13¼", punch, ftd.	425.00
Bowl, 4½", rnd.	12.00	Bowl, 14", fruit	60.00
Bowl, 4¾", finger	55.00	Butter dish, ¼ lb.	50.00
Bowl, 4¾", hdld.	12.00	Candlestick, 3½"	17.50
Bowl, 5", bonbon	12.00	Candlestick, 6½", double	45.00
Bowl, 5", cream soup	60.00	Candlestick, 7"	37.50
Bowl, 5", hdld.	15.00	Candlestick, 7½", w/8 prisms	77.50
Bowl, 5½", sq.	22.00	Candlestick, 9"	40.00
Bowl, 5¾", high ft.	16.00	Candlestick, 9¾", w/prisms	100.00
Bowl, 5", rnd.	15.00	Candlestick, 14½", w/10 prisms	175.00
Bowl, 6", rose	25.00	Candy, w/cover, 6½"	45.00
Bowl, 7", bonbon, 3 ftd.	14.00	Candy, w/cover, ftd., ½ lb.	75.00
Bowl, 7", olive, oblong	14.00	Cheese & cracker	55.00
Bowl, 7¾", salad	25.00	Cigarette box	58.00
Bowl, 8", cupped	47.50	Comport, 4"	17.50
Bowl, 8", hdld.	40.00	Comport, cover, 6½"	45.00
Bowl, 9", rolled console	40.00	Creamer, 3¼", indiv.	12.50
Bowl, 9½", pickle	20.00	Creamer, 3¾"	9.00
Bowl, 9¾", salad	50.00	Cup, 6 oz., ftd.	7.50
Bowl, 10", fruit	40.00	Cup, punch	15.00
Bowl, 10½", low ft.	85.00	Ice bucket	85.00
Bowl, 10½", high ft.	125.00	Ice bucket, plain edge	195.00
Bowl, 10½", oval	60.00	Lamp, electric	175.00

	Crystal
Mayonnaise, 3 pc.	35.00
Oil w/stopper, 4½ oz.	45.00
Pitcher, 16 oz., milk	75.00
Pitcher, 48 oz., ice lip	210.00
Pitcher, 2 qt., ice lip	125.00
Plate, ctr. hdld., sandwich	35.00
Plate, 6", bread & butter	7.00
Plate, 6½", lemon, hdld.	12.00
Plate, 7", salad	10.00
Plate, 8", luncheon	13.00
Plate, 9", dinner	27.50
Plate, 10", hdld., cake	27.50
Plate, 12", ftd., salver	85.00
Plate, 13", torte	30.00
Plate, 15", torte	65.00
Plate, 18", torte	110.00
Platter, 12"	52.50
Relish, 10½", hdld., 3 part	27.50
Salt, 2½" indiv., pr.	20.00
Salt & pepper, pr., 3⅝"	28.00

	Crystal
Saucer	2.00
Stem, 3⅜", 4 oz., oyster cocktail	12.00
Stem, 3⅝", 5 oz., sherbet	10.00
Stem, 4", 3½ oz., cocktail	12.00
Stem, 4¼", 3¼ oz., wine	22.00
Stem, 5¼", 9 oz., goblet	17.00
Sugar, 2¾", indiv.	12.50
Sugar, 3½"	9.00
Tray for indiv. sugar/cream	15.00
Tumbler, 3⅝", 5 oz., juice	25.00
Tumbler, 3⅞", 9 oz., water	22.00
Tumbler, 4⅞", 12 oz., tea	40.00
Tumbler, 4½", 5 oz., ftd.	18.00
Tumbler, 5¾", 12 oz., ftd.	22.00
Vase, 6", bud, flared	16.00
Vase, 7", cupped	50.00
Vase, 7½", flared	65.00
Vase, 9", cornucopia	85.00
Vase, 12", straight	195.00

Colors: crystal, Zircon/Limelight, Sahara, and rare in amber

Crystolite is one of the most recognized Heisey patterns since most pieces are marked with the well-known H inside a diamond. That easily found mark means you will seldom find a bargain piece of Crystolite in today's market. Pattern recognition always helps collectors, but depending upon finding an embossed mark can be a big mistake. Many pieces of Heisey are not marked. They had paper labels that were removed with use.

You can spot the harder to find items by their high prices. Non-scratched dinner plates, 5" comport, 6" basket, rye bottle, cocktail shaker, and pressed tumblers have always been difficult to locate. Note the added decoration to the perfume and puff box on page 66. These were added outside the glass factory.

	Crystal
Ashtray, 3½", sq.	6.00
Ashtray, 4½", sq.	10.00
Ashtray, 5", w/book match holder	45.00
Ashtray (coaster), 4", rnd.	8.00
Basket, 6", hdld.	550.00
Bonbon, 7", shell	22.00
Bonbon, 7½", 2 hdld.	15.00
Bottle, 1 qt., rye, #107 stopper	300.00
Bottle, 4 oz., bitters, w/short tube	175.00
Bottle, 4 oz., cologne, w/#108 stopper	75.00
w/drip stop	150.00
Bottle, syrup, w/drip & cut top	135.00
Bowl, 7½ quart, punch	120.00
Bowl, 2", indiv. swan nut (or ashtray)	20.00
Bowl, 3", indiv. nut, hdld.	20.00
Bowl, 4½", dessert (or nappy)	20.00
Bowl, 5", preserve	20.00
Bowl, 5", 1000 island dressing, ruffled top	30.00
Bowl, 5½", dessert	14.00
Bowl, 6", oval jelly, 4 ft.	22.00
Bowl, 6", preserve, 2 hdld.	20.00
Bowl, 7", shell praline	35.00
Bowl, 8", dessert (sauce)	30.00
Bowl, 8", 2 pt. conserve, hdld.	55.00
Bowl, 9", leaf pickle	30.00

	Crystal
Bowl, 10", salad, rnd.	50.00
Bowl, 11", w/attached mayonnaise (chip 'n dip)	225.00
Bowl, 12", gardenia, shallow	65.00
Bowl, 13", oval floral, deep	60.00
Candle block, 1-lite, sq.	25.00
Candle block, 1-lite, swirl	25.00
Candlestick, 1-lite, ftd.	25.00
Candlestick, 1-lite, w/#4233, 5", vase	35.00
Candlestick, 2-lite	35.00
Candlestick, 2-lite, bobeche & 10 "D" prisms	65.00
Candlestick sans vase, 3-lite	45.00
Candlestick, w/#4233, 5", vase, 3-lite	55.00
Candy, 5½", shell and cover	55.00
Candy box, w/cover, 7", 3 part	70.00
Candy box, w/cover, 7"	60.00
Cheese, 5½", ftd.	27.00
Cigarette box, w/cover, 4"	35.00
Cigarette box, w/cover, 4½"	40.00
Cigarette holder, ftd.	35.00
Cigarette holder, oval	25.00
Cigarette holder, rnd.	25.00
Cigarette lighter	30.00
Coaster, 4"	12.00
Cocktail shaker, 1 qt. w/#1 strainer; #86 stopper	325.00
Comport, 5", ftd., deep, #5003, blown rare	300.00

	Crystal
Creamer, indiv.	20.00
Creamer, reg.	30.00
Creamer, round	40.00
Cup	22.00
Cup, punch or custard	9.00
Hurricane block, 1-lite, sq.	40.00
Hurricane block, w/#4061, 10" plain globe, 1-lite, sq.	120.00
Ice tub, w/silver plate handle	120.00
Jar, covered cherry	110.00
Jam jar, w/cover	70.00
Ladle, glass, punch	35.00
Ladle, plastic	10.00
Mayonnaise, 5½", shell, 3 ft.	35.00
Mayonnaise, 6", oval, hdld.	40.00
Mayonnaise ladle	12.00
Mustard & cover	55.00
Oil bottle, 3 oz.	45.00
Oil bottle, w/stopper, 2 oz.	35.00
Oval creamer, sugar, w/tray, set	70.00
Pitcher, ½ gallon, ice, blown	140.00
Pitcher, 2 quart swan, ice lip	700.00
Plate, 7", salad	15.00
Plate, 7", shell	32.00
Plate, 7", underliner for 1000 island dressing bowl	20.00
Plate, 7½", coupe	40.00
Plate, 8", oval, mayonnaise liner	20.00
Plate, 8½", salad	20.00
Plate, 10½", dinner	100.00
Plate, 11", ftd., cake salver	350.00
Plate, 11", torte	40.00
Plate, 12", sandwich	45.00
Plate, 13", shell torte	100.00

	Crystal
Plate, 14", sandwich	55.00
Plate, 14", torte	50.00
Plate, 20", buffet or punch liner	125.00
Puff box, w/cover, 4¾"	75.00
Salad dressing set, 3 pc.	38.00
Salt & pepper, pr.	45.00
Saucer	6.00
Stem, 1 oz., cordial, wide optic, blown, #5003	130.00
Stem, 3½ oz., cocktail, w.o., blown, #5003	28.00
Stem, 3½ oz., claret, w.o., blown, #5003	38.00
Stem, 3½ oz., oyster cocktail, w.o. blown, #5003	28.00
Stem, 6 oz., sherbet/saucer champagne, #5003	18.00
Stem, 10 oz., water, #1503, pressed	500.00
Stem, 10 oz., w.o., blown, #5003	35.00
Sugar, indiv.	20.00
Sugar, reg.	30.00
Sugar, round	40.00
Syrup pitcher, drip cut	135.00
Tray, 5½", oval, liner indiv. creamer/sugar set	40.00
Tray, 9", 4 pt., leaf relish	40.00
Tray, 10", 5 pt., rnd. relish	45.00
Tray, 12", 3 pt., relish, oval	35.00
Tray, 12", rect., celery	38.00
Tray, 12", rect., celery/olive	35.00
Tumbler, 5 oz., ftd., juice, w.o., blown, #5003	38.00
Tumbler, 8 oz., pressed, #5003	60.00
Tumbler, 10 oz., pressed	70.00
Tumbler, 10 oz., iced tea, w.o., blown, #5003	40.00
Tumbler, 12 oz., ftd., iced tea, w.o., blown, #5003	38.00
Urn, 7", flower	75.00
Vase, 3", short stem	45.00
Vase, 6", ftd.	40.00
Vase, 12"	225.00

Colors: crystal, crystal w/gold encrusting

Daffodil is a later Cambridge pattern that is beginning to be noticed by new collectors. I will be transferring it to my *Collectible Glassware from the 40s, 50s, and 60s* book with the next edition so this will be the last time you will find it in this book. I am trying to adjust the time frame set by my books.

	Crystal
Basket, 6", 2 hdld., low ft., #55	40.00
Bonbon, #1181	30.00
Bonbon, 5¼", 2 hdld., #3400/1180	40.00
Bowl, 11" oval, tuck hdld., #384	75.00
Bowl, 12", belled, #430	85.00
Candle, 2 lite, arch, #3900/72	65.00
Candlestick, 3½", #628	55.00
Candy box & cover, cut hexagon knob, #306	145.00
Celery, 11", #248	65.00
Comport, 5½", ftd., #533	45.00
Comport, 6½", 2 hdld., low ftd., #54	55.00
Comport, 6" tall, pulled stem, #532	65.00
Creamer, #254	25.00
Creamer, indiv., #253	30.00
Cup, #11770	25.00
Jug, #3400/140	275.00
Jug, 76 oz., #3400/141	300.00
Mayonnaise, 3 pc., ftd., w ladle & liner plate, #533	95.00
Mayonnaise, ftd., w/ladle and plate	95.00
Oil, 6 oz., #293	135.00
Plate, #1174	30.00
Plate, 6", 2 hdld., bonbon, #3400/1181	22.50
Plate, 8½", salad	18.00
Plate, 8", sq., #1176	20.00
Plate, 8", 2 hdld., low ft., #56	30.00
Plate, 11½" cake, #1495	75.00
Plate, 13½", cabaret, #166	95.00
Relish, 10", 3 pt., #214	65.00
Salad dressing set, twin, 4 pc. w/ladles & liner, #1491	110.00

	Crystal
Salt & pepper, squat, pr., #360	65.00
Saucer, #1170	5.00
Stem, brandy, ¾ oz., #1937	75.00
Stem, claret, 4½ oz., #3779	65.00
Stem, claret, 4½ oz., #1937	65.00
Stem, cocktail, 3½ oz., #1937	35.00
Stem, cocktail, 3 oz., #3779	35.00
Stem, cordial, 1 oz., #3779	90.00
Stem, cordial, 1 oz., #1937	90.00
Stem, oyster cocktail, 5 oz., #1937	20.00
Stem, oyster cocktail, 4½ oz., #3779	20.00
Stem, sherbet, 6 oz., low, #1937	18.00
Stem, sherbet, 6 oz., low, #3779	18.00
Stem, sherbet, 6 oz., tall, #1937	22.00
Stem, sherbet, 6 oz., tall, #3779	22.00
Stem, sherry, 2 oz., #1937	65.00
Stem, water, 9 oz., low, #3779	30.00
Stem, water, 9 oz., tall, #3779	35.00
Stem, water, 11 oz., #1937	47.50
Stem, wine, 2½ oz., #3779	57.50
Stem, wine, 3 oz., #1937	55.00
Sugar, #254	25.00
Sugar, indiv., #253	30.00
Tumbler, ftd., 5 oz., #1937	22.00
Tumbler, ftd., 5 oz., #3779	22.00
Tumbler, ftd., 10 oz., #1937	27.50
Tumbler, ftd., 12 oz., iced tea, #3779	37.50
Tumbler, ftd., 12 oz., #1937	37.50
Vase, 8", ftd., #6004	110.00
Vase, 11", ftd., #278	135.00

and Glass Co., 1926 – 1940s

Colors: crystal, French crystal, frosted crystal, green and frosted green, pink and frosted pink, Ruby flashed, white, and assorted ceramic colors

Dancing Nymph is the Consolidated name for this pattern that has been referred to as "Dance of the Nudes" for over 30 years. Securely established names are almost impossible to just toss away in the collecting world, even after the correct name has surfaced all these years later. When the expensive Ruba Rombic was first listed in this book ten years ago, bargains in that pattern became infrequent. Dancing Nymph has not been quite so sensational since glassware depicting nudes has always been popular. People may not have known its proper name, but it captured their attention. Dancing Nymph prices are, in fact, reasonable when contrasted with other Consolidated patterns. This pattern is one of a few 3-D patterns that exist in this collecting field and was influenced in its concept by the graceful curves of the Art Nouveau movement as well as European wares, particularly Lalique, popular at this time. We searched for this pattern for years trying to find enough to picture. The ceramic green bowl shown, as a pattern shot, is the only different piece I could acquire since the last book.

Green color has an aqua cast to it as shown in the photograph. French Crystal is clear nudes with satin background like the plate in the bottom row, really illustrating the Lalique influence. Other colors are self-explanatory except for the unusual ceramic colors. Ceramic colors were obtained by covering the bottom of a crystal piece with color, wiping the nude designs clear, and firing the plate. The Honey (yellow) plate in row 3 is an example. (Older glassware often involved several hand processes that would be prohibitive to perform today due to labor costs.) Ceramic colors are highly desirable and costly. Other colors with this process are Sepia (brown), white, dark blue, light blue, pinkish lavender, and light green.

Dancing Nymph was introduced in 1926 and made until Consolidated closed in 1932. In 1936 the plant was reopened and a cupped saucer and sherbet plates were added to this production. You can see the cupped saucer in row 2 and the cupped sherbet plates in several colors. These sherbet plates are like a shallow bowl and were often referred to as ice cream plates in other patterns of the time. The flatter version is shown in row 1 with sherbets atop. Salad plates usually came with basic sets, but sherbet plates were often special order items, which, of course, makes them harder to find today. Candlesticks in Dancing Nymph are rare. Notice the two different styles pictured. I have been advised the crystal items were never sold, but were supposed to be frosted. I have seen enough crystal to wonder about that. However, one story I heard was that the crystal came out of the factory when it closed for good in the 1940s. It was supposed to be frosted, but had not received the treatment before the plant went out of business. Before being introduced in my book, I saw the crystal Dancing Nymph pieces in Florida regularly with reasonable prices. No longer!

	Crystal	Frosted Crystal French Crystal	*Frosted Pink or Green	Ceramic Colors
Bowl, 4½"	35.00	65.00	85.00	110.00
Bowl, 8"	75.00	125.00	200.00	275.00
Bowl, 16", palace	600.00	1250.00		1600.00
Candle, pr.	395.00	600.00		750.00
Cup	35.00	55.00	85.00	110.00
Plate, 6", cupped			75.00	
Plate, 6", sherbet	25.00	45.00	75.00	100.00
Plate, 8", salad	35.00	65.00		125.00
Plate, 10"	65.00	95.00	150.00	195.00
Platter, 18", palace	600.00	1000.00		1250.00
Saucer, coupe			35.00	
Saucer, flat	15.00	20.00	35.00	40.00
Sherbet	35.00	65.00	85.00	
Tumbler, 3½", cocktail	45.00	65.00		
Tumbler, 5½", goblet	55.00	75.00	125.00	175.00
Vase, 5½", crimped	75.00	135.00		165.00
Vase, 5½", fan	75.00	135.00		165.00

*Subtract 10% to 15% for unfrosted.

DECAGON, Cambridge Glass Company, 1930s – 1940s

Colors: Amber, amethyst, crystal Emerald green, Peach-Blo, Carmen, Royal blue, Moonlight blue, Ebony

Decagon is the company designation for the ten-sided mould blank on which many of Cambridge's etchings were set. The blank makes no difference when patterns like Cleo, Rosalie, and Imperial Hunt Scene are etched on it. Collectors definitely see the pattern itself rather than the Decagon blank. Yet, there are some fervent collectors of this plain, geometric Decagon "pattern." Amber Decagon has admirers, but not as many as Willow blue. Some Cleo collectors pursue Decagon to enrich their etched collections. Why spend $500.00 for a gravy and liner when you can buy a Decagon one for 25% of that?

You will find that Peach-Blo (pink), Emerald (green), and amber are more plentiful, but Willow blue is the preferred color. Pattern availability is only one important issue in collecting. Color also plays a fundamental role; and blue wins out more often than not.

Flat soups, cordials, and pitchers are not easily spotted. Many collectors are searching for serving pieces both for this pattern and to fill in spots in their etched wares. This makes finding what you need even more challenging.

	Pastel Colors	Blue
Basket, 7", 2 hdld. (upturned sides)	15.00	30.00
Bowl, bouillon, w/liner	15.00	35.00
Bowl, cream soup, w/liner	22.00	35.00
Bowl, 2½", indiv., almond	30.00	50.00
Bowl, 3¾", flat rim, cranberry	20.00	32.00
Bowl, 3½" belled, cranberry	20.00	32.00
Bowl, 5½", 2 hdld., bonbon	12.00	22.00
Bowl, 5½", belled, fruit	10.00	20.00
Bowl, 5¾", flat rim, fruit	10.00	20.00
Bowl, 6", belled, cereal	20.00	30.00
Bowl, 6", flat rim, cereal	22.00	40.00
Bowl, 6", ftd., almond	30.00	50.00
Bowl, 6¼", 2 hdld., bonbon	12.00	22.00
Bowl, 8½", flat rim, soup "plate"	25.00	50.00
Bowl, 9", rnd., veg.	30.00	55.00
Bowl, 9", 2 pt., relish	30.00	40.00
Bowl, 9½", oval, veg.	35.00	50.00
Bowl, 10", berry	35.00	50.00
Bowl, 10½", oval, veg.	35.00	50.00
Bowl, 11", rnd. veg.	40.00	48.00
Bowl, 11", 2 pt., relish	38.00	40.00
Comport, 5¾"	20.00	35.00
Comport, 6½", low ft.	20.00	35.00
Comport, 7", tall	25.00	48.00
Creamer, ftd.	10.00	20.00
Creamer, scalloped edge	9.00	18.00
Creamer, lightning bolt handles	10.00	15.00
Creamer, tall, lg. ft.	10.00	22.00
Cup	6.00	11.00
French dressing bottle, "Oil/Vinegar"	90.00	150.00
Gravy boat, w/2 hdld. liner (like spouted cream soup)	100.00	125.00
Ice bucket	45.00	75.00
Ice tub	45.00	65.00
Mayonnaise, 2 hdld., w/2 hdld. liner and ladle	27.00	45.00
Mayonnaise, w/liner & ladle	25.00	65.00
Oil, 6 oz., tall, w/hdld. & stopper	70.00	175.00
Plate, 6¼", bread/butter	5.00	10.00
Plate, 7", 2 hdld.	9.00	15.00
Plate, 7½"	8.00	12.00
Plate, 8½", salad	15.00	25.00
Plate, 9½", dinner	50.00	70.00
Plate, 10", grill	35.00	50.00
Plate, 10", service	35.00	50.00
Plate, 12½", service	30.00	60.00
Relish, 6 inserts	100.00	165.00
Salt dip, 1½", ftd.	25.00	40.00
Sauce boat & plate	100.00	125.00
Saucer	3.00	4.00
Server, center hdld.	30.00	45.00
Stem, 1 oz., cordial	45.00	70.00
Stem, 3½ oz., cocktail	15.00	24.00
Stem, 6 oz., low sherbet	12.00	18.00
Stem, 6 oz., high sherbet	15.00	25.00
Stem, 9 oz., water	20.00	35.00
Sugar, lightning bolt handles	10.00	15.00
Sugar, ftd.	9.00	20.00
Sugar, scalloped edge	9.00	20.00
Sugar, tall, lg. ft.	20.00	35.00
Tray, 8", 2 hdld., flat pickle	25.00	40.00
Tray, 9", pickle	25.00	40.00
Tray, 11", oval, service	30.00	50.00
Tray, 11", celery	30.00	50.00
Tray, 12", center handled	30.00	45.00
Tray, 12", oval, service	25.00	45.00
Tray, 13", 2 hdld., service	35.00	50.00
Tray, 15", oval, service	45.00	75.00
Tumbler, 2½ oz., ftd.	20.00	25.00
Tumbler, 5 oz., ftd.	15.00	20.00
Tumbler, 8 oz., ftd.	18.00	25.00
Tumbler, 10 oz., ftd.	20.00	30.00
Tumbler, 12 oz., ftd.	25.00	38.00

"DEERWOOD" or "BIRCH TREE," U.S. Glass Company, late 1920s – early 1930s

Colors: light amber, green, pink, black, crystal

Look on page 23 for the Black Forest pattern photo if you tend to confuse these two patterns. Deer and trees are depicted on "Deerwood"; moose and trees are illustrated on Black Forest. I trust you know the difference between deer and moose. Hopefully, you won't be like the hunter in Maine who wouldn't let the guy take his saddle off the "moose" she shot out from under him.

Gold decorated, black "Deerwood" is being bought by people who are not necessarily collectors, but who just like it. Those using Internet auctions have also discovered "Deerwood." These occurrences have caused some price modifications. "Deerwood," itself, is not commonly found but gold decoration on black really makes the pattern stand out, and pieces of this are particularly hard to acquire. Large sets can only be garnered in green and pink. You will have to settle for an occasional piece or two in the other colors.

That #300 flat, three-part, pink candy in the top photo is a Paden City mould and not U.S. Glass. This makes a researcher's job more interesting than necessary! A U.S. Glass etching on a Paden City candy is a definite oddity. We are obtaining more and more case histories of "shared" wares between companies, for whatever reasons. Some authors have flatly stated that didn't happen, but I am positive that it did.

There is some catalog documentation for "Deerwood," but not nearly enough. That is why new pieces keep turning up after 30 years of serious collecting. It makes you wonder if some other company did some etchings of "Deerwood." The moulds definitely were produced at Tiffin, but perhaps etching contracts were sublet to someone else.

The mayonnaise was listed at Tiffin as a whipped cream rather than a mayonnaise. Terminology of the old glass companies often differed from their competitors — just as today's ideas change, too.

	*Black	Amber	Green	Pink
Bowl, 10", ftd.	165.00			
Bowl, 10", straight edge				75.00
Bowl, 12", console			85.00	80.00
Cake plate, low pede.			75.00	75.00
Candlestick, 2½"	75.00		40.00	
Candlestick, 4"				60.00
Candy dish, w/cover, 3 part, flat				150.00
Candy jar, w/cover, ftd. cone			165.00	165.00
Celery, 12"			75.00	
Cheese and cracker			125.00	125.00
Comport, 10", low, ftd., flared	150.00			75.00
Creamer, 2 styles	70.00		45.00	45.00
Cup				80.00
Plate, 5½"			15.00	15.00
Plate, 7½", salad				25.00
Plate, 9½", dinner				100.00
Plate, 10¼", 2 hdld.	145.00			
Saucer				20.00
Server, center hdld.			75.00	75.00
Stem, 2 oz., wine, 4½"				60.00
Stem, 6 oz., sherbet, 4¾"			30.00	
Stem, 6 oz., cocktail, 5"			40.00	
Stem, 9 oz., water, 7"	135.00		65.00	65.00
Sugar, 2 styles	70.00		45.00	45.00
Tumbler, 9 oz.			37.50	37.50
Tumbler, 12 oz., tea, 5½"		55.00		
Vase, 7", sweet pea, rolled edge			145.00	145.00
Vase, 10", ruffled top			145.00	145.00
Vase, 12", 2 handles	225.00			
Whipped cream pail, w/ladle			75.00	75.00

*Add 20% for gold decorated.

Colors: crystal; some pink, yellow, blue, Heatherbloom, Emerald green, amber, Crown Tuscan w/gold

Cambridge's Diane pattern can be found in numerous colors; but only crystal can be collected in more than a small set. You might be able to obtain a luncheon set in color, but after that only an occasional bowl, candle, or tumbler will be seen. Apparently the price of making this colored, handmade glass contributed to its scarcity; in any case, colored Diane is scarce.

Mostly crystal is presently pictured; you will have to search earlier books for Diane in color. As with other Cambridge patterns in this book, you will have to look at Rose Point listings for pricing any unlisted Diane items. Diane will run 30% to 40% less than comparable items listed in Rose Point. Remember that Rose Point is the highest priced Cambridge pattern and other patterns sell for less. Demand for Rose Point pushes prices to new levels; other patterns increase in price rather slowly.

The bitters bottle and round ball shaker are difficult to find, but not impossible. That ball shaker has a square, screw-on glass base that is often damaged. I wonder why they were so designed because holding them upside down to fill should cause the salt or pepper to run out the holes I assume the "deco" look was the goal here.

You have several choices for stemware collecting in Diane; pick whichever you like. Each line looks excellent with the set. In my travels, I see more #3122 stems than any other; they might be the easiest to find.

	Crystal		Crystal
Basket, 6", 2 hdld., ftd.	35.00	Comport, 5½"	40.00
Bottle, bitters	175.00	Comport, 5⅜", blown	60.00
Bowl, #3106, finger, w/liner	47.50	Creamer	20.00
Bowl, #3122	25.00	Creamer, indiv., #3500 (pie crust edge)	22.00
Bowl, #3400, cream soup, w/liner	50.00	Creamer, indiv., #3900, scalloped edge	22.00
Bowl, 3", indiv. nut, 4 ftd.	60.00	Creamer, scroll handle, #3400	22.00
Bowl, 5", berry	32.00	Cup	20.00
Bowl, 5¼", 2 hdld., bonbon	25.00	Decanter, ball	250.00
Bowl, 6", 2 hdld., ftd., bonbon	25.00	Decanter, lg. ftd.	210.00
Bowl, 6", 2 pt., relish	25.00	Decanter, short ft., cordial	265.00
Bowl, 6", cereal	40.00	Hurricane lamp, candlestick base	195.00
Bowl, 6½", 3 pt., relish	35.00	Hurricane lamp, keyhole base w/prisms	235.00
Bowl, 7", 2 hdld., ftd., bonbon	38.00	Ice bucket, w/chrome hand	100.00
Bowl, 7", 2 pt., relish	35.00	Mayonnaise, div., w/liner & ladles	65.00
Bowl, 7", relish or pickle	35.00	Mayonnaise (sherbet type w/ladle)	55.00
Bowl, 9", 3 pt., celery or relish	40.00	Mayonnaise, w/liner, ladle	50.00
Bowl, 9½", pickle (like corn)	40.00	Oil, 6 oz., w/stopper	135.00
Bowl, 10", 4 ft., flared	65.00	Pitcher, ball	225.00
Bowl, 10", baker	60.00	Pitcher, Doulton	350.00
Bowl, 11", 2 hdld.	65.00	Pitcher, martini	795.00
Bowl, 11", 4 ftd.	65.00	Pitcher, upright	235.00
Bowl, 11½", tab hdld., ftd.	62.00	Plate, 6", 2 hdld., plate.	15.00
Bowl, 12", 3 pt., celery & relish	55.00	Plate, 6", sq., bread/butter	10.00
Bowl, 12", 4 ft.	70.00	Plate, 6½", bread/butter	8.00
Bowl, 12", 4 ft., flared	80.00	Plate, 8", 2 hdld., ftd., bonbon	18.00
Bowl, 12", 4 ft., oval	80.00	Plate, 8", salad	14.00
Bowl, 12", 4 ft., oval, w/"ears," hdld.	85.00	Plate, 8½"	20.00
Bowl, 12", 5 pt., celery & relish	65.00	Plate, 10½", dinner	95.00
Butter, rnd.	165.00	Plate, 12", 4 ft., service	55.00
Cabinet flask	295.00	Plate, 13", 4 ft., torte	60.00
Candelabrum, 2-lite, keyhole	33.00	Plate, 13½", 2 hdld.	60.00
Candelabrum, 3-lite, keyhole	40.00	Plate, 14", torte	75.00
Candlestick, 1-lite, keyhole	35.00	Platter, 13½"	95.00
Candlestick, 5"	20.00	Salt & pepper, ftd., w/glass tops, pr.	50.00
Candlestick, 6", 2-lite, "fleur-de-lis"	40.00	Salt & pepper, pr., flat	50.00
Candlestick, 6", 3-lite	45.00	Saucer	6.00
Candy box, w/cover, rnd.	95.00	Stem, #1066, 1 oz., cordial	75.00
Cigarette urn	75.00	Stem, #1066, 3 oz., cocktail	27.50
Cocktail shaker, glass top	250.00	Stem, #1066, 3 oz., wine	35.00
Cocktail shaker, metal top	135.00	Stem, #1066, 3½ oz., tall cocktail	30.00
Cocktail icer, 2 pc.	85.00	Stem, #1066, 4½ oz., claret	60.00

	Crystal
Stem, #1066, 5 oz., oyster/cocktail	25.00
Stem, #1066, 7 oz., low sherbet	22.00
Stem, #1066, 7 oz., tall sherbet	25.00
Stem, #1066, 11 oz., water	35.00
Stem, #3122, 1 oz., cordial	70.00
Stem, #3122, 2½ oz., wine	35.00
Stem, #3122, 3 oz., cocktail	25.00
Stem, #3122, 4½ oz., claret	60.00
Stem, #3122, 4½ oz., oyster/cocktail	22.00
Stem, #3122, 7 oz., low sherbet	22.00
Stem, #3122, 7 oz., tall sherbet	25.00
Stem, #3122, 9 oz., water goblet	30.00
Sugar, indiv., #3500 (pie crust edge)	22.00
Sugar, indiv., #3900, scalloped edge	22.00
Sugar, scroll handle, #3400	22.00
Tumbler, 2½ oz., sham bottom	60.00
Tumbler, 5 oz., ft., juice	40.00
Tumbler, 5 oz., sham bottom	45.00
Tumbler, 7 oz., old-fashion, w/sham bottom	55.00
Tumbler, 8 oz., ft.	30.00
Tumbler, 10 oz., sham bottom	35.00
Tumbler, 12 oz., sham bottom	40.00
Tumbler, 13 oz.	35.00
Tumbler, 14 oz., sham bottom	45.00

	Crystal
Tumbler, #1066, 3 oz.	30.00
Tumbler, #1066, 5 oz., juice	25.00
Tumbler, #1066, 9 oz., water	22.00
Tumbler, #1066, 12 oz., tea	28.00
Tumbler, #3106, 3 oz., ftd.	26.00
Tumbler, #3106, 5 oz., ftd., juice	22.00
Tumbler, #3106, 9 oz., ftd., water	20.00
Tumbler, #3106, 12 oz., ftd., tea	26.00
Tumbler, #3122, 2½ oz.	40.00
Tumbler, #3122, 5 oz., juice	20.00
Tumbler, #3122, 9 oz., water	25.00
Tumbler, #3122, 12 oz., tea	30.00
Tumbler, #3135, 2½ oz., ftd., bar	45.00
Tumbler, #3135, 10 oz., ftd., tumbler	22.00
Tumbler, #3135, 12 oz., ftd., tea	33.00
Vase, 5", globe	75.00
Vase, 6", high ft., flower	55.00
Vase, 8", high ft., flower	70.00
Vase, 9", keyhole base	95.00
Vase, 10", bud	65.00
Vase, 11", flower	115.00
Vase, 11", ped. ft., flower	110.00
Vase, 12", keyhole base	125.00
Vase, 13", flower	165.00

Note: See pages 236 – 237 for stem identification.

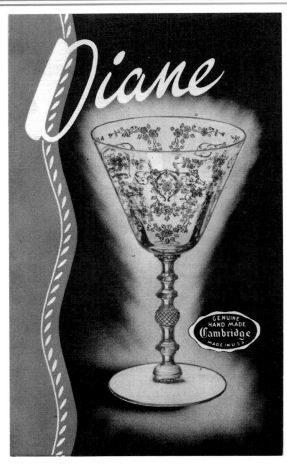

LIST OF DIANE ITEMS

3122	9 oz. Goblet
3122	7 oz. Tall Sherbet
3122	7 oz. Low Sherbet
3122	3 oz. Cocktail
3122	2½ oz. Wine
3122	4½ oz. Claret
3122	4½ oz. Oyster Cockta
3122	1 oz. Cordial
3122	12 oz. Ftd. Ice Tea
3122	9 oz. Ftd. Tumbler
3122	5 oz. Ftd. Tumbler
477	9½ in. Pickle
3400/1180	5¼ in. 2 Hdl. Bonbon
3400/1181	6 in. 2 Hdl. Plate
3400/90	6 in. 2 part Relish
3500/15	Ind. Sugar & Cream
3500/54	6 in. 2 Hdl. Ftd. Bonbon
3500/55	6 in. 2 Hdl. Ftd. Basket
3500/69	6½ in. 3 part Relish
3500/161	8 in. 2 Hdl. Ftd. Plate
3500/57	8 in. 3 part Candy Box & Cover (not illus.)
3900/17	Cup & Saucer
3900/19	2 pc. Mayonnaise Set
3900/20	6½ in. Bread & Butter Plate
3900/22	8 in. Salad Plate
3900/24	10½ in. Dinner Plate
3900/26	12 in. 4 Ftd. Plate
3900/28	11½ in. Ftd. Bowl
3900/33	13 in. 4 Ftd. Torte Plate, R. E.
3900/34	11 in. 2 Handled Bowl
3900/35	13½ in. 2 Handled Cake Plate
3900/40	Ind. Sugar & Cream
3900/41	Sugar & Cream
3900/54	10 in. 4 Ftd. Bowl, flared
3900/62	12 in. 4 Ftd. Bowl, flared
3900/65	12 in. 4 Ftd. Oval Bowl
3900/67	5 in. Candlestick
3900/72	6 in. 2 lite Candlestick
3900/74	6 in. 3 lite Candlestick
3900/100	6 oz. Oil, q.s.
3900/111	4 pc. Mayonnaise Set
3900/115	13 oz. Tumbler
3900/120	12 in. 5 part Celery & Relish
3900/123	7 in. Relish or Pickle
3900/124	7 in. 2 part Relish
3900/125	9 in. 3 part Celery & Relish
3900/126	12 in. 3 part Celery & Relish
3900/129	3 pc. Mayonnaise Set
3900/130	7 in. 2 handled Ftd. Bonbon
3900/131	8 in. 2 handled Ftd. Bonbon Plate
3900/136	5½ in. Comport
3900/165	Candy Box & Cover
3900/166	14 in. Plate, r.e.
3900/671	Ice Bucket
3900/671	Ice Bucket with chrome handle
	Chrome Ice Tongs (long)
3900/1177	Salt & Pepper Shaker (doz. pr.)
274	10 in. Bud Flower Holder
278	11 in. Ftd. Flower Holder
279	13 in. Ftd. Flower Holder
968	2 pc. Cocktail Icer
1237	9 in. Ftd. Flower Holder
1238	12 in. Ftd. Flower Holder
1299	11 in. Ftd. Flower Holder
1309	5 in. Glode Flower Holder
1603	Hurricane Lamp (Etch. Chimney only)
1617	Hurricane Lamp (Etch. Chimney only)
3121	5-⅜ in. Blown Comport
6004	6 in. Ftd. Flower Holder
6004	8 in. Ftd Flower Holder

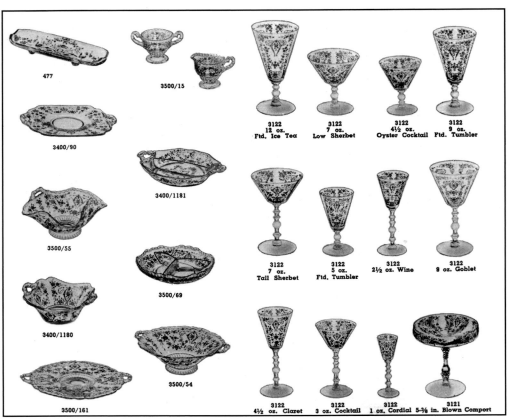

477

3500/15

3400/90

3400/1181

3500/55

3500/69

3400/1180

3500/54

3500/161

3122 12 oz. Ftd. Ice Tea

3122 7 oz. Low Sherbet

3122 4½ oz. Oyster Cocktail

3122 9 oz. Ftd. Tumbler

3122 7 oz. Tall Sherbet

3122 5 oz. Ftd. Tumbler

3122 2½ oz. Wine

3122 9 oz. Goblet

3122 4½ oz. Claret

3122 3 oz. Cocktail

3122 1 oz. Cordial

3121 5-⅜ in. Blown Comport

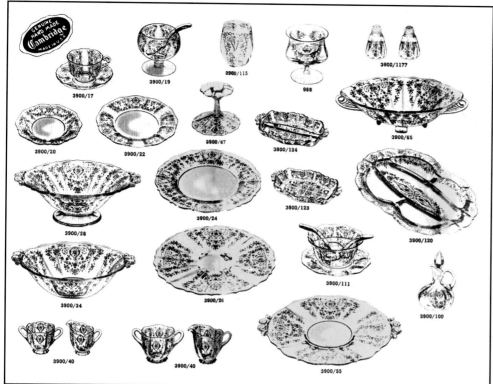

Colors: crystal

Elaine is repeatedly confused with Chantilly, and not only by new collectors. A seasoned dealer of Depression glass admitted to such confusion until Cathy showed him the difference in a way he'll never forget! The Elaine design has a thin and angled scroll like the top of the capital letter "E" (for Elaine) as you write it in script. Be sure to look at our outlined design at the top of the page.

Elaine is most often found on Cambridge's #3500 Gadroon line that has the ornate "pie crust" edge shown in the photographs. Seasoned Cambridge dealers and collectors cringe at that description as they do the "lightning bolt" description of handles on Decagon. However, those terms have caught on — even with other writers. You will find accessory pieces not listed here since I have used as much listing space as I have. Many pieces listed under Rose Point etch are found etched Elaine. Bear in mind that prices for Elaine will be 30% to 40% lower than those listed under Rose Point.

	Crystal		Crystal
Basket, 6", 2 hdld. (upturned sides)	30.00	Salt & pepper, ftd., pr	45.00
Bowl, #3104, finger, w/liner	50.00	Salt & pepper, hdld., pr	50.00
Bowl, 3", indiv. nut, 4 ftd.	60.00	Saucer	5.00
Bowl, 5¼", 2 hdld., bonbon	30.00	Stem, #1402, 1 oz., cordial	125.00
Bowl, 6", 2 hdld., ftd., bonbon	32.00	Stem, #1402, 3 oz., wine	45.00
Bowl, 6", 2 pt. relish	30.00	Stem, #1402, 3½ oz., cocktail	35.00
Bowl, 6½", 3 pt., relish	30.00	Stem, #1402, 5 oz., claret	45.00
Bowl, 7", 2 pt. pickle or relish	35.00	Stem, #1402, low sherbet	20.00
Bowl, 7", ftd., tab hdld., bonbon	40.00	Stem, #1402, tall sherbet	22.00
Bowl, 7", pickle or relish	35.00	Stem, #1402, goblet	35.00
Bowl, 9", 3 pt. celery & relish	45.00	Stem, #3104 (very tall stems), ¾ oz., brandy	195.00
Bowl, 9½", pickle (like corn dish)	50.00	Stem, #3104, 1 oz., cordial	195.00
Bowl, 10", 4 ftd., flared	75.00	Stem, #3104, 1 oz., pousse-cafe	195.00
Bowl, 11", tab hdld.	95.00	Stem, #3104, 2 oz., sherry	195.00
Bowl, 11½", ftd., tab hdld.	85.00	Stem, #3104, 2½ oz., creme de menthe	150.00
Bowl, 12", 3 pt. celery & relish	65.00	Stem, #3104, 3 oz., wine	150.00
Bowl, 12", 4 ftd., flared	75.00	Stem, #3104, 3½ oz., cocktail	100.00
Bowl, 12", 4 ftd., oval, "ear" hdld.	95.00	Stem, #3104, 4½ oz., claret	150.00
Bowl, 12", 5 pt. celery & relish	75.00	Stem, #3104, 5 oz., roemer	150.00
Candlestick, 5"	35.00	Stem, #3104, 5 oz., tall hock	150.00
Candlestick, 6", 2-lite	45.00	Stem, #3104, 7 oz., tall sherbet	125.00
Candlestick, 6", 3-lite	60.00	Stem, #3104, 9 oz., goblet	150.00
Candy box, w/cover, rnd.	100.00	Stem, #3121, 1 oz., cordial	75.00
Cocktail icer, 2 pc.	85.00	Stem, #3121, 3 oz., cocktail	35.00
Comport, 5½"	45.00	Stem, #3121, 3½ oz., wine	45.00
Comport, 5⅜", #3500 stem	50.00	Stem, #3121, 4½ oz., claret	50.00
Comport, 5⅜", blown	55.00	Stem, #3121, 4½ oz., oyster cocktail	30.00
Creamer (several styles)	22.00	Stem, #3121, 5 oz., parfait, low stem	45.00
Creamer, indiv.	22.00	Stem, #3121, 6 oz., low sherbet	22.00
Cup	22.00	Stem, #3121, 6 oz., tall sherbet	25.00
Decanter, lg., ftd.	235.00	Stem, #3121, 10 oz., water	32.00
Hat, 9"	395.00	Stem, #3500, 1 oz., cordial	75.00
Hurricane lamp, candlestick base	190.00	Stem, #3500, 2½ oz., wine	45.00
Hurricane lamp, keyhole ft., w/prisms	235.00	Stem, #3500, 3 oz., cocktail	35.00
Ice bucket, w/chrome handle	125.00	Stem, #3500, 4½ oz., claret	55.00
Mayonnaise (cupped sherbet w/ladle)	50.00	Stem, #3500, 4½ oz., oyster cocktail	30.00
Mayonnaise (div. bowl, liner, 2 ladles)	60.00	Stem, #3500, 5 oz., parfait, low stem	45.00
Mayonnaise, w/liner & ladle	55.00	Stem, #3500, 7 oz., low sherbet	22.00
Oil, 6 oz., hdld., w/stopper	125.00	Stem, #3500, 7 oz., tall sherbet	25.00
Pitcher, ball, 80 oz.	295.00	Stem, #3500, 10 oz., water	35.00
Pitcher, Doulton	350.00	Sugar (several styles)	22.00
Pitcher, upright	250.00	Sugar, indiv.	22.00
Plate, 6", 2 hdld.	15.00	Tumbler, #1402, 9 oz., ftd., water	25.00
Plate, 6½", bread/butter	12.00	Tumbler, #1402, 12 oz., tea	40.00
Plate, 8", 2 hdld., ftd.	22.00	Tumbler, #1402, 12 oz., tall ftd., tea	40.00
Plate, 8", salad	22.00	Tumbler, #3121, 5 oz., ftd., juice	30.00
Plate, 8", tab hdld., bonbon	25.00	Tumbler, #3121, 10 oz., ftd., water	40.00
Plate, 10½", dinner	85.00	Tumbler, #3121, 12 oz., ftd., tea	40.00
Plate, 11½" 2 hdld., ringed "Tally Ho" sandwich	65.00	Tumbler, #3500, 5 oz., ftd., juice	30.00
Plate, 12", 4 ftd., service	60.00	Tumbler, #3500, 10 oz., ftd., water	35.00
Plate, 13", 4 ftd., torte	55.00	Tumbler, #3500, 12 oz., ftd., tea	40.00
Plate, 13½", tab hdld., cake	75.00	Vase, 6", ftd.	75.00
Plate, 14", torte	65.00	Vase, 8", ftd.	100.00
Salt & pepper, flat, pr.	50.00	Vase, 9", keyhole, ftd.	145.00

LIST OF ELAINE ITEMS

3121	10 oz. Goblet
3121	6 oz. Tall Sherbet
3121	6 oz. Low Sherbet
3121	3 oz. Cocktail
3121	3½ oz. Wine
3121	4½ oz. Claret
3121	4½ oz. Oyster Cocktail
3121	1 oz. Cordial
3121	5 oz. Cafe Parfait
3121	12 oz. Ftd. Ice Tea
3121	10 oz. Ftd. Tumbler
3121	5 oz. Ftd. Tumbler
477	9½ in. Pickle
3400/1180	5¼ in. 2 Hdl. Bonbon
3400/1181	6 in. 2 Hdl. Plate
3400/90	6 in. 2 part Relish
3500/15	Ind. Sugar & Cream
3500/54	6 in. 2 Hdl. Ftd. Bonbon
3500/55	6 in. 2 Hdl. Ftd. Basket
3500/69	6½ in. 2 part Relish
3500/161	8 in. 2 Hdl. Plate
3500/57	8 in. 3 part Candy Box & Cover (not illus.)
3900/17	Cup & Saucer
3900/19	2 pc. Mayonnaise Set
3900/20	6½ in. Bread & Butter Plate
3900/22	8 in. Salad Plate
3900/24	10½ in. Dinner Plate
3900/26	12 in. 4 Ftd. Plate
3900/28	11½ in. Ftd. Bowl
3900/33	13 in. 4 Ftd. Torte Plate, R.E.
3900/34	11 in. 2 Handled Bowl
3900/35	13½ in. 2 Handled Cake Plate
3900/40	Ind. Sugar & Cream
3900/41	Sugar & Cream
3900/54	10 in. 4 Ftd. Bowl, flared
3900/62	12 in. 4 Ftd. Bowl, flared
3900/65	12 in. 4 Ftd. Oval Bowl
3900/67	5 in. Candlestick
3900/72	6 in. 2 lite Candlestick
3900/74	6 in. 3 lite Candlestick
3900/100	6 oz. Oil, g.s.
3900/111	4 pc. Mayonnaise Set
3900/115	13 oz. Tumbler
3900/120	12 in. 5 part Celery & Relish
3900/123	7 in. Relish or Pickle
3900/124	7 in. 2 part Relish
3900/125	9 in. 3 part Celery & Relish
3900/126	12 in. 3 part Celery & Relish
3900/129	3 pc. Mayonnaise Set
3900/130	7 in. 2 handled Ftd. Bonbon
3900/131	8 in. 2 handled Ftd. Bonbon Plate
3900/136	5½ in. Comport
3900/165	Candy Box & Cover
3900/166	14 in. Plate, r.e.
3900/671	Ice Bucket
3900/671	Ice Bucket with chrome Handle
	Chrome Ice Tongs (long)
3900/1177	Salt & Pepper Shaker (doz. pr.)
274	10 in. Bud Flower Holder
278	11 in. Ftd. Flower Holder
279	13 in. Ftd. Flower Holder
968	2 pc. Cocktail Icer
1237	9 in. Ftd. Flower Holder
1238	12 in. Ftd. Flower Holder
1299	11 in. Ftd. Flower Holder
1309	5 in. Glode Flower Holder
1603	Hurricane Lamp (Etch., Chimney only)
1617	Hurricane Lamp (Etch., Chimney only)
3121	5-3/8 in. Blown Comport
6004	6 in. Ftd. Flower Holder
6004	8 in. Ftd. Flower Holder

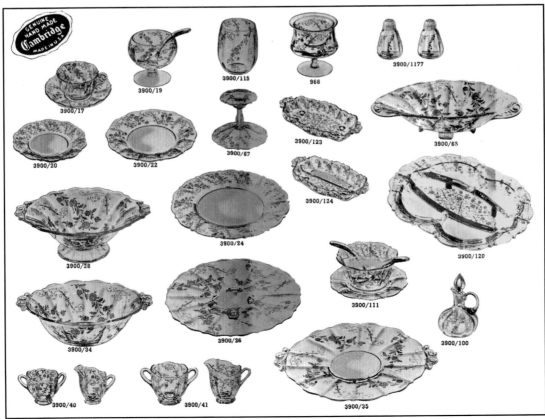

3900/19   968   3900/1177
3900/17   3900/123   3900/65
3900/20   3900/22   3900/67   3900/124
3900/28   3900/24   3900/120
3900/34   3900/26   3900/111   3900/100
3900/40   3900/41   3900/35

3900/54
3900/126
3900/131
3900/165
3900/130
3900/72
3900/166
3900/62
3900/74
3900/125
1603
3900/33
3900/136
3900/671
274
1299

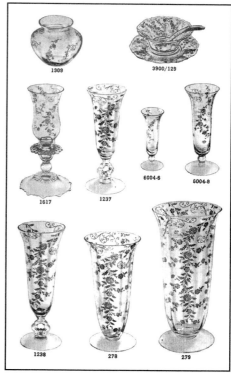

1309
3900/129
1617
1237
6004-6
6004-8
1238
278
279

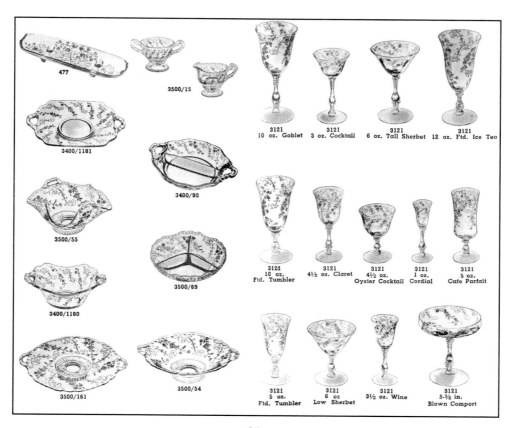

477
3500/15
3400/1181
3400/90
3500/55
3500/69
3400/1180
3500/161
3500/54

3121
10 oz. Goblet

3121
3 oz. Cocktail

3121
6 oz. Tall Sherbet

3121
12 oz. Ftd. Ice Tea

3121
10 oz.
Ftd. Tumbler

3121
4½ oz. Claret

3121
4½ oz.
Oyster Cocktail

3121
1 oz.
Cordial

3121
5 oz.
Cafe Parfait

3121
5 oz.
Ftd. Tumbler

3121
6 oz
Low Sherbet

3121
3½ oz. Wine

3121
5-3/8 in.
Blown Comport

Colors: Flamingo pink, Sahara yellow, Moongleam green, cobalt, and Alexandrite; some Tangerine

   Empress is shown in Sahara on page 83 and Alexandrite on page 82. Alexandrite is Heisey's purple/pink color that changes looks depending upon the lighting source. Under natural light it appears pink and under florescent light it appears blue. My photographers and printers have always done a remarkable job in showing it just right.

   Crystal listings are now found under the pattern Queen Ann. When the colors were made, this pattern was called Empress; but later on, when crystal was produced, the pattern name was changed to Queen Ann. Note that Empress can be found on both round and square blanks. I have always preferred square plates because you can load more food on them than you can round ones.

	Flamingo	Sahara	Moongleam	Cobalt	Alexandrite
Ashtray	175.00	185.00	250.00	300.00	225.00
Bonbon, 6"	20.00	25.00	30.00		
Bowl, cream soup	30.00	30.00	50.00		110.00
Bowl, cream soup, w/sq. liner	40.00	40.00	55.00		175.00
Bowl, frappe, w/center	45.00	60.00	75.00		
Bowl, nut, dolphin ftd., indiv.	30.00	32.00	45.00		170.00
Bowl, 4½", nappy	40.00	40.00	60.00		
Bowl, 5", preserve, 2 hdld.	20.00	25.00	30.00		
Bowl, 6", ftd., jelly, 2 hdld.	20.00	25.00	30.00		
Bowl, 6", dolphin ftd., mint	35.00	40.00	45.00		230.00
Bowl, 6", grapefruit, sq. top, grnd. bottom	12.50	20.00	25.00		
Bowl, 6½", oval, lemon, w/cover	65.00	80.00	150.00		
Bowl, 7", 3 pt., relish, triplex	40.00	45.00	50.00		300.00
Bowl, 7", 3 pt., relish, ctr. hand.	45.00	50.00	75.00		
Bowl, 7½", dolphin ftd., nappy	65.00	65.00	80.00	300.00	350.00
Bowl, 7½", dolphin ftd., nasturtium	130.00	130.00	150.00	350.00	425.00
Bowl, 8", nappy	35.00	37.00	45.00		

	Flamingo	Sahara	Moongleam	Cobalt	Alexandrite
Bowl, 8½", ftd., floral, 2 hdld	45.00	50.00	70.00		
Bowl, 9", floral, rolled edge	40.00	42.00	50.00		
Bowl, 9", floral, flared	70.00	75.00	90.00		
Bowl, 10", 2 hdld., oval dessert	50.00	60.00	70.00		
Bowl, 10", lion head, floral	550.00	550.00	700.00		
Bowl, 10", oval, veg.	50.00	55.00	75.00		
Bowl, 10", square, salad, 2 hdld.	55.00	60.00	80.00		
Bowl, 10", triplex, relish	50.00	55.00	65.00		
Bowl, 11", dolphin ftd., floral	65.00	75.00	100.00	400.00	500.00
Bowl, 13", pickle/olive, 2 pt.	35.00	45.00	50.00		
Bowl, 15", dolphin ftd., punch	900.00	900.00	1,100.00		
Candlestick, low, 4 ftd., w/2 hdld.	100.00	100.00	170.00		
Candlestick, 6", dolphin ftd.	170.00	125.00	155.00	260.00	300.00
Candy, w/cover, 6", dolphin ftd.	150.00	150.00	200.00	450.00	
Comport, 6", ftd.	110.00	70.00	100.00		
Comport, 6", square	70.00	75.00	85.00		
Comport, 7", oval	85.00	80.00	90.00		
Compotier, 6", dolphin ftd.	260.00	225.00	275.00		
Creamer, dolphin ftd.	50.00	45.00	45.00		250.00
Creamer, indiv.	45.00	45.00	50.00		210.00
Cup	30.00	30.00	35.00		115.00
Cup, after dinner	60.00	60.00	70.00		
Cup, bouillon, 2 hdld.	35.00	35.00	45.00		
Cup, 4 oz., custard or punch	30.00	35.00	45.00		
Cup, #1401½, has rim as demi-cup	28.00	32.00	40.00		
Grapefruit, w/square liner	30.00	30.00	35.00		
Ice tub, w/metal handles	100.00	150.00	165.00		
Jug, 3 pint, ftd.	200.00	210.00	250.00		

	Flamingo	Sahara	Moongleam	Cobalt	Alexandrite
Jug, flat			175.00		
Marmalade, w/cover, dolphin ftd.	200.00	200.00	225.00		
Mayonnaise, 5½", ftd. with ladle	85.00	90.00	110.00		400.00
Mustard, w/cover	85.00	80.00	95.00		
Oil bottle, 4 oz.	125.00	125.00	135.00		
Plate, bouillon liner	12.00	15.00	17.50		25.00
Plate, 4½"	10.00	15.00	20.00		
Plate, 6"	11.00	14.00	16.00		40.00
Plate, 6", sq.	10.00	13.00	15.00		40.00
Plate, 7"	12.00	15.00	17.00		50.00
Plate, 7", sq.	12.00	15.00	17.00	60.00	65.00
Plate, 8", sq.	18.00	22.00	35.00	80.00	75.00
Plate, 8"	16.00	20.00	24.00	70.00	75.00
Plate, 9"	25.00	35.00	40.00		
Plate, 10½"	100.00	100.00	140.00		335.00
Plate, 10½", sq.	100.00	100.00	140.00		335.00
Plate, 12"	45.00	55.00	65.00		
Plate, 12", muffin, sides upturned	55.00	80.00	90.00		
Plate, 12", sandwich, 2 hdld.	35.00	45.00	60.00		180.00
Plate, 13", hors d'oeuvre, 2 hdld.	50.00	60.00	70.00		
Plate, 13", sq., 2 hdld.	40.00	45.00	55.00		
Platter, 14"	40.00	45.00	80.00		
Salt & pepper, pr.	100.00	110.00	135.00		450.00
Saucer, sq.	10.00	10.00	15.00		25.00
Saucer, after dinner	10.00	10.00	15.00		
Saucer, rnd.	10.00	10.00	15.00		25.00
Stem, 2½ oz., oyster cocktail	20.00	25.00	30.00		
Stem, 4 oz., saucer champagne	35.00	40.00	60.00		
Stem, 4 oz., sherbet	22.00	28.00	35.00		
Stem, 9 oz., Empress stemware, unusual	55.00	65.00	75.00		
Sugar, indiv.	45.00	45.00	50.00		210.00
Sugar, dolphin ftd., 3 hdld.	50.00	45.00	45.00		250.00
Tray, condiment & liner for indiv. sugar/creamer	75.00	75.00	85.00		
Tray, 10", 3 pt., relish	50.00	55.00	65.00		
Tray, 10", 7 pt., hors d'oeuvre	160.00	150.00	200.00		
Tray, 10", celery	25.00	35.00	40.00		150.00
Tray, 12", ctr. hdld., sandwich	48.00	57.00	65.00		
Tray, 12", sq. ctr. hdld., sandwich	52.00	60.00	67.50		
Tray, 13", celery	30.00	40.00	45.00		
Tray, 16", 4 pt., buffet relish	75.00	75.00	86.00		160.00
Tumbler, 8 oz., dolphin ftd., unusual	150.00	170.00	160.00		
Tumbler, 8 oz., grnd. bottom	60.00	50.00	70.00		
Tumbler, 12 oz., tea, grnd. bottom	70.00	65.00	75.00		
Vase, 8", flared	140.00	150.00	190.00		
Vase, 9", dolphin ftd.	200.00	200.00	220.00		850.00

Colors: Blue, Azure blue, Orchid, amber, Rose, green, Topaz; some Ruby, Ebony, and Wisteria

Fairfax (the name of this mould blank #2375) was the line used by Fostoria for several of their most popular etchings, particularly June, Versailles, and Trojan. Illustrated on page 86 are Orchid and green colors. The Orchid is a darker lavender color that is occasionally confused with Wisteria. Wisteria changes color depending upon the light source (natural or florescent), but Orchid does not. See Hermitage on page 108 – 109 for an example of Wisteria. The stems and tumblers pictured in Orchid have the Spartan pattern needle etch on them. You can also find unetched Orchid stems. Orchid and Azure blue are the colors most popular in Fairfax. Amber is readily available, but traditionally has had fewer collectors seeking it.

Fortunately, Fairfax collectors have a choice of two stemware lines, which does not happen in some etched patterns. The Fostoria stems and shapes shown on page 87 are the #5298 stem and tumbler line (even though the pieces shown are etched June and Versailles). More collectors adopt this line especially in pink and blue. The other stem line, #5299, is commonly found in yellow with Trojan etch. Collectors call this stem "waterfall." All Wisteria stems are found on the #5299 line. Some collectors mix stem lines; but tumblers are more difficult to mix because they have distinctly different shapes. The #5299 tumblers (oyster cocktail on page 87) are more flared at the top than the #5298 (all other tumblers on page 87).

I have shown the array of Fostoria's stemware on page 87 so that all shapes can be seen. The claret and high sherbets are major concerns. Each is 6" high. The claret is shaped like the wine. I recently had to show that difference to someone who told me he had some blue June clarets which unfortunately, turned out to be crystal high sherbets, a few hundred dollars difference! The parfait is also taller than the juice, although shaped similarly.

	Rose, Blue, Orchid	Amber	Green, Topaz
Ashtray, 2½"	15.00	8.00	11.00
Ashtray, 4"	17.50	10.00	12.50
Ashtray, 5½"	20.00	13.00	17.50
Baker, 9", oval	45.00	16.00	30.00
Baker, 10½", oval	50.00	20.00	30.00
Bonbon	12.50	9.00	10.00
Bottle, salad dressing	210.00	75.00	110.00
Bouillon, ftd.	15.00	8.00	10.00
Bowl, 9", lemon, 2 hdld.	20.00	10.00	13.00
Bowl, sweetmeat	22.00	12.00	16.00
Bowl, 5", fruit	20.00	8.00	10.00
Bowl, 6", cereal	30.00	10.00	15.00
Bowl, 6⅞", 3 ftd.	25.00	15.00	20.00
Bowl, 7", soup	60.00	30.00	40.00
Bowl, 8", rnd., nappy	45.00	20.00	30.00
Bowl, lg., hdld., dessert	45.00	20.00	30.00
Bowl, 12"	50.00	25.00	35.00
Bowl, 12", centerpiece	50.00	25.00	35.00
Bowl, 13", oval, centerpiece	50.00	25.00	35.00
Bowl, 15", centerpiece	55.00	30.00	40.00
Butter dish, w/cover	165.00	80.00	125.00
Candlestick, flattened top	25.00	12.00	15.00
Candlestick, 3"	25.00	12.00	18.00
Candy w/cover, flat, 3 pt.	75.00	45.00	55.00
Candy w/cover, ftd.	85.00	50.00	65.00
Celery, 11½"	30.00	15.00	18.00
Cheese & cracker set (2 styles)	45.00	20.00	25.00
Cigarette box	32.00	20.00	25.00
Comport, 5"	35.00	15.00	25.00
Comport, 7"	40.00	15.00	25.00
Cream soup, ftd.	23.00	10.00	15.00
Creamer, flat		10.00	14.00
Creamer, ftd.	15.00	7.00	10.00
Creamer, tea	25.00	8.00	12.00
Cup, after dinner	30.00	12.00	18.00
Cup, flat		4.00	6.00
Cup, ftd.	14.00	6.00	7.00
Flower holder, oval, window box	125.00	75.00	60.00
Grapefruit	35.00	18.00	25.00
Grapefruit liner	30.00	12.00	20.00
Ice bucket	95.00	50.00	65.00
Ice bowl	25.00	15.00	20.00
Ice bowl liner	20.00	15.00	* 15.00
Mayonnaise	25.00	12.00	15.00
Mayonnaise ladle	35.00	20.00	25.00
Mayonnaise liner, 7"	10.00	5.00	6.00

	Rose, Blue, Orchid	Amber	Green, Topaz
Nut cup, blown	35.00	22.00	25.00
Oil, ftd.	175.00	85.00	110.00
Pickle, 8½"	25.00	8.00	12.00
Pitcher, #5000	300.00	130.00	175.00
Plate, canape	20.00	10.00	10.00
Plate, whipped cream	11.00	8.00	9.00
Plate, 6", bread/butter	8.00	3.00	4.00
Plate, 7½", salad	10.00	4.00	5.00
Plate, 7½", cream soup or mayonnaise liner	10.00	5.00	6.00
Plate, 8¾", salad	14.00	7.00	8.00
Plate, 9½", luncheon	17.00	7.00	10.00
Plate, 10¼", dinner	45.00	20.00	32.00
Plate, 10¼", grill	40.00	18.00	22.00
Plate, 10", cake	22.00	13.00	15.00
Plate, 12", bread, oval	45.00	25.00	27.50
Plate, 13", chop	30.00	15.00	20.00
Platter, 10½", oval	38.00	20.00	30.00
Platter, 12", oval	65.00	30.00	45.00
Platter, 15", oval	95.00	35.00	60.00
Relish, 3 part, 8½"	30.00	10.00	15.00
Relish, 11½"	22.00	11.00	13.00
Sauce boat	50.00	20.00	30.00
Sauce boat liner	20.00	10.00	15.00
Saucer, after dinner	8.00	4.00	5.00
Saucer	4.00	2.50	3.00
Shaker, ftd., pr	70.00	30.00	45.00
Shaker, indiv., ftd., pr.		20.00	25.00
Stem, 4", ¾ oz., cordial	70.00	30.00	50.00
Stem, 4¼", 6 oz., low sherbet	18.00	9.00	11.00
Stem, 5¼", 3 oz., cocktail	24.00	12.00	18.00
Stem, 5½", 3 oz., wine	35.00	18.00	25.00
Stem, 6", 4 oz., claret	45.00	25.00	35.00
Stem, 6", 6 oz., high sherbet	22.00	10.00	15.00
Stem, 8¼", 10 oz., water	32.00	16.00	22.00
Sugar, flat		10.00	12.00
Sugar, ftd.	15.00	6.00	8.00
Sugar cover	35.00	20.00	25.00
Sugar pail	80.00	35.00	55.00
Sugar, tea	25.00	8.00	12.00
Tray, 11", ctr. hdld.	40.00	20.00	30.00
Tumbler, 2½ oz., ftd.	32.00	12.00	18.00
Tumbler, 4½", 5 oz., ftd.	18.00	10.00	11.00
Tumbler, 5¼", 9 oz., ftd.	22.00	12.00	13.00
Tumbler, 6", 12 oz., ftd.	28.00	13.50	18.00
Vase, 8" (2 styles)	95.00	40.00	60.00
Whipped cream pail	75.00	35.00	50.00

FOSTORIA STEMS AND SHAPES

Top Row: Left to Right
1. Water, 10 oz., 8¼"
2. Claret, 4 oz., 6"
3. Wine, 3 oz., 5½"
4. Cordial, ¾ oz., 4"
5. Sherbet, low, 6 oz., 4¼"
6. Cocktail, 3 oz., 5¼"
7. Sherbet, high, 6 oz., 6"

Bottom Row: Left to Right
1. Grapefruit and liner
2. Ice tea tumbler, 12 oz., 6"
3. Water tumbler, 9 oz., 5¼"
4. Parfait, 6 oz., 5¼"
5. Juice tumbler, 5 oz., 4½"
6. Oyster cocktail, 5½ oz.
7. Bar tumbler, 2½ oz.

Color: crystal

First Love is likely the most recognized Duncan & Miller etching. Various mould lines were adapted for this large pattern. Among those are #30 (Pall Mall), #111 (Terrace), #115 (Canterbury), #117 (Three Feathers), #126 (Venetian), and #5111½ (Terrace blown stemware). Canterbury can be found on pages 38 to 40 and Terrace can be seen on pages 209 and 210. You will have to check earlier editions of this book for catalog pages showing details of those other lines. Most pieces of First Love will be found on lines #111 or #115.

I received numerous letters from collectors who thought the darker background highlighted the pattern much better. If you see the pattern better, then I am all for it.

	Crystal		Crystal
Ashtray, 3½", sq., #111	17.50	Candy jar, 5" x 7¼", w/lid, ftd., #25	85.00
Ashtray, 3½" x 2½", #30	16.50	Candy, 6½", w/5" lid, #115	75.00
Ashtray, 5" x 3", #12, club	37.50	Carafe, w/stopper, water, #5200	195.00
Ashtray, 5" x 3¼", #30	24.00	Cheese stand, 3" x 5¼", #111	25.00
Ashtray, 6½" x 4¼", #30	35.00	Cheese stand, 5¾" x 3½", #115	25.00
Basket, 9¼" x 10" x 7¼", #115	175.00	Cigarette box w/lid, 4" x 4¼"	32.00
Basket, 10" x 4¼" x 7", oval hdld., #115	195.00	Cigarette box w/lid, 4½" x 3½", #30	35.00
Bottle, oil w/stopper, 8", #5200	60.00	Cigarette box w/lid, 4¾" x 3¾"	35.00
Bowl, 3" x 5", rose, #115	40.00	Cocktail shaker, 14 oz., #5200	135.00
Bowl, 4" x 1½", finger, #30	32.00	Cocktail shaker, 16 oz., #5200	135.00
Bowl, 4¼", finger, #5111½	35.00	Cocktail shaker, 32 oz., #5200	175.00
Bowl, 6" x 2½", oval, olive, #115	25.00	Comport w/lid, 8¾" x 5½", #111	135.00
Bowl, 6¾" x 4¼", ftd., flared rim, #111	30.00	Comport, 3½"x 4¾"w, #111	30.00
Bowl, 7½" x 3", 3 pt., ftd., #117	35.00	Comport, 5" x 5½", flared rim, #115	32.00
Bowl, 8" sq. x 2½", hdld., #111	60.00	Comport, 5¼" x 6¾", flat top, #115	32.00
Bowl, 8½" x 4", #115	37.50	Comport, 6" x 4¾", low #115	37.50
Bowl, 9" x 4½", ftd., #111	42.00	Creamer, 2½", individual, #115	18.00
Bowl, 9½" x 2½", hdld., #111	45.00	Creamer, 3", 10 oz., #111	18.00
Bowl, 10" x 3¾", ftd., flared rim, #111	55.00	Creamer, 3¾", 7 oz., #115	15.00
Bowl, 10" x 4½", #115	45.00	Creamer, sugar w/butter pat lid, breakfast set, #28	75.00
Bowl, 10½" x 5", crimped, #115	44.00	Cruet, #25	90.00
Bowl, 10½" x 7" x 7", #126	62.00	Cruet, #30	90.00
Bowl, 10¾" x 4¾", #115	42.50	Cup, #115	18.00
Bowl, 11" x 1 ¾", #30	55.00	Decanter w/stopper, 16 oz., #5200	150.00
Bowl, 11" x 3¼", flared rim, #111	62.50	Decanter w/stopper, 32 oz., #30	175.00
Bowl, 11" x 5¼", flared rim, #6	70.00	Decanter w/stopper, 32 oz., #5200	175.00
Bowl, 11½" x 8¼", oval, #115	45.00	Hat, 4½", #30	395.00
Bowl, 12" x 3½", #6	70.00	Hat, 5½" x 8½" x 6¼", #30	350.00
Bowl, 12" x 3¼", flared, #115	60.00	Honey dish, 5" x 3", #91	30.00
Bowl, 12" x 4" x 7½", oval, #117	65.00	Ice bucket, 6", #30	110.00
Bowl, 12½", flat, ftd., #126	75.00	Lamp, hurricane, w/prisms, 15", #115	175.00
Bowl, 13" x 3¼" x 8¾", oval, flared, #115	55.00	Lamp shade only, #115	125.00
Bowl, 13" x 7" x 9¼", #126	67.50	Lid for candy urn, #111	35.00
Bowl, 13" x 7", #117	62.50	Mayonnaise, 4¾" x 4½", div. w/7½" underplate	35.00
Bowl, 14" x 7½" x 6", oval, #126	65.00	Mayonnaise, 5¼" x 3", div. w/6½" plate, #115	35.00
Box, candy w/lid, 4¾" x 6¼"	60.00	Mayonnaise, 5½" x 2½", ftd., hdld., #111	35.00
Butter or cheese, 7" sq. x 1¼", #111	130.00	Mayonnaise, 5½" x 2¾", #115	35.00
Candelabra, 2-lite, #41	35.00	Mayonnaise, 5½" x 3½", crimped, #111	32.00
Candelabrum, 6", 2-lite w/prisms, #30	60.00	Mayonnaise, 5¾" x 3", w/dish hdld. tray, #111	35.00
Candle, 3", 1-lite, #111	25.00	Mayonnaise, w/7" tray hdld., #111	35.00
Candle, 3", low, #115	25.00	Mustard w/lid & underplate	57.50
Candle, 3½", #115	25.00	Nappy, 5" x 1", w/bottom star, #25	20.00
Candle, 4", cornucopia, #117	25.00	Nappy, 5" x 1¾", one hdld., #115	18.00
Candle, 4", low, #111	25.00	Nappy, 5½" x 2", div., hdld., #111	18.00
Candle, 5¼", 2-lite, globe, #30	35.00	Nappy, 5½" x 2", one hdld., heart, #115	28.00
Candle, 6", 2-lite, #30	35.00	Nappy, 6" x 1¾", hdld., #111	22.00
Candy box, 6" x 3½", 3 hdld., 3 pt., w/lid, #115	85.00		
Candy box, 6" x 3½", 3 pt., w/lid, crown finial, #106	90.00		

	Crystal
Perfume tray, 8" x 5", #5200	25.00
Perfume, 5", #5200	85.00
Pitcher, #5200	195.00
Pitcher, 9", 80 oz., ice lip, #5202	225.00
Plate, 6", #111	12.00
Plate, 6", #115	12.00
Plate, 6", hdld., lemon, #111	14.00
Plate, 6", sq., #111	14.00
Plate, 7", #111	17.50
Plate, 7½", #111	18.00
Plate, 7½", #115	18.00
Plate, 7½", mayonnaise liner, hdld. #115	15.00
Plate, 7½", sq., #111	19.00
Plate, 7½", 2 hdld., #115	19.00
Plate, 8½", #30	20.00
Plate, 8½", #111	20.00
Plate, 8½", #115	20.00
Plate, 11", #111	47.50
Plate, 11", 2 hdld., sandwich, #115	30.00
Plate, 11", hdld., #111	40.00
Plate, 11", hdld., cracker w/ring, #115	40.00
Plate, 11", hdld., cracker w/ring, #111	40.00
Plate, 11", hdld., sandwich, #111	40.00
Plate, 11¼", dinner, #115	55.00
Plate, 12", egg, #30	150.00
Plate, 12", torte, rolled edge, #111	40.00
Plate, 13", torte, flat edge, #111	50.00
Plate, 13", torte, rolled edge, #111	60.00
Plate, 13¼", torte, #111	60.00
Plate, 13½", cake, hdld., #115	50.00
Plate, 14", #115	50.00
Plate, 14", cake, #115	50.00
Plate, 14½", cake, lg. base, #30	55.00
Plate, 14½", cake, sm. base, #30	55.00
Relish, 6" x 1¾", hdld., 2 pt., #111	20.00
Relish, 6" x 1¾", hdld., 2 pt., #115	20.00
Relish, 8" x 4½", pickle, 2 pt., #115	25.00
Relish, 8", 3 pt., hdld., #115	25.00
Relish, 9" x 1½", 2 pt. pickle, #115	25.00
Relish, 9" x 1½", 3 hdld, 3 pt., #115	32.50
Relish, 9" x 1½", 3 hdld., flared, #115	32.50
Relish, 10", 5 pt. tray, #30	65.00
Relish, 10½" x 1½", hdld., 5 pt., #111	85.00
Relish, 10½" x 1¼", 2 hdld, 3 pt., #115	60.00
Relish, 10½" x 7", #115	37.50
Relish, 11¾", tray, #115	45.00
Relish, 12", 4 pt., hdld., #111	40.00
Relish, 12", 5 pt., hdld., #111	55.00
Salt and pepper pr., #30	30.00
Salt and pepper pr., #115	40.00
Sandwich tray, 12" x 5¼", ctr. handle, #115	80.00
Saucer, #115	8.50
Stem, 3¾", 1 oz., cordial, #5111½	65.00
Stem, 3¾", 4½ oz., oyster cocktail, #5111½	22.50
Stem, 4", 5 oz., ice cream, #5111½	14.00
Stem, 4¼", 3 oz., cocktail, #115	22.50

	Crystal
Stem, 4½", 3½ oz., cocktail, #5111½	22.50
Stem, 5", 5 oz., saucer champagne, #5111½	18.00
Stem, 5¼", 3 oz., wine, #5111½	32.50
Stem, 5¼", 5 oz., ftd. juice, #5111½	24.00
Stem, 5¾", 10 oz., low luncheon goblet, #5111½	17.50
Stem, 6", 4½ oz., claret, #5111½	50.00
Stem, 6½", 12 oz., ftd. ice tea, #5111½	35.00
Stem, 6¾", 14 oz., ftd. ice tea, #5111½	35.00
Stem, cordial, #111	20.00
Sugar, 2½", individual, #115	15.00
Sugar, 3", 7 oz., #115	14.00
Sugar, 3", 10 oz., #111	15.00
Tray, 8" x 2", hdld. celery, #111	17.50
Tray, 8" x 4¾", individual sug/cr., #115	17.50
Tray, 8¾", celery, #91	30.00
Tray, 11", celery, #91	40.00
Tumbler, 2", 1½ oz., whiskey, #5200	65.00
Tumbler, 2½" x 3⅜", sham, Teardrop, ftd.	60.00
Tumbler, 3", sham, #5200	32.50
Tumbler, 4¾", 10 oz., sham, #5200	37.50
Tumbler, 5½", 12 oz., sham, #5200	37.50
Tumbler, 6", 14 oz., sham, #5200	37.50
Tumbler, 8 oz., flat, #115	30.00
Urn, 4½" x 4½", #111	27.50
Urn, 4½" x 4½", #115	27.50
Urn, 4¾", rnd ft.	27.50
Urn, 5", #525	37.50
Urn, 5½", ring hdld., sq. ft.	65.00
Urn, 5½", sq. ft.	37.50
Urn, 6½", sq. hdld.	70.00
Urn, 7", #529	37.50
Vase, 4", flared rim, #115	25.00
Vase, 4½" x 4¾", #115	30.00
Vase, 5" x 5", crimped, #115	35.00
Vase, 6", #507	55.00
Vase, 8" x 4¾", cornucopia, #117	65.00
Vase, 8", ftd., #506	90.00
Vase, 8", ftd., #507	90.00
Vase, 8½" x 2¾", #505	110.00
Vase, 8½" x 6", #115	90.00
Vase, 9" x 4½", #505	95.00
Vase, 9", #509	90.00
Vase, 9", bud, #506	80.00
Vase, 9½" x 3½", #506	125.00
Vase, 10" x 4¾", #5200	90.00
Vase, 10", #507	95.00
Vase, 10", ftd., #111	115.00
Vase, 10", ftd., #505	115.00
Vase, 10", ftd., #506	115.00
Vase, 10½" x 12 x 9½", #126	155.00
Vase, 10½", #126	175.00
Vase, 11" x 5¼", #505	145.00
Vase, 11½ x 4½", #506	140.00
Vase, 12", flared #115	145.00
Vase, 12", ftd., #506	145.00
Vase, 12", ftd., #507	155.00

Colors: crystal, pink, yellow, and rare in green

Tiffin's Flanders is regularly mistaken for Cambridge's Gloria by collectors, particularly yellow or crystal. Refer to Gloria to see that curved stem floral design. I still remember my Mom calling me in Florida a few years before her death all excited about a pink Gloria pitcher she had just bought. That "Gloria" pitcher is the one shown here. As with most Tiffin pitchers of this time, you can find Flanders with and without a cover. Keep in mind that the pitcher top is plain with no pattern etched on it. When Cathy returned from Florida last fall, she stumbled upon a large set of pink Flanders in a shop. She just stopped on a whim. Internet activity was rather heavy when we ran pieces of this set on it. An entire new wave of collectors has discovered these patterns via the net. This is bound to impact prices on these already scarce wares. I do not expect those supplies advertised now to be long lived. More glassware has been delivered into collector's hands through the Internet than by any other way in the last few years. If you want a pattern, do not procrastinate about getting it.

Flanders stems are customarily found on Tiffin's #17024 blank. Frequently these have a crystal foot and stem with tops of crystal, pink, or yellow. Color blending that is seen infrequently includes green foot with pink stems, and pink tumblers as well as pitchers with crystal handle and foot. One green Flanders vase was found a couple of years ago and is pictured in *Very Rare Glassware of the Depression Years, Fifth Series.* Round plates are Tiffin's line #8800 and each size plate has a different number. Scalloped plates are line #5831. I see more of the round plates than I do the scalloped ones.

Shakers are being found in crystal occasionally, but only a few pink shakers have been seen. I have had a few reports of yellow, but I have never seen one. Lamps are found only in crystal. That cylindrical shade is sometimes found over a candlestick and designated a Chinese hurricane lamp. I have pictured an electric one here.

FLANDERS

	Crystal	Pink	Yellow
Ashtray, 2¼x3¾", w/cigarette rest	55.00		
Bowl, 2 hdld., bouillon	50.00	135.00	85.00
Bowl, finger, w/liner	35.00	95.00	60.00
Bowl, 2 hdld., bonbon	30.00	100.00	65.00
Bowl, 8", ftd., blown	75.00	295.00	
Bowl, 11", ftd., console	75.00	175.00	95.00
Bowl, 12", flanged rim, console	75.00	175.00	95.00
Candlestick, 2 styles	40.00	75.00	50.00
Candy jar, w/cover, flat	135.00	350.00	250.00
Candy jar, w/cover, ftd.	100.00	250.00	185.00
Celery, 11"	40.00	95.00	60.00
Cheese & cracker	55.00	130.00	100.00
Comport, 3½"	40.00	95.00	60.00
Comport, 6"	65.00	175.00	95.00
Creamer, flat	45.00	135.00	90.00
Creamer, ftd.	40.00	120.00	70.00
Cup, 2 styles	50.00	100.00	65.00
Decanter	195.00	350.00	275.00
Electric lamp	325.00		
Grapefruit, w/liner	75.00	195.00	125.00
Hurricane lamp, Chinese style	275.00		
Mayonnaise, w/liner	50.00	125.00	80.00
Nut cup, ftd., blown	40.00	80.00	60.00
Oil bottle & stopper	150.00	350.00	250.00
Parfait, 5⅝", hdld.	75.00	195.00	125.00
Pitcher & cover	250.00	395.00	295.00
Plate, 6"	7.00	18.00	12.00

	Crystal	Pink	Yellow
Plate, 8"	12.00	26.00	15.50
Plate, 10¼", dinner	65.00	125.00	75.00
Relish, 3 pt.	60.00	125.00	80.00
Salt & pepper, pr.	175.00	395.00	275.00
Sandwich server, center hdld.		165.00	
Saucer	8.00	15.00	10.00
Stem, 4½", oyster cocktail	20.00	55.00	25.00
Stem, 4½", sherbet	15.00	40.00	17.50
Stem, 4¾", cocktail	22.00	50.00	30.00
Stem, 5", cordial	60.00	125.00	85.00
Stem, 5⅝", parfait	40.00	110.00	80.00
Stem, 6⅛", wine	35.00	85.00	45.00
Stem, 6¼", saucer champagne	18.00	40.00	20.00
Stem, claret	40.00	150.00	95.00
Stem, 8¼", water	35.00	60.00	35.00
Sugar, flat	45.00	135.00	90.00
Sugar, ftd.	40.00	120.00	70.00
Tumbler, 2¾", 2½ oz., ftd.	45.00	100.00	60.00
Tumbler, 4¾", 9 oz., ftd., water	22.00	65.00	25.00
Tumbler, 4¾", 10 oz., ftd.	22.00	65.00	30.00
Tumbler, 5⅞", 12 oz., ftd., tea	35.00	100.00	40.00
Vase, bud	50.00	125.00	70.00
Vase, ftd.	100.00	250.00	175.00
Vase, Dahlia style	150.00	275.00	200.00
Vase, fan	100.00	250.00	150.00

Colors: crystal w/green, Twilight, Twilight w/crystal, pink, crystal w/amber

Fontaine is a Tiffin pattern that would attract more collectors were they ever given the chance to see much of it. The purple color in the photograph is Tiffin's earlier Twilight color that does not change colors when exposed to different light sources. Tiffin's later Twilight changes from pink to purple depending upon fluorescent or natural light. The only additional piece I have added since the last book is a pink goblet. Some Twilight has appeared at shows, but not at a price that enticed me to own it.

Several different companies — even on earlier carnival glass used this fountain theme. Tiffin added their version to come up with Fontaine. As with all Tiffin patterns, cup and saucers are rarely found. I bought the set pictured years ago, before I even considered this pattern for the book. I knew cups and saucers were hard to find in Tiffin patterns. I have never found cup and saucers in any other Fontaine colors — which doesn't mean they don't exist. I just haven't found them!

The cordial pictured is from my collection. I once saw one in pink, but left it for some forgotten reason — probably price. Water goblets seem to be more plentiful than sherbets as I now have three different colors. I fancy the crystal tops with colored stems over the monotone colored pieces; but they're all pretty.

The only covered pitchers I have seen were at the Houston Depression glass show years ago. Both were Twilight and both sold. One sold reasonably; the other went for a bunch of money — even back then. If you are lucky enough to spot some Fontaine, buy it no matter the color. Some collector will thank you. I'm speaking from experience here.

	Amber Green Pink	Twilight
Bowl, 13" ctrpc., #8153	75.00	175.00
Candlestick, low, #9758	35.00	80.00
Creamer, ftd., #4	35.00	65.00
Cup, #8869	60.00	125.00
Finger bowl, #022	45.00	85.00
Grape fruit, #251 & footed		
liner, #881	65.00	125.00
Jug & cover, #194	395.00	1195.00
Plate, 6", #8814	12.50	20.00
Plate, 8", #8833	20.00	35.00
Plate, 10", #8818	75.00	145.00
Plate, 10", cake w/ctr. hdld., #345	65.00	125.00
Saucer, #8869	12.50	25.00
Stem, cafe parfait, #033	65.00	135.00
Stem, claret, #033	60.00	115.00
Stem, cocktail, #033	35.00	65.00
Stem, cordial	100.00	165.00
Stem, saucer champagne, #033	30.00	65.00

	Amber Green Pink	Twilight
Stem, sundae, #033	25.00	55.00
Stem, water, #033	55.00	95.00
Stem, wine, 2½ oz., #033	65.00	125.00
Sugar, ftd., #4	35.00	65.00
Tumbler, 9 oz. table, #032	35.00	65.00
Vase, 8" ftd., #2	95.00	195.00
Vase, 9¼", bowed top, #7	125.00	225.00

Colors: crystal and crystal w/Wisteria base

Fostoria's Fuchsia was included as a new pattern last book. I had a scolding letter from a reader who said she was upset that I put Fostoria Fuchsia in since the prices have now gone up! Be sure to look at Tiffin's Fuchsia pattern on the next page so that you do not confuse these. This Fuchsia is mostly etched on Fostoria's Lafayette mould blank #2244, which can be found on page 126. Stemware line #6044 was also used for Fuchsia.

I know one collector who collects both Fostoria's and Tiffin's Fuchsia as well as Cambridge's Marjorie, which is a Fuchsia design and several pottery designs featuring Fuchsia. Guess she can never have too many Fuchsias in her house. Notice that champagne with the Wisteria stem. Most of those were sold to go with Lafayette Wisteria tableware that was unetched. I have run into several sets that had this Wisteria stem, but they all had plain Wisteria cups, saucers, plates, and creamers and sugars.

The plain center surface areas are easily scratched from use or from stacking due to the flat, ground bottoms. I have seen some recently that were cloudy looking from all the marks. These will not sell for much, if at all.

Collectors do put a premium on mint condition, and few value shopworn glassware. I have been told a few people around the country are trying their hand at buffing out the scratches from these plates; but I understand it's expensive and not always successful since most of the glassware made at this time is very soft compared to highly polished glass.

	Crystal	Wisteria		Crystal	Wisteria
Bonbon, #2470	33.00		Saucer, #2440	7.50	
Bowl, 10", #2395	95.00		Stem, ¾ oz., cordial, #6004	65.00	175.00
Bowl, 10½", #2470½	75.00		Stem, 2½ oz., wine, #6004	35.00	65.00
Bowl 11½", "B," #2440	75.00		Stem, 3 oz., cocktail, #6004	25.00	65.00
Bowl, 12" #2470	90.00	175.00	Stem, 4 oz., claret, #6004	45.00	85.00
Candlestick, 3", #2375	35.00		Stem, 5 oz., low sherbet, #6004	22.50	40.00
Candlestick, 5", #2395½	55.00		Stem, 5½ oz., 6" parfait, #6004	37.50	75.00
Candlestick, 5½", #2470½	75.00		Stem, 5½ oz., 5⅜", saucer		
Candlestick, 5½", #2470	75.00	195.00	champagne, #6004	27.50	55.00
Comport, 6" low, #2470	40.00	95.00	Stem, 9 oz., water, #6004	35.00	75.00
Comport, 6" tall, #2470	75.00	150.00	Sugar, ftd., #2440	35.00	
Creamer, ftd., #2440	35.00		Sweetmeat, #2470	38.00	
Cup, #2440	20.00		Tumbler, 2 oz., #833	25.00	
Finger bowl, #869	35.00		Tumbler, 2½ oz., ftd. whiskey,		
Lemon dish, #2470	32.00		#6004	35.00	60.00
Oyster cocktail, 4½ oz., #6004	17.50	35.00	Tumbler, 5 oz., #833	22.50	
Plate, 10", cake	65.00		Tumbler, 5 oz., ftd. juice, #6004	20.00	45.00
Plate, 6", bread & butter, #2440	10.00		Tumbler, 8 oz., #833	22.00	
Plate, 7", salad, #2440	15.00		Tumbler, 9 oz., ftd., #6004	18.00	45.00
Plate, 8", luncheon, #2440	22.00		Tumbler, 12 oz., #833	30.00	
Plate, 9", dinner, #2440	67.50		Tumbler, 12 oz., ftd., #6004	32.00	60.00

Colors: crystal

Be sure to check out Fostoria's Fuchsia pattern on page 94. The patterns are similar, but the shapes are not. You need to realize pattern names were not exclusive to one particular company.

New pieces continue to be unearthed. Like Cambridge's Rose Point that appears etched on almost every line that Cambridge made, Tiffin's Fuchsia seems to have followed this same path. Fuchsia has always attracted collectors; and because of this, dealers are searching every nook and cranny, explaining why so many new pieces are being found.

There are many rarely seen pieces including the bitters bottle, icers with inserts, cocktail shaker, hurricane and electric lamps as well as the #17457 stems of all varieties. The cordial in that line is especially hard to get. As with most Tiffin patterns, cups, saucers, and dinner plates are not found often enough to supply all collectors' needs. There are footed as well as flat finger bowls; so you can pick the style you like or the one you find. There are three styles of double candlesticks. The #5831, pointed knob type, is the most difficult to find.

You will be able to find a multitude of different serving bowls in Fuchsia unlike most other Tiffin patterns where serving pieces come at a premium. The large handled urn vase must have found favor with customers for years as I see that one vase more than any other Tiffin vase made. I also see some ridiculously high prices on it; my experience has been they have a hard time fetching more than $100.00 on a good day.

	Crystal
Ashtray, 2¼" x 3¾", w/cigarette rest	35.00
Bell, 5", #15083	75.00
Bitters bottle	450.00
Bowl, 4", finger, ftd., #041	60.00
Bowl, 4½" finger, w/#8814 liner	75.00
Bowl, 5³⁄₁₆", 2 hdld., #5831	35.00
Bowl, 6¼", cream soup, ftd., #5831	50.00
Bowl, 7¼", salad, #5902	40.00

	Crystal
Bowl, 8⅜", 2 hdld., #5831	55.00
Bowl, 9¾", deep salad	75.00
Bowl, 10", salad	65.00
Bowl, 10½", console, fan shaped sides, #319	70.00
Bowl, 11⅞", console, flared, #5902	80.00
Bowl, 12", flanged rim, console, #5831	60.00
Bowl, 12⅝", console, flared, #5902	90.00
Bowl, 13", crimped, #5902	80.00

	Crystal
Candlestick, 2-lite, w/pointed center, #5831	80.00
Candlestick, 2-lite, tapered center, #15306	80.00
Candlestick, 5", 2-lite, ball center	80.00
Candlestick, 5⅝", 2-lite, w/fan center, #5902	80.00
Candlestick, single, #348	40.00
Celery, 10", oval, #5831	35.00
Celery, 10½", rectangular, #5902	37.50
Cigarette box, w/lid, 4" x 2¾", #9305	120.00
Cocktail shaker, 8", w/metal top	250.00
Comport, 6¼", #5831	30.00
Comport, 6½", w/beaded stem, #15082	35.00
Creamer, 2⅞", individual, #5831	45.00
Creamer, 3⅜", flat w/beaded handle, #5902	27.50
Creamer, 4½", ftd., #5831	22.50
Creamer, pearl edge	45.00
Cup, #5831	80.00
Electric lamp	350.00
Hurricane, 12", Chinese style	250.00
Icer, with insert	165.00
Mayonnaise, flat, w/6¼" liner, #5902 w/ladle	50.00
Mayonnaise, ftd., w/ladle, #5831	50.00
Nut dish, 6¼"	40.00
Pickle, 7⅜", #5831	40.00
Pitcher & cover, #194	395.00
Pitcher, flat	395.00
Plate, 6¼", bread and butter, #5902	8.00
Plate, 6¼", sherbet, #8814	10.00
Plate, 6⅜", 2 hdld., #5831	12.50
Plate, 7", marmalade, 3-ftd., #310½	27.50
Plate, 7½", salad, #5831	15.00
Plate, 7⅞", cream soup or mayo liner, #5831	12.50
Plate, 7⅞", salad, #8814	15.00
Plate, 8⅛", luncheon, #8833	22.50
Plate, 8¼", luncheon, #5902	17.50
Plate, 8⅜", bonbon, pearl edge	27.50
Plate, 9½", dinner, #5902	75.00
Plate, 10½", 2 hdld., cake, #5831	75.00
Plate, 10½", muffin tray, pearl edge	55.00
Plate, 13", lily rolled and crimped edge	65.00
Plate, 14¼", sandwich, #8833	55.00
Relish, 6⅜", 3 pt., #5902	25.00
Relish, 9¼", sq., 3 pt.	40.00
Relish, 10½" x 12½", hdld., 3 pt., #5902	60.00

	Crystal
Relish, 10½" x 12½", hdld., 5 pt.	70.00
Salt and pepper, pr., #2	125.00
Saucer, #5831	15.00
Stem, 4 1/16", cordial, #15083	32.50
Stem, 4⅛", sherbet, #15083	12.00
Stem, 4¼", cocktail, #15083	18.00
Stem, 4⅝", 3½ oz., cocktail, #17453	37.50
Stem, 4⅞", saucer champagne, hollow stem	110.00
Stem, 5 1/16", wine, #15083	30.00
Stem, 5¼", claret, #15083	37.50
Stem, 5⅜", cocktail, "S" stem, #17457	50.00
Stem, 5⅜", cordial, "S" stem, #17457	125.00
Stem, 5⅜", 7 oz., saucer champagne, #17453	30.00
Stem, 5⅜", saucer champagne, #15083	15.00
Stem, 5⅜", saucer champagne, "S" stem, #17457	45.00
Stem, 5 15/16", parfait, #15083	40.00
Stem, 6¼", low water, #15083	25.00
Stem, 7⅜", 9 oz., water, #17453	40.00
Stem, 7½", water, high, #15083	25.00
Stem, 7⅝", water, "S" stem, #17457	65.00
Sugar, 2⅞", individual, #5831	40.00
Sugar, 3⅜", flat, w/beaded handle, #5902	27.50
Sugar, 4½", ftd., #5831	22.50
Sugar, pearl edge	45.00
Tray, sugar/creamer	55.00
Tray, 9½", 2 hdld. for cream/sugar	45.00
Tumbler, 2 7/16", 2 oz., bar, flat, #506	65.00
Tumbler, 3 5/16", oyster cocktail, #14196	14.00
Tumbler, 3⅜", old-fashioned, flat, #580	55.00
Tumbler, 4 13/16" flat, juice	35.00
Tumbler, 4 5/16", 5 oz., ftd., juice, #15083	25.00
Tumbler, 5⅛", water, flat, #517	35.00
Tumbler, 5 5/16", 9 oz., ftd., water, #15083	25.00
Tumbler, 6 5/16", 12 oz., ftd., tea, #15083	35.00
Vase, 6½", bud, #14185	32.00
Vase, 8 13/16", flared, crimped	95.00
Vase, 8¼", bud, #14185	40.00
Vase, 10½", bud, #14185	50.00
Vase, 10¾", bulbous bottom, #5872	195.00
Vase, 10⅞", beaded stem, #15082	75.00
Vase, 11¾", urn, 2 hdld., trophy.	125.00
Whipped cream, 3-ftd., #310	40.00

Colors: black, blue, crystal, green, red, and yellow

Gazebo and another Paden City pattern, Utopia, are two very similar designs, which we are combing for the time being. The images on Utopia are larger and fuller than those on Gazebo. Utopia may have been converted from Gazebo for use on larger items or Gazebo downsized from Utopia. Yes, we are theorizing, as no one knows why the glass companies did some of the things they did. Thirty years ago when I first started researching, I believed all of the retired workers' reminiscences and anecdotal testaments; time has proved many of those stories false or exaggerated — as well as some quite true!

The limited availability of Paden City's patterns creates major problems for collectors today. There is just enough to whet your appetite. Until I listed this pattern a couple of books back, you could find most pieces in the $45.00 range due to size more than anything else. Most people selling Gazebo had no idea about the pattern. It looked old and elegant and was never priced inexpensively.

Several different Paden City mould lines were used for this etching. All measurements in our listing are taken from actual pieces, as catalog pages are not abundant for Gazebo. We have not yet found a punch bowl to go with our punch cups. However, it was the fashion of the day to include "custard" cups with a set. There may be no punch bowl per se. We have found a flat, heart-shaped candy dish. There are crystal ones and blue bottoms with crystal tops being found. If you find one with a blue top, please let me know. We spotted another blue cheese dish, but I have not observed one in crystal yet. That cheese has also been spotted in Ruby, but without an etching. All pieces may not be found in color. Blue seems only to be found on the beaded edge pieces. The yellow and black vases are the only pieces I have spotted in those colors. If you have other pieces, please let me know.

	Crystal	Blue		Crystal	Blue
Bowl, 9", fan handles	45.00		Mayonnaise liner	15.00	225.00
Bowl, 9", bead handles	45.00	80.00	Mayonnaise, bead handles	25.00	
Bowl, 13", flat edge	55.00		Plate, 10¾"	45.00	
Bowl, 14", low flat	55.00		Plate, 12½", bead handles	55.00	90.00
Cake stand	65.00		Plate, 13", fan handles	50.00	
Candlestick, 5¼"	45.00		Plate, 16", beaded edge		100.00
Candlestick, double, 2 styles	60.00		Relish, 9¾", three part	35.00	65.00
Candy dish w/lid, "heart"	110.00	250.00	Server, 10", swan handle	50.00	
Candy w/lid, 10¼", small	75.00	125.00	Server, 11", center handle	40.00	85.00
Candy w/lid, 11", large	90.00		Sugar	22.50	
Cheese dish and cover	100.00	250.00	Tumbler, ftd. juice	22.00	
Cocktail shaker, w/glass stopper	135.00		Vase, 10¼"	75.00	195.00*
Creamer	22.50				

*Black or yellow

Colors: crystal, yellow, Peach-Blo, green, Emerald green (light and dark), amber, blue, Heatherbloom, Ebony with white gold

Cambridge's Gloria is regularly confused with Tiffin's Flanders. Look closely at these two similar patterns and notice that the flower on Gloria bends the stem. Both are renditions of poppies but they are easily identified once you place them side by side. You may note the seven colors of ice buckets pictured. The blue and Ebony with white gold ones are rarely seen. Gloria can be gathered in large sets of yellow or crystal if you so desire; but any other color will vex you. Yellow Gloria is more obtainable than is crystal; so if you like that color, buy it when you can. A luncheon set in blue and Peach-Blo (pink) is found occasionally, but larger sets may not be possible to assemble. For some inexplicable reason, I have always been drawn to the dark Emerald green, but I have only owned a dozen or so pieces in that color as it is rarely found; no ice bucket has been seen in that color to my knowledge.

Gold encrusted items bring 20% to 25% more than those without gold. However, pieces with worn gold are difficult to sell at present. That may change with all the decorators touting the "distressed" look. Distressed glass may soon be fashionable as well.

Amber footed, yellow stem Gloria turns up once in a while, but there is little of this color combination available. Gloria might make an ideal candidate for blending of colors, since there are so many from which to choose.

I am amazed at the amount of Elegant glass that is being found in the West. When I travel out there, I see some glassware that I never see in the East. Distribution of patterns was unmistakably geographical, and the best way to discover this is to visit different areas of the country.

As with other Cambridge patterns in this book, not all Gloria pieces are listed. A more complete listing of Cambridge etched pieces is found under Rose Point. Prices for crystal Gloria will run 30% to 40% less than the prices listed there.

	Crystal	Green Pink Yellow		Crystal	Green Pink Yellow
Basket, 6", 2 hdld. (sides up)	40.00	65.00	Bowl, finger, flared edge, w/rnd. plate	35.00	65.00
Bowl, 3", indiv. nut, 4 ftd.	65.00	85.00	Bowl, finger, ftd.	35.00	60.00
Bowl, 3½", cranberry	40.00	75.00	Bowl, finger, w/rnd. plate	40.00	65.00
Bowl, 5", ftd., crimped edge, bonbon	30.00	50.00	Butter, w/cover, 2 hdld.	225.00	395.00
Bowl, 5", sq., fruit, "saucer"	22.00	38.00	Candlestick, 6", ea.	45.00	75.00
Bowl, 5½", bonbon, 2 hdld.	25.00	38.00	Candy box, w/cover, 4 ftd., w/tab hdld.	145.00	225.00
Bowl, 5½", bonbon, ftd.	25.00	35.00	Cheese compote w/11½" cracker plate, tab hdld.	60.00	95.00
Bowl, 5½", flattened, ftd., bonbon	25.00	35.00	Cocktail shaker, grnd. stopper, spout (like pitcher)	145.00	250.00
Bowl, 5½", fruit, "saucer"	22.00	35.00	Comport, 4", fruit cocktail	18.00	33.00
Bowl, 6", rnd., cereal	35.00	55.00	Comport, 5", 4 ftd.	25.00	75.00
Bowl, 6", sq., cereal	35.00	55.00	Comport, 6", 4 ftd.	30.00	80.00
Bowl, 8", 2 pt., 2 hdld., relish	35.00	45.00	Comport, 7", low	40.00	100.00
Bowl, 8", 3 pt., 3 hdld., relish	38.00	50.00	Comport, 7", tall	45.00	125.00
Bowl, 8¾", 2 hdld., figure, "8" pickle	30.00	50.00	Comport, 9½", tall, 2 hdld., ftd. bowl	80.00	195.00
Bowl, 8¾", 2 pt., 2 hdld., figure "8" relish	30.00	50.00	Creamer, ftd.	20.00	30.00
Bowl, 9", salad, tab hdld.	50.00	100.00	Creamer, tall, ftd.	20.00	35.00
Bowl, 9½", 2 hdld., veg.	75.00	120.00	Cup, rnd. or sq.	20.00	33.00
Bowl, 10", oblong, tab hdld., "baker"	65.00	100.00	Cup, 4 ftd., sq.	50.00	100.00
Bowl, 10", 2 hdld.	55.00	90.00	Cup, after dinner (demitasse), rnd. or sq.	80.00	125.00
Bowl, 11", 2 hdld., fruit	60.00	95.00	Fruit cocktail, 6 oz., ftd. (3 styles)	15.00	25.00
Bowl, 12", 4 ftd., console	60.00	95.00	Ice pail, metal handle w/tongs	75.00	150.00
Bowl, 12", 4 ftd., flared rim	60.00	95.00	Icer, w/insert	65.00	110.00
Bowl, 12", 4 ftd., oval	85.00	150.00	Mayonnaise, w/liner & ladle (4 ftd. bowl)	45.00	95.00
Bowl, 12", 5 pt., celery & relish	60.00	90.00	Oil, w/stopper, tall, ftd., hdld.	110.00	250.00
Bowl, 13", flared rim	65.00	100.00			
Bowl, cream soup, w/rnd. liner	55.00	85.00			
Bowl, cream soup, w/sq. saucer	55.00	85.00			

	Crystal	Green Pink Yellow			Crystal	Green Pink Yellow
Oyster cocktail, #3035, 4½ oz.	20.00	30.00		Stem, #3035, 2½ oz., wine	30.00	60.00
Oyster cocktail, 4½ oz., low stem	20.00	30.00		Stem, #3035, 3 oz., cocktail	20.00	35.00
Pitcher, 67 oz., middle indent	225.00	395.00		Stem, #3035, 3½ oz., cocktail	20.00	35.00
Pitcher, 80 oz., ball	295.00	495.00		Stem, #3035, 4½ oz., claret	45.00	85.00
Pitcher, w/cover, 64 oz.	295.00	595.00		Stem, #3035, 6 oz., low sherbet	18.00	26.00
Plate, 6", 2 hdld.	15.00	20.00		Stem, #3035, 6 oz., tall sherbet	22.00	30.00
Plate, 6", bread/butter	12.00	15.00		Stem, #3035, 9 oz., water	28.00	50.00
Plate, 7½", tea	14.00	18.00		Stem, #3035, 3½ oz., cocktail	20.00	35.00
Plate, 8½"	16.00	25.00		Stem, #3115, 9 oz., goblet	28.00	50.00
Plate, 9½", dinner	65.00	100.00		Stem, #3120, 1 oz., cordial	70.00	155.00
Plate, 10", tab hdld., salad	45.00	65.00		Stem, #3120, 4½ oz., claret	45.00	85.00
Plate, 11", 2 hdld.	50.00	70.00		Stem, #3120, 6 oz., low sherbet	18.00	26.00
Plate, 11", sq., ftd. cake	100.00	265.00		Stem, #3120, 6 oz., tall sherbet	20.00	30.00
Plate, 11½", tab hdld., sandwich	60.00	80.00		Stem, #3120, 9 oz., water	28.00	50.00
Plate, 14", chop or salad	65.00	100.00		Stem, #3130, 1 oz., cordial	70.00	125.00
Plate, sq., bread/butter	12.00	15.00		Stem, #3130, 2½ oz., wine	30.00	62.50
Plate, sq., dinner	70.00	110.00		Stem, #3130, 6 oz., low sherbet	18.00	26.00
Plate, sq., salad	14.00	20.00		Stem, #3130, 6 oz., tall sherbet	20.00	30.00
Plate, sq., service	45.00	80.00		Stem, #3130, 8 oz., water	28.00	50.00
Platter, 11½"	75.00	150.00		Stem, #3135, 6 oz., low sherbet	18.00	26.00
Salt & pepper, pr., short	45.00	125.00		Stem, #3135, 6 oz., tall sherbet	20.00	30.00
Salt & pepper, pr., w/glass top, tall	70.00	150.00		Stem, #3135, 8 oz., water	28.00	50.00
Salt & pepper, ftd., metal tops	60.00	150.00		Sugar, ftd.	20.00	30.00
Saucer, rnd.	4.00	6.00		Sugar, tall, ftd.	25.00	35.00
Saucer, rnd. after dinner	12.00	20.00		Sugar shaker, w/glass top	195.00	395.00
Saucer, sq., after dinner (demitasse)	15.00	25.00		Syrup, tall, ftd.	95.00	195.00
Saucer, sq.	4.00	6.00		Tray, 11", ctr. hdld., sandwich	35.00	75.00

	Crystal	Green Pink Yellow
Tray, 2 pt., ctr. hdld., relish	30.00	50.00
Tray, 4 pt., ctr. hdld., relish	35.00	65.00
Tray, 9", pickle, tab hdld.	35.00	70.00
Tumbler, #3035, 5 oz., high ftd.	20.00	30.00
Tumbler, #3035, 10 oz., high ftd.	22.00	42.50
Tumbler, #3035, 12 oz., high ftd.	30.00	55.00
Tumbler, #3115, 5 oz., ftd., juice	22.00	35.00
Tumbler, #3115, 8 oz., ftd.	22.00	40.00
Tumbler, #3115, 10 oz., ftd.	25.00	45.00
Tumbler, #3115, 12 oz., ftd.	30.00	50.00
Tumbler, #3120, 2½ oz., ftd. (used w/cocktail shaker)	30.00	65.00
Tumbler, #3120, 5 oz., ftd.	22.00	35.00
Tumbler, #3120, 10 oz., ftd.	25.00	42.00
Tumbler, #3120, 12 oz., ftd.	30.00	50.00
Tumbler, #3130, 5 oz., ftd.	22.00	35.00
Tumbler, #3130, 10 oz., ftd.	30.00	50.00
Tumbler, #3130, 12 oz., ftd.	30.00	50.00
Tumbler, #3135, 5 oz., juice	22.00	40.00
Tumbler, #3135, 10 oz., water	25.00	45.00
Tumbler, #3135, 12 oz., tea	32.00	55.00
Tumbler, 12 oz., flat (2 styles), one indent side to match 67 oz. pitcher	25.00	45.00
Vase, 9", oval, 4 indent	115.00	215.00
Vase, 10", keyhole base	95.00	160.00

Note: See pages 236 – 237 for stem identification.

	Crystal	Green Pink Yellow
Vase, 10", squarish top	150.00	275.00
Vase, 11"	125.00	195.00
Vase, 11", neck indent	145.00	225.00
Vase, 12", keyhole base, flared rim	165.00	250.00
Vase, 12", squarish top	195.00	295.00
Vase, 14", keyhole base, flared rim	175.00	250.00

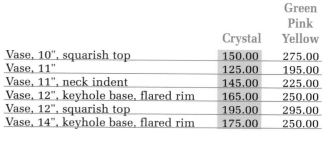

Colors: crystal, Spanish red, Ritz blue, Stiegel green, 14K Topaz, Anna Rose, Old Amethyst, India Black, Venetian (shamrock) green, Azure blue, Aquamarine, Peach, Caramel, Meadow green, Copen blue, Smoke, Light amethyst, Mission gold, Milk

Morgantown's Golf Ball is the most acknowledged and collected design of this company. It is often confused with Cambridge's #1066 which is similar to Golf Ball at first glance, Cambridge's #1066 has cut, indented "dimples" at intervals around the stem. I bought the Ritz blue (cobalt) 6" torch candle (middle of the vases on Row 3, page 103) as well as the 4" Jacobi candle (row 1, #4) at an antique show in Ohio a few years ago. Both were tagged hard to find Cambridge and priced more reasonably than they would have been as Morgantown. Morgantown's Golf Ball has crosshatched bumps symmetrically overlaid all over the stem. See my *Stemware Identification* book for further clarification.

The Spanish red item between the two Jacobi candles in the top row was a damaged candlestick that someone "cut down" to make it usable. I found it intriguing.

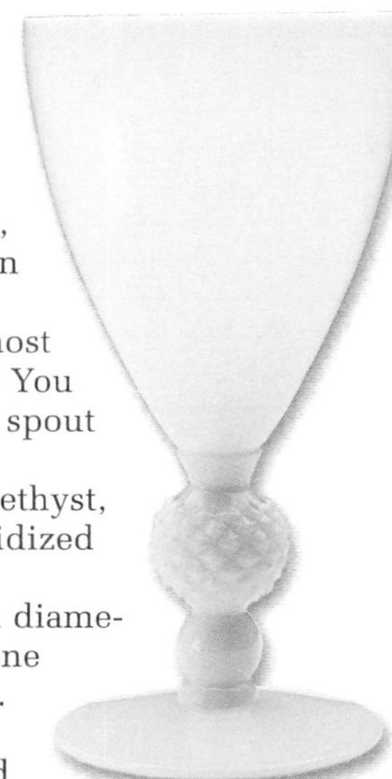

A major problem for everyone is color identification of Golf Ball. I am having my new finds added to the top of page 104 so those items should be grouped as row 1. Page 104 the second row shows Anna Rose, Smoke, Azure blue, Light amethyst, and Peach. Unfortunately the Peach has picked up the spotlight and appears somewhat yellow. Row 3 illustrates Topaz Mist, 14K Topaz, Copen blue, and Meadow green. Row 4 includes crystal, Spanish red, Smoke, Meadow green, and Azure blue. On page 103 additional colors shown are India Black, Old Amethyst (dark), Stiegel green (blue/green), and Milk.

As a general rule, all pieces of Golf Ball are hard to find except for stems, most vases, and candles. The Dupont (inverted two tiers) candle is not easily found. You should note the Irish coffee (row 2 #5 page 103). It became a creamer when a spout was added. Some square-footed stems can be found.

The Harlequin pastel colors, often marketed in sets of eight, include Amethyst, Copen blue, Gloria blue, Peach, Smoke, Topaz Mist, Shamrock green, and iridized yellow. Additional Harlequin sets include Coral and Pink Champagne.

Row 3 on page103 shows ivy balls with and without a rim. They are 4" in diameter but stand a little under 6" without rim and a little over 7" with one. The one with the ruffled top is the most difficult to find and few of them have been seen. The Spanish red piece in the bottom row is the urn.

To be consistent in terminology for collectors, in the listings I have used name designations found in *Gallagher's Handbook of Old Morgantown Glass,* that unfortunately is no longer in print.

	Steigel Green Spanish Red *Ritz Blue	Other colors
Amherst water lamp, super rare	1000.00+	
Bell	125.00	60.00
Candle, pr., 4⅝", Dupont (inverted 2 tier)	300.00	200.00
Candle, 6" torch	200.00	125.00
Candlestick, 4" Jacobi (top flat rim)	195.00	135.00
Candy, flat w/golf ball knob cover, 6"x 5½" (Alexandra)	1000.00	750.00
Creamer	175.00	
Compote, 10" diam., 7½" high, w/14 crimp rim (Truman)	475.00	375.00
Compote w/cover, 6" diam. (Celeste)	750.00	550.00
Compote, 6" diam. (Celeste)	450.00	300.00
Irish coffee, 5¼", 6 oz.	195.00	150.00
Pilsner, 9⅛", 11 oz.	175.00	135.00
Schooner, 8½", 32 oz.	295.00	195.00
Stem, brandy snifter, 6½", 21 oz.	155.00	125.00
Stem, cafe parfait, 6¼", 4 oz.	100.00	60.00
Stem, champagne, 5", 5½ oz.	37.50	27.50
Stem, claret, 5¼", 4½ oz.	75.00	45.00
Stem, cocktail, 4⅛", 3½ oz.	26.00	20.00
Stem, cordial, 3½", 1½ oz.	50.00	40.00

	Steigel Green Spanish Red *Ritz Blue	Other colors
Stem, oyster cocktail, 4⅜", 4½ oz., cupped	60.00	35.00
Stem, oyster cocktail, 4¼", 4 oz., flared	45.00	30.00
Stem, sherbet/sundae, 4⅛", 5½ oz.	30.00	22.00
Stem, sherry, 4⅝", 2½ oz.	65.00	40.00
Stem, water, 6¾", 9 oz.	50.00	35.00
Stem, wine, 4¾", 3 oz.	50.00	35.00
Sugar, no handles, cone	175.00	
Tumbler, 4⅜", ftd., wine	40.00	22.00
Tumbler, 5", 5 oz., ftd., juice	35.00	22.00
Tumbler, 6⅛", 9 oz., ftd., water	40.00	24.00
Tumbler, 6¾", 12 oz., ftd., tea	50.00	33.50
Urn, 6½" high.	125.00	65.00
Vase, 4", Ivy ball, ruff	300.00	150.00
Vase, 4", Ivy ball w/rim (Kimball)	75.00	55.00
Vase, 4", Ivy ball, no rim (Kennon)	75.00	50.00
Vase, 6½", "brandy," w/short standing rm. (Stephanie)	155.00	125.00
Vase, 8" high, Charlotte w/crimped rim	275.00	175.00
Vase, 8" high, flair rim flute (Charlotte)	265.00	175.00
Vase, 10½", #78 Lancaster (cupped w/tiny stand up rim)	425.00	250.00
Vase, 11", #79 Montague (flair rim)	450.00	300.00

*Add 10% for Ritz Blue.

Colors: crystal; Flamingo pink punch bowl and cups only

Greek Key is an older Heisey pattern that is easily recognized by collectors. Other companies made similar patterns but most Heisey pieces are marked. Note all four ice tubs are shown. Stemware in all sizes is troublesome to find and the prices indicate that reality.

	Crystal
Bowl, finger	40.00
Bowl, jelly, w/cover, 2 hdld., ftd	145.00
Bowl, indiv., ftd., almond	45.00
Bowl, 4", nappy	25.00
Bowl, 4", shallow, low ft., jelly	40.00
Bowl, 4½", nappy	25.00
Bowl, 4½", scalloped, nappy	25.00
Bowl, 4½", shallow, low ft., jelly	40.00
Bowl, 5", ftd., almond	40.00
Bowl, 5", ftd., almond, w/cover	110.00
Bowl, 5", hdld., jelly	95.00
Bowl, 5", low ft., jelly, w/cover	110.00
Bowl, 5", nappy	30.00
Bowl, 5½", nappy	40.00
Bowl, 5½", shallow nappy, ftd.	65.00
Bowl, 6", nappy	30.00
Bowl, 6", shallow nappy	30.00
Bowl, 6½", nappy	35.00
Bowl, 7", low ft., straight side	90.00
Bowl, 7", nappy	80.00
Bowl, 8", low ft., straight side	70.00
Bowl, 8", nappy	70.00
Bowl, 8", scalloped nappy	65.00
Bowl, 8", shallow, low ft.	75.00
Bowl, 8½", shallow nappy	75.00
Bowl, 9", flat, banana split	45.00
Bowl, 9", ftd., banana split	55.00
Bowl, 9", low ft., straight side	65.00
Bowl, 9", nappy	70.00
Bowl, 9", shallow, low ft.	70.00
Bowl, 9½", shallow nappy	70.00
Bowl, 10", shallow, low ft.	85.00
Bowl, 11", shallow nappy	70.00
Bowl, 12", orange bowl	500.00
Bowl, 12", punch, ftd.,	300.00
Flamingo	750.00
Bowl, 12", orange, flared rim	450.00
Bowl, 14½", orange, flared rim	500.00
Bowl, 15", punch, ftd.	400.00
Bowl, 18", punch, shallow	400.00
Butter, indiv. (plate)	35.00
Butter/jelly, 2 hdld., w/cover	200.00
Candy, w/cover, ½ lb.	140.00
Candy, w/cover, 1 lb.	170.00
Candy, w/cover, 2 lb.	210.00
Cheese & cracker set, 10"	150.00
Compote, 5"	90.00
Compote, 5", w/cover	130.00
Creamer	50.00
Creamer, oval, hotel	55.00
Creamer, rnd., hotel	50.00

	Crystal
Cup, 4½ oz., punch	20.00
Cup, punch, Flamingo	45.00
Coaster	20.00
Egg cup, 5 oz.	80.00
Hair receiver	170.00
Ice tub, lg., tab hdld.	150.00
Ice tub, sm., tab hdld.	130.00
Ice tub, w/cover, hotel	235.00
Ice tub, w/cover, 5", individual, w/5" plate	200.00
Jar, 1 qt., crushed fruit, w/cover	400.00
Jar, 2 qt., crushed fruit, w/cover	400.00
Jar, lg. cover, horseradish	140.00
Jar, sm. cover, horseradish	130.00
Jar, tall celery	140.00
Jar, w/knob cover, pickle	160.00
Pitcher, 1 pint (jug)	130.00
Pitcher, 1 quart (jug)	210.00
Pitcher, 3 pint (jug)	250.00
Pitcher, ½ gal. (tankard)	240.00
Oil bottle, 2 oz., squat, w/#8 stopper	100.00
Oil bottle, 2 oz., w/#6 stopper	110.00
Oil bottle, 4 oz., squat, w/#8 stopper	100.00
Oil bottle, 4 oz., w/#6 stopper	100.00
Oil bottle, 6 oz., w/#6 stopper	100.00
Oil bottle, 6 oz., squat, w/#8 stopper	100.00
Plate, 4½"	20.00
Plate, 5"	25.00
Plate, 5½"	25.00
Plate, 6"	35.00
Plate, 6½"	35.00
Plate, 7"	50.00
Plate, 8"	70.00
Plate, 9"	90.00
Plate, 10"	110.00
Plate, 16", orange bowl liner	180.00
Puff box, #1, w/cover	175.00
Puff box, #3, w/cover	175.00
Salt & pepper, pr.	125.00

	Crystal
Sherbet, 4½ oz., ftd., straight rim	30.00
Sherbet, 4½ oz., ftd., flared rim	30.00
Sherbet, 4½ oz., high ft., shallow	30.00
Sherbet, 4½ oz., ftd., shallow	30.00
Sherbet, 4½ oz., ftd., cupped rim	30.00
Sherbet, 6 oz., low ft.	35.00
Spooner, lg.	110.00
Spooner, 4½" (or straw jar)	110.00
Stem, ¾ oz., cordial	250.00
Stem, 2 oz., wine	110.00
Stem, 2 oz., sherry	200.00
Stem, 3 oz., cocktail	50.00
Stem, 3½ oz., burgundy	125.00
Stem, 4½ oz., saucer champagne	60.00
Stem, 4½ oz., claret	170.00
Stem, 7 oz.	95.00
Stem, 9 oz.	160.00
Stem, 9 oz., low ft.	145.00
Straw jar, w/cover	425.00
Sugar	50.00
Sugar, oval, hotel	55.00
Sugar, rnd., hotel	50.00

	Crystal
Sugar & creamer, oval, individual	140.00
Tray, 9", oval celery	50.00
Tray, 12", oval celery	60.00
Tray, 12½", French roll	140.00
Tray, 13", oblong	260.00
Tray, 15", oblong	300.00
Tumbler, 2½ oz. (or toothpick)	475.00
Tumbler, 5 oz., flared rim	50.00
Tumbler, 5 oz., straight side	50.00
Tumbler, 5½ oz., water	50.00
Tumbler, 7 oz., flared rim	60.00
Tumbler, 7 oz., straight side	60.00
Tumbler, 8 oz., w/straight, flared, cupped, shallow	60.00
Tumbler, 10 oz., flared rim	90.00
Tumbler, 10 oz., straight wide	90.00
Tumbler, 12 oz., flared rim	100.00
Tumbler, 12 oz., straight side	100.00
Tumbler, 13 oz., straight side	100.00
Tumbler, 13 oz., flared rim	100.00
Water bottle	220.00

"HARDING," No. 401 Deep Plate Etch Optic, Central Glass Works, Pat. June 1, 1920

Colors: pink, crystal, crystal w/green trim, crystal w/gold, green; w/optic

Central's No. 401 etch was given the name "Harding" when President and Mrs. Harding selected a set of this "Dragon" design consisting of over 300 pieces; it was etched with gold. Thereafter, Central advertised it as glass "for America's first families." There are few pieces available, today, but well worth your search. We have bought all the "Harding" pictured over the last seven years.

	*All colors
Bowl, 12", console, octagon	85.00
Bowl, finger, #800	35.00
Bowl, soup, flat	60.00
Candlestick, octagon collar	50.00
Candlestick, rnd. collar	45.00
Comport, 4½", short stem	35.00
Comport, 6", short stem	35.00
Comport, 6", 10 oz., tall stem	45.00
Creamer, ftd.	40.00
Cup, handled custard	20.00
Decanter, qt. w/cut stop	325.00
Ice tub, 2 hdld.	425.00
Jug, tall, flat bottom	395.00
Plate, 5" sherbet	12.00
Plate, 6" finger bowl liner	15.00
Plate, dinner	75.00
Plate, lunch	25.00
Server, center handle	65.00
Shaker, ftd. indiv.	75.00
Stem style, indiv., almond	20.00

	*All colors
Stem, 5½ oz. sherbet	20.00
Stem, 6 oz., saucer champagne, #780	25.00
Stem, 9 oz., water, #780	27.50
Stem, cordial	75.00
Stem, oyster cocktail	20.00
Stem, wine	28.00
Sugar, ftd.	40.00
Tumbler, 5 oz	18.00
Tumbler, 8 oz.	20.00
Tumbler, 10 oz., #530	20.00
Tumbler, 12 oz.	20.00
Tumbler, ftd., hdld., tea	45.00
Vase, 8"	125.00
Vase, 10", ruffled top	195.00

* 25% less for crystal

HERMITAGE, #2449, Fostoria Glass Company, 1932 – 1945

Colors: Amber, Azure (blue), crystal, Ebony, green, Topaz, Wisteria

Hermitage is a Fostoria pattern that has only a small number of devotees at present; however, a few collectors are beginning to notice the Wisteria color. Other Fostoria patterns found in Wisteria are being priced out of sight. Hermitage prices are reasonable; so if you like this color, now is the time to start buying it.

My listings are from a Fostoria catalog that had January 1, 1933, entered on the front page in pencil. We have several different colored ice buckets to show you.

	Crystal	Amber/Green/Topaz	Azure	Wisteria
Ashtray holder, #2449	5.00	8.00	12.00	
*Ashtray, #2449	3.00	5.00	8.00	
Bottle, 3 oz., oil, #2449	20.00	40.00		
Bottle, 27 oz., bar w/stopper, #2449	45.00			
Bowl, 4½", finger, #2449½	4.00	6.00	10.00	22.50
Bowl, 5", fruit, #2449½	5.00	8.00	15.00	
Bowl, 6", cereal, #2449½	6.00	10.00	20.00	
Bowl, 6½", salad, #2449½	6.00	9.00	20.00	
Bowl, 7", soup, #2449½	8.00	12.00	22.00	45.00
Bowl, 7½", salad, #2449½	8.00	12.00	30.00	
Bowl, 8", deep, ped., ft., #2449	17.50	35.00	60.00	
Bowl, 10", ftd., #2449	20.00	35.00		125.00
Bowl, grapefruit, w/crystal liner, #2449	20.00	40.00		
Candle, 6", #2449	12.50	22.00	35.00	
Coaster, 5⅝", #2449	5.00	7.50	11.00	
Comport, 6", #2449	12.00	17.50	27.50	40.00
Creamer, ftd., #2449	4.00	6.00	10.00	30.00
Cup, ftd., #2449	6.00	10.00	15.00	22.00
Decanter, 28 oz., w/stopper, #2449	40.00	110.00	150.00	
Fruit cocktail, 2⅜", 5 oz., ftd., #2449	5.00	7.50	12.00	
Ice tub, 6", #2449	17.50	35.00	50.00	225.00
Icer, #2449	10.00	18.00	30.00	900.00
Icer, insert	10.00	20.00	25.00	35.00
Mayonnaise, 5⅝" w/7" plate, #2449	20.00	35.00		
Mug, 9 oz., ftd., #2449	15.00			

108

	Crystal	Amber/Green/Topaz	Azure	Wisteria
Mug, 12 oz., ftd., #2449	17.50			
Mustard w/cover & spoon, #2449	17.50	35.00		
Pitcher, pint, #2449	22.50	40.00	60.00	
Pitcher, 3 pint, #2449	75.00	90.00	150.00	595.00
Plate, 6", #2449½	3.00	5.00	8.00	
Plate, 7", ice dish liner	4.00	6.00	10.00	20.00
Plate, 7", #2449½	4.00	6.00	10.00	
Plate, 7⅜", crescent salad, #2449	10.00	17.50	35.00	70.00
Plate, 8", #2449½	6.00	10.00	15.00	25.00
Plate, 9", #2449½	12.50	20.00	30.00	
Plate, 12", sandwich, #2449		12.50	20.00	
Relish, 6", 2 pt., #2449	6.00	10.00	15.00	25.00
Relish, 7¼", 3 pt., #2449	8.00	11.00	17.50	50.00
Relish, 8", pickle, #2449	8.00	11.00	17.50	
Relish, 11", celery, #2449	10.00	15.00	25.00	50.00
Salt & pepper, 3⅜", #2449	25.00	50.00	75.00	100.00
Salt, indiv., #2449	4.00	6.00	10.00	
Saucer, #2449	2.00	3.50	5.00	8.00
Sherbet, 3", 7 oz., low, ftd., #2449	6.00	8.00	12.50	15.00
Stem, 3¼", 5½ oz., high sherbet, #2449	8.00	11.00	17.50	25.00
Stem, 4⅝", 4 oz., claret, #2449	10.00	15.00		
Stem, 5¼", 9 oz., water goblet, #2449	10.00	15.00	25.00	40.00
Sugar, ftd., #2449	4.00	6.00	10.00	30.00
Tray, 6½", condiment, #2449	6.00	12.00	20.00	30.00
Tumbler, 2½", 2 oz., #2449½	8.00	10.00	20.00	40.00
Tumbler, 2½", 2 oz., ftd., #2449	5.00	10.00		
Tumbler, 3", 4 oz., cocktail, ftd., #2449	5.00	7.50	14.00	25.00
Tumbler, 3¼", 6 oz. old-fashion, #2449½	6.00	10.00	18.00	30.00
Tumbler, 3⅞", 5 oz., #2449½	5.00	8.00	12.00	25.00
Tumbler, 4", 5 oz., ftd., #2449	5.00	8.00	12.00	25.00
Tumbler, 4⅛", 9 oz., ftd., #2449	6.00	10.00	15.00	30.00
Tumbler, 4¾", 9 oz., #2449½	6.00	10.00	15.00	32.50
Tumbler, 5¼", 12 oz., ftd., iced tea, #2449	10.00	16.00	28.00	
Tumbler, 5⅞", 13 oz., #2449½	10.00	16.00	28.00	40.00
Vase, 6", ftd.	22.00	32.50		

* Ebony – $15.00

Colors: amber, black, crystal, Emerald green, Peach Blo, Willow blue

Imperial Hunt Scene displays well when the design is gold encrusted. Gold decoration adds 10% to 20% to the price listed. Be wary of worn gold; it is not as alluring for collectors! Has anyone found a creamer to match the sugar and lid I have been picturing? None of Cambridge's catalogs show either a sugar or creamer with this etching, but I'd be highly surprised if they made a sugar and no creamer.

The Internet has effected climbing prices on this pattern. Collectors seem to succumb to glassware that depicts animals. Cathy says she ran into a lady at a market exclaiming over an 1880 flamingo patterned bowl. So, it appears to have always been thus! Cups, saucers, creamers, sugars, and shakers have always been scarce, but now more collectors are searching for them. Sets can be put together in pink (Peach Blo) and possibly Emerald green.

Stems are plentiful, but pricey, in most sizes other than cordials and clarets. That is "plentiful" in comparison to serving pieces rather than plentiful in comparison to other patterns. You will find bi-colored Hunt Scene stemware. Pink bowl with a green stem or foot is the characteristic form — and the choice of most collectors.

Black and Emerald green (dark) with gold decorations sell 25% to 50% higher than prices listed if you should find any.

	Crystal	Colors
Bowl, 6", cereal	20.00	40.00
Bowl, 8"	40.00	90.00
Bowl, 8½", 3 pt.	45.00	95.00
Candlestick, 2-lite, keyhole	35.00	75.00
Candlestick, 3-lite, keyhole	45.00	95.00
Comport, 5½", #3085		60.00
Creamer, flat	15.00	50.00
Creamer, ftd.	20.00	65.00
Cup	50.00	65.00
Decanter		295.00
Finger bowl, w/plate, #3085		75.00
Humidor, tobacco		595.00
Ice bucket	100.00	195.00
Ice tub	65.00	125.00
Mayonnaise, w/liner	40.00	85.00
Pitcher, w/cover, 63 oz., #3085		495.00
Pitcher, w/cover, 76 oz., #711	195.00	395.00
Plate, 8"	20.00	22.50

	Crystal	Colors
Salt & pepper, pr.	100.00	275.00
Saucer	10.00	15.00
Stem, 1 oz., cordial, #1402	100.00	
Stem, 2½ oz., wine, #1402	65.00	
Stem, 3 oz., cocktail, #1402	50.00	
Stem, 6 oz., tomato, #1402	45.00	
Stem, 6½ oz., sherbet, #1402	40.00	
Stem, 7½ oz., sherbet, #1402	45.00	
Stem, 10 oz., water, #1402	50.00	
Stem, 14 oz., #1402	55.00	
Stem, 18 oz., #1402	65.00	
Stem, 1 oz., cordial, #3085		195.00
Stem, 2½ oz., cocktail, #3085		50.00
Stem, 2½ oz., wine, #3085		55.00
Stem, 4½ oz., claret, #3085		67.50
Stem, 5½ oz., parfait, #3085		75.00
Stem, 6 oz., low sherbet, #3085		22.50
Stem, 6 oz., high sherbet, #3085		35.00
Stem, 9 oz., water, #3085		55.00
Sugar, flat w/ lid	50.00	125.00
Sugar, ftd.	20.00	75.00
Tumbler, 2½ oz., 2⅞", flat, #1402	25.00	
Tumbler, 5 oz., flat, #1402	20.00	
Tumbler, 7 oz., flat, #1402	20.00	
Tumbler, 10 oz., flat, #1402	23.00	
Tumbler, 10 oz., flat, tall, #1402	25.00	
Tumbler, 15 oz., flat, #1402	35.00	
Tumbler, 2½ oz., ftd., #3085		65.00
Tumbler, 5 oz., 3⅞", ftd., #3085		45.00
Tumbler, 8 oz., ftd., #3085		50.00
Tumbler, 10 oz., ftd., #3085		55.00
Tumbler, 12 oz., 5⅜", ftd., #3085.		50.00

Colors: crystal, Flamingo pink, Sahara yellow, Moongleam green, cobalt, and Alexandrite

I wish to reiterate that if you find any colored piece of Ipswich, other than those listed, it was made at Imperial and not Heisey. It may be marked Heisey, but it was manufactured at Imperial from purchased Heisey moulds and, as such, is pretty much ignored at this point by true Heisey collectors. Mostly, I get letters on (Alexandrite) candy jars that are actually Imperial's Heather (purple) color. Imperial is now out of business; their wares are collectible; but, so far, not the Heisey patterns they made in their own colors.

Moongleam is the color of preference with collectors of Ipswich, and there are collectors who would love a pitcher in that color.

	Crystal	Pink	Sahara	Green	Cobalt	Alexandrite
Bowl, finger, w/underplate	40.00	90.00	80.00	120.00		
Bowl, 11", ftd., floral	80.00		300.00		450.00	
Candlestick, 6", 1-lite	150.00	275.00	200.00	300.00	400.00	
Candlestick centerpiece, ftd., vase, "A" prisms, complete	160.00	300.00	350.00	450.00	500.00	
Candy jar, ¼ lb., w/cover	175.00					
Candy jar, ½ lb., w/cover	175.00	325.00	300.00	400.00		
Cocktail shaker, 1 quart, strainer, #86 stopper	225.00	600.00	700.00	800.00		
Creamer	35.00	70.00	90.00	125.00		
Stem, 4 oz., oyster cocktail, ftd.	25.00	60.00	50.00	70.00		
Stem, 5 oz., saucer champagne (knob in stem)	25.00	60.00	50.00	70.00		
Stem, 10 oz., goblet (knob in stem)	35.00	85.00	70.00	90.00		750.00
Stem, 12 oz., schoppen, flat bottom	100.00					
Pitcher, ½ gal.	350.00	600.00	550.00	750.00		
Oil bottle, 2 oz., ftd., #86 stopper	125.00	285.00	275.00	300.00		
Plate, 7", sq.	30.00	60.00	50.00	70.00		
Plate, 8", sq.	35.00	65.00	55.00	75.00		
Sherbet, 4 oz., ftd. (knob in stem)	15.00	35.00	30.00	45.00		
Sugar	35.00	70.00	90.00	125.00		
Tumbler, 5 oz., ftd. (soda)	30.00	45.00	40.00	85.00		
Tumbler, 8 oz., ftd. (soda)	30.00	45.00	40.00	85.00		
Tumbler, 10 oz., cupped rim, flat bottom	70.00	110.00	100.00	140.00		
Tumbler, 10 oz., straight rim, flat bottom	70.00	110.00	100.00	140.00		
Tumbler, 12 oz., ftd. (soda)	40.00	80.00	70.00	95.00		

Colors: crystal, Cobalt, Ruby, Light Blue, Emerald, Amethyst

Janice was one of the latest additions to this book, and now there are many new collectors seeking it. In the last edition I reported that Dalzell Viking was making or had recently made both candlesticks pictured on the ends of row 2. These were made in crystal, cobalt blue, and red that I can confirm. Dalzell Viking has now gone out of business, but they made a bunch of Janice candles. The light blue was not made to my knowledge, but be wary of other colors. The only significant difference is that the newer ones are slightly heavier and not as fire polished as the old. The reissued ones have an oily feel, as does much of the newly made glass.

Ice buckets are rare in Janice, but you couldn't prove it from our photo. The really unusual one is the glass handled one that looks like a basket rather than a bucket. I have been assured it is listed as an ice bucket in the catalogs of New Martinsville; in any case, the handle surviving all these years is a miracle.

There is a separate line of swan handled items in the Janice pattern that I have not listed here, but note the covered candy which I found fascinating.

	Crystal	Blue Red		Crystal	Blue Red
Basket, 6½", 9" high	75.00	145.00	Ice tub, 6", ftd.	115.00	265.00
Basket, 11"	75.00	215.00	Jam jar w/cover, 6"	20.00	45.00
Basket, 12", oval, 10" high	85.00	250.00	Mayonnaise liner, 7", 2 hdld.	9.00	14.00
Bonbon, 5½", 2 hdld., 4½" high	18.00	30.00	Mayonnaise plate, 6"	7.50	12.50
Bonbon, 6", 2 hdld., 4" high	20.00	33.00	Mayonnaise, 6", 2 hdld.	18.00	30.00
Bonbon, 7", 2 hdld., 4¾" high	25.00	40.00	Mayonnaise, round	15.00	27.50
Bowl, 5½", flower, w/eight crimps	22.00	35.00	Oil, 5 oz., w/stopper	40.00	100.00
Bowl, 6", 2 hdld., crimped	20.00	33.00	Pitcher, 15 oz., berry cream	50.00	150.00
Bowl, 9½", cupped	35.00	65.00	Plate, 7", 2 hdld.	9.00	14.00
Bowl, 9½", flared	35.00	65.00	Plate, 8½", salad	10.00	17.50
Bowl, 9", 2 hdld.	37.50	75.00	Plate, 11", cheese	22.50	40.00
Bowl, 10"	37.50	75.00	Plate, 11", ftd., rolled edge	27.50	50.00
Bowl, 10½", cupped, 3 toed	45.00	75.00	Plate, 12", 2 hdld.	30.00	55.00
Bowl, 10½", flared, 3 toed	45.00	85.00	Plate, 13"	30.00	60.00
Bowl, 11", oval	40.00	75.00	Plate, 13", 2 hdld.	32.50	65.00
Bowl, 11", cupped, ftd.	45.00	85.00	Plate, 14", ftd., rolled edge	40.00	85.00
Bowl, 11", flared	40.00	65.00	Plate, 15"	40.00	
Bowl, 12", flared	42.50	90.00	Plate, 15", rolled edge torte	50.00	
Bowl, 12", fruit, ruffled top	50.00	110.00	Platter, 13", oval	35.00	90.00
Bowl, 12", oval	42.50	70.00	Relish, 6", 2 part, 2 hdld.	15.00	37.50
Bowl, 12", salad, scalloped top	50.00	85.00	Salt and pepper, pr.	40.00	85.00
Bowl, 12", six crimps	52.50	125.00	Saucer	2.00	4.50
Bowl, 13", flared	50.00	100.00	Sherbet	12.00	26.00
Canape set: tray w/ftd. juice	30.00		Sugar, 6 oz.	12.00	20.00
Candelbra, 5", 2-lt., 5" wide	40.00		Sugar, individual, flat	10.00	22.00
Candlestick, 5½", 1-lt., 5" wide	35.00	50.00	Sugar, individual, ftd.	12.50	25.00
Candlestick, 6", 1-lt., 4½" wide	37.50	60.00	Sugar, tall	15.00	45.00
Candy box w/cover, 5½"	55.00	150.00	Syrup, w/dripcut top	75.00	
Celery, 11"	20.00	45.00	Tray, oval, 2 hdld., ind. sug/cr	12.00	20.00
Comport, cracker for cheese plate	14.00	25.00	Tray, oval, 2 hdld., cr/sug	15.00	25.00
Condiment set: tray and 2 cov. jars	55.00	125.00	Tumbler	14.00	30.00
Creamer, 6 oz.	12.00	20.00	Vase, 4", ivy, 3½" high	22.00	50.00
Creamer, individual, flat	12.00	22.00	Vase, 4", ivy, 4½" high, w/base peg	25.00	60.00
Creamer, individual, ftd.	12.50	25.00	Vase, 7", ftd.	35.00	75.00
Creamer, tall	15.00	45.00	Vase, 8", ball, 7½" high	45.00	110.00
Cup	8.00	23.00	Vase, 8", cupped, 3 toed	50.00	125.00
Guest set: bottle w/tumbler	85.00		Vase, 8", flared, 3 toed	50.00	125.00
Ice pail, 10", hdld.	85.00	225.00	Vase, 9", ball	55.00	135.00

Color: crystal w/amber trim, wide optic

Julia is a Tiffin pattern that is just being discovered by collectors. A long-time collector told me that it was only manufactured for about five years. Notice that the plates are wholly amber while stems and other pieces are crystal with amber stems, feet or handles. Unfortunately, the pattern does not show as well on those amber flat pieces. When set flat, the design practically disappears. However, it really zings against the crystal. It was the fashion in the late twenties and early thirties to make bi-colored glass. This is an excellent example of that practice. You can probably gather this pattern without much immediate competition, but I would not count on that lasting too long. There are just a few Tiffin patterns that can be collected in amber; so, if you like Tiffin styling and design, as a growing number of collectors do, this would be an ideal pattern to pursue. Too, there is a growing group of collectors whose main focus is bi-colored glass!

	Amber
Bowl, finger	25.00
Candy jar and cover, ftd.	135.00
Creamer	35.00
Jug and cover, ftd.	325.00
Plate, 8", luncheon	20.00
Plate, dessert	12.00
Plate, salad	14.00
Stem, cafe parfait	40.00
Stem, claret	45.00
Stem, cocktail	25.00

	Amber
Stem, cordial	55.00
Stem, saucer champagne	22.00
Stem, sundae	18.00
Stem, water	30.00
Stem, wine	40.00
Sugar	35.00
Tumbler, ftd., seltzer	22.00
Tumbler, ftd., table	25.00
Tumbler, ftd., tea	30.00

Colors: crystal, Azure blue, Topaz yellow, Rose pink

June is the most collected etched Fostoria pattern. Azure and Rose have continued to rise in price. Prices for crystal and Topaz have remained fairly stable, but a few more collectors have taken a fancy to crystal of late. If you have been putting off buying crystal or yellow, better start gathering now before prices catch blue and pink.

Shakers came with both glass and metal tops. Collectors prefer the glass ones first used. In later years, only metal tops were made; all replacement tops were metal; so if you are seeking tops, you will have to settle for metal.

If you will refer to Versailles (page 221), I have listed all the Fostoria line numbers for each piece. Since these are fundamentally the same listings as June, you can use the ware number listings from Versailles should you need them. Be sure to see the stemware illustrations on page 87. You would not want to pay for a 6" claret and receive a 6" high sherbet simply because you didn't realize they were shaped differently.

	Crystal	Rose Blue	Topaz
Ashtray	25.00	55.00	40.00
Bottle, salad dressing, #2083 or #2375	300.00	995.00	495.00
Bowl, baker, 9", oval	50.00	150.00	85.00
Bowl, baker, 10", oval	40.00	135.00	75.00
Bowl, bonbon	12.50	30.00	23.00
Bowl, bouillon, ftd.	18.00	50.00	27.00
Bowl, finger, w/liner	35.00	75.00	50.00
Bowl, mint, 3 ftd., 4½"	15.00	45.00	30.00
Bowl, 6", nappy, 3 ftd., jelly	15.00	45.00	25.00
Bowl, 6½", cereal	25.00	95.00	45.00
Bowl, 7", soup	65.00	195.00	175.00
Bowl, lg., dessert, hdld.	35.00	150.00	95.00
Bowl, 10"	35.00	150.00	85.00
Bowl, 10", Grecian	50.00	175.00	95.00
Bowl, 11", centerpiece	35.00	110.00	75.00
Bowl, 12", centerpiece, three types	55.00	125.00	75.00

	Crystal	Rose Blue	Topaz
Bowl, 13", oval centerpiece, w/flower frog	90.00	275.00	150.00
Candlestick, 2"	14.00	33.00	22.00
Candlestick, 3"	20.00	50.00	30.00
Candlestick, 3", Grecian	20.00	60.00	30.00
Candlestick, 5", Grecian	30.00	75.00	45.00
Candy, w/cover, 3 pt.		350.00	
Candy, w/cover, ½ lb., ¼ lb.			225.00
Celery, 11½"	35.00	110.00	65.00
Cheese & cracker set, #2368 or #2375	50.00	135.00	95.00
Comport, 5", #2400	30.00	75.00	50.00
Comport, 6", #5298 or #5299	30.00	95.00	55.00
Comport, 7", #2375	35.00	125.00	70.00
Comport, 8", #2400	50.00	165.00	80.00
Cream soup, ftd.	25.00	60.00	40.00
Creamer, ftd.	15.00	30.00	20.00

	Crystal	Rose Blue	Topaz
Creamer, tea	30.00	80.00	50.00
Cup, after dinner	25.00	100.00	50.00
Cup, ftd.	15.00	33.00	25.00
Decanter	425.00	2,000.00	645.00
Goblet, claret, 6", 4 oz.	50.00	165.00	90.00
Goblet, cocktail, 5¼", 3 oz.	24.00	48.00	35.00
Goblet, cordial, 4", ¾ oz.	60.00	155.00	85.00
Goblet, water, 8¼", 10 oz.	35.00	75.00	50.00
Goblet, wine, 5½", 3 oz.	25.00	110.00	50.00
Grapefruit	40.00	110.00	75.00
Grapefruit liner	35.00	90.00	50.00
Ice bucket	85.00	165.00	100.00
Ice dish	35.00	75.00	45.00
Ice dish liner (tomato, crab, fruit)	8.00	22.00	12.00
Mayonnaise, w/liner	30.00	85.00	50.00
Oil, ftd.	250.00	750.00	350.00
Oyster cocktail, 5½ oz.	20.00	40.00	28.00
Parfait, 5¼"	40.00	125.00	75.00
Pitcher	275.00	695.00	395.00
Plate, canape	20.00	50.00	30.00
Plate, lemon	16.00	30.00	25.00
Plate, 6", bread/butter	7.00	15.00	9.00
Plate, 6", finger bowl liner	4.50	15.00	10.00
Plate, 7½", salad	10.00	18.00	13.00
Plate, 7½, cream soup	7.00	20.00	15.00
Plate, 8¾", luncheon	6.00	25.00	18.00
Plate, 9½", sm. dinner	15.00	50.00	30.00
Plate, 10", cake, hdld. (no indent)	35.00	75.00	45.00
Plate, 10", cheese with indent, hdld.	35.00	75.00	45.00

	Crystal	Rose Blue	Topaz
Plate, 10¼", dinner	40.00	125.00	75.00
Plate, 10¼", grill	40.00	125.00	75.00
Plate, 13", chop	25.00	90.00	65.00
Plate, 14", torte		135.00	75.00
Platter, 12"	40.00	135.00	85.00
Platter, 15"	75.00	250.00	135.00
Relish, 8½", 3 part	35.00		60.00
Sauce boat	40.00	295.00	125.00
Sauce boat liner	15.00	90.00	45.00
Saucer, after dinner	6.00	20.00	10.00
Saucer	4.00	8.00	5.00
Shaker, ftd., pr	60.00	225.00	150.00
Sherbet, high, 6", 6 oz.	20.00	40.00	27.50
Sherbet, low, 4¼", 6 oz.	18.00	33.00	25.00
Sugar, ftd., straight or scalloped top	15.00	30.00	22.00
Sugar cover	55.00	250.00	150.00
Sugar pail	70.00	250.00	150.00
Sugar, tea	25.00	80.00	45.00
Sweetmeat	25.00	40.00	25.00
Tray, service and lemon		350.00	300.00
Tray, 11", ctr. hdld.	25.00	50.00	40.00
Tumbler, 2½ oz., ftd.	20.00	100.00	65.00
Tumbler, 5 oz., 4½", ftd.	15.00	50.00	30.00
Tumbler, 9 oz., 5¼", ftd.	18.00	45.00	25.00
Tumbler, 12 oz., 6", ftd.	25.00	70.00	40.00
Vase, 8", 2 styles	80.00	325.00	225.00
Vase, 8½", fan, ftd.	90.00	275.00	175.00
Whipped cream bowl	12.00	30.00	20.00
Whipped cream pail	95.00	250.00	195.00

Note: See stemware identification on page 87.

Colors: crystal

June Night stemware is obtainable. Apparently, Tiffin promoted this rival of Cambridge's Rose Point for clientele to use with their china. I see hundreds of stems for every bowl or candle. June Night can be found on several different stemware lines, but the one most often encountered is Tiffin's #17392 that is shown in the photograph. You will also find line numbers #17378 (prism stem with pearl edge top), #17441 (quadrangle flowing to hexagonal cut), and #17471. The latter line has a bow tie stem, but I have never personally seen June Night on it. I need one for photography. More of this pattern is being displayed at shows. I've noticed that similar pieces of Cherokee Rose have created an identity problem with many novices and part-time dealers. There is a flower encircled on June Night and an urn on Cherokee Rose. Shapes are important, but it is the design that makes the pattern. Since both of these patterns are on the same Tiffin mould blank, a dealer needs to be sure which one he has before labeling it.

Shakers and the pitcher seem to be the most difficult components of a set to obtain. I have finally found a pitcher to show you along with the elusive shakers. The small bowl in the right hand corner is a mayonnaise without a liner. The finger bowl is thin and has a smooth rim and is not shown.

Gold-trimmed June Night stemware was called Cherry Laurel. Name changing within same patterns is another glass company gimmick. Any different treatment done to a pattern often resulted in a separate name. In the case of gold trim, often they would just add "golden" to the pattern name. Remember that gold trim did not and still does not hold up well with frequent use. Never put gold-trimmed items in the dishwasher especially if you use any soap with lemon in it. Lemon will remove gold trim.

	Crystal			Crystal
Bowl, 5", finger.	22.00		Shaker, pr.	200.00
Bowl, 6", fruit or nut	27.50		Stem, 1 oz., cordial	45.00
Bowl, 7", salad	35.00		Stem, 2 oz., sherry	35.00
Bowl, 10", deep salad	70.00		Stem, 3½ oz., cocktail	18.00
Bowl, 12", crimped	75.00		Stem, 3½ oz., wine	27.50
Bowl, 12½" centerpiece, flared	75.00		Stem, 4 oz., claret	37.50
Bowl, 13", centerpiece	75.00		Stem, 4½ oz., parfait	38.00
Candlestick, double branch	50.00		Stem, 5½ oz., sherbet/champagne	16.00
Celery, 10½", oblong	40.00		Stem, 9 oz., water	22.00
Creamer	20.00		Sugar	20.00
Mayonnaise, liner and ladle	45.00		Table bell	85.00
Pitcher	495.00		Tumbler, 4½ oz., oyster cocktail	20.00
Plate, 6", sherbet	8.00		Tumbler, 5 oz., ftd., juice	16.00
Plate, 8", luncheon	12.50		Tumbler, 8 oz., ftd., water	17.50
Plate, 13½", turned-up edge, lily	45.00		Tumbler, 10½ oz., ftd., ice tea	22.50
Plate, 14", sandwich	45.00		Vase, 6", bud	25.00
Relish, 6½", 3 pt.	35.00		Vase, 8", bud	35.00
Relish, 12½", 3 pt.	65.00		Vase, 10", bud	45.00

JUNGLE ASSORTMENT, Satin Decoration #14 Parrot, Tiffin Glass Company, et. al.
c. 1922 – 34

Colors: Green, pink and crystal satin; various flashed colors

Jungle Assortment is a Tiffin pattern that only a few collectors have paid much attention to over the years. Cathy started accumulating pieces for display in Florida until she found enough to photograph for the book. Over the years, I kept running into reasonably priced pieces, so we accumulated quite a variety. I prefer the flashed colors to the satinized, but each treatment has evidence of problems keeping those parrots from flying off their perches. Actually, the painted birds just wore off with use, but "flying off" seems more apropos. This is one pattern where you might like to pick up some slightly worn pieces until mint condition ones appear. You will not find these birds every day!

All of the items pictured in the photo below were picked up in a three-month period after we first photographed the larger shot. Since then, we have been limited to finding that cute little lamp.

We have found three styles of candles, and I wonder how many colors were produced in each type. You will certainly find additional items not listed, so let me know what you discover.

Basket, 6", #151	95.00
Bonbon & cover, 5½" high ftd., #330	60.00
Bonbon and cover, 5", low ftd., #330	60.00
Bowl, centerpiece, #320	55.00
Candle, hdld., #330	37.50
Candle, hdld. tall, octagonal base	45.00
Candle, low, #10	25.00
Candy and cover, ftd., #15179	75.00
Candy box & cover, flat, #329	65.00
Candy jar and cover, ftd., cone, #330	75.00
Cologne bottle, #5722	125.00
Decanter & stopper	125.00
Jug and cover, 2 quart, #127	210.00
Lamp	100.00
Marmalade & cover, 2 hdld., #330	45.00
Night cap set, #6712	100.00
Puff box and cover, hexagonal	95.00
Shaker, ftd., #6205	35.00
Smoking set, 3 pc., #188	40.00
Tumbler, 12 oz., #444	32.00
Vase, 6", 2 hdld., #151	45.00

Vase, 7" ftd., flair from base, #330	65.00
Vase, 7" ftd., flair rim, #151	65.00
Vase, 7" sweet pea, #151	75.00
Vase, wall, #320	75.00

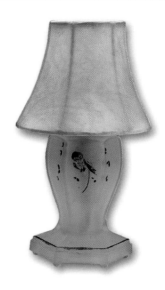

This pattern was produced primarily in crystal; however, some pieces with ruby stain have surfaced. It is generally marked with the Heisey logo, consisting of an H enclosed in a diamond. Because of its pattern number (1776), it became extremely popular with collectors in 1976, during the Bicentennial and has remained desirable since that time.

Bottle, hdld., molasses, 13 oz.	185.00
Bottle, hdld., oil, 2 oz.	140.00
Bottle, hdld., oil, 4 oz.	130.00
Bottle, hdld., oil, 6 oz.	130.00
Bottle, water	175.00
Bowl, 4½", deep	30.00
Bowl, 5", deep	35.00
Bowl, 5", flared	35.00
Bowl, 5", hdld.	38.00
Bowl, 5", crimped	35.00
Bowl, 6", shallow	35.00
Bowl, 7", deep, straight sided	45.00
Bowl, 7", deep, flared	45.00
Bowl, 8", flared	65.00
Bowl, 9", shallow	65.00
Bowl, 10", shallow	70.00
Bowl, 11", shallow	70.00
Bowl, 12", punch and stand	225.00
Butter and cover, domed	150.00
Cake plate, 9", ftd.	225.00
Celery, tall	90.00
Celery tray, 12"	65.00
Comport, deep ftd. jelly, 5"	110.00
Comport, shallow ftd. jelly, 5½"	110.00
Comport, deep or shallow, 8", ftd.	185.00
Comport, deep or shallow, 9", ftd.	190.00
Comport, deep or shallow, 10", ftd.	200.00
Creamer, tall	90.00
Creamer, hotel	70.00
Cup, punch, 3 oz.	26.00

Cup, punch, 3½ oz.	26.00
Mug, hdld., 8 oz.	175.00
Mustard and cover	235.00
Pickle jar and cover	195.00
Pickle tray	65.00
Pitcher, ½ gallon	300.00
Plate, 5½"	30.00
Plate, 6"	35.00
Plate, 8", fruit	55.00
Shaker, salt & pepper, 3 styles, pr.	180.00
Shaker, sugar	145.00
Spoon tray	60.00
Spooner, tall	65.00
Stem, egg cup, 9½ oz.	75.00
Stem, goblet, 9 oz.	190.00
Stem, champagne, 6½ oz.	45.00
Stem, sherbet, 6 oz.	40.00
Stem, sherbet, 5½ oz., straight sided or scalloped	40.00
Stem, claret, 5 oz.	165.00
Stem, sherbet, 4½ oz., scalloped	40.00
Stem, sherbet, 3½ oz., scalloped	40.00
Stem, burgundy, 3 oz.	150.00
Stem, wine, 2 oz.	175.00
Stem, cordial, 1¼ oz.	300.00
Sugar and cover, tall	95.00
Sugar, hotel (no cover)	70.00
Toothpick	425.00
Tumbler, 8 oz.	65.00

Colors: Topaz yellow, Azure blue, some green

Kashmir was not as expansively distributed as other Fostoria patterns, so collecting it will take longer unless you luckily live in one of those areas where it was sold. Blue Kashmir would be the Fostoria pattern to collect if you like that color. Other Azure Fostoria etched patterns have thousands of collectors searching for them; but few collectors pay attention to Kashmir. Of course finding blue Kashmir is the major problem.

I found Kashmir more in the Midwest than anywhere else; you can see from my pictures how well green Kashmir has been eluding me; and I have been looking for it! Supposedly there are some 6", 7", and 8" plates to be had along with the two styles of cups and saucers.

Unfortunately, what little Kashmir offered for sale does not immediately disappear, as do some of the other Fostoria patterns. The right collector has to come along; and since there are so few Kashmir admirers, it frequently takes a while to find that collector. Demand always wins over scarcity.

I would sincerely recommend you look at this pattern. While everyone else is fighting over the price on June and Versailles, you might gather a beautiful Kashmir set for a lot less investment. I run across settings of yellow for sale. You could complete a set of yellow Kashmir more economically than any other etched, yellow Fostoria pattern.

The stemware and tumbler line is #5099, which is the same line on which Trojan is found. This is the "cascading waterfall" stem.

Both styles of after dinner cups are shown in the picture of blue. The square #2419 (Mayfair blank) saucer set is more difficult to find than the round; but I have only found that in green, though it was supposedly made in Azure and Topaz.

	Yellow Green	Blue
Ashtray	25.00	30.00
Bowl, cream soup	22.00	30.00
Bowl, finger	15.00	40.00
Bowl, 5", fruit	13.00	25.00
Bowl, 6", cereal	30.00	35.00
Bowl, 7", soup	35.00	95.00
Bowl, 8½", pickle	20.00	30.00
Bowl, 9", baker	37.50	85.00
Bowl, 10", 2 hdld.	40.00	65.00
Bowl, 12", centerpiece	40.00	50.00
Candlestick, 2"	15.00	17.50
Candlestick, 3"	20.00	25.00
Candlestick, 5"	22.50	27.50
Candlestick, 9½"	40.00	60.00
Candy, w/cover	90.00	165.00
Cheese and cracker set	65.00	85.00
Comport, 6"	35.00	45.00
Creamer, ftd.	17.50	20.00
Cup	15.00	20.00
Cup, after dinner, flat	40.00	
Cup, after dinner, ftd.	40.00	55.00
Grapefruit	60.00	
Grapefruit liner	50.00	
Ice bucket	95.00	110.00
Oil, ftd.	295.00	495.00
Pitcher, ftd.	325.00	425.00
Plate, 6", bread & butter	5.00	6.00
Plate, 7", salad, rnd.	6.00	7.00
Plate, 7", salad, sq.	6.00	7.00
Plate, 8", salad	8.00	10.00
Plate, 9", luncheon	9.00	15.00

	Yellow Green	Blue
Plate, 10", dinner	45.00	70.00
Plate, 10", grill	35.00	55.00
Plate, cake, 10"	35.00	
Salt & pepper, pr.	120.00	175.00
Sandwich, center hdld.	35.00	40.00
Sauce boat, w/liner	125.00	165.00
Saucer, rnd.	5.00	10.00
Saucer, after dinner, sq.	8.00	
Saucer, after dinner, rnd.	8.00	15.00
Stem, ¾ oz., cordial	85.00	115.00
Stem, 2½ oz., ftd.	30.00	45.00
Stem, 2 oz., ftd., whiskey	30.00	50.00
Stem, 2½ oz., wine	32.00	60.00
Stem, 3 oz., cocktail	22.00	25.00
Stem, 3½ oz., ftd., cocktail	22.00	25.00
Stem, 4 oz., claret	35.00	55.00
Stem, 4½ oz., oyster cocktail	16.00	18.00
Stem, 5½ oz., parfait	30.00	40.00
Stem, 5 oz., ftd., juice	15.00	25.00
Stem, 5 oz., low sherbet	13.00	20.00
Stem, 6 oz., high sherbet	17.50	30.00
Stem, 9 oz., water	20.00	35.00
Sugar, ftd.	15.00	20.00
Sugar lid	50.00	85.00
Tumbler, 10 oz., ftd., water	22.00	35.00
Tumbler, 11 oz.	22.50	
Tumbler, 12 oz., ftd.	25.00	35.00
Tumbler, 13 oz., ftd., tea	25.00	
Tumbler, 16 oz., ftd., tea	35.00	
Vase, 8"	100.00	175.00

Note: See stemware identification on page 87.

Colors: crystal, Topaz/Gold Tint (every piece of pattern); at least 12 pieces of Regal Blue, Empire Green, Burgundy; 6 pieces of Ruby & Silver Mist; some amber, green, Wisteria, and rose

Crystal Lafayette is the mould line used for many of Fostoria's later etchings, with Navarre being the most recognized. Colored pieces of Lafayette are collected for themselves. The most favored color is Wisteria, but yellow can also be gathered into a large set. I finally found some Regal blue (cobalt) and will show it next time. You might blend some of the colors with crystal in order to achieve a larger set.

	Crystal/Amber	Rose/Green/Topaz	Wisteria	Regal Blue	Burgundy	Empire Green
Almond, indiv.	12.00	15.00	25.00			
Bonbon, 5", 2 hdld.	15.00	22.50	40.00	35.00	30.00	33.00
Bowl, 4½", sweetmeat	18.00	22.50	40.00	35.00	35.00	33.00
Bowl, cream soup	22.50	35.00	85.00			
Bowl, 5", fruit		22.50	32.50			
Bowl, 6", cereal	20.00	25.00	45.00			
Bowl, 6½", olive	18.00	25.00	50.00			
Bowl, 6½", 2-pt. relish	22.50	30.00	55.00	55.00	45.00	45.00
Ruby 50.00; Silver Mist 25.00						
Bowl, 6½", oval sauce	25.00	35.00	125.00	55.00	50.00	45.00
Ruby 65.00; Silver Mist 27.50						
Bowl, 7", "D" cupped	30.00	40.00	135.00			
Bowl, 7½", 3-pt. relish	25.00	35.00	110.00	55.00	45.00	45.00
Ruby 55.00; Silver Mist 30.00						
Bowl, 8", nappy	30.00	40.00	85.00			
Bowl, 8½", pickle	18.00	27.50	55.00			
Bowl, 10", oval baker	35.00		75.00	75.00		
Bowl, 10", "B," flair	35.00	40.00				
Bowl, 12", salad, flair	38.00	45.00	155.00			
Cake, 10½", oval, 2 hdld.	40.00	45.00		60.00	60.00	60.00
Celery, 11½"	30.00	35.00	135.00			
Creamer, 4½", ftd.	15.00	25.00	55.00	40.00	40.00	40.00
Cup	15.00	18.00	22.50	35.00	35.00	35.00
Cup, demi	17.50	45.00	75.00			
Tray, 5", 2-hdld., lemon	17.50	22.50	40.00	35.00	30.00	33.00
Tray, 8½", oval, 2-hdld.	22.50	30.00	155.00	55.00	45.00	45.00
Ruby 55.00; Silver Mist 25.00						
Mayonnaise, 6½", 2 pt.	24.00	30.00	155.00	55.00	55.00	55.00
Ruby 55.00; Silver Mist 30.00						
Plate, 6"	8.00	12.00	14.00			
Plate, 7¼"	8.00	12.00	20.00			
Plate, 8½"	10.00	15.00	22.50			
Plate, 9½"	22.50	27.50	50.00			
Plate, 10¼"	35.00	45.00	95.00			
Plate, 13", torte	40.00	50.00	125.00	115.00	95.00	110.00
Ruby 110.00; Silver Mist 40.00						
Platter, 12"	40.00	52.50	115.00			
Platter, 15"	50.00	65.00				
Saucer	4.00	6.00	5.00	8.00	8.00	6.00
Saucer, demi	8.00	15.00	20.00			
Sugar, 3⅝", ftd.	15.00	25.00	50.00	40.00	40.00	40.00
Vase, 7", rim ft., flair	45.00	60.00				

Colors: crystal; rare in black and amber

Lariat prices have remained rather steady; but the rarer pieces sell well since there are many collectors looking for seldom-found items. Conversely, the horse head candy has softened in price since more have been found than there are collectors willing to pay the former high price. Common Lariat pieces are still available; you can ascertain scarce pieces by their prices in my listing. The cutting most often seen on Lariat is Moonglo. Many non-Lariat collectors adore this cut; strangely, few Lariat collectors try to rope it! We have tried to entice you with the abundance of pieces shown. Enjoy! The ads that I have shown in the past are becoming collectible themselves. Watch for them in women's magazines of the 1940s and 1950s.

Amber and black pieces pictured are rarely seen; note that in your travels in case you should find a piece or two in those colors.

	Crystal
Ashtray, 4"	15.00
Basket, 7½", bonbon	100.00
Basket, 8½", ftd.	165.00
Basket, 10", ftd.	195.00
Bowl, 2 hdld., cream soup	50.00
Bowl, 7 quart, punch	130.00
Bowl, 4", nut, individual	32.00
Bowl, 7", 2 pt., mayonnaise	24.00
Bowl, 7", nappy	20.00
Bowl, 8", flat, nougat	24.00
Bowl, 9½", camellia	28.00
Bowl, 10", hdld., celery	35.00
Bowl, 10½", 2 hdld., salad	38.00
Bowl, 10½", salad	40.00
Bowl, 11", 2 hdld., oblong, relish	30.00
Bowl, 12", floral or fruit	40.00
Bowl, 13", celery	50.00
Bowl, 13", gardenia	35.00
Bowl, 13", oval, floral	35.00
Candlestick, 1-lite, individual	30.00
Candlestick, 2-lite	40.00
Candlestick, 3-lite	45.00
Candy box, w/cover, caramel	75.00
Candy, w/cover, 7"	90.00
Candy, w/cover, 8", w/horse head finial (rare)	1,400.00
Cheese, 5", ftd., w/cover	50.00
Cheese dish, w/cover, 8"	60.00
Cigarette box	55.00
Coaster, 4"	12.00
Cologne	85.00
Compote, 10", w/cover	100.00
Creamer	20.00

	Crystal
Creamer & sugar, w/tray, indiv.	45.00
Cup	20.00
Cup, punch	8.00
Ice tub	75.00
Jar, w/cover, 12", urn	175.00
Lamp & globe, 7", black-out	120.00
Lamp & globe, 8", candle, hdld.	95.00
Mayonnaise, 5" bowl, 7" plate w/ladle set	60.00
Oil bottle, 4 oz., hdld., w/#133 stopper	180.00
Oil bottle, 6 oz., oval	85.00
Plate, 6", finger bowl liner	8.00
Plate, 7", salad	14.00
Plate, 8", salad	22.00
Plate, 10½", dinner	125.00
Plate, 11", cookie	35.00
Plate, 12", demi-torte, rolled edge	40.00
Plate, 13", deviled egg, round	290.00
Plate, 14", 2 hdld., sandwich	50.00
Plate, 15", deviled egg, oval	290.00
Plate, 21", buffet	70.00
Platter, 15", oval	60.00
Salt & pepper, pr.	200.00
Saucer	5.00
Stem, 1 oz., cordial, double loop	250.00
Stem, 1 oz., cordial blown, single loop	150.00
Stem, 2½ oz., wine, blown	25.00
Stem, 3½ oz., cocktail, pressed	20.00
Stem, 3½ oz., cocktail, blown	20.00
Stem, 3½ oz., wine, pressed	24.00
Stem, 4 oz., claret, blown	28.00
Stem, 4¼ oz., oyster cocktail or fruit	18.00
Stem, 4½ oz., oyster cocktail, blown	18.00
Stem, 5½ oz., sherbet/saucer champagne, blown	17.00
Stem, 6 oz., low sherbet	10.00
Stem, 6 oz., sherbet/saucer champagne, pressed	17.00
Stem, 9 oz., pressed	22.00
Stem, 10 oz., blown	22.00
Sugar	20.00
Tray, rnd., center hdld., w/ball finial	165.00
Tray for sugar & creamer, 8", 2 hdld.	24.00
Tumbler, 5 oz., ftd., juice	22.00
Tumbler, 5 oz., ftd., juice, blown	22.00
Tumbler, 12 oz., ftd., ice tea	28.00
Tumbler, 12 oz., ftd., ice tea, blown	28.00
Vase, 7", ftd., fan	30.00
Vase, swung	135.00

CORDIAL, YET CAREFREE··· *that's Heisey* *Lariat*

Lariat carries an air of matchless charm, expressed in its lighthearted loop design. Cordial, yet carefree, it will be esteemed by you as highly as any of your treasures. Rare as the western air, this hand-cast crystal gaily blends your own good taste with the trend that is today. Your Heisey dealer will be pleased to show you the complete selection of LARIAT stemware and table accessories.

Lariat is one of several patterns pictured in "CHOOSING YOUR CRYSTAL PATTERN," an informal, streamlined guide to proper crystal, china and silver. Send 10c to Department H8, A. H. HEISEY & CO., NEWARK, OHIO.

THE FINEST IN GLASSWARE, MADE IN AMERICA BY HAND

Color: crystal

A question I have been asked more often than any other is "Where can I find more of this beautiful pattern?" Actually, we just unpacked some glassware at a new antique mall this afternoon and there was a cordial sitting in the glass case next to ours. It does appear occasionally; so keep a sharp eye open.

Duncan's Lily of the Valley is a pattern that even non-collectors appreciate. I first became aware of it from seeing a cordial when I began collecting them in the mid-1970s. I had to be told that it was Lily of the Valley, but bought it for my cordial collection without hesitation because of its wonderful carved stem. Stemware has the Lily of the Valley cut into the stem itself, but the bowls atop of the stem are found with or without the cutting. The cutting on the bowl is the icing on the cake for me. Duncan's designation for this stem was D-4 and the cut variety was DC-4. Prices below are for cut (DC-4) bowl items; deduct about a third (or more) for plain bowl stems. Once you see this pattern, you will understand why collectors want the cut version.

Canterbury #115 and Pall Mall #30 blanks were used for this cutting. The mayonnaise pictured is #30 and the bowl and plate are #115. I have not seen a cup or saucer in this cut. Have you?

	Crystal		Crystal
Ashtray, 3"	25.00	Mayonnaise liner	15.00
Ashtray, 6"	35.00	Plate, 8"	30.00
Bowl, 12"	55.00	Plate, 9"	45.00
Candlestick, double	55.00	Relish, 3-part	25.00
Candy, w/lid	85.00	Stem, cocktail	25.00
Celery, 10½"	35.00	Stem, cordial	80.00
Cheese and cracker	75.00	Stem, high sherbet	25.00
Creamer	25.00	Stem, water goblet	40.00
Mayonnaise	30.00	Stem, wine	42.00
Mayonnaise ladle	8.00	Sugar	25.00

Co., c. 1934

Colors: black, crystal, green, pink

I have dubbed this New Martinsville "coat of arms style" etch "Lions." I almost called it "Lions Rampant"; but not being a heraldry expert, I was not quite sure they were in the correct attitude to be so labeled." I will be more than happy to convert to the original name if one can be determined. I can already tell you, hunting "Lions" will be a challenge. Nearly all "Lions" etch is found on New Martinsville's Line #34 as pictured in color below. The only crystal items shown are on Line #37 known as "Moondrops" to collectors. I have not seen this etch on colored pieces of Line #37 or crystal pieces of Line #34, but it would not be startling if those appear.

You can round up a luncheon set in color, but adding serving pieces may be another matter. Note the pink candy with missing lid. I buy whatever I can find when I am adding new patterns to a book. Maybe one of you have a spare lid that will fit my candy bottom.

I am positive that additional pieces not in the list are available; so let me know what else you have seen.

	Crystal	Pink/Green	Black		Crystal	Pink/Green	Black
Candleholder, #37	25.00			Cup		25.00	35.00
Candlestick, #34		35.00		Plate, 8"		20.00	30.00
Candy w/lid		60.00	95.00	Plate, 12"		30.00	40.00
Center handle server		45.00		Saucer		7.50	10.00
Creamer, #34		25.00	35.00	Sugar, #34		25.00	35.00
Creamer, #37	15.00			Sugar, #37	15.00		

Although it was produced primarily in crystal, it may be found with gold trim or ruby flashing and there have been a few pieces surface in cobalt. The piece in cobalt that I have seen is a small tray, perhaps a pickle tray, that rests on a metal (chrome) base. There seems to be an abundance of this pattern available and one could put a collection together rather quickly.

Bottle, bitters	75.00	Plate, 5"	8.00
Bottle, molasses, hdld.	85.00	Plate, 6"	9.00
Bottle, oil, hdld.	40.00	Plate, 7"	9.00
Bottle, water	65.00	Plate, 8"	20.00
Bowl, berry, 4"	20.00	Salt & pepper	55.00
Bowl, shallow, 6"	24.00	Salt, open, individual	12.00
Bowl, round, 8"	55.00	Spooner, tall	65.00
Bowl, fruit, 10"	75.00	Spooner, individual	50.00
Bowl, punch, 13½", and stand	165.00	Stem, goblet	45.00
Box, powder and cover	165.00	Stem, claret	50.00
Butter and cover, domed	75.00	Stem, champagne/sherbet, 2 styles	22.00
Butter and cover, imdividual	165.00	Stem, cocktail	24.00
Cake plate, ftd.	110.00	Stem, wine	28.00
Celery, tall	65.00	Stem, sherry, straight sided and flared	35.00
Cracker jar and cover, tall	145.00	Stem, cordial	60.00
Creamer, regular	35.00	Sugar and cover, regular	50.00
Creamer, individual	100.00	Sugar and cover, individual	150.00
Cup, punch	10.00	Toothpick	45.00
Egg cup, ftd.	45.00	Tumbler, water	24.00
Jug, honey, individual	65.00	Tumbler, juice	20.00
Mustard and cover	75.00	Tumbler, bar (2 oz.)	20.00
Pitcher, straight sided	150.00	Vase, ball, individual, 1½"	165.00
Pitcher, bulbous	175.00	Vase, ball, 4"	40.00
Pitcher, syrup, individual	75.00	Vase, tall, footed, 10"	55.00
Plate, 3", butter	26.00		

Stemline #7606 (shown) c. 1920: Stemline #3750 (hexagon stem) c. 1940s

Colors: amethyst w/gold, crystal, Emerald green

Cambridge's Marjorie was rechristened Fuchsia in the 1930s; do not confuse it with Tiffin's or Fostoria's Fuchsia. The #7606 stems were advertised in the 1927 Sears catalog.

	Crystal
Comport, #4011	45.00
Comport, 5", #4004	35.00
Comport, 5", jelly (sherbet), #2090	35.00
Cream, flat, curved in side, #1917/10	75.00
Cream, flat, straight side, #1917/18	75.00
Cup	30.00
Decanter, 28 oz., cut stop, #17	195.00
Decanter, 28 oz. #7606	175.00
Finger bowl, #7606	40.00
Grapefruit w/liner inside, #7606	85.00
Jug, 30 oz. #104	165.00
Jug w/cover, 30 oz., #106	225.00
Jug, 3 pint, #93	155.00
Jug, 3½ pint, #108 short, flair bottom	195.00
Jug, 3½ pint, rim bottom, bulbous, #111	195.00
Jug, 54 oz., flat bottom, #51	225.00
Jug w/cover, 66 oz., #106	250.00
Jug, 4 pint, tall, flat bottom, #110	235.00
Jug, guest room 38 oz. w/tumbler fitting inside, #103	335.00
Marmalade & cover, #145	85.00
Nappie, 4", #4111	20.00
Nappie, 4" ftd., #5000	22.50
Nappie, 8", #4111	60.00
Nappie, 8" ftd., #5000	65.00
Night bottle, 20 oz. w/tumbler, #4002	300.00
Oil w/hex cone cut stop, #32	135.00
Plate, 7", finger bowl liner or salad, #7606	15.00
Plate, finger bowl liner, #7606	15.00

	Crystal
Stem, ⅞ oz., cordial, #7606	110.00
Stem, 1 oz., cordial, #3750	110.00
Stem, 2½ oz., wine, #7606	65.00
Stem, 2 oz., creme de menthe, #7606	100.00
Stem, 3 oz., cocktail, #7606	25.00
Stem, 3 oz., wine, #3750	35.00
Stem, 3½ oz., cocktail, #3750	25.00
Stem, 4½ oz., claret, #3750	55.00
Stem, 4½ oz., claret, #7606	55.00
Stem, 5½ oz., cafe parfait, #7606	45.00
Stem, 6 oz., low sherbet, #3750	15.00
Stem, 6 oz., low fruit/sherbet, #7606	15.00
Stem, 6 oz., high sherbet, #3750	18.00
Stem, 6 oz., high sherbet, #7606	18.00
Stem, 10 oz., water, #3750	22.00
Stem, 10 oz., water, #7606	22.00
Sugar, flat, curved in side, #1917/10	75.00
Sugar, flat, straight side, #1917/18	75.00
Syrup & cover, 8 oz., #106	150.00
Tumbler, #8851	20.00
Tumbler, 1½ oz. whiskey, #7606	25.00
Tumbler, 5 oz., #8858	15.00
Tumbler, 5 oz., #7606	15.00
Tumbler, 5 oz. ftd., #3750	18.00
Tumbler, 8 oz., #7606	20.00
Tumbler, 9 oz., #8858	20.00
Tumbler, 10 oz., ftd. & hdld., #7606	35.00
Tumbler, 10 oz., hdld. & ftd., #8023	25.00
Tumbler, 10 oz., table, #7606	25.00
Tumbler, 10 oz., ftd., #3750	25.00
Tumbler, 12 oz., #8858	22.00
Tumbler, 12 oz., ftd., #3750	25.00
Tumbler, 12 oz., tea, #7606	22.00
Tumbler, 12 oz., hdld., #8858	25.00

Glass Co, 1926 – 1944

Colors: crystal and some blue

New Martinsville's Meadow Wreath is prevalently found etched on Radiance Line #42, but there are a few exceptions. The #4457 Teardrop two-light candlestick in the center of the picture is Janice blank, a contemporary of Radiance. The Meadow Wreath etch sometimes irritates Radiance collectors searching for light blue. I see more Meadow Wreath etched candles than I do ones without the etch. If a collector were willing to mix the etched Meadow Wreath with unetched wares, a wider range of pieces would be opened.

There is an abundance of bowls and serving pieces available in Meadow Wreath, but essential luncheon items are absent except for the omnipresent sugars and creamers. I would propose using these serving items to complement some of those patterns where serving items are almost nonexistent. Blending color is already a trend; so blending patterns does not seem such a long stretch in this day of ever more expensive and hard to find glassware.

	Crystal
Bowl, 7", 2 pt. relish, #4223/26	18.00
Bowl, 8", 3 pt. relish, #4228/26	32.50
Bowl, 10", comport, #4218/26	35.00
Bowl, 10", crimped, #4220/26	40.00
Bowl, 10", oval celery, #42/26	35.00
Bowl, 10", flat, flared	35.00
Bowl, 11", crimped, ftd. #4266/26	40.00
Bowl, 11", ftd., flared, #4265/26	40.00
Bowl, 12", crimped, flat, #4212	45.00
Bowl, 12", flat, flared, deep, #42/26	47.50
Bowl, 12", flat, flared, #4213/26	47.50
Bowl, 13", crimped, flat	50.00
Bowl, 5 qt., punch, #4221/26	135.00

	Crystal
Candle, 2 light, rnd. ft.	42.50
Candy box (3 pt.) & cover, #42/26	67.50
Cheese & cracker, 11", #42/26	50.00
Creamer, ftd., tab hdld., #42/26	15.00
Cup, 4 oz., punch, tab hdld.	9.00
Ladle, punch, #4226	55.00
Mayonnaise set, liner & ladle, #42/26	45.00
Plate, 11"	35.00
Plate, 14", #42/26	45.00
Salver, 12", ftd., #42/26	40.00
Sugar, ftd., tab hdld., #42/26	15.00
Tray, oval for sugar & creamer, #42/26	15.00
Vase, 10", crimped, #4232/26	55.00
Vase, 10", flared, #42/26	50.00

Colors: crystal

The manufacture of Minuet began in 1939 making it a precarious case for moving it into *Collectible Glassware from the 40s, 50s, and 60s.* This decision will be determined by how many new patterns I can fit into the allotted pages of the books. There are 11 new patterns in this book after adding 22 last book. Those 33 patterns have really pushed the limits to what we can put into this book.

Minuet is one Heisey pattern where stable prices have prevailed, although a few price adjustments have been noted for basic pieces like dinner plates, creamer, and sugars. By the way, dinner plates are listed as service plates in Heisey catalogs. That was generally the case in Cambridge catalogs, also.

Minuet stemware is copious as is the case in most Heisey patterns, but most tumblers are elusive. As with many other stemware lines, Minuet was purchased to go with china settings. Serving pieces were rarely bought since china was mostly used for serving. Only the three-part relish and the three-footed bowl seem to be found with regularity. You will meet devoted competition looking to purchase this pattern.

	Crystal
Bell, dinner, #3408	75.00
Bowl, finger, #3309	50.00
Bowl, 6", ftd., dolphin, mint	45.00
Bowl, 6", ftd., 2 hdld., jelly	30.00
Bowl, 6½", salad dressings	35.00
Bowl, 7", salad dressings	40.00
Bowl, 7", triplex, relish	60.00
Bowl, 7½", sauce, ftd.	70.00
Bowl, 9½", 3 pt., "5 o'clock," relish	70.00
Bowl, 10", salad, #1511 Toujours	65.00
Bowl, 11", 3 pt., "5 o'clock," relish	80.00
Bowl, 11", ftd., dolphin, floral	120.00
Bowl, 12", oval, floral, #1511 Toujours	65.00
Bowl, 12", oval, #1514	65.00
Bowl, 13", floral, #1511 Toujours	60.00
Bowl, 13", pickle & olive	45.00
Bowl, 13½", shallow salad	75.00
Candelabrum, 1-lite, w/prisms	110.00
Candelabrum, 2-lite, bobeche & prisms	175.00
Candlestick, 1-lite, #112	35.00
Candlestick, 2-lite, #1511 Toujours	150.00
Candlestick, 3-lite, #142 Cascade	90.00
Candlestick, 5", 2-lite, #134 Trident	60.00
Centerpiece vase & prisms, #1511 Toujours	200.00
Cocktail icer, w/liner, #3304 Universal	125.00
Comport, 5½", #5010	40.00
Comport, 7½", #1511 Toujours	60.00
Creamer, #1511 Toujours	60.00
Creamer, dolphin ft.	42.50
Creamer, indiv., #1509 Queen Ann	37.50
Creamer, indiv., #1511 Toujours	70.00

	Crystal
Cup	30.00
Ice bucket, dolphin ft.	160.00
Marmalade, w/cover, #1511 Toujours (apple shape)	175.00
Mayonnaise, 5½", dolphin ft.	60.00
Mayonnaise, ftd., #1511 Toujours	75.00
Pitcher, 73 oz., #4164	450.00
Plate, 7", mayonnaise liner	10.00
Plate, 7", salad	18.00
Plate, 7", salad, #1511 Toujours	15.00
Plate, 8", luncheon	30.00
Plate, 8", luncheon, #1511 Toujours	25.00
Plate, 10½", service	190.00
Plate, 12", rnd., 2 hdld., sandwich	150.00

	Crystal
Plate, 13", floral, salver, #1511 Toujours	60.00
Plate, 14", torte, #1511 Toujours	60.00
Plate, 15", sandwich, #1511 Toujours	65.00
Plate, 16", snack rack, w/#1477 center	80.00
Salt & pepper, pr. (#10)	75.00
Saucer	10.00
Stem, #5010, Symphone, 1 oz., cordial	135.00
Stem, #5010, 2½ oz., wine	50.00
Stem, #5010, 3½ oz., cocktail	35.00
Stem, #5010, 4 oz., claret	40.00
Stem, #5010, 4½ oz., oyster cocktail	25.00
Stem, #5010, 6 oz., saucer champagne	25.00
Stem, #5010, 6 oz., sherbet	25.00
Stem, #5010, 9 oz., water	35.00
Sugar, indiv., #1511 Toujours	70.00
Sugar, indiv., #1509 Queen Ann	37.50
Sugar, dolphin ftd., #1509 Queen Ann	40.00

	Crystal
Sugar, #1511 Toujours	60.00
Tray, 12", celery, #1511 Toujours	50.00
Tray, 15", social hour	90.00
Tray for indiv. sugar & creamer	30.00
Tumbler, #5010, 5 oz., fruit juice	34.00
Tumbler, #5010, 9 oz., low ftd., water	35.00
Tumbler, #5010, 12 oz., tea	60.00
Tumbler, #2351, 12 oz., tea	60.00
Vase, 5", #5013	50.00
Vase, 5½", ftd., #1511 Toujours	95.00
Vase, 6", urn, #5012	75.00
Vase, 7½", urn, #5012	90.00
Vase, 8", #4196	95.00
Vase, 9", urn, #5012	110.00
Vase, 10", #4192	110.00
Vase, 10", #4192, Saturn optic	115.00

Colors: amber, amethyst, black, blue, crystal, green, pink, lilac, crystal stems w/color bowls

Joseph Balda designed Morgan in 1920. He was better known for his designs made for Heisey. A family named Morgan allegedly adopted Morgan for use in the West Virginia governor's mansion. Thus, the very masculine pattern name attached to this swinging, fairy design.

Morgan has attracted a multitude of followers. Cathy found it intriguing about 15 years ago and began acquiring anything she could find. Since most dealers did not know what it was, very little was offered for sale at shows or markets. After introducing it in my book, many new collectors began searching for this sparsely distributed pattern. It has been even more difficult to find additional pieces to include in the book. Page 137 shows all the colors we have located except for green and black. We have seen very little of the lilac, represented by a dinner plate and high sherbet in the photo, although a large set of lilac was marketed a few years ago. This was before the days of the Internet and I was never able to trace the West Virginia buyer.

There are even fewer pieces of amber being found, but there are fewer collectors buying it. Pieces of black being found include a candy, 6" bonbon, and a bud vase with a gold encrusted fairy. Newly pictured items in pink are the ice bucket, diamond-shaped divided candy, an octagonal plate, and a blown candy or powder jar. The pattern is found only on the lid of the covered items; so, do not fret too much about condition of the bottom. Other bottoms will turn up as pieces without etchings. Cups and saucers in color are the items missing from most collections of this Central Glass Works pattern. I have only heard of crystal and pink cup and saucers, with crystal leading the way.

The gold-decorated bud vase shown is dramatic against its dark amethyst background. We have now found this golden design on a black bud vase. Does anyone have a gold decorated piece other than a bud vase?

Stemware has become more difficult to find, with blue and lilac stems commanding some royal prices. Internet auctions have increased the demand for Morgan tremendously. Note that there are three styles of stemware. The beaded stems seem to come in solid colors of crystal, pink, or green. The "wafer" stem is found all pink, green stems with crystal tops, and crystal stems with blue tops. All lilac stems are solid lilac, but the bowls are shaped differently than other colors. This is the same mould line as "Balda" shown on page 17.

If you have knowledge of additional pieces, please let me know.

	*All Colors		*All Colors
Bonbon, 6", two hdld.	65.00	Server, 11", octagonal, flat, center hdld.	100.00
Bonbon, 9", two hdld.	95.00	Stem, 3¼", sherbet	35.00
Bowl, 4¼", ftd., fruit	60.00	Stem, 4⅜", sherbet, beaded stem	40.00
Bowl, 10", console	100.00	Stem, 5⅛", cocktail, beaded stem	40.00
Bowl, 13", console	125.00	Stem, 5⅜", high, sherbet, beaded stem	45.00
Candlestick, 3"	75.00	Stem, 5⅞", high sherbet, straight stem	65.00
Candy, blown, pattern on top	595.00	Stem, 5⅞", wine	65.00
Candy w/lid, diamond shaped, 4 ftd.	495.00	Stem, 7¼", 10 oz., water	75.00
Cheese & cracker	150.00	Stem, 8¼", water	75.00
Comport, 6½" tall, 5" wide	75.00	Sugar, ftd.	75.00
Comport, 6½" tall, 6" wide	85.00	Tumbler, oyster cocktail	40.00
Creamer, ftd.	75.00	Tumbler, 2⅛", whiskey	100.00
Cup	150.00	Tumbler, 10 oz., flat water	40.00
Decanter, w/stopper	495.00	Tumbler, 4⅜", ftd. juice	40.00
Ice bucket, 4¾" x7½", 2 hdld.	650.00	Tumbler, 5⅜", ftd., 10 oz., water	40.00
Mayonnaise	75.00	Tumbler, 5¾", ftd., water	40.00
Mayonnaise liner	20.00	Tumbler, 5⅞", ftd., 12 oz., tea	65.00
Oil bottle	295.00	Vase, fan shaped	395.00
Pitcher	495.00	Vase, 8", drape optic	195.00
Plate, 6½", fruit bowl liner	15.00	Vase, 9⅞", straight w/flared top	395.00
Plate, 7¼", salad	25.00	**Vase, 10", bud	200.00
Plate, 8½", luncheon	35.00	Vase, 10", ribbed, flared top	395.00
Plate, 9¼", dinner	125.00	Vase, 10", ruffled top	595.00
Salt & pepper, pr.	100.00		
Saucer	25.00	* Crystal 10% to 20% lower.	
Server, 9½", octagonal, center hdld.	125.00	Blue, lilac 25% to 30% higher.	
Server, 10⅜", round, center hdld.	100.00	** Gold decorated $300.00.	

Colors: amber, crystal, Carmen, Royal Blue, Heatherbloom, Emerald green (light and dark); rare in Violet

Sets of Mt. Vernon can only be gathered in amber or crystal. You could obtain small luncheon sets in red, cobalt blue, or Heatherbloom; but only a few additional pieces are available in those colors. However, prices for any of those colors can double the prices listed for amber and crystal. Many collectors are combining their crystal Mt. Vernon with a spatter of color. That makes a more judicious investment in a set than buying only hard to find and expensive colored pieces that are rarely seen.

	Amber Crystal		Amber Crystal
Ashtray, 3½", #63	8.00	Bowl, 12½", flanged, rolled edge, #45	35.00
Ashtray, 4", #68	12.00	Bowl, 12½", flared, #121	35.00
Ashtray, 6" x 4½", oval, #71	12.00	Bowl, 12½", flared, #44	35.00
Bonbon, 7", ftd., #10	12.50	Bowl, 13", shallow, crimped, #116	35.00
Bottle, bitters, 2½ oz., #62	65.00	Box, 3", w/cover, round, #16	30.00
Bottle, 7 oz., sq., toilet, #18	75.00	Box, 4", w/cover, sq., #17	32.50
Bowl, finger, #23	10.00	Box, 4½", w/cover, ftd., round, #15	37.50
Bowl, 4½", ivy ball or rose, ftd., #12	27.50	Butter tub, w/cover, #73	65.00
Bowl, 5¼", fruit, #6	10.00	Cake stand, 10½" ftd., #150	35.00
Bowl, 6", cereal, #32	12.50	Candelabrum, 13½", #38	150.00
Bowl, 6", preserve, #76	12.00	Candlestick, 4", #130	10.00
Bowl, 6½", rose, #106	18.00	Candlestick, 5", 2-lite, #110	25.00
Bowl, 8", pickle, #65	17.50	Candlestick, 8", #35	27.50
Bowl, 8½", 4 pt. 2 hdld., sweetmeat, #105	32.00	Candy, w/cover, 1 lb., ftd., #9	85.00
Bowl, 10", 2 hdld., #39	20.00	Celery, 10½", #79	15.00
Bowl, 10½", deep, #43	30.00	Celery, 11", #98	17.50
Bowl, 10½", salad, #120	25.00	Celery, 12", #79	20.00
Bowl, 11", oval, 4 ftd., #136	27.50	Cigarette box, 6", w/cover, oval, #69	32.00
Bowl, 11", oval, #135	25.00	Cigarette holder, #66	15.00
Bowl, 11½", belled, #128	30.00	Coaster, 3", plain, #60	5.00
Bowl, 11½", shallow, #126	30.00	Coaster, 3", ribbed, #70	5.00
Bowl, 11½", shallow cupped, #61	30.00	Cocktail icer, 2 pc., #85	27.50
Bowl, 12", flanged, rolled edge, #129	32.50	Cologne, 2½ oz., w/stopper, #1340	45.00
Bowl, 12", oblong, crimped, #118	32.50	Comport, 4½", #33	12.00
Bowl, 12", rolled edge, crimped, #117	32.50	Comport, 5½", 2 hdld., #77	15.00

	Amber Crystal
Comport, 6", #34	15.00
Comport, 6½", #97	17.50
Comport, 6½", belled, #96	22.50
Comport, 7½" #11	25.00
Comport, 8", #81	25.00
Comport, 9", oval, 2 hdld., #100	35.00
Comport, 9½", #99	30.00
Creamer, ftd., #8	10.00
Creamer, indiv., #4	10.00
Creamer, #86	10.00
Cup, #7	6.50
Decanter, 11 oz., #47	60.00
Decanter, 40 oz., w/stopper, #52	85.00
Honey jar, w/cover (marmalade), #74	35.00
Ice bucket, w/tongs, #92	35.00
Lamp, 9" hurricane, #1607	85.00
Mayonnaise, divided, 2 spoons, #107	25.00
Mug, 14 oz., stein, #84	30.00
Mustard, w/cover, 2½ oz., #28	25.00
Pickle, 6", 1 hdld., #78	12.00
Pitcher, 50 oz., #90	90.00
Pitcher, 66 oz., #13	95.00
Pitcher, 80 oz., ball, #95	105.00
Pitcher, 86 oz., #91	125.00
Plate, finger bowl liner, #23	4.00
Plate, 6", bread & butter, #4	3.00
Plate, 6⅜", bread & butter, #19	4.00
Plate, 8½", salad, #5	7.00
Plate, 10½", dinner, #40	35.00
Plate, 11½", hdld., #37	20.00
Relish, 6", 2 pt., 2 hdld., #106	12.00
Relish, 8", 2 pt., hdld., #101	17.50
Relish, 8", 3 pt., 3 hdld., #103	20.00
Relish, 11", 3 part, #200	25.00
Relish, 12", 2 part, #80	30.00
Relish, 12", 5 part, #104	30.00
Salt, indiv., #24	7.00
Salt, oval, 2 hdld., #102	12.00

	Amber Crystal
Salt & pepper, pr., #28	22.50
Salt & pepper, pr., short, #88	20.00
Salt & pepper, tall, #89	25.00
Salt dip, #24	9.00
Sauce boat & ladle, tab hdld., #30-445	75.00
Saucer, #7	7.50
Stem, 3 oz., wine, #27	15.00
Stem, 3½ oz., cocktail, #26	9.00
Stem, 4 oz., oyster cocktail, #41	9.00
Stem, 4½ oz., claret, #25	13.50
Stem, 4½ oz., low sherbet, #42	7.50
Stem, 6½ oz., tall sherbet, #2	10.00
Stem, 10 oz., water, #1	15.00
Sugar, ftd., #8	10.00
Sugar, indiv., #4	12.00
Sugar, #86	10.00
Tray, for indiv., sugar & creamer, #4	10.00
Tumbler, 1 oz., ftd., cordial, #87	22.00
Tumbler, 2 oz., whiskey, #55	10.00
Tumbler, 3 oz., ftd., juice, #22	9.00
Tumbler, 5 oz., #56	12.00
Tumbler, 5 oz., ftd., #21	12.00
Tumbler, 7 oz., old-fashion, #57	15.00
Tumbler, 10 oz., ftd., water, #3	15.00
Tumbler, 10 oz., table, #51	12.00
Tumbler, 10 oz., tall, #58	12.00
Tumbler, 12 oz., barrel shape, #13	15.00
Tumbler, 12 oz., ftd., tea, #20	17.00
Tumbler, 14 oz., barrel shape, #14	20.00
Tumbler, 14 oz., tall, #59	22.00
Urn, w/cover (same as candy), #9	85.00
Vase, 5", #42	15.00
Vase, 6", crimped, #119	20.00
Vase, 6", ftd., #50	25.00
Vase, 6½", squat, #107	27.50
Vase, 7", #58	30.00
Vase, 7", ftd., #54	35.00
Vase, 10", ftd., #46	60.00

This was a cutting applied to glassware by the A.H. Heisey Company, Newark, Ohio, from the early 1940s until 1957. Narcissus, Heisey cutting number 965 was applied to a number of Heisey blanks but more often on the Jamestown stemware line (#3408) and the Waverly general line blanks (#1519). This cutting was very popular because of its beauty and the wide application which would allow for a complete set of glassware.

Bottle, oil (#1519)	175.00
Bowl, floral, ftd., 11" (#1519)	65.00
Bowl, floral, 13" (#1519)	60.00
Bowl, gardenia, 13 (#1519)	50.00
Candlestick, 2-light (#134)	35.00
Candlestick, 3-light (#1519)	65.00
Candy and cover, ftd., 5" (#1519)	185.00
Celery tray, 12" (#1519)	35.00
Comport, low ftd., 6" (#1519)	35.00
Comport, ftd. honey, 7" (#1519)	40.00
Comport, ftd., nut, 7" (#1519)	70.00
Creamer, ftd. (#1519)	30.00
Cup (#1519)	30.00
Mayonnaise, ftd. and underplate (#1519)	55.00
Relish, oval, 3-part, 11" (#1519)	40.00

Relish, round, 3-part, 8" (#1519)	35.00
Plate luncheon, 8" (#1519)	16.00
Plate, party, 14" (#1519)	45.00
Salt & pepper (#1519)	75.00
Saucer (#1519)	10.00
Stem, goblet, 9 oz. (#3408)	28.00
Stem,sherbet/saucer-champ., 6 oz. (#3408)	16.00
Stem,claret, 4½ oz. (#3408)	32.00
Stem, cocktail, 3 oz. (#3408)	18.00
Stem, wine, 2-oz. (#3408)	26.00
Stem, cordial, 1 oz. (#3408)	85.00
Sugar (#1519)	30.00
Tumbler, ice tea, ftd., 12 oz. (#3408)	26.00
Tumbler, juice, ftd., 5 oz. (#3408)	24.00
Vase, round, ftd., 7" (#1519)	85.00

Color: crystal, blue, blue and pink opalescent

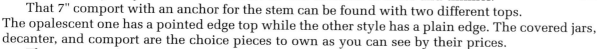

The inclusion of Nautical a few years ago created quite a commotion among long-time collectors who had been buying this pattern reasonably. Most Nautical is easily recognized; but various pieces slip through the cracks. It is hard to miss items with anchors and rope; however some pieces do not have the anchor, which means they can elude you unless you are attentive. Blue, and particularly, the opalescent, is the most sought color; but collectors are inclined to mix blue with crystal in order to have more pieces. Prices for blue continue to rise, but opalescent prices have slowed a bit due to the higher range they have now achieved. Notice the difference in the decanter and covered jar that are pictured side by side in the bottom row on page 142. The jars are listed as candy jars and the decanter is the taller opalescent covered piece in the row. I confused the decanter with a jar myself when I first saw it. The decanter is taller and thinner.

That 7" comport with an anchor for the stem can be found with two different tops. The opalescent one has a pointed edge top while the other style has a plain edge. The covered jars, decanter, and comport are the choice pieces to own as you can see by their prices.

There are similar pieces that are confused with Nautical. You can find a pair of bookends that have a leaning anchor across the base. You will often see this same shaped bookend with a horse head. Those anchor bookends can be found in blue or crystal. There are crystal lamps and an ashtray made to look like a captain's wheel that will blend well with Nautical as long as you do not pay Nautical prices for them.

NAUTICAL

	*Blue	Crystal	Opalescent
Ashtray, 3"	30.00	8.00	
Ashtray, 6"	40.00	12.50	
Candy jar, w/lid	550.00	295.00	650.00
Cigarette holder	55.00	15.00	
Cigarette jar	75.00	25.00	
Cocktail shaker (fish design)	150.00	60.00	
Comport, 7"	295.00	110.00	595.00
Creamer	45.00	15.00	
Decanter	495.00	225.00	650.00
Ice bucket	125.00	55.00	
Marmalade	75.00	25.00	
Plate, 6½", 2 hdld., cake	35.00	12.00	
Plate, 8"	40.00	10.00	
Plate, 10"	100.00	25.00	
Relish, 12", 7 part	75.00	35.00	
Relish, 2-part, 2 hdld.	45.00	22.50	
Shakers, pr.		35.00	
Sugar	45.00	15.00	
Tumbler, 2 oz., bar	25.00	12.50	
Tumbler, 8 oz., whiskey & soda	25.00	12.00	
Tumbler, 9 oz., water, ftd.	28.00	15.00	
Tumbler, cocktail	22.00	12.00	
Tumbler, ftd., orange juice	28.00	15.00	
Tumbler, high ball	30.00	18.00	

*Add 10% for satinized.

Colors: crystal; all other colors found made very late

Fostoria's Navarre pattern has become the creme de la creme of crystal etchings made by Fostoria! (American is the most widely collected pressed Fostoria crystal pattern; but it was made for about 70 years and several generations came to know it.) Navarre was made for over 40 years; and the thin delicate stems still enhance modern day china patterns. Navarre was distributed nationally, but prices on the West Coast were always more expensive due to shipping costs. With the price of gasoline and postage shooting upwards, transportation costs may seriously have to factor into dealers' prices of merchandise once again.

Only older crystal pieces of Navarre are priced in this Elegant book. Pink and blue were made in the 1970s and 1980s as were additional crystal pieces not originally made in the late 1930s and 1940s. These later pieces include carafes; roemer wines, continental champagnes, and brandies. You can find these later pieces in my *Collectible Glassware from the 40s, 50s, and 60s....* Most of these pieces are acid signed on base "Fostoria" although some carried only a sticker. I am telling you this to make you aware of the colors made in Navarre. You will even find a few pieces of Navarre that are signed Lenox. These were made after Fostoria closed. Some collectors shy away from the Lenox pieces since the color is lighter than the original; but it does not seem to make much difference to most Navarre collectors. A few Depression era glass shows have not allowed these pieces or colors to be sold since they were of so recent manufacture. However, most shows are changing these stricter rules to allow patterns to be included as long as production began earlier.

Note the footed shakers in the photo below. They came with both glass and metal lids. Glass tops were used in the early production years, but soon gave way to metal. Metal lids were the ones most often shipped as replacements when customers ordered new lids.

	Crystal		Crystal
Bell, dinner	75.00	Bowl, #2496, 10½", hdld., ftd.	95.00
Bowl, #2496, 4", sq., hdld.	20.00	Bowl, #2470½, 10½", ftd.	70.00
Bowl, #2496, 4⅜", hdld.	17.50	Bowl, #2496, 12", flared	75.00
Bowl, #869, 4½", finger	75.00	Bowl, #2545, 12½", oval, "Flame"	95.00
Bowl, #2496, 4⅝", tri-cornered	25.00	Candlestick, #2496, 4"	27.50
Bowl, #2496, 5", hdld., ftd.	20.00	Candlestick, #2496, 4½", double	42.50
Bowl, #2496, 6", square, sweetmeat	32.50	Candlestick, #2472, 5", double	55.00
Bowl, #2496, 6¼", 3 ftd., nut	25.00	Candlestick, #2496, 5½"	40.00
Bowl, #2496, 7⅜", ftd., bonbon	32.50	Candlestick, #2496, 6", triple	65.00
Bowl, #2496, 10", oval, floating garden	67.50	Candlestick, #2545, 6¾", double, "Flame"	85.00

	Crystal
Candlestick, #2482, 6¾", triple	90.00
Candy, w/cover, #2496, 3 part	150.00
Celery, #2440, 9"	35.00
Celery, #2496, 11"	50.00
Comport, #2496, 3¼", cheese	37.50
Comport, #2400, 4½"	35.00
Comport, #2496, 4¾"	37.50
Cracker, #2496, 11", plate	50.00
Creamer, #2440, 4¼", ftd.	20.00
Creamer, #2496, individual	20.00
Cup, #2440	20.00
Ice bucket, #2496, 4⅜" high	130.00
Ice bucket, #2375, 6" high	157.50
Mayonnaise, #2375, 3 piece	75.00
Mayonnaise, #2496½", 3 piece	75.00
Pickle, #2496, 8"	27.50
Pickle, #2440, 8½"	32.50
Pitcher, #5000, 48 oz., ftd.	375.00
Plate, #2440, 6", bread/butter	12.00
Plate, #2440, 7½", salad	16.00
Plate, #2440, 8½", luncheon	24.00
Plate, #2440, 9½", dinner	52.50
Plate, #2496, 10", hdld., cake	60.00
Plate, #2440, 10½", oval cake	65.00
Plate, #2496, 14", torte	75.00
Plate, #2464, 16", torte	135.00
Relish, #2496, 6", 2 part, sq.	35.00
Relish, #2496, 10" x 7½", 3 part	55.00

	Crystal
Relish, #2496, 10", 4 part	65.00
Relish, #2419, 13¼", 5 part	100.00
Salt & pepper, #2364, 3¼", flat, pr.	85.00
Salt & pepper, #2375, 3½", ftd., pr.	125.00
Salad dressing bottle, #2083, 6½"	495.00
Sauce dish, #2496, div. mayonnaise, 6½"	40.00
Sauce dish, #2496, 6½" x 5¼"	135.00
Sauce dish liner, #2496, 8", oval	30.00
Saucer, #2440	5.00
Stem, #6106, 1 oz., cordial, 3⅞"	60.00
Stem, #6106, 3¼ oz., wine, 5½"	37.50
Stem, #6106, 3½ oz., cocktail, 6"	27.50
Stem, #6106, 4 oz., oyster cocktail, 3⅝"	27.50
Stem, #6106, 4½ oz., claret, 6½"	47.50
Stem, #6106, 6 oz., low sherbet, 4⅜"	25.00
Stem, #6106, 6 oz., saucer champagne, 5⅝"	27.50
Stem, #6106, 10 oz., water, 7⅝"	35.00
Sugar, #2440, 3⅝", ftd.	20.00
Sugar, #2496, individual	20.00
Syrup, #2586, metal cut-off top, 5½"	475.00
Tid bit, #2496, 8¼", 3 ftd., turned up edge	30.00
Tray, #2496½", for ind. sugar/creamer	25.00
Tumbler, #6106, 5 oz., ftd., juice, 4⅝"	25.00
Tumbler, #6106, 10 oz., ftd., water, 5⅜"	27.50
Tumbler, #6106, 13 oz., ftd., tea, 5⅞"	37.50
Vase, #4128, 5"	125.00
Vase, #4121, 5"	120.00

Colors: crystal, frosted crystal, some cobalt with crystal stem and foot

Except for stems, the celery tray, and candlesticks, the production of New Era falls outside production dates of this book; so, be warned, New Era will be transferred into my *Collectible Glassware from the 40s, 50s, and 60s* book after this Elegant edition. The New Era double-branched candelabrum with bobeches is probably the most acknowledged Heisey candle. Stemware abounds; but keep your eye peeled for flat pieces of New Era that often goes unrecognized as Heisey!

	Crystal
Ashtray or indiv. nut	30.00
Bottle, rye, w/stopper	120.00
Bowl, 11", floral	35.00
Candelabra, 2-lite, w/2 #4044 bobeche & prisms	120.00
Creamer	37.50
Cup	10.00
Cup, after dinner	62.50
Pilsner, 8 oz.	27.50
Pilsner, 12 oz.	32.50
Plate, 5½" x 4½", bread & butter	15.00
Plate, 9" x 7"	25.00
Plate, 10" x 8"	45.00
Relish, 13", 3 part	25.00
Saucer	5.00
Saucer, after dinner	12.50
Stem, 1 oz. cordial	35.00
Stem, 3 oz. wine	25.00
Stem, 3½ oz., high, cocktail	12.00

	Crystal
Stem, 3½ oz., oyster cocktail	12.00
Stem, 4 oz., claret	18.00
Stem, 6 oz., champagne	13.00
Stem, 6 oz., sherbet, low	12.50
Stem, 10 oz., goblet	16.00
Sugar	37.50
Tray, 13", celery	30.00
Tumbler, 5 oz., ftd., soda	8.00
Tumbler, 8 oz., ftd., soda	11.00
Tumbler, 10 oz., low, ftd.	11.00
Tumbler, 12 oz., ftd., soda	18.00
Tumbler, 14 oz., ftd., soda	20.00

Colors: Amber, Rose, and Topaz

New Garland is a Fostoria pattern that is beginning to be gathered by collectors. Notice the ice buckets, which do not show up often. Some new collectors have been attracted to its older, squared mould shape of Fostoria's #2419 Mayfair line. Which, by the way, was designed by George Sakier, the man behind many of Fostoria's more avant garde designs of that era.

Pink appears to be the color of choice, but we are getting a few requests for yellow recently.

	Amber Topaz	Rose
Bonbon, 2 hdld.	15.00	20.00
Bottle, salad dressing	135.00	225.00
Bowl, 5", fruit	10.00	12.50
Bowl, 6", cereal	12.00	18.00
Bowl, 7", soup	22.00	30.00
Bowl, 7½"	25.00	40.00
Bowl, 10", baker	35.00	45.00
Bowl, 11", ftd.	50.00	70.00
Bowl, 12"	55.00	70.00
Candlestick, 2"	15.00	20.00
Candlestick, 3"	17.50	22.50
Candlestick, 9½"	30.00	40.00
Candy jar, cover, ½ lb.	55.00	85.00
Celery, 11"	22.00	30.00
Comport, 6"	20.00	28.00
Comport, tall	30.00	40.00
Cream soup	18.00	22.50
Creamer	12.50	15.00
Creamer, ftd.	15.00	17.50
Creamer, tea	17.50	20.00
Cup, after dinner	20.00	25.00
Cup, ftd.	14.00	17.50
Decanter	125.00	195.00
Finger bowl, #4121	12.00	15.00
Finger bowl, #6002, ftd.	15.00	18.00
Ice bucket	65.00	95.00
Ice dish	20.00	25.00
Jelly, 7"	18.00	22.50
Lemon dish, 2 hdld.	15.00	18.00
Mayonnaise, 2 hdld.	18.00	22.50
Mint, 5½"	12.50	16.00
Nut, individual	10.00	13.00
Oil, ftd.	135.00	195.00
Pickle, 8½"	16.00	20.00
Pitcher, ftd.	250.00	310.00
Plate, 6"	4.00	6.00
Plate, 7"	7.00	10.00
Plate, 8"	12.00	15.00
Plate, 9"	25.00	35.00
Plate, 10" cake, 2 hdld.	27.50	35.00
Platter, 12"	35.00	45.00
Platter, 15"	50.00	75.00
Relish, 4 part	20.00	27.50
Relish, 8½"	14.00	18.00
Sauce boat	50.00	75.00
Sauce boat liner	20.00	25.00
Saucer	3.00	4.00
Saucer, after dinner	8.00	10.00
Shaker, pr.	40.00	60.00

	Amber Topaz	Rose
Shaker, pr., ftd.	75.00	100.00
Stem, #4120, 2 oz., whiskey	20.00	28.00
Stem, #4120, 3½ oz., cocktail	20.00	24.00
Stem, #4120, 5 oz., low sherbet	14.00	16.00
Stem, #4120, 7 oz., low sherbet	15.00	18.00
Stem, #4120, high sherbet	18.00	20.00
Stem, #4120, water goblet	22.00	25.00
Stem, #6002, claret	25.00	32.50
Stem, #6002, cordial	30.00	37.50
Stem, #6002, goblet	22.00	25.00
Stem, #6002, high sherbet	18.00	20.00
Stem, #6002, low sherbet	14.00	16.00
Stem, #6002, oyster cocktail	16.00	20.00
Stem, #6002, wine	22.00	25.00
Sugar	12.50	15.00
Sugar, ftd.	15.00	17.50
Sugar, tea	17.50	20.00
Tumbler, #4120, 5 oz.	12.00	15.00
Tumbler, #4120, 10 oz.	14.00	17.50
Tumbler, #4120, 13 oz.	15.00	18.00
Tumbler, #4120, 16 oz.	20.00	24.00
Tumbler, #6002, ftd., 2 oz.	18.00	22.00
Tumbler, #6002, ftd., 5 oz.	12.00	15.00
Tumbler, #6002, ftd., 10 oz.	14.00	17.50
Tumbler, #6002, ftd., 13 oz.	15.00	18.00
Vase, 8"	65.00	85.00

Colors: Emerald green, Peach Blo; #3095 colored Peach-blo w/ribbed bowl, crystal stem & foot, optic

Cambridge's Number 520 and Number 704, which follows on the next page, are usually designated as "one of those Cambridge numbered patterns," but few members of the public take the trouble to learn which one. There are some avid collectors of both of these lines, and hopefully adding names, "Byzantine" and "Windows Border" may help identify the patterns as did "Rosalie" for Number 731. Collectors like names. Since no factory name has been forthcoming, let's adopt one collector's idea. She told me it reminded her of the elaborate designs seen in her travels. "It's very Byzantine," she said.

I see equal amounts of Peach Blo (pink) and Emerald, but apparently there are more admirers of the green. That green butter dish would fetch a king's ransom in some other pattern. Perhaps someday it will in "Byzantine."

	Peach Blo Green			Peach Blo Green
Bouillon, 2 hdld. soup cup, #934	22.50		Plate, finger bowl liner, #3060	12.50
Bowl, 5¼", fruit, #928	22.50		Platter for gravy boat	45.00
Bowl, 6½", cereal or grapefruit, #466	32.50		Saucer, #933	7.00
Bowl, cream soup	25.00		Saucer, cupped, liner for bouillon	12.00
Bowl, finger, #3060	25.00		Stem, 2½ oz., cocktail, #3060	22.50
Butter w/cover	195.00		Stem, 2½ oz., wine, #3060	35.00
Candy box, #300	110.00		Stem, 6 oz., hi sherbet, #3060	22.50
Comport, 7¼" h., #531	40.00		Stem, 7 oz., sherbet, #3060	22.50
Comport, jelly, #2900	35.00		Stem, 9 oz., water, #3060	30.00
Comport, #3095 (twist stem)	40.00		Stem, cocktail, #3095	22.50
Creamer, rim ft., #138	20.00		Stem, high sherbet, #3095	20.00
Cup, #933	18.00		Stem, low sherbet, #3095	18.00
Gravy or sauce boat	95.00		Sugar, rim ft., #138	20.00
Oil bottle, #193	175.00		Tumbler, 3 oz., ftd., #3060	20.00
Oil bottle w/cut flattened stop, 6 oz., #197	195.00		Tumbler, 5 oz., ftd., #3060	22.50
Plate, 6", sherbet	10.00		Tumbler, 10 oz., ftd., #3060	25.00
Plate, 8", luncheon	18.00		Tumbler, 12 oz., low ft., #3095	30.00
Plate, 9½" dinner, #810	60.00			

Colors: amber, Bluebell, crystal, Emerald, Peach-blo

Number 704 has been referred to by a collector as "Windows Border" and that might stick better than Number 704 which usually is forgotten once it has been looked up.

"Windows Border" is often displayed in sets in malls without an identifying name, but labeled Cambridge since most pieces are marked with that telltale C in a triangle signifying Cambridge. I am hoping this exposure will enhance its appeal to collectors and bring it the recognition it truly deserves. Look at it! It's a wonderful etch and it can be found with searching.

	All Colors
Bottle, decanter, #0315	195.00
Bottle, decanter, #3075	225.00
Bowl, 5¼", fruit	16.00
Bowl, 6", cereal	25.00
Bowl, 8½", soup	30.00
Bowl, 8¾", oval	33.00
Bowl, 10½", #912 casserole and cover	175.00
Bowl, 12", oval, #914	50.00
Bowl, 12", oval w/cover, #915	125.00
Bowl, 2 hdld. cream soup, #922	20.00
Bowl, finger, #3060	35.00
Bowl, finger, #3075	35.00
Butter and cover, #920	125.00
Candlestick, 2", #227½	22.50
Candlestick, 3½", #628	27.50
Candlestick, 7½", #439	35.00
Candlestick, 8½", #438	40.00
Candlestick, 9½", #437	45.00
Candy box and cover, 5", #98, 3-part, flat	95.00
Candy box and cover, 5", #299, 3-ftd.	95.00
Candy box and cover, 6", #300, 3-ftd.	110.00
Celery, 11", #908	35.00

	All Colors
Celery tray, 11", #652	45.00
Cheese plate, #468	35.00
Cheese plate & cover, #3075	125.00
Cigarette box, #430	50.00
Cigarette box, #616	50.00
Cologne, 1 oz., #198 or #199	125.00
Comport, 5", #3075	30.00
Creamer, flat, #137	22.50
Creamer, flat, #942	22.50
Creamer, flat, #943	22.50
Creamer, flat, #944	22.50
Cup, #933	15.00
Cup, demi, #925	35.00
Gravy boat, double and stand, #917	125.00
Ice bucket w/bail, short, #970	95.00
Ice bucket w/bail, tall, #957	110.00
Ice tub, straight up tab hdlds., #394	100.00
Jug, nite set, #103, 38 oz. w/tumbler	195.00

	All Colors
Jug, #107	150.00
Jug, #124, 68 oz., w/lid	250.00
Jug, 62 oz., flat, #955	210.00
Jug, #3077 w/lid	325.00
Mayonnaise, 3 pc., #169	75.00
Mayonnaise, 3 pc., #533	65.00
Oil, 6 oz., #193	65.00
Oyster cocktail, 4½ oz., ftd., #3060	14.00
Pickle tray, 9", #907	30.00
Plate, 6"	6.00
Plate, 7"	8.00
Plate, 8"	15.00
Plate, 8½"	22.50
Plate, 9½", dinner	65.00
Plate, 10½", service	75.00
Plate, 13½"	75.00
Plate, cupped, liner for creme soup, #922	8.00
Plate, liner for finger bowl, #3060	8.00
Plate, liner for finger bowl, #3075	8.00
Platter, 12½", oval service, #901	75.00
Platter, 16", oval, #904	95.00
Puff & cover, 3" or 4", #578, blown	85.00
Puff & cover, 4", #582	55.00
Saucer, #933	5.00
Saucer, demi, #925	10.00
Stem, 1 oz., cordial, #3075	65.00
Stem, 2½ oz., cocktail (wide bowl), #3075	18.00
Stem, 2½ oz., wine (slender bowl), #3075	35.00
Stem, 4½ oz., claret, #3075	50.00
Stem, 5 oz., parfait, #3060	40.00

	All Colors
Stem, 5½ oz., cafe parfait, #3075	40.00
Stem, 6 oz., high sherbet, #3060	20.00
Stem, 9 oz., #3060	28.00
Stem, 9 oz., #3075	28.00
Stem, low sherbet, #3075	15.00
Stem, hi sherbet, #3075	20.00
Sugar, flat, #137	20.00
Sugar, flat, #942	20.00
Sugar, flat, #943	20.00
Sugar, flat, #944	20.00
Syrup, 9 oz., w/metal cover, #170	150.00
Syrup, tall jug, #814	160.00
Toast dish and cover, 9", #951	195.00
Tray, 10", center handle	45.00
Tumbler, 2 oz., flat, #3060	33.00
Tumbler, 2 oz., whiskey, #3075	35.00
Tumbler, 3 oz., ftd., #3075	27.50
Tumbler, 5 oz., ftd., #3075	20.00
Tumbler, 5 oz., #3075	20.00
Tumbler, 6 oz., ftd. fruit salad (sherbet)	15.00
Tumbler, 8 oz., ftd., #3075	20.00
Tumbler, 10 oz., #3075	22.50
Tumbler, 10 oz., flat, #3060	20.00
Tumbler, 10 oz., ftd., #3075	22.50
Tumbler, 12 oz., #3075	27.50
Tumbler, 12 oz., flat, #3060	25.00
Tumbler, 12 oz., ftd., #3060	28.00
Tumbler, 12 oz., ftd., #3075	30.00
Vase, 6½", ftd., #1005	100.00
Vase, 9½", ftd., #787	150.00

Color: crystal

One of the more entertaining aspects of researching glass comes from finding the same cut pattern on different company's blanks.

The Oak cutting here is an extreme example, but one I felt compelled to show to confirm why there is sometimes difficulty identifying a cutting using just the company blank. Because the blank is recognized as Heisey or Fostoria does not mean the cutting came from that factory.

Pictured are groups of Fostoria Glass Company items including nine different pieces of Century Blank #2630, one piece of Baroque Blank #2496, and a #2482 trindle candlestick. That is eleven pieces of Fostoria on three different blanks. Oak is cut on two different Heisey blanks including Lariat #1540 stems and Queen Ann #1509 mould blank. Viking Glass is represented by three different pieces including a butter dish and #5247 creamer and sugar. There are six unidentified pieces although I feel sure the two tumblers are Libbey due to their characteristic safety edged rim. I have priced items by what uncut pieces bring and what I had to pay to get this glass to illustrate this point.

FOSTORIA GLASS COMPANY

CENTURY BLANK #2630 Line

Bonbon, 7¼", 3-ftd.	25.00
Bowl, 9½", 2 hdld.	40.00
Creamer, individual	12.50
Mayonnaise	25.00
Mayonnaise liner	10.00
Relish, 11⅛", 3-part	30.00
Sugar, individual	12.50
Tidbit, 8⅛", 3-ftd.	
Tray, 7⅛", individual sugar/creamer	17.50

BAROQUE BLANK #2496

Bowl, 10", hdld.	45.00
Blank #2482	
Trindle candlestick, 6¾" high	65.00

BLANK #2482

Trindle candlestick, 6¾" high	65.00

A. H. HEISEY GLASS COMPANY

LARIAT BLANK #1540

Stem, 9 oz., pressed water goblet	25.00
Stem, 5½ oz., pressed saucer champagne	20.00

QUEEN ANN BLANK #1509

Relish, 10", triplex	35.00

VIKING GLASS COMPANY

Creamer,# 5247	15.00
Sugar, #5247	15.00
Butter dish, ¼ pound	40.00

UNIDENTIFIED COMPANIES

Paperweight, rectangular	35.00
Pitcher, 16 oz.	20.00
Pitcher, 32 oz.	30.00
Salt dip w/spoon	20.00
Tumbler, juice (possibly Libbey)	10.00
Tumbler, water (possibly Libbey)	12.50

Colors: crystal, Flamingo pink, Sahara yellow, Moongleam green, Hawthorne orchid, Marigold deep amber/yellow, and Dawn

Octagon was consistently marked by Heisey's trademark H within a diamond; so, it is one pattern that everyone can readily ascertain is Heisey. Only a small number of collectors search for this plainer pattern, but it does come in an array of colors. In the price list below, the only piece that stands out is the very last listing of a 12", four-part tray. Octagon is reasonably priced and is often just waiting for a new home. This tray can be found in the rare gray/black color Dawn.

Marigold pieces are found occasionally in Octagon. This is a seldom seen Heisey color; but be cautious when buying it because the color is subject to peeling. If that should happen, it becomes uninviting to collectors.

	Crystal	Flamingo	Sahara	Moongleam	Hawthorne	Marigold
Basket, 5", #500	100.00	300.00	300.00	425.00	450.00	350.00
Bonbon, 6", sides up, #1229	10.00	40.00	25.00	25.00	40.00	
Bowl, cream soup, 2 hdld.	10.00	20.00	25.00	30.00	40.00	
Bowl, 2 hdld, ind. nut bowl	15.00	25.00	25.00	25.00	60.00	65.00
Bowl, 5½", jelly, #1229	15.00	30.00	25.00	25.00	50.00	
Bowl, 6", mint, #1229	10.00	20.00	25.00	25.00	45.00	30.00
Bowl, 6", #500	14.00	20.00	22.00	25.00	35.00	
Bowl, 6½", grapefruit	10.00	20.00	22.00	25.00	35.00	
Bowl, 8", ftd., #1229 comport	15.00	25.00	35.00	45.00	55.00	
Bowl, 9", flat soup	10.00	15.00	20.00	27.50	30.00	
Bowl, 9", vegetable	15.00	32.00	25.00	30.00	50.00	
Candlestick, 3", 1-lite	15.00	30.00	30.00	40.00	50.00	
Cheese dish, 6", 2 hdld., #1229	7.00	15.00	10.00	15.00	15.00	
Creamer, #500	10.00	30.00	35.00	35.00	50.00	
Creamer, hotel	10.00	30.00	30.00	35.00	50.00	
Cup, after dinner	10.00	20.00	20.00	25.00	42.00	
Cup, #1231	5.00	15.00	20.00	20.00	35.00	
Dish, frozen dessert, #500	15.00	30.00	20.00	30.00	35.00	50.00
Ice tub, #500	30.00	70.00	75.00	80.00	115.00	150.00
Mayonnaise, 5½", ftd., #1229	10.00	25.00	30.00	35.00	55.00	
Nut, two hdld.	10.00	25.00	18.00	25.00	65.00	70.00
Plate, cream soup liner	3.00	5.00	7.00	9.00	12.00	
Plate, 6"	4.00	8.00	8.00	10.00	15.00	
Plate, 7", bread	5.00	10.00	10.00	15.00	20.00	
Plate, 8", luncheon	7.00	10.00	10.00	15.00	25.00	
Plate, 10", sand., #1229	15.00	20.00	25.00	30.00	80.00	

	Crystal	Flamingo	Sahara	Moongleam	Hawthorne	Marigold
Plate, 10", muffin, #1229, sides up	15.00	25.00	30.00	35.00	40.00	
Plate, 10½"	17.00	25.00	30.00	35.00	45.00	
Plate, 10½", ctr. hdld., sandwich	25.00	40.00	40.00	45.00	70.00	
Plate, 12", muffin, #1229, sides up	20.00	27.00	30.00	35.00	45.00	
Plate, 13", hors d'oeuvre, #1229	20.00	35.00	35.00	45.00	60.00	
Plate, 14"	22.00	25.00	30.00	35.00	50.00	
Platter, 12¾", oval	20.00	25.00	30.00	40.00	50.00	
Saucer, after dinner	5.00	8.00	10.00	10.00	12.00	
Saucer, #1231	5.00	8.00	10.00	10.00	12.00	
Sugar, #500	10.00	25.00	35.00	35.00	50.00	
Sugar, hotel	10.00	30.00	30.00	35.00	50.00	
Tray, 6", oblong, #500	8.00	15.00	15.00	15.00	30.00	
Tray, 9", celery	10.00	20.00	20.00	25.00	45.00	
Tray, 12", celery	10.00	25.00	25.00	30.00	50.00	
Tray, 12", 4 pt., #500 variety	60.00	120.00	140.00	160.00	250.00	*350.00

*Dawn

Blank #3380, A.H. Heisey & Co., 1930 – 1939

Colors: crystal, Flamingo pink, Sahara yellow, Moongleam green, Marigold deep amber/yellow

Due to the abundance of Sahara (yellow), Old Colony pricing will be based on Sahara as follows: crystal — Subtract 50%; Flamingo — Subtract 10%; Moongleam — add 10%; Marigold — add 20%. Space does not permit pricing each color separately.

	Sahara
Bouillon cup, 2 hdld., ftd.	25.00
Bowl, finger, #4075	15.00
Bowl, ftd., finger, #3390	25.00
Bowl, 4½", nappy	14.00
Bowl, 5", ftd., 2 hdld.	24.00
Bowl, 6", ftd., 2 hdld., jelly	30.00
Bowl, 6", dolphin ftd., mint	35.00
Bowl, 7", triplex, dish	35.00
Bowl, 7½", dolphin ftd., nappy	70.00
Bowl, 8", nappy	40.00
Bowl, 8½", ftd., floral, 2 hdld.	60.00
Bowl, 9", 3 hdld.	90.00
Bowl, 10", rnd., 2 hdld., salad	60.00
Bowl, 10", sq., salad, 2 hdld.	55.00
Bowl, 10", oval, dessert, 2 hdld.	50.00
Bowl, 10", oval, veg.	42.00
Bowl, 11", floral, dolphin ft.	80.00
Bowl, 13", ftd., flared	40.00
Bowl, 13", 2 pt., pickle & olive	24.00
Cigarette holder, #3390	44.00
Comport, 7", oval, ftd.	80.00
Comport, 7", ftd., #3368	70.00
Cream soup, 2 hdld.	22.00
Creamer, dolphin ft.	45.00
Creamer, indiv.	40.00
Cup, after dinner	40.00
Cup	32.00
Decanter, 1 pt.	325.00
Flagon, 12 oz., #3390	100.00
Grapefruit, 6"	30.00
Grapefruit, ftd., #3380	20.00
Ice tub, dolphin ft.	115.00
Mayonnaise, 5½", dolphin ft.	70.00

	Sahara
Oil, 4 oz., ftd.	105.00
Pitcher, 3 pt., #3390	230.00
Pitcher, 3 pt., dolphin ft.	240.00
Plate, bouillon	15.00
Plate, cream soup	12.00
Plate, 4½", rnd.	7.00
Plate, 6", rnd.	15.00
Plate, 6", sq.	15.00
Plate, 7", rnd.	20.00
Plate, 7", sq.	20.00
Plate, 8", rnd.	24.00
Plate, 8", sq.	24.00
Plate, 9", rnd.	23.00
Plate, 10½", rnd.	80.00
Plate, 10½", sq.	70.00
Plate, 12", rnd.	75.00
Plate, 12", 2 hdld., rnd., muffin	75.00
Plate, 12", 2 hdld., rnd., sand.	70.00
Plate, 13", 2 hdld., sq., sand.	50.00
Plate, 13", 2 hdld., sq., muffin	50.00
Platter, 14", oval	45.00
Salt & pepper, pr.	125.00
Saucer, sq.	10.00
Saucer, rnd.	10.00
Stem, #3380, 1 oz., cordial	135.00
Stem, #3380, 2½ oz., wine	35.00
Stem, #3380, 3 oz., cocktail	25.00
Stem, #3380, 4 oz., oyster/cocktail	20.00
Stem, #3380, 4 oz., claret	40.00
Stem, #3380, 5 oz., parfait	20.00
Stem, #3380, 6 oz., champagne	20.00
Stem, #3380, 6 oz., sherbet	20.00
Stem, #3380, 10 oz., short soda	20.00
Stem, #3380, 10 oz., tall soda	25.00
Stem, #3390, 1 oz., cordial	125.00
Stem, #3390, 2½ oz., wine	35.00
Stem, #3390, 3 oz., cocktail	20.00

	Sahara
Stem, #3390, 3 oz., oyster/cocktail	20.00
Stem, #3390, 4 oz., claret	30.00
Stem, #3390, 6 oz., champagne	25.00
Stem, #3390, 6 oz., sherbet	25.00
Stem, #3390, 11 oz., low water	25.00
Stem, #3390, 11 oz., tall water	27.00
Sugar, dolphin ft.	45.00
Sugar, indiv.	40.00
Tray, 10", celery	30.00
Tray, 12", ctr. hdld., sandwich	75.00
Tray, 12", ctr. hdld., sq.	75.00
Tray, 13", celery	40.00
Tray, 13", 2 hdld., hors d'oeuvre	75.00

	Sahara
Tumbler, dolphin ft.	165.00
Tumbler, #3380, 1 oz., ftd., bar	45.00
Tumbler, #3380, 2 oz., ftd., bar	20.00
Tumbler, #3380, 5 oz., ftd., bar	16.00
Tumbler, #3380, 8 oz., ftd., soda	18.00
Tumbler, #3380, 10 oz., ftd., soda	20.00
Tumbler, #3380, 12 oz., ftd., tea	22.00
Tumbler, #3390, 2 oz., ftd.	24.00
Tumbler, #3390, 5 oz., ftd., juice	20.00
Tumbler, #3390, 8 oz., ftd., soda	25.00
Tumbler, #3390, 12 oz., ftd., tea	27.00
Vase, 9", ftd.	150.00

Colors: crystal, Flamingo pink, Sahara yellow, Moongleam green, cobalt, amber

Moongleam is the most desired Old Sandwich color as is so with its sister pattern Ipswich. However, we are showing colors other than Moongleam. Sets can be gathered in crystal, but other colored sets would be difficult and costly. Notice there are four sizes of creamers and one sugar. Cobalt blue pieces of Old Sandwich are rare and usually expensive should you spot any.

	Crystal	Flamingo	Sahara	Moongleam	Cobalt
Ashtray, individual	9.00	60.00	35.00	60.00	45.00
Beer mug, 12 oz.	50.00	300.00	210.00	400.00	240.00
* Beer mug, 14 oz.	55.00	325.00	225.00	425.00	250.00
Beer mug, 18 oz.	65.00	400.00	270.00	475.00	380.00
Bottle, catsup, w/#3 stopper (like large cruet)	70.00	200.00	175.00	225.00	
Bowl, finger	12.00	50.00	60.00	60.00	
Bowl, ftd., popcorn, cupped	80.00	110.00	110.00	135.00	
Bowl, 11", rnd., ftd., floral	50.00	85.00	65.00	100.00	
Bowl, 12", oval, ftd., floral	50.00	80.00	70.00	80.00	
Candlestick, 6"	60.00	120.00	110.00	150.00	325.00
Cigarette holder	50.00	65.00	60.00	65.00	
Comport, 6"	60.00	95.00	90.00	100.00	
Creamer, oval	25.00	90.00	85.00	50.00	
Creamer, 12 oz.	32.00	185.00	170.00	175.00	575.00
Creamer, 14 oz.	35.00	175.00	180.00	185.00	
Creamer, 18 oz.	40.00	185.00	190.00	195.00	
Cup	40.00	65.00	65.00	125.00	
Decanter, 1 pint, w/#98 stopper	75.00	185.00	200.00	225.00	425.00
Floral block, #22	15.00	25.00	30.00	35.00	
Oil bottle, 2½ oz., #85 stopper	65.00	200.00	170.00	180.00	

	Crystal	Flamingo	Sahara	Moongleam	Cobalt
Parfait, 4½ oz.	15.00	50.00	50.00	60.00	
Pilsner, 8 oz.	14.00	28.00	32.00	38.00	
Pilsner, 10 oz.	16.00	32.00	37.00	42.00	
Pitcher, ½ gallon, ice lip	100.00	175.00	165.00	185.00	
Pitcher, ½ gallon, reg.	100.00	175.00	165.00	185.00	
Plate, 6", sq., ground bottom	10.00	20.00	17.00	22.00	
Plate, 7", sq.	10.00	27.00	25.00	30.00	
Plate, 8", sq.	15.00	30.00	27.00	32.00	
Salt & pepper, pr.	40.00	65.00	75.00	85.00	
Saucer	10.00	15.00	15.00	25.00	
Stem, 2½ oz., wine	18.00	45.00	45.00	55.00	
Stem, 3 oz., cocktail	20.00	30.00	32.00	40.00	
Stem, 4 oz., claret	17.00	35.00	35.00	50.00	150.00
Stem, 4 oz., oyster cocktail	12.00	27.00	27.00	32.00	
Stem, 4 oz., sherbet	7.00	17.00	17.00	20.00	
Stem, 5 oz., saucer champagne	12.00	32.00	32.00	35.00	
Stem, 10 oz., low ft.	20.00	30.00	35.00	40.00	
Sugar, oval	25.00	90.00	55.00	60.00	
Sundae, 6 oz.	18.00	30.00	30.00	35.00	
Tumbler, 1½ oz., bar, ground bottom	20.00	130.00	120.00	135.00	100.00
Tumbler, 5 oz., juice	7.00	15.00	15.00	25.00	
Tumbler, 6½ oz., toddy	20.00	35.00	40.00	40.00	
Tumbler, 8 oz., ground bottom, cupped & straight rim	20.00	35.00	35.00	40.00	
Tumbler, 10 oz.	20.00	40.00	40.00	45.00	
Tumbler, 10 oz., low ft.	15.00	40.00	42.00	45.00	
Tumbler, 12 oz., ftd., iced tea	20.00	45.00	45.00	55.00	
Tumbler, 12 oz., iced tea	20.00	45.00	45.00	55.00	

*Amber; $300.00. Whimsey crystal basket made from footed soda, $725.00.

Colors: amber, Blue, crystal, green, Rose

Fostoria's Pioneer is the mould blank on which Seville and Vesper are etched. There are collectors of #2350 Pioneer who search for the less expensive unetched. Blue, as the color pictured here was called, can be bought at prices well below those of Vesper. The Blue butter dish pictured could be bought for $125.00, but one etched Vesper would break the bank. Gathering undecorated glassware can enhance your etched settings. Numerous collectors have informed me that that is true.

Row 1: Cup and saucer, creamer, 6" plate, butter, cup and saucer. Row 2: Footed water, sugar and lid, 12" platter, urn, 12" plate, 8" plate.

*Regal Blue 22.50, Burgundy 22.50,
   Empire Green 22.50, Ruby 25.00
**Regal Blue 6.00, Burgundy 6.00,
   Empire Green 6.00, Ruby 7.50

	Crystal/Amber Green	Ebony	Rose Topaz	Azure Orchid	Blue
Ashtray, 3¾"	16.00	18.00	20.00	24.00	
Ashtray, lg., deep	18.00	18.00	22.00	25.00	
Bouillon, flat	12.00				14.00
Bouillon, ftd.	10.00				
Bowl, 5", fruit (shallow)	8.00				15.00
Bowl, 6", cereal	10.00				20.00
Bowl, 7", rnd. soup	15.00				25.00
Bowl, 8", nappy	20.00				25.00
Bowl, 8", oval pickle	17.50				22.50
Bowl, 9", nappy	17.50				25.00
Bowl, 9", oval baker	35.00				45.00
Bowl, 10", oval baker	40.00				50.00
Bowl, 10", salad	25.00				40.00
Bowl, creme soup, flat	15.00				27.50
Bowl, creme soup, ftd.	18.00				
Butter & cover	75.00				125.00
Celery, 11", oval narrow	20.00				24.00
Comport, 8"	27.50		30.00	35.00	
Creamer, flat	9.00				15.00
Creamer, ftd.	9.00	10.00	12.00		15.00
Ruby 17.50					
Cup, flat	12.00				15.00
* Cup, ftd.	10.00	12.50			15.00
Egg cup	20.00		25.00		

	Crystal/Amber Green	Ebony	Rose Topaz	Azure Orchid	Blue
Grapefruit liner (looks like straight crystal glass)	6.00				
Grapefruit, strt. side	25.00				33.00
Plate, 6"	5.00	8.00			
Plate, 7", salad	6.00	9.00			9.00
Plate, 8"	8.00	10.00			15.00
Plate, 9"	12.50	14.00			20.00
Plate, 10"	17.50	20.00			30.00
Plate, 12", chop	18.00				32.50
Plate, 15", service	22.50				35.00
Plate, bouillon liner	5.00				
Plate, creme soup	6.00				7.00
Plate, oval sauce boat	10.00				12.50
Platter, 10½"	22.50				30.00
Platter, 12"	15.00				32.50
Platter, 15"	27.50				35.00
Relish, rnd., 3 pt.	12.50		15.00	17.50	
Sauce boat, flat	22.50				35.00
** Saucer	3.00	4.00			5.00
Sugar cover	17.50				32.50
Sugar, flat	9.00				15.00
Sugar, ftd.	9.00	10.00	12.00		15.00
Ruby 17.50					
Tumbler, ftd., water					25.00
Urn					55.00

Colors: amber, crystal, green, pink, cobalt blue, red

Plaza was Duncan & Miller's pattern #21 that was made in an assortment of colors. I see more amber in my travels as evidenced by my photograph. You buy what you find when you are trying to add a new pattern to a book.

More collectors seek pink or green than other colors. Were blue and red more readily available, those would be the desired colors. I see very little of those colors except in the Pittsburgh area; and in that part of the country, everyone knows Duncan and it is priced for the serious collector. Let me know what you find as I am quite sure my listing is incomplete at this first attempt of putting it in a book.

	Amber/Crystal	*Pink/Green
Bowl, 4⅜", finger	8.00	15.00
Bowl, 6¼", cereal	10.00	20.00
Bowl, 9", oval vegetable	35.00	60.00
Bowl, 10", deep vegetable	30.00	55.00
Bowl, 14", flared, console	50.00	95.00
Candle, 4¾"h. x 7"w. double	27.50	52.50
Candy and lid, 4½", round	20.00	40.00
Cup	6.00	12.00
Mustard, w/slotted lid	17.50	30.00
Oil bottle	27.50	60.00
Parfait	15.00	30.00
Pitcher, flat	50.00	125.00
Plate, 5¼", finger bowl liner	5.00	10.00
Plate, 6½", bread and butter	4.00	9.00
Plate, 7½", salad	6.00	12.00
Plate, 8½", luncheon	8.00	15.00
Plate, 10½", hdld.	20.00	37.50

	Amber/Crystal	*Pink/Green
Salt and pepper, pr.	35.00	
Saucer	2.00	4.00
Stem, cocktail	12.50	20.00
Stem, cordial	22.50	42.50
Stem, saucer champagne	10.00	17.50
Stem, 3¾, sherbet	8.00	15.00
Stem, water	15.00	30.00
Stem, wine	15.00	30.00
Tumbler, flat juice	8.00	15.00
Tumbler, flat tea	12.50	25.00
Tumbler, flat water	10.00	17.50
Tumbler, flat whiskey	8.00	15.00
Tumbler, 3½", ftd., juice	8.00	15.00
Tumbler, ftd., tea	15.00	30.00
Tumbler, ftd., water	12.00	20.00
Vase, 8"	30.00	65.00

*Add 50% for any cobalt blue or red

PLEAT & PANEL, Blank #1170, A.H. Heisey & Co., c. 1926

Colors: crystal, Flamingo pink, Moongleam green

Many novices call this Depression glass; and several elite Heisey dealers I know would rather put Pleat and Panel in that category. They don't want to claim it as being Heisey. There are color variations in the pink. Only inexpensively made Depression glass companies were supposed to have color deviations. Yes, even Heisey had difficulty maintaining color consistencies! However, it does evidence the ushering in of the Deco influence in its design.

Most Pleat & Panel pieces carry the well-known H in a diamond mark. Stems are marked on the stem itself and not the foot; so look there if you are searching for a mark.

	Crystal	Flamingo	Moongleam
Bowl, 4", chow chow	6.00	11.00	14.00
Bowl, 4½", nappy	6.00	11.00	14.00
Bowl, 5", 2 hdld., bouillon	7.00	14.00	17.50
Bowl, 5", 2 hdld., jelly	9.00	14.00	17.50
Bowl, 5", lemon, w/cover	20.00	60.00	65.00
Bowl, 6½", grapefruit/cereal	5.00	14.00	17.50
Bowl, 8", nappy	10.00	32.50	40.00
Bowl, 9", oval, vegetable	12.50	35.00	40.00
Cheese & cracker set, 10½", tray, w/compote	25.00	75.00	80.00
Compotier, w/cover, 5", high ftd.	35.00	75.00	80.00
Creamer, hotel	10.00	25.00	30.00
Cup	7.00	15.00	17.50
Marmalade, 4¾"	10.00	30.00	35.00
Oil bottle, 3 oz., w/pressed stopper	30.00	75.00	110.00
Pitcher, 3 pint, ice lip	45.00	140.00	165.00
Pitcher, 3 pint	45.00	140.00	165.00

	Crystal	Flamingo	Moongleam
Plate, 6"	4.00	8.00	8.00
Plate, 6¾", bouillon underliner	4.00	8.00	8.00
Plate, 7", bread	4.00	8.00	10.00
Plate, 8", luncheon	5.00	12.50	15.00
Plate, 10¾", dinner	15.00	48.00	52.00
Plate, 14", sandwich	15.00	32.50	40.00
Platter, 12", oval	15.00	42.50	47.50
Saucer	3.00	5.00	5.00
Sherbet, 5 oz., footed	4.00	10.00	12.00
Stem, 5 oz., saucer champagne	5.00	14.00	18.00
Stem, 7½ oz., low foot	12.00	30.00	35.00
Stem, 8 oz.	15.00	35.00	40.00
Sugar w/lid, hotel	10.00	30.00	35.00
Tray, 10", compartmented spice	10.00	25.00	30.00
Tumbler, 8 oz., ground bottom	5.00	17.50	22.50
Tumbler, 12 oz., tea, ground bottom	7.00	25.00	30.00
Vase, 8"	30.00	80.00	100.00

Colors: crystal, yellow, Heatherbloom, green, amber, Carmen, and Crown Tuscan w/gold

Portia crystal items not listed here may be found under Rose Point, which has a more detailed listing of Cambridge pieces. Prices for the Portia items will run 40% to 50% less than the same item in Rose Point.

	Crystal
Basket, 2 hdld. (upturned sides)	30.00
Basket, 7", 1 hdld.	325.00
Bowl, 3", indiv. nut, 4 ftd.	60.00
Bowl, 3½", cranberry	45.00
Bowl, 3½", sq., cranberry	45.00
Bowl, 5¼", 2 hdld., bonbon	30.00
Bowl, 6", 2 pt., relish	27.50
Bowl, 6", ftd., 2 hdld., bonbon	30.00
Bowl, 6", grapefruit or oyster	35.00
Bowl, 6½", 3 pt., relish	30.00
Bowl, 7", 2 pt., relish	35.00
Bowl, 7", ftd., bonbon, tab hdld.	35.00
Bowl, 7", pickle or relish	40.00
Bowl, 9", 3 pt., celery & relish, tab hdld.	50.00
Bowl, 9½", ftd., pickle (like corn bowl)	40.00

	Crystal
Bowl, 10", flared, 4 ftd.	50.00
Bowl, 11", 2 pt., 2 hdld., "figure 8" relish	40.00
Bowl, 11", 2 hdld.	65.00
Bowl, 12", 3 pt., celery & relish, tab hdld.	60.00
Bowl, 12", 5 pt., celery & relish	60.00
Bowl, 12", flared, 4 ftd.	65.00
Bowl, 12", oval, 4 ftd., "ears" handles	95.00
Bowl, finger, w/liner, #3124	50.00
Bowl, seafood (fruit cocktail w/liner)	75.00
Candlestick, 5"	35.00
Candlestick, 6", 2-lite, "fleur-de-lis"	45.00
Candlestick, 6", 3-lite	55.00
Candy box, w/cover, rnd.	125.00
Cigarette holder, urn shape	65.00
Cocktail icer, 2 pt.	75.00
Cocktail shaker, w/stopper	195.00
Cocktail shaker, 80 oz., hdld. ball w/chrome top	235.00
Cologne, 2 oz., hdld. ball w/stopper	195.00
Comport, 5½"	50.00
Comport, 5⅜", blown	65.00
Creamer, ftd.	22.00
Creamer, hdld. ball	45.00
Creamer, indiv.	22.00
Cup, ftd., sq.	25.00
Cup, rd.	20.00
Decanter, 29 oz., ftd., sherry, w/stopper	250.00
Hurricane lamp, candlestick base	175.00
Hurricane lamp, keyhole base, w/prisms	235.00
Ice bucket, w/chrome handle	115.00
Ivy ball, 5¼"	95.00

	Crystal
Mayonnaise, div. bowl, w/liner & 2 ladles	65.00
Mayonnaise, w/liner & ladle	65.00
Oil, 6 oz., loop hdld., w/stopper	120.00
Oil, 6 oz., hdld. ball, w/stopper	100.00
Pitcher, ball	275.00
Pitcher, Doulton	355.00
Plate, 6", 2 hdld.	15.00
Plate, 6½", bread/butter	7.50
Plate, 8", salad	15.00
Plate, 8", ftd., 2 hdld.	22.00
Plate, 8", ftd., bonbon, tab hdld.	22.00
Plate, 8½", sq.	18.00
Plate, 10½", dinner	95.00
Plate, 13", 4 ftd., torte	65.00
Plate, 13½", 2 hdld., cake	65.00
Plate, 14", torte	75.00
Puff box, 3½", ball shape, w/lid	195.00
Salt & pepper, pr., flat	45.00
Saucer, sq. or rnd.	5.00
Set: 3 pc. frappe (bowl, 2 plain inserts)	65.00
Stem, #3121, 1 oz., cordial	75.00
Stem, #3121, 1 oz., low ftd., brandy	65.00
Stem, #3121, 2½ oz., wine	40.00
Stem, #3121, 3 oz., cocktail	30.00
Stem, #3121, 4½ oz., claret	50.00
Stem, #3121, 4½ oz., oyster cocktail	20.00
Stem, #3121, 5 oz., parfait	43.00
Stem, #3121, 6 oz., low sherbet	20.00
Stem, #3121, 6 oz., tall sherbet	22.00
Stem, #3121, 10 oz., goblet	30.00
Stem, #3124, 3 oz., cocktail	20.00
Stem, #3124, 3 oz., wine	35.00
Stem, #3124, 4½ oz., claret	50.00
Stem, #3124, 7 oz., low sherbet	18.00
Stem, #3124, 7 oz., tall sherbet	20.00
Stem, #3124, 10 oz., goblet	28.00

	Crystal		Crystal
Stem, #3126, 1 oz., cordial	65.00	Tumbler, #3121, 10 oz., ftd., water	25.00
Stem, #3126, 1 oz., low ft., brandy	65.00	Tumbler, #3121, 12 oz., ftd., tea	30.00
Stem, #3126, 2½ oz., wine	40.00	Tumbler, #3124, 3 oz.	18.00
Stem, #3126, 3 oz., cocktail	22.00	Tumbler, #3124, 5 oz., juice	20.00
Stem, #3126, 4½ oz., claret	45.00	Tumbler, #3124, 10 oz., water	25.00
Stem, #3126, 4½ oz., low ft., oyster cocktail	18.00	Tumbler, #3124, 12 oz., tea	30.00
Stem, #3126, 7 oz., low sherbet	18.00	Tumbler, #3126, 2½ oz.	40.00
Stem, #3126, 7 oz., tall sherbet	20.00	Tumbler, #3126, 5 oz., juice	20.00
Stem, #3126, 9 oz., goblet	30.00	Tumbler, #3126, 10 oz., water	25.00
Stem, #3130, 1 oz., cordial	70.00	Tumbler, #3126, 12 oz., tea	30.00
Stem, #3130, 2½ oz., wine	40.00	Tumbler, #3130, 5 oz., juice	25.00
Stem, #3130, 3 oz., cocktail	20.00	Tumbler, #3130, 10 oz., water	25.00
Stem, #3130, 4½ oz., claret	45.00	Tumbler, #3130, 12 oz., tea	30.00
Stem, #3130, 4½ oz., fruit/oyster cocktail	20.00	Tumbler, 12 oz., "roly-poly"	30.00
Stem, #3130, 7 oz., low sherbet	18.00	Vase, 5", globe	75.00
Stem, #3130, 7 oz., tall sherbet	20.00	Vase, 6", ftd.	85.00
Stem, #3130, 9 oz., goblet	30.00	Vase, 8", ftd.	95.00
Sugar, ftd., hdld. ball	45.00	Vase, 9", keyhole ft.	90.00
Sugar, ftd.	22.00	Vase, 10", bud	70.00
Sugar, indiv.	22.00	Vase, 11", flower	95.00
Tray, 11", celery	40.00	Vase, 11", pedestal ft.	100.00
Tumbler, #3121, 2½ oz., bar	40.00	Vase, 12", keyhole ft.	120.00
Tumbler, #3121, 5 oz., ftd., juice	20.00	Vase, 13", flower	150.00

PRINCESS FEATHER, #201 Westmoreland Glass Company, late 1924 – early 1950s; reissued as Golden Sunset (amber) in 1960s.

Colors: blue, crystal, crystal w/black base, crystal w/lavender or red flash, green, pink

Princess Feather is often confused with other companies' Sandwich patterns. Note the back to back quarter moons tied together in the pattern. If that visual is kept in mind, you'll never confuse this with any Sandwich pattern again. The color most often seen is Golden Sunset (amber) which was not made until the 1960s. Originally made in crystal in the mid-1920s this long-lived pattern can be collected in crystal more easily than any color.

More collectors seek pink or green and sets can be collected in either color with work and patience. I have seen little of the lavender or red flashed, but if I were a collector, I'd be buying every piece of the lilac flashed that I could find.

	Amber/Crystal	*Pink/Green
Basket, 8", hdld.	45.00	
Bonbon, 6", hdld.	20.00	
Bonbon, 7½", crimped	25.00	
Bowl, finger	8.00	15.00
Bowl, 5", nappy	8.00	15.00
Bowl, 6½", nappy	12.50	20.00
Bowl, 6½", grapefruit	12.00	20.00
Bowl, 9½", bell, ftd.	40.00	
Bowl, 10", banana, ftd.	55.00	
Bowl, 10", crimped, ftd.	55.00	
Bowl, 11" x 8", oval, hdld.	45.00	
Bowl, 12" nappy	35.00	55.00
Cake salver, 10"	37.50	
Candle, one lite	15.00	25.00
Candle, double	25.00	37.50
Creamer	10.00	20.00
Cup	8.00	5.00
Decanter w/stopper	30.00	
Jelly w/lid, 5"	25.00	
Pitcher, 54 oz.	75.00	
Plate, 6½", liner finger bowl	5.00	10.00
Plate, 7"	6.00	12.50

	Amber/Crystal	*Pink/Green
Plate, 8"	8.00	17.50
Plate, 10½", dinner	20.00	35.00
Plate, 13", service	22.50	40.00
Plate, 18"	30.00	
Relish, 5 part, 2 hdld.	35.00	
Salt and pepper	25.00	55.00
Saucer	3.00	4.00
Stem, 2 oz., cordial	15.00	
Stem, 2½ oz., wine	12.00	22.50
Stem, 3 oz., cocktail	10.00	17.50
Stem, 5 oz., high sherbet	10.00	17.50
Stem, 5 oz.. saucer champagne	10.00	17.50
Stem, 6 oz., sherbet	8.00	15.00
Stem, 8 oz., water	12.50	22.50
Sugar	10.00	20.00
Tray, creamer/sugar	12.00	
Tumbler, 6 oz., juice	8.00	15.00
Tumbler, 9 oz., ftd.	10.00	20.00
Tumbler, 10 oz., water, flat	12.50	22.50
Tumbler, 12 oz., ice tea, flat		
Vase, 14", flat	65.00	

* Add 25% for blue or ruby/lavender flash.

Colors: crystal, Limelight green

This pattern was first called Whirlpool in the 1930s; but Heisey changed its name to Provincial for the 1952 reissue. Limelight colored Provincial was Heisey's attempt at rejuvenating the earlier, popular Zircon color.

	Crystal	Limelight Green
Ashtray, 3", sq.	12.50	
Bonbon dish, 7", 2 hdld., upturned sides	12.00	45.00
Bowl, 5 quart, punch	120.00	
Bowl, individual, nut/jelly	20.00	40.00
Bowl, 4½", nappy	15.00	70.00
Bowl, 5", 2 hdld., nut/jelly	20.00	
Bowl, 5½", nappy	20.00	40.00
Bowl, 5½", round, hdld., nappy	20.00	
Bowl, 5½", tri-corner, hdld., nappy	20.00	55.00
Bowl, 10", 4 part, relish	40.00	150.00
Bowl, 12", floral	40.00	
Bowl, 13", gardenia	40.00	
Box, 5½", footed, candy, w/cover	85.00	550.00
Butter dish, w/cover	100.00	
Candle, 1-lite, block	35.00	
Candle, 2-lite	80.00	
Candle, 3-lite, #4233, 5", vase	95.00	
Cigarette box w/cover	70.00	
Cigarette lighter	30.00	
Coaster, 4"	15.00	
Creamer, ftd.	25.00	95.00
Creamer & sugar, w/tray, individual	80.00	
Cup, punch	10.00	

	Crystal	Limelight Green
Mayonnaise, 7" (plate, ladle, bowl)	40.00	150.00
Mustard	140.00	
Oil bottle, 4 oz., #1 stopper	45.00	
Oil & vinegar bottle (french dressing)	65.00	
Plate, 5", footed, cheese	20.00	
Plate, 7", 2 hdld., snack	25.00	
Plate, 7", bread	10.00	
Plate, 8", luncheon	15.00	50.00
Plate, 14", torte	45.00	
Plate, 18", buffet	70.00	175.00
Salt & pepper, pr.	40.00	
Stem, 3½ oz., oyster cocktail	20.00	
Stem, 3½ oz., wine	20.00	
Stem, 5 oz., sherbet/champagne	10.00	
Stem, 10 oz.	20.00	
Sugar, footed	25.00	95.00
Tray, 13", oval, celery	22.00	
Tumbler, 5 oz., ftd., juice	14.00	60.00
Tumbler, 8 oz.	17.00	
Tumbler, 9 oz., ftd.	17.00	80.00
Tumbler, 12 oz., ftd., iced tea	20.00	80.00
Tumbler, 13", flat, ice tea	20.00	
Vase, 3½", violet	30.00	95.00
Vase, 4", pansy	35.00	
Vase, 6", sweet pea	45.00	

Color: crystal and crystal w/green

Psyche is a Tiffin pattern that attracts collectors. The design speaks of elegance and quality. It is not a plentiful pattern, but enough can be found to keep your appetite whetted.

The cordial pictured is one from a set of Tiffin cordials found at the National Heisey show about fifteen years ago. A dealer had a large set of Tiffin on the same stemware line as Psyche. It was priced as a set, not individually. If memory serves me correctly (and it doesn't do as well as it used to do), the pattern was a floral design. Most observers of the set marveled at the wild price, but one observant dealer noticed that several of the cordials were Psyche and not the floral design. He persuaded the dealer to sell those cordials. I was able to obtain my cordial that way. The price of that set may now have caught up with prices on it then — but I doubt it!

As with most Tiffin patterns of this era, you can find tumblers and stems, but finding basic serving pieces is a chore. I found a creamer, but no sugar to accompany it. I see the green stem and handled pieces more than the all crystal pieces, but finding plates or bowls is not easily done.

Bonbon	65.00	Stem, cocktail	40.00
Bowl, 13", centerpiece	125.00	Stem, cordial	150.00
Bowl, finger, ftd.	40.00	Stem, grapefruit w/liner	85.00
Candleholder, #9758	75.00	Stem, saucer champagne	35.00
Cream	65.00	Stem, sherbet	30.00
Cup	85.00	Stem, water goblet	50.00
Pitcher	395.00	Stem, wine	75.00
Pitcher w/cover	495.00	Sugar	65.00
Plate, 6"	20.00	Tumbler, iced tea	50.00
Plate, 8"	30.00	Tumbler, juice	40.00
Saucer	20.00	Tumbler, oyster cocktail	40.00
Plate, 10"	150.00	Tumbler, water	40.00
Stem, café parfait	55.00	Vase, bud	125.00
Stem, claret	65.00		

Colors: crystal, green, pink

Puritan has driven me slightly bonkers getting enough pieces to photograph. Last spring, I finally ran into a large amount of green in a mall in Florida. I bought one of each piece.

Interestingly, I had a dealer ask what was the pattern name of the green glass she bought last year where I had bought one of each piece. She had to show me so I would know what she meant. It was the set of Puritan. Unfortunately, all of that green I bought didn't get to the photo session as it is still in one of the boxes never unpacked before we photographed.

Thankfully, there were a couple of ice buckets to help fill the photo. You will find a lot of crystal Puritan pieces have a floral cut. I have not been able to determine what that pattern is called.

	*All colors
Bowl, cream soup, 2-hdld.	20.00
Bowl, 5"	12.50
Bowl, 9", oval vegetable	55.00
Bowl, 9¼"	50.00
Bowl, 12", rolled console	65.00
Candlestick	25.00
Comport	35.00
Creamer	17.50
Cup	15.00
Cup, demi	17.50
Ice bucket	100.00

	*All colors
Pitcher	125.00
Plate, 7½", salad	10.00
Plate, cream soup liner	8.00
Saucer	3.00
Saucer, demi	5.00
Server, center hdld.	35.00
Stem, water goblet	22.50
Sugar	17.50
Tumbler, flat tea	25.00
Vase	65.00

* Crystal 25% less.

Colors: crystal

When Empress (#1401) was produced in crystal, it was generally named Queen Ann (c. 1938). Although this has been acknowledged by almost everyone, it is not entirely factual. According to Heisey experts, there is a slight difference between Queen Ann and Empress. Most collectors and dealers cannot distinguish a difference; so pricing is the same.

Queen Ann's mould blank was used for several of Heisey's most popular etched patterns including Orchid, Heisey Rose, Minuet, etc. This plainer, unetched line has been easy to find and inexpensive in the past; however, the prices are now adjusting to demand, particularly for rarely found pieces.

	Crystal
Ashtray	30.00
Bonbon, 6"	12.00
Bowl, cream soup	18.00
Bowl, cream soup, w/sq. liner	25.00
Bowl, frappe, w/center	25.00
Bowl, nut, dolphin ftd., indiv.	35.00
Bowl, 4½", nappy	8.00
Bowl, 5", preserve, 2 hdld.	15.00
Bowl, 6", ftd., jelly, 2 hdld.	15.00
Bowl, 6", dolphin ftd., mint	20.00
Bowl, 6", grapefruit, sq. top, ground bottom	12.00
Bowl, 6½", oval, lemon, w/cover	45.00
Bowl, 7", 3 pt., relish, triplex	18.00
Bowl, 7", 3 pt., relish, ctr. hand.	25.00
Bowl, 7½", dolphin ftd., nappy	28.00
Bowl, 7½", dolphin ftd., nasturtium	35.00
Bowl, 8", nappy	25.00
Bowl, 8½", ftd., floral, 2 hdld	32.00
Bowl, 9", floral, rolled edge	25.00
Bowl, 9", floral, flared	32.00
Bowl, 10", 2 hdld., oval dessert	30.00
Bowl, 10", lion head, floral	250.00
Bowl, 10", oval, veg.	30.00
Bowl, 10", square, salad, 2 hdld.	35.00
Bowl, 10", triplex, relish	25.00
Bowl, 11", dolphin ftd., floral	38.00
Bowl, 13", pickle/olive, 2 pt.	20.00
Bowl, 15", dolphin ftd., punch	400.00
Candlestick, 3", 3 ftd	50.00
Candlestick, low, 4 ftd., w/2 hdld.	30.00
Candlestick, 6", dolphin ftd.	70.00
Candy, w/cover, 6", dolphin ftd.	50.00
Comport, 6", ftd.	25.00
Comport, 6", square	40.00

	Crystal
Comport, 7", oval	35.00
Compotier, 6", dolphin ftd.	70.00
Creamer, dolphin ftd.	30.00
Creamer, indiv.	20.00
Cup	15.00
Cup, after dinner	20.00
Cup, bouillon, 2 hdld.	20.00
Cup, 4 oz., custard or punch	12.00
Cup, #1401½, has rim as demi-cup	20.00
Grapefruit, w/sq. liner	20.00

	Crystal			Crystal
Ice tub, w/metal handles	60.00		Salt & pepper, pr.	50.00
Jug, 3 pint, ftd.	100.00		Saucer, sq.	5.00
Marmalade, w/cover, dolphin ftd.	60.00		Saucer, after dinner	5.00
Mayonnaise, 5½", ftd., w/ladle	30.00		Saucer	5.00
Mustard, w/cover	60.00		Stem, 2½ oz., oyster cocktail	15.00
Oil bottle, 4 oz.	40.00		Stem, 4 oz., saucer champagne	20.00
Plate, bouillon liner	8.00		Stem, 4 oz., sherbet	15.00
Plate, cream soup liner	8.00		Stem, 9 oz., Empress stemware,	
Plate, 4½"	5.00		unusual	40.00
Plate, 6"	5.00		Sugar, indiv.	20.00
Plate, 6", sq.	5.00		Sugar, dolphin ftd., 3 hdld.	30.00
Plate, 7"	8.00		Tray, condiment & liner for indiv.	
Plate, 7", sq.	7.00		sugar/creamer	20.00
Plate, 8", sq.	10.00		Tray, 10", 3 pt., relish	20.00
Plate, 8"	9.00		Tray, 10", 7 pt., hors d'oeuvre	60.00
Plate, 9"	12.00		Tray, 10", celery	12.00
Plate, 10½"	40.00		Tray, 12", ctr. hdld., sand.	30.00
Plate, 10½", sq.	40.00		Tray, 12", sq. ctr. hdld., sand.	32.50
Plate, 12"	25.00		Tray, 13", celery	20.00
Plate, 12", muffin, sides upturned	35.00		Tray, 16", 4 pt., buffet relish	35.00
Plate, 12", sandwich, 2 hdld.	30.00		Tumbler, 8 oz., dolphin ftd., unusual	75.00
Plate, 13", hors d'oeuvre, 2 hdld.	60.00		Tumbler, 8 oz., ground bottom	20.00
Plate, 13", sq., 2 hdld.	35.00		Tumbler, 12 oz., tea, ground bottom	20.00
Platter, 14"	30.00		Vase, 8", flared	55.00

c. 1928

Color: crystal bowl w/Anna Rose (pink) stem and foot

Queen Louise is one of my favorite Elegant patterns. It is absolutely magnificent with that silk screen process that must have cost a fortune when originally sold. It still commands a substantial price, but may be under valued considering its dearth today. The only new item I was able to find was used as a close-up pattern shot. I paid dearly just to have a different piece to show you.

Looking for this has been an adventure of almost ten years. Evidently Queen Louise was sold in the Chicago and St. Louis areas since that is where it is being found today. Even the Internet auctions have been void of offerings of this pattern recently.

For purposes of identification I will point out that the stem on the far left is a wine and next to that is the parfait. The bowl in the center is a footed finger bowl although shaped like some of the Depression era sherbets. On the right are a cocktail and a water goblet. Personal observations on this pattern show that all stems sell in the same price range with waters being found the most often. Champagnes and parfaits may be the most difficult stems to find. Plates are rare and the footed bowl is seldom seen. No substantiation of the rumored dinner plate has been forthcoming.

	Crystal w/pink			Crystal w/pink
Bowl, finger, ftd.	225.00		Stem, 5½ oz., saucer champagne	375.00
Plate, 6", finger bowl liner	125.00		Stem, 5½ oz., sherbet	300.00
Plate, salad	150.00		Stem, 7 oz., parfait	450.00
Stem, 2½ oz., wine	375.00		Stem, 9 oz., water	400.00
Stem, 3 oz., cocktail	375.00			

RIDGELEIGH, Blanks #1467, #1468, and #1469, A.H. Heisey & Co. 1935 to mid 1940s

Colors: crystal, Sahara, Zircon, rare

	Crystal
Ashtray, rnd.	14.00
Ashtray, sq.	10.00
Ashtray, 4", rnd.	22.00
Ashtray, 6", sq.	35.00
Ashtrays, bridge set (heart, diamond, spade, club)	65.00
Basket, bonbon, metal handle	25.00
Bottle, rock & rye, w/#104 stopper	240.00
Bottle, 4 oz., cologne	130.00
Bottle, 5 oz., bitters, w/tube	130.00
Bowl, indiv., nut	15.00
Bowl, oval, indiv., jelly	20.00
Bowl, indiv., nut, 2 part	20.00
Bowl, 4½", nappy, bell or cupped	20.00
Bowl, 4½", nappy, scalloped	20.00
Bowl, 5", lemon, w/cover	65.00
Bowl, 5", nappy, straight	18.00
Bowl, 5", nappy, sq.	25.00
Bowl, 6", 2 hdld., div., jelly	40.00
Bowl, 6", 2 hdld., jelly	30.00
Bowl, 7", 2 part, oval, relish	30.00
Bowl, 8", centerpiece	55.00
Bowl, 8", nappy, sq.	55.00
Bowl, 9", nappy, sq.	65.00
Bowl, 9", salad	50.00
Bowl, 10", flared, fruit	45.00
Bowl, 10", floral	45.00
Bowl, 11", centerpiece	50.00
Bowl, 11", punch	200.00
Bowl, 11½", floral	50.00
Bowl, 12", oval, floral	55.00
Bowl, 12", flared, fruit	50.00
Bowl, 13", cone, floral	65.00
Bowl, 14", oblong, floral	70.00
Bowl, 14", oblong, swan hdld., floral	280.00
Box, 8", floral	70.00
Candle block, 3", #1469½	30.00
Candle vase, 6"	35.00
Candlestick, 2", 1-lite	35.00
Candlestick, 2-lite, bobeche & "A" prisms	80.00
Candlestick, 7", w/bobeche & "A" prisms	120.00
Cheese, 6", 2 hdld.	22.00
Cigarette box, w/cover, oval	90.00
Cigarette box, w/cover, 6"	35.00
Cigarette holder, oval, w/2 comp. ashtrays	70.00
Cigarette holder, rnd.	18.00
Cigarette holder, sq.	18.00
Cigarette holder, w/cover	30.00
Coaster or cocktail rest	15.00
Cocktail shaker, 1 qt., w/#1 strainer & #86 stopper	300.00
Comport, 6", low ft., flared	25.00
Comport, 6", low ft., w/cover	40.00
Creamer	30.00
Creamer, indiv.	20.00
Cup	16.00
Cup, beverage	12.00
Cup, punch	10.00
Decanter, 1 pint, w/#95 stopper	210.00
Ice tub, 2 hdld.	100.00
Marmalade, w/cover (scarce)	90.00
Mayonnaise and under plate	55.00
Mustard, w/cover	80.00
Oil bottle, 3 oz., w/#103 stopper	50.00

	Crystal
Pitcher, ½ gallon, ball shape	380.00
Pitcher, ½ gallon, ice lip, ball shape	380.00
Plate, oval, hors d'oeuvres	500.00
Plate, 2 hdld., ice tub liner	50.00
Plate, 6", rnd.	12.00
Plate, 6", sq.	24.00
Plate, 7", sq.	28.00
Plate, 8", rnd.	20.00
Plate, 8", sq.	32.00
Plate, 13½", sandwich	45.00
Plate, 13½", ftd., torte	45.00
Plate, 14", salver	50.00
Plate, 20", punch bowl underplate	140.00
Puff box, 5", and cover	90.00
Salt & pepper, pr.	45.00
Salt dip, indiv.	13.00
Saucer	5.00
Soda, 12 oz., ftd., no knob in stem (rare)	50.00
Stem, cocktail, pressed	25.00
Stem, claret, pressed	50.00
Stem, oyster cocktail, pressed	35.00
Stem, sherbet, pressed	20.00
Stem, saucer champagne, pressed	30.00
Stem, wine, pressed	40.00
Stem, 1 oz., cordial, blown	160.00
Stem, 2 oz., sherry, blown	90.00
Stem, 2½ oz., wine, blown	80.00
Stem, 3½ oz., cocktail, blown	35.00
Stem, 4 oz., claret, blown	55.00
Stem, 4 oz., oyster cocktail, blown	30.00
Stem, 5 oz., saucer champagne, blown	25.00
Stem, 5 oz., sherbet, blown	20.00
Stem, 8 oz., luncheon, low stem	30.00
Stem, 8 oz., tall stem	40.00
Sugar	30.00
Sugar, indiv.	20.00
Tray, for indiv. sugar & creamer	20.00
Tray, 10½", oblong	40.00
Tray, 11", 3 part, relish	50.00
Tray, 12", celery & olive, divided	50.00
Tray, 12", celery	40.00
Tumbler, 2½ oz., bar, pressed	45.00
Tumbler, 5 oz., juice, blown	30.00
Tumbler, 5 oz., soda, ftd., pressed	30.00
Tumbler, 8 oz., #1469¾, pressed	35.00
Tumbler, 8 oz., old-fashion, pressed	40.00
Tumbler, 8 oz., soda, blown	40.00
Tumbler, 10 oz., #1469½, pressed	45.00
Tumbler, 12 oz., ftd., soda, pressed	50.00
Tumbler, 12 oz., soda, #1469½, pressed	50.00

	Crystal
Tumbler, 13 oz., iced tea, blown	40.00
Vase, #1 indiv., cuspidor shape	40.00
Vase, #2 indiv., cupped top	45.00
Vase, #3 indiv., flared rim	30.00
Vase, #4 indiv., fan out top	55.00

	Crystal
Vase, #5 indiv., scalloped top	55.00
Vase, 3½"	25.00
Vase, 6" (also flared)	35.00
Vase, 8"	75.00
Vase, 8", triangular, #1469¾	110.00

Colors: crystal

Rogene is an early Fostoria pattern that has recently been discovered by some new collectors searching for something different to collect. There are multitudes of pieces that are reasonably priced by standards set by other Fostoria patterns. Since its introduction in my last book, there has been some slight price hikes in the more rarely seen items.

	Crystal
Almond, ftd., #4095	8.00
Comport, 5" tall, #5078	30.00
Comport, 6", #5078	30.00
Creamer, flat, #1851	30.00
Decanter, qt., cut neck, #300	85.00
Finger bowl, #766	20.00
Jelly, #825	22.50
Jelly & cover, #825	40.00
Jug 4, ftd., #4095	100.00
Jug 7, #318	150.00
Jug 7, #2270	165.00
Jug 7, #4095	195.00
Jug 7, covered, #2270	250.00
Marmalade & cover, #1968	45.00
Mayonnaise bowl, #766	30.00
Mayonnaise ladle	22.50
Mayonnaise set, 3 pc., #2138 (ftd. compote, ladle, liner)	60.00
Nappy, 5" ftd. (comport/sherbet), #5078	17.50
Nappy, 6" ftd., #5078	25.00
Nappy, 7" ftd., #5078	30.00
Night set, 2 pc., #1697 (carafe & tumbler)	110.00
Oil bottle w/cut stop, 5 oz., #1495	55.00
Oyster cocktail, ftd., #837	12.50
Plate, 5"	6.00
Plate, 6"	7.50
Plate, 6", #2283	7.00
Plate, 7" salad, #2283	10.00

	Crystal
Plate, 8"	15.00
Plate, 11"	25.00
Plate, 11", w/cut star	27.50
Plate, finger bowl liner	7.50
Plate, mayonnaise liner, #766	12.50
Shaker, pr., glass (pearl) top, #2283	60.00
Stem, ¾ oz., cordial, #5082	45.00
Stem, 2½ oz., wine, #5082	25.00
Stem, 3 oz., cocktail, #5082	18.00
Stem, 4½ oz., claret, #5082	30.00
Stem, 5 oz., fruit, #5082	12.50
Stem, 5 oz., saucer champagne, #5082	17.50
Stem, 6 oz., parfait, #5082	22.50
Stem, 9 oz., #5082	22.50
Stem, grapefruit, #945½	30.00
Stem, grapefruit liner, #945½	12.50
Sugar, flat, #1851	30.00
Tumbler, 2½ oz., whiskey, #887	17.50
Tumbler, 2½ oz., ftd., #4095	17.50
Tumbler, 5 oz., flat, #889	12.50
Tumbler, 5 oz., ftd., #4095	12.50
Tumbler, 8 oz., flat,, #889	14.00
Tumbler, 10 oz., ftd., #4095	15.00
Tumbler, 12 oz., flat, hdld., #837	25.00
Tumbler, 13 oz., flat, #889	17.50
Tumbler, 13 oz., ftd., #4095	20.00
Tumbler, flat, table, #4076	14.00
Vase, 8½" rolled edge	95.00

Colors: Amber, Bluebell, Carmen, crystal, Emerald green, Heatherbloom, Peach-Blo, Topaz, Willow blue

Rosalie, Cambridge's #731 line, is a Cambridge pattern that can be collected in several colors; but finding a complete set will take years of searching unless you are extremely lucky. The good news is that Rosalie is one of Cambridge's least expensive colored wares especially in pink and green. Perhaps a small set of Willow Blue is possible; but Carmen, Bluebell, or Heatherbloom are colors that are too infrequently seen to be gathered into sets. Note how well the pattern shows on the green and blue pieces that have been emphasized by highlighted color. These are factory made; and for photography purposes, I wish all patterns were made that way.

The Ebony vase pictured here belongs to a collector in Michigan. Hopefully the Rosalie pattern will show against the black. It has an additional gold decorated pattern along the rim, but it is the Rosalie decoration on black that is highly unusual.

	Blue Pink Green	Amber/ Crystal		Blue Pink Green	Amber/ Crystal
Bottle, French dressing	195.00	100.00	Bowl, 11"	75.00	40.00
Bowl, bouillon, 2 hdld.	30.00	15.00	Bowl, 11", basket, 2 hdld.	75.00	45.00
Bowl, cream soup	30.00	20.00	Bowl, 11½"	90.00	55.00
Bowl, finger, w/liner	70.00	55.00	Bowl, 12", decagon	125.00	85.00
Bowl, finger, ftd., w/liner	75.00	60.00	Bowl, 13", console	125.00	
Bowl, 3½", cranberry	50.00	35.00	Bowl, 14", decagon, deep	245.00	195.00
Bowl, 5½", fruit	22.00	15.00	Bowl, 15", oval console	135.00	75.00
Bowl, 5½", 2 hdld., bonbon	25.00	15.00	Bowl, 15", oval, flanged	135.00	75.00
Bowl, 6¼", 2 hdld., bonbon	25.00	18.00	Bowl, 15½", oval	145.00	85.00
Bowl, 7", basket, 2 hdld.	35.00	22.00	Candlestick, 4", 2 styles	40.00	25.00
Bowl, 8½", soup	60.00	35.00	Candlestick, 5", keyhole	45.00	30.00
Bowl, 8½", 2 hdld.	75.00	35.00	Candlestick, 6", 3-lite keyhole	80.00	45.00
Bowl, 8½", w/cover, 3 pt.	125.00	65.00	Candy and cover, 6"	150.00	75.00
Bowl, 10"	75.00	40.00	Celery, 11"	40.00	25.00
Bowl, 10", 2 hdld.	75.00	40.00	Cheese & cracker, 11", plate	75.00	45.00

	Blue Pink Green	Amber/ Crystal		Blue Pink Green	Amber/ Crystal
Cigarette jar & cover	95.00	60.00	Relish, 9", 2 pt.	45.00	20.00
Comport, 5½", 2 hdld.	30.00	15.00	Relish, 11", 2 pt.	50.00	30.00
Comport, 5¾"	30.00	15.00	Salt dip, 1½", ftd.	65.00	40.00
Comport, 6", ftd., almond	45.00	30.00	Saucer	5.00	4.00
Comport, 6½", low ft.	45.00	30.00	Stem, 1 oz., cordial, #3077	100.00	65.00
Comport, 6½", high ft.	45.00	30.00	Stem, 3½ oz., cocktail, #3077	22.00	16.00
Comport, 6¾"	55.00	35.00	Stem, 6 oz., low sherbet, #3077	18.00	14.00
Creamer, ftd.	20.00	15.00	Stem, 6 oz., high sherbet, #3077	20.00	16.00
Creamer, ftd., tall, ewer	65.00	35.00	Stem, 9 oz., water goblet, #3077	28.00	22.00
Cup	35.00	25.00	Stem, 10 oz., goblet, #801	35.00	22.00
Gravy, double, w/platter	175.00	100.00	Sugar, ftd.	20.00	13.00
Ice bucket or pail	110.00	55.00	Sugar shaker	325.00	225.00
Icer, w/liner	85.00	50.00	Tray for sugar shaker/creamer	30.00	20.00
Ice tub	100.00	65.00	Tray, ctr. hdld., for sugar/creamer	20.00	14.00
Mayonnaise, ftd., w/liner	75.00	35.00	Tray, 11", ctr. hdld.	30.00	20.00
Nut, 2½", ftd.	65.00	50.00	Tumbler, 2½ oz., ftd., #3077	45.00	25.00
Pitcher, 62 oz., #955	295.00	195.00	Tumbler, 5 oz., ftd., #3077	35.00	20.00
Plate, 6¾", bread/butter	10.00	7.00	Tumbler, 8 oz., ftd., #3077	20.00	16.00
Plate, 7", 2 hdld.	16.00	10.00	Tumbler, 10 oz., ftd., #3077	30.00	20.00
Plate, 7½", salad	15.00	8.00	Tumbler, 12 oz., ftd., #3077	40.00	25.00
Plate, 8⅜"	20.00	10.00	Vase, 5½", ftd.	85.00	50.00
Plate, 9½", dinner	70.00	45.00	Vase, 6"	90.00	55.00
Plate, 11", 2 hdld.	40.00	25.00	Vase, 6½", ftd.	125.00	60.00
Platter, 12"	100.00	55.00	Wafer tray	135.00	85.00
Platter, 15"	150.00	100.00			

Colors: crystal; some crystal with gold

Without question, Rose Point is the most collected pattern of Cambridge and most likely the most collected pattern in this book. Only Fostoria American might approach the collecting numbers of Rose Point. American was made for over 70 years; so more sets were used and passed down over the decades.

There were so many mould lines used to make the pattern that individual collectors can choose what they prefer. Consequently, not all are always looking for the same pieces. Variety is a good thing!

Take note of the two gold encrusted nude stem goblets pictured on page 178. These were the first Statuesque table stems to be found decorated with Rose Point. Also note the amber, gold decorated ice bucket pictured as a pattern shot. A Louisiana collector lent it.

Pages 179 and 180 show a Rose Point brochure with a listing where pieces are identified by number and that should help you distinguish pieces. There are limitations to how much catalog information we can do and still show you the actual glass. An uncertainty confronting new collectors is identifying different blanks on which Rose Point is found. At the top of the brochure is line #3900 and at the bottom are #3400 and #3500. These are the major mould lines upon which Rose Point was etched. The bottom of page 180 pictures the #3500 stem and tumblers. Be sure to note the shape differences in the parfait and the footed, five-ounce juice. They are often confused and there is quite a price difference. You might not mind buying juices for parfait prices, but you wouldn't want to sell parfaits as juices.

	Crystal
Ashtray, stack set on metal pole, #1715	255.00
Ashtray, 2½", sq., #721	35.00
Ashtray, 3¼", #3500/124	40.00
Ashtray, 3¼", sq., #3500/129	60.00
Ashtray, 3½", #3500/125	40.00
Ashtray, 4", #3500/126	42.50
Ashtray, 4", oval, #3500/130	100.00
Ashtray, 4¼", #3500/127	47.50
Ashtray, 4½", #3500/128	60.00
Ashtray, 4½", oval, #3500/131	70.00
Basket, 3", favor, #3500/79	425.00
Basket, 5", 1 hdld., #3500/51	325.00
Basket, 6", 1 hdld., #3500/52	375.00
Basket, 6", 2 hdld., #3400/1182	42.50
Basket, 6", sq., ftd., 2 hdld, #3500/55	47.50
Basket, 7", 1 hdld., #119	550.00
Basket, 7", wide, #3500/56	65.00
Basket, sugar, w/handle and tongs, #3500/13	325.00
Bell, dinner, #3121	150.00
Bowl, 3", 4 ftd., nut, #3400/71	75.00
Bowl, 3½", bonbon, cupped, deep, #3400/204	90.00
Bowl, 3½", cranberry, #3400/70	95.00
Bowl, 5", hdld., #3500/49	50.00
Bowl, 5", fruit, #3500/10	85.00
Bowl, 5", fruit, blown, #1534	90.00
Bowl, 5¼", fruit, #3400/56	85.00
Bowl, 5½", nappy, #3400/56	75.00
Bowl, 5½", 2 hdld., bonbon, #3400/1179	42.50
Bowl, 5½", 2 hdld., bonbon, #3400/1180	42.50
Bowl, 6", bonbon, crimped, #3400/203	100.00
Bowl, 6", bonbon, cupped, shallow, #3400/205	85.00
Bowl, 6", cereal, #3400/53	115.00
Bowl, 6", cereal, #3400/10	110.00
Bowl, 6", cereal, #3500/11	110.00
Bowl, 6", hdld., #3500/50	47.50
Bowl, 6", 2 hdld., #1402/89	45.00
Bowl, 6", 2 hdld., ftd., bonbon, #3500/54	40.00
Bowl, 6", 4 ftd., fancy rim, #3400/136	165.00
Bowl, 6½", bonbon, crimped, #3400/202	90.00
Bowl, 7", bonbon, crimped, shallow, #3400/201	125.00
Bowl, 7", tab hdld., ftd., bonbon, #3900/130	40.00

	Crystal
Bowl, 8", ram's head, squared, #3500/27	495.00
Bowl, 8½", rimmed soup, #361	295.00
Bowl, 8½", 3 part, #221	225.00
Bowl, 9", 4 ftd., #3400/135	250.00
Bowl, 9", ram's head, #3500/25	495.00
Bowl, 9½", pickle like corn, #477	55.00
Bowl, 9½", ftd., w/hdl., #3500/115	160.00
Bowl, 9½", 2 hdld., #3400/34	90.00
Bowl, 9½", 2 part, blown, #225	495.00
Bowl, 2 hdld., #3400/1185	100.00
Bowl, 10", 2 hdld., #3500/28	100.00
Bowl, 10", 4 tab ftd., flared, #3900/54	80.00
Bowl, 10", salad Pristine, #427	175.00
Bowl, 10½", crimp edge, #1351	100.00
Bowl, 10½", flared, #3400/168	85.00
Bowl, 10½", 3 part, #222	375.00
Bowl, 10½", 3 part, #1401/122	375.00
Bowl, 11", ftd., #3500/16	115.00
Bowl, 11", ftd., fancy edge, #3500/19	195.00
Bowl, 11", 4 ftd., oval, #3500/109	395.00
Bowl, 11", 4 ftd., shallow, fancy edge, #3400/48	120.00
Bowl, 11", fruit, #3400/1188	120.00
Bowl, 11", low foot, #3400/3	175.00
Bowl, 11", tab hdld., #3900/34	90.00
Bowl, 11½", ftd., w/tab hdl., #3900/28	90.00
Bowl, 12", crimped, pan Pristine, #136	350.00
Bowl, 12", 4 ftd., oval, #3400/1240	145.00
Bowl, 12", 4 ftd., oval, w/"ears" hdl., #3900/65	110.00
Bowl, 12", 4 ftd., fancy rim oblong, #3400/160	100.00
Bowl, 12", 4 ftd., flared, #3400/4	90.00
Bowl, 12", 4 tab ftd., flared, #3900/62	90.00
Bowl, 12", ftd., #3500/17	150.00
Bowl, 12", ftd., oblong, #3500/118	190.00
Bowl, 12", ftd., oval w/hdld., #3500/21	245.00
Bowl, 12½", flared, rolled edge, #3400/2	185.00
Bowl, 12½", 4 ftd., #993	110.00
Bowl, 13", #1398	150.00
Bowl, 13", 4 ftd., narrow, crimped, #3400/47	150.00
Bowl, 13", flared, #3400/1	90.00
Bowl, 14", 4 ftd., crimp edge, oblong, #1247	165.00
Bowl, 18", crimped, pan Pristine, #136	695.00

ROSE POINT

	Crystal
Bowl, cream soup, w/liner, #3400	195.00
Bowl, cream soup, w/liner, #3500/2	195.00
Bowl, finger, w/liner, #3106	110.00
Bowl, finger, w/liner, #3121	110.00
Butter, w/cover, round, #506	195.00
Butter, w/cover, 5", #3400/52	210.00
Butter dish, ¼ lb., #3900/52	495.00
Candelabrum, 2-lite w/bobeches & prisms, #1268	225.00
Candelabrum, 2-lite, #3500/94	150.00
Candelabrum, 3-lite, #1338	95.00
Candelabrum, 5½", 3-lite w/#19 bobeche & #1 prisms, #1545	175.00
Candelabrum, 6½", 2-lite, w/bobeches & prisms Martha, #496	195.00
Candle, torchere, cup ft., #3500/90	275.00
Candle, torchere, flat ft., #3500/88	250.00
Candlestick Pristine, #500	150.00
Candlestick, sq. base & lites, #1700/501	225.00
Candlestick, 2½", #3500/108	40.00
Candlestick, 3½", #628	45.00
Candlestick, 4", #627	75.00
Candlestick, 4", ram's head, #3500/74	125.00
Candlestick, 5", 1-lite keyhole, #3400/646	55.00
Candlestick, 5", inverts to comport, #3900/68	95.00
Candlestick, 5½", 2-lite Martha, #495	125.00
Candlestick, 6", #3500/31	150.00
Candlestick, 6", 2-lite keyhole, #3400/647	55.00
Candlestick, 6", 2-lite, #3900/72	65.00
Candlestick, 6", 3-lite, #3900/74	75.00
Candlestick, 6", 3-lite keyhole, #3400/638	80.00
Candlestick, 6", 3-tiered lite, #1338	95.00
Candlestick, 6½", Calla Lily, #499	125.00
Candlestick, 7", #3121	110.00
Candlestick, 7½", w/prism Martha, #497	145.00
Candy box, w/cover, 5", apple shape, #316	1,250.00
Candy box, w/cover, 5⅜", #1066 stem	210.00

	Crystal
Candy box, w/cover, 5⅜", tall stem, #3121/3	185.00
Candy box, w/cover, 5⅜", short stem, #3121/4	175.00
Candy box, w/cover, blown, 5⅜", #3500/103	210.00
Candy box, w/cover, 6", ram's head, #3500/78	325.00
Candy box, w/rose finial, 6", 3 ftd., #300	395.00
Candy box, w/cover, 7", #3400/9	175.00
Candy box, w/cover, 7", rnd., 3 pt., #103	195.00
Candy box, w/cover, 8", 3 pt., #3500/57	120.00
Candy box, w/cover, rnd., #3900/165	150.00
Celery, 12", #3400/652	65.00
Celery, 12", #3500/652	75.00
Celery, 12", 5 pt., #3400/67	95.00
Celery, 14", 4 pt., 2 hdld., #3500/97	185.00
Celery & relish, 9", 3 pt., #3900/125	65.00
Celery & relish, 12", 3 pt., #3900/126	80.00
Celery & relish, 12", 5 pt., #3900/120	95.00
Cheese, 5", comport & cracker, 13", plate, #3900/135	145.00
Cheese, 5½", comport & cracker, 11½", plate, #3400/6	145.00
Cheese, 6", comport & cracker, 12", plate, #3500/162	165.00
Cheese dish, w/cover, 5", #980	625.00
Cigarette box, w/cover, #615	175.00
Cigarette box, w/cover, #747	195.00
Cigarette holder, oval, w/ashtray ft., #1066	195.00
Cigarette holder, rnd., w/ashtray ft., #1337	175.00
Coaster, 3½", #1628	65.00
Cocktail icer, 2 pc., #3600	85.00
Cocktail shaker, metal top, #3400/157	210.00
Cocktail shaker, metal top, #3400/175	200.00
Cocktail shaker, 12 oz., metal top, #97	400.00
Cocktail shaker, 32 oz., w/glass stopper, #101	275.00
Cocktail shaker, 46 oz., metal top, #98	225.00
Cocktail shaker, 48 oz., glass stopper, #102	225.00
Comport, 5", #3900/135	50.00
Comport, 5", 4 ftd., #3400/74	75.00
Comport, 5½", scalloped edge, #3900/136	85.00
Comport, 5⅜", blown, #3500/101	90.00
Comport, 5⅜", blown, #3121 stem	95.00
Comport, 5⅜", blown, #1066 stem	85.00
Comport, 6", #3500/36	160.00
Comport, 6", #3500/111	195.00
Comport, 6", 4 ftd., #3400/13	65.00
Comport, 7", 2 hdld., #3500/37	150.00
Comport, 7", keyhole, #3400/29	150.00
Comport, 7", keyhole, low, #3400/28	110.00
Creamer, #3400/68	25.00
Creamer, #3500/14	30.00
Creamer, flat, #137	150.00
Creamer, flat, #944	165.00
Creamer, ftd., #3400/16	100.00
Creamer, ftd., #3900/41	25.00
Creamer, indiv., #3500/15 pie crust edge	27.50
Creamer, indiv., #3900/40 scalloped edge	25.00
Cup, 3 styles, #3400/54, #3500/1, #3900/17	32.50
Cup, 5 oz., punch, #488	40.00
Cup, after dinner, #3400/69	300.00

LIST OF ROSE POINT ITEMS

No.	Description
3500	10 oz. Goblet
3500	7 oz. Tall Sherbet
3500	7 oz. Low Sherbet
3500	3 oz. Cocktail
3500	2½ oz. Wine
3500	4½ oz. Claret
3500	4½ oz. Oyster Cocktail
3500	1 oz. Cordial
3500	5 oz Cafe Parfait
3500	12 oz. Ftd. Ice Tea
3500	10 oz. Ftd. Tumbler
3500	5 oz. Ftd. Tumbler
477	9½ in. Pickle
3400/1180	5¼ in. 2 Hdl. Bonbon
3400/1181	6 in. 2 Hdl. Plate
3400/90	6 in. 2 part Relish
3500/15	Ind. Sugar & Cream
3500/54	6 in. 2 Hdl. Ftd. Bonbon
3500/55	6 in. 2 Hdl. Ftd. Basket
3500/69	6½ in. 3 part Relish
3500/161	8 in. 2 Hdl. Ftd. Plate
3400/91	8 in. 3 part Relish
3500/57	8 in. 3 part Candy Box & Cover
3500/101	5⅜ in. Tall Comport
3900/17	Cup & Saucer
3900/19	2 pc. Mayonnaise Set
3900/20	6½ in. Bread & Butter Plate
3900/22	8 in. Salad Plate
3900/24	10½ in. Dinner Plate
3900/26	12 in. 4 Ftd. Plate
3900/28	11½ in. Ftd. Bowl
3900/33	13 in. 4 Ftd. Torte Plate, R. E.
3900/34	11 in. 2 Handled Bowl
3900/35	13½ in. 2 Handled Cake Plate
3900/40	Ind. Sugar & Cream
3900/41	Sugar & Cream
3900/54	10 in. 4 Ftd. Bowl, flared
3900/62	12 in. 4 Ftd. Bowl, flared
3900/65	12 in. 4 Ftd. Oval Bowl
3900/67	5 in. Candlestick
3900/72	6 in. 2 lite Candlestick
3900/74	6 in. 3 lite Candlestick
3900/100	6 oz. Oil, g. s.
3900/111	4 pc. Mayonnaise Set
3900/115	13 oz. Tumbler
3900/120	12 in. 5 part Celery & Relish
3900/123	7 in. Relish or Pickle
3900/124	7 in. 2 part Relish
3900/125	9 in. 3 part Celery & Relish
3900/126	12 in. 3 part Celery & Relish
3900/129	3 pc. Mayonnaise Set
3900/130	7 in. 2 handled Ftd. Bonbon
3900/131	8 in. 2 handled Ftd. Bonbon Plate
3900/136	5½ in. Comport
3900/165	Candy Box & Cover
3900/166	14 in. Plate, r. e.
3900/671	Ice Bucket
3900/671	Ice Bucket with chrome Handle Chrome Ice Tongs (long)
3900/1177	Salt & Pepper Shaker (doz. pr.)
274	10 in. Bud Flower Holder
278	11 in. Ftd. Flower Holder
279	13 in. Ftd. Flower Holder
968	2 pc. Cocktail Icer
1237	9 in. Ftd. Flower Holder
1238	12 in. Ftd. Flower Holder
1299	11 in. Ftd. Flower Holder
1309	5 in. Glode Flower Holder
1603	Hurricane Lamp (Etch. Chimney only)
1617	Hurricane Lamp (Etch. Chimney only)
6004	6 in. Ftd. Flower Holder
6004	8 in. Ftd. Flower Holder
P. 101	Cocktail Shaker (Patent—D133,198)

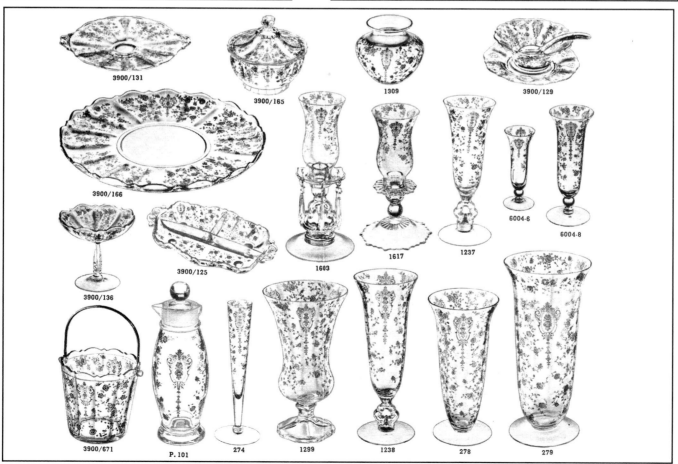

968
3900/1177
3900/54
3900/126
3900/65
3900/130
3900/123
3900/74
3900/124
3500/57
3900/120
3900/111
3900/62
3400/91
3900/100
3900/35
3900/33
3900/72

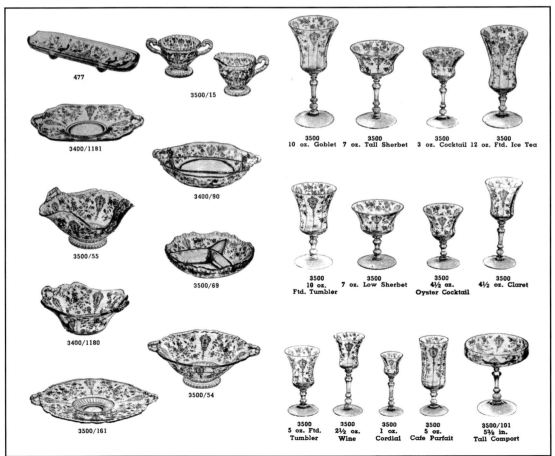

477
3500/15
3400/1181
3400/90
3500/55
3500/69
3400/1180
3500/54
3500/161

3500
10 oz. Goblet
3500
7 oz. Tall Sherbet
3500
3 oz. Cocktail
3500
12 oz. Ftd. Ice Tea

3500
10 oz.
Ftd. Tumbler
3500
7 oz. Low Sherbet
3500
4½ oz.
Oyster Cocktail
3500
4½ oz. Claret

3500
5 oz. Ftd.
Tumbler
3500
2½ oz.
Wine
3500
1 oz.
Cordial
3500
5 oz.
Cafe Parfait
3500/101
5⅜ in.
Tall Comport

	Crystal
Decanter, 12 oz., ball, w/stopper, #3400/119	350.00
Decanter, 14 oz., ftd., #1320	500.00
Decanter, 26 oz., sq., #1380	600.00
Decanter, 28 oz., tall, #1372	795.00
Decanter, 28 oz., w/stopper, #1321	425.00
Decanter, 32 oz., ball, w/stopper, #3400/92	495.00
Dressing bottle, flat, #1263	400.00
Dressing bottle, ftd., #1261	375.00
Epergne candle w/vases, #3900/75	275.00
Grapefruit, w/liner, #187	125.00
Hat, 5", #1704	495.00
Hat, 6", #1703	525.00
Hat, 8", #1702	650.00
Hat, 9", #1701	795.00
Honey dish, w/cover, #3500/139	400.00
Hot plate or trivet	125.00
Hurricane lamp, w/prisms, #1613	400.00
Hurricane lamp, candlestick base, #1617	300.00
Hurricane lamp, keyhole base, w/prisms, #1603	300.00
Hurricane lamp, 8", etched chimney, #1601	300.00
Hurricane lamp, 10", etched chimney & base, #1604	400.00
Ice bucket, #1402/52	235.00
Ice bucket, w/chrome hand., #3900/671	195.00
Ice pail, #1705	275.00
Ice pail, #3400/851	185.00
Ice tub, Pristine, #671	300.00
Icer, cocktail, #968 or, #18	80.00
Marmalade, 8 oz., #147	195.00
Marmalade, w/cover, 7 oz., ftd., #157	215.00

	Crystal
Mayonnaise sherbet type w/ladle, #19	85.00
Mayonnaise, div., w/liner & 2 ladles, #3900/111	95.00
Mayonnaise, 3 pc., #3400/11	85.00
Mayonnaise, 3 pc., #3900/129	85.00
Mayonnaise, w/liner & ladle, #3500/59	85.00
Mustard, 3 oz., #151	185.00
Mustard, 4½ oz., ftd., #1329	400.00
Oil, 2 oz., ball, w/stopper, #3400/96	120.00
Oil, 6 oz., ball, w/stopper, #3400/99	175.00
Oil, 6 oz., hdld., #3400/193	135.00
Oil, 6 oz., loop hdld., w/stopper, #3900/100	175.00
Oil, 6 oz., w/stopper, ftd., hdld., #3400/161	275.00
Pickle, 9", #3400/59	70.00
Pickle or relish, 7", #3900/123	45.00
Pitcher, 20 oz., #3900/117	350.00
Pitcher, 20 oz., w/ice lip, #70	375.00
Pitcher, 32 oz., #3900/118	400.00
Pitcher, 32 oz., martini slender, w/metal insert, #3900/114	550.00
Pitcher, 60 oz., martini, #1408	1,995.00
Pitcher, 76 oz., #3900/115	310.00
Pitcher, 76 oz., ice lip, #3400/100	250.00
Pitcher, 76 oz., ice lip, #3400/152	400.00
Pitcher, 80 oz., ball, #3400/38	300.00
Pitcher, 80 oz., ball, #3900/116	300.00
Pitcher, 80 oz., Doulton, #3400/141	400.00
Pitcher, nite set, 2 pc., w/tumbler insert top, #103	950.00
Plate, 6", bread/butter, #3400/60	15.00
Plate, 6", bread/butter, #3500/3	16.00
Plate, 6", 2 hdld., #3400/1181	22.00

	Crystal
Plate, 6⅛", canape, #693	195.00
Plate, 6½", bread/butter, #3900/20	16.00
Plate, 7½", #3500/4	20.00
Plate, 7½", salad, #3400/176	20.00
Plate, 8", salad, #3900/22	22.00
Plate, 8", 2 hdld., ftd., #3500/161	45.00
Plate, 8", tab hdld., ftd., bonbon, #3900/131	42.00
Plate, 8½", breakfast, #3400/62	25.00
Plate, 8½", salad, #3500/5	25.00
Plate, 9½", crescent salad, #485	295.00
Plate, 9½", luncheon, #3400/63	42.00
Plate, 10½", dinner, #3400/64	165.00
Plate, 10½", dinner, #3900/24	165.00
Plate, 11", 2 hdld., #3400/35	65.00
Plate, 12", 4 ftd., service, #3900/26	75.00
Plate, 12", ftd., #3500/39	92.00
Plate, 12½", 2 hdld., #3400/1186	75.00
Plate, 13", rolled edge, ftd., #3900/33	75.00
Plate, 13", 4 ftd., torte, #3500/110	130.00
Plate, 13", ftd., cake Martha, #170	250.00
Plate, 13", torte, #3500/38	185.00
Plate, 13½", #242	150.00
Plate, 13½", rolled edge, #1397	75.00
Plate, 13½", tab hdld., cake, #3900/35	75.00
Plate, 14", rolled edge, #3900/166	80.00
Plate, 14", service, #3900/167	80.00
Plate, 14", torte, #3400/65	155.00
Plate, 18", punch bowl liner, Martha, #129	595.00
Punch bowl, 15", Martha, #478	4,000.00
Punch set, 15-pc., Martha	5,100.00

	Crystal
Relish, 5½", 2 pt., #3500/68	30.00
Relish, 5½", 2 pt., hdld., #3500/60	40.00
Relish, 6", 2 pt., #3400/90	40.00
Relish, 6", 2 pt., 1 hdl., #3400/1093	100.00
Relish, 6½", 3 pt., #3500/69	60.00
Relish, 6½", 3 pt., hdld., #3500/61	65.00
Relish, 7", 2 pt., #3900/124	42.50
Relish, 7½", 3 pt., center hdld., #3500/71	150.00
Relish, 7½", 4 pt., #3500/70	65.00
Relish, 7½", 4 pt., 2 hdld., #3500/62	90.00
Relish, 8", 3 pt., 3 hdld., #3400/91	40.00
Relish, 10", 2 hdld., #3500/85	100.00
Relish, 10", 3 pt., 2 hdld., #3500/86	90.00
Relish, 10", 3 pt., 4 ftd., 2 hdld., #3500/64	75.00
Relish, 10", 4 pt., 4 ftd., #3500/65	90.00
Relish, 10", 4 pt., 2 hdld., #3500/87	90.00
Relish, 11", 2 pt., 2 hdld., #3400/89	100.00
Relish, 11", 3 pt., #3400/200	70.00
Relish, 12", 5 pt., #3400/67	90.00
Relish, 12", 5 pt., Pristine, #419	295.00
Relish, 12", 6 pc., #3500/67	285.00
Relish, 14", w/cover, 4 pt., 2 hdld., #3500/142	1,100.00
Relish, 15", 4 pt., hdld., #3500/113	250.00
Salt & pepper, egg shape, pr., #1468	125.00
Salt & pepper, individual, rnd., glass base, pr., #1470	125.00
Salt & pepper, individual, w/chrome tops, pr., #360	90.00
Salt & pepper, lg., rnd., glass base, pr., #1471	125.00
Salt & pepper, w/chrome tops, pr., ftd. #3400/77	60.00

	Crystal
Salt & pepper w/chrome tops, pr., flat, #3900/1177	60.00
Sandwich tray, 11", center handled, #3400/10	145.00
Saucer, after dinner, #3400/69	65.00
Saucer, 3 styles, #3400, #3500, #3900	7.00
Stem, #3104, 3½ oz., cocktail	295.00
Stem, #3106, ¾ oz., brandy	135.00
Stem, #3106, 1 oz., cordial	135.00
Stem, #3106, 1 oz., pousse cafe	145.00
Stem, #3106, 2 oz., sherry	60.00
Stem, #3106, 2½ oz., wine	55.00
Stem, #3106, 3 oz., cocktail	40.00
Stem, #3106, 4½ oz., claret	60.00
Stem, #3106, 5 oz., oyster cocktail	35.00
Stem, #3106, 7 oz., high sherbet	33.00
Stem, #3106, 7 oz., low sherbet	26.00
Stem, #3106, 10 oz., water goblet	40.00
Stem, #3121, 1 oz., brandy	135.00
Stem, #3121, 1 oz., cordial	75.00
Stem, #3121, 3 oz., cocktail	35.00
Stem, #3121, 3½ oz., wine	65.00
Stem, #3121, 4½ oz., claret	100.00
Stem, #3121, 4½ oz., low oyster cocktail	37.50
Stem, #3121, 5 oz., low ft. parfait	110.00
Stem, #3121, 6 oz., low sherbet	22.00
Stem, #3121, 6 oz., tall sherbet	24.00
Stem, #3121, 10 oz., water	42.00
Stem, #3500, 1 oz., cordial	75.00
Stem, #3500, 2½ oz., wine	75.00
Stem, #3500, 3 oz., cocktail	40.00
Stem, #3500, 4½ oz., claret	110.00
Stem, #3500, 4½ oz., low oyster cocktail	40.00
Stem, #3500, 5 oz., low ft. parfait	125.00
Stem, #3500, 7 oz., low ft. sherbet	24.00
Stem, #3500, 7 oz., tall sherbet	32.50
Stem, #3500, 10 oz., water	45.00
Stem, #7801, 4 oz., cocktail, plain stem	45.00
Stem, #7966, 1 oz., cordial, plain ft.	150.00
Stem, #7966, 2 oz., sherry, plain ft.	125.00
Sugar, #3400/68	22.00
Sugar, #3500/14	25.00
Sugar, flat, #137	150.00
Sugar, flat, #944	165.00
Sugar, ftd., #3400/16	100.00
Sugar, ftd., #3900/41	25.00
Sugar, indiv., #3500/15, pie crust edge	27.50
Sugar, indiv., #3900/40, scalloped edge	22.00
Syrup, w/drip stop top, #1670	450.00
Tray, 6", 2 hdld., sq., #3500/91	195.00
Tray, 12", 2 hdld., oval, service, #3500/99	275.00
Tray, 12", rnd., #3500/67	210.00
Tray, 13", 2 hdld., rnd., #3500/72	210.00
Tray, sugar/creamer, #3900/37	35.00
Tumbler, #498, 2 oz., straight side	130.00
Tumbler, #498, 5 oz., straight side	52.50
Tumbler, #498, 8 oz., straight side	50.00
Tumbler, #498, 10 oz., straight side	50.00

	Crystal
Tumbler, #498, 12 oz., straight side	65.00
Tumbler, #3000, 3½ oz., cone, ftd.	120.00
Tumbler, #3000, 5 oz., cone, ftd.	135.00
Tumbler, #3106, 3 oz., ftd.	40.00
Tumbler, #3106, 5 oz., ftd.	37.50
Tumbler, #3106, 9 oz., ftd.	40.00
Tumbler, #3106, 12 oz., ftd.	45.00
Tumbler, #3121, 2½ oz., ftd.	75.00
Tumbler, #3121, 5 oz., low ft., juice	40.00
Tumbler, #3121, 10 oz., low ft., water	35.00
Tumbler, #3121, 12 oz., low ft., ice tea	45.00
Tumbler, #3400/1341, 1 oz., cordial	125.00
Tumbler, #3400/92, 2½ oz.	125.00
Tumbler, #3400/38, 5 oz.	110.00
Tumbler, #3400/38, 12 oz.	67.50
Tumbler, #3900/115, 13 oz.	55.00
Tumbler, #3500, 2½ oz., ftd.	75.00
Tumbler, #3500, 5 oz., low ft., juice	45.00
Tumbler, #3500, 10 oz., low ft., water	35.00
Tumbler, #3500, 13 oz., low ftd.	47.50
Tumbler, #3500, 12 oz., tall ft., ice tea	47.50
Tumbler, #7801, 5 oz., ftd.	60.00
Tumbler, #7801, 12 oz., ftd., ice tea	85.00
Tumbler, #3900/117, 5 oz.	70.00
Tumbler, #3400/115, 13 oz.	60.00
Urn, 10", w/cover, #3500/41	695.00
Urn, 12", w/cover, #3500/42	795.00
Vase, 5", #1309	125.00
Vase, 5", globe, #3400/102	110.00
Vase, 5", ftd., #6004	70.00
Vase, 6", high ftd., flower, #6004	75.00
Vase, 6", #572	175.00
Vase, 6½", globe, #3400/103	130.00
Vase, 7", ivy, ftd., ball, #1066	295.00
Vase, 8", #1430	295.00
Vase, 8", flat, flared, #797	195.00
Vase, 8", ftd., #3500/44	175.00
Vase, 8", high ftd., flower, #6004	85.00
Vase, 9", ftd., keyhole, #1237	120.00
Vase, 9", ftd., #1620	175.00
Vase, 9½" ftd., keyhole, #1233	135.00
Vase, 10", ball bottom, #400	250.00
Vase, 10", bud, #1528	150.00
Vase, 10", cornucopia, #3900/575	250.00
Vase, 10", flat, #1242	175.00
Vase, 10", ftd., #1301	110.00
Vase, 10", ftd., #6004	125.00
Vase, 10", ftd., #3500/45	220.00
Vase, 10", slender, #274	75.00
Vase, 11", ftd., flower, #278	165.00
Vase, 11", ped. ftd., flower, #1299	225.00
Vase, 12", ftd., #6004	150.00
Vase, 12", ftd., keyhole, #1234	165.00
Vase, 12", ftd., keyhole, #1238	175.00
Vase, 13", ftd., flower, #279	275.00
Vase 18", #1336	2,500.00
Vase, sweet pea, #629	350.00

Colors: amber, Ebony, blue, green

Fostoria's Royal is occasionally erroneously mislabeled as Vesper since both etchings are similar. Both were made on the #2350 blank and both were manufactured in the same colors. Royal does not entice as many collectors as Vesper, possibly due to a limited distribution. New collectors should find Royal priced more to their liking since there is less demand. Remember that demand raises prices more than scarcity.

Unusual and hard to find pieces of Royal include both styles of pitchers, covered cheese and butter dishes, cologne bottle, and sugar lid. The cologne bottle is a combination powder jar and cologne. The dauber is the hardest part of the three-piece set to find.

Adequate amber or green can be found to acquire a set; but only a minuscule number of pieces can be found in blue or black. Fostoria's blue color found with Royal etching was called "Blue" as opposed to the "Azure" blue which is a lighter color found etched with June or other patterns.

Published material indicates production of Royal continued until 1934 although the January 1, 1933, Fostoria catalog no longer listed Royal as being for sale. I have changed my cutoff date of production to 1932. If you can find a May 1928 copy of *House and Garden,* there is a fascinating Fostoria Royal advertisement displayed.

	*Amber Green		*Amber Green
Ashtray, #2350, 3½"	22.50	Bowl, #2324, 10", ftd.	45.00
Bowl, #2350, bouillon, flat	15.00	Bowl, #2350, 10", salad	35.00
Bowl, #2350½, bouillon, ftd.	18.00	Bowl, #2350, 10½", oval, baker	60.00
Bowl, #2350, cream soup, flat	18.00	Bowl, #2315, 10½", ftd.	45.00
Bowl, #2350½, cream soup, ftd.	20.00	Bowl, #2329, 11", console	22.00
Bowl, #869, 4½", finger	20.00	Bowl, #2297, 12", deep	22.00
Bowl, #2350, 5½", fruit	15.00	Bowl, #2329, 13", console	30.00
Bowl, #2350, 6½", cereal	25.00	Bowl, #2324, 13", ftd.	50.00
Bowl, #2267, 7", ftd.	35.00	Bowl, #2371, 13", oval, w/flower frog	175.00
Bowl, #2350, 7¾", soup	30.00	Butter, w/cover, #2350	325.00
Bowl, #2350, 8", nappy	30.00	Candlestick, #2324, 4"	22.00
Bowl, #2350, 9", nappy	32.00	Candlestick, #2324, 9"	75.00
Bowl, #2350, 9", oval, baker	45.00	Candy, w/cover, #2331, 3 part	85.00

*Add up to 50% more for blue or black.

	*Amber / Green
Candy, w/cover, ftd., ½ lb.	195.00
Celery, #2350, 11"	25.00
Cheese, w/cover/plate, #2276 (plate 11")	175.00
Cologne, #2322, tall	125.00
Cologne, #2323, short	100.00
Cologne/powder jar combination	295.00
Comport, #1861½, 6", jelly	25.00
Comport, #2327, 7"	28.00
Comport, #2358, 8" wide	30.00
Creamer, flat	18.00
Creamer, #2315½, ftd., fat	18.00
Creamer, #2350½, ftd.	15.00
Cup, #2350, flat	12.00
Cup, #2350½, ftd.	13.00
Cup, #2350, demi	25.00
Egg cup, #2350	30.00
Grapefruit, w/insert	100.00
Ice bucket, #2378	65.00
Mayonnaise, #2315	25.00
Pickle, 8", #2350	20.00
Pitcher, #1236	425.00
Pitcher, #5000, 48 oz.	325.00
Plate, 8½", deep soup/underplate	37.50
Plate, #2350, 6", bread/butter	3.00
Plate, #2350, 7½", salad	4.00
Plate, #2350, 8½", luncheon	8.00
Plate, #2321, 8¾, Maj Jongg (canape)	40.00
Plate, #2350, 9½", small dinner	13.00
Plate, #2350, 10½", dinner	30.00
Plate, #2350, 13", chop	35.00

	*Amber / Green
Plate, #2350, 15", chop	60.00
Platter, #2350, 10½"	30.00
Platter, #2350, 12"	65.00
Platter, #2350, 15½"	135.00
Salt and pepper, #5100, pr.	75.00
Sauce boat, w/liner	165.00
Saucer, #2350/#2350½	3.00
Saucer, #2350, demi	8.00
Server, #2287, 11", center hdld.	25.00
Stem, #869, ¾ oz., cordial	75.00
Stem, #869, 2¾ oz., wine	32.50
Stem, #869, 3 oz., cocktail	22.50
Stem, #869, 5½ oz., oyster cocktail	20.00
Stem, #869, 5½ oz., parfait	32.50
Stem, #869, 6 oz., low sherbet	15.00
Stem, #869, 6 oz., high sherbet	18.00
Stem, #869, 9 oz., water	23.00
Sugar, flat, w/lid	175.00
Sugar, #2315, ftd., fat	18.00
Sugar, #2350½, ftd.	15.00
Sugar lid, #2350½	135.00
Tumbler, #869, 5 oz., flat	22.50
Tumbler, #859, 9 oz., flat	25.00
Tumbler, #859, 12 oz., flat	30.00
Tumbler, #5000, 2½ oz., ftd.	35.00
Tumbler, #5000, 5 oz., ftd.	15.00
Tumbler, #5000, 9 oz., ftd.	18.00
Tumbler, #5000, 12 oz., ftd.	27.50
Vase, #2324, urn, ftd.	125.00
Vase, #2292, flared	135.00

Colors: Smokey Topaz, Jungle Green, French Crystal, Silver Gray, Lilac, Sunshine, Jade; some milk glass, Apple Green, black, French Opalescent

Ruba Rombic has seen a few price adjustments, and amazingly not on the downward side as has happened to some patterns. Mostly prices have held steady, but steady here is way beyond the pocket of most collectors of glass. There are collectors who feel this is the most wonderful pattern in the book. If you see a piece for sale, inexpensively priced, buy it regardless of your feelings. Someone will love it.

The color shown in the larger photo here is Smokey Topaz, priced below with the Jungle Green. Both of these colors are transparent as opposed to the other colors that are cased (layered). Smokey Topaz will be the color you are most likely to find if you are lucky enough to spot a piece.

The cased color column below includes three colors. They are Lilac (lavender), Sunshine (yellow), and Jade (green). French crystal is a white, applied color except that the raised edges are crystal with no white coloring at all. Silver is sometimes referred to as Gray Silver.

A couple of collections have been broken up and supplied the market with more pieces than in several years. Once a piece of glass reaches four digit prices, there are a limited number of collectors willing to pay that price. Once five digit prices are realized, there is only a handful. You can get a fairly good used car or a new import in that range. Ruba Rombic has always sold in a specialized market that eluded most dealers who did not have an outlet where they could sell it. The Internet is changing that. Dealers who specialized in patterns such as this are having difficulty in buying it cheaply, and selling it at big bucks. Now, when new pieces are found, they seem to go directly to the Internet.

In the past, Ruba Rombic was sporadically exhibited at Depression glass shows; but upper echelon Art Deco collectors and museums started displaying Ruba Rombic, and prices ascended beyond the checkbook of the average collector.

	Smokey Topaz Jungle Green	Cased Colors	French Opal French Crystal Silver
Ashtray, 3½"	600.00	750.00	850.00
Bonbon, flat, 3 part	250.00	350.00	400.00
Bottle, decanter, 9"	1,800.00	2,200.00	2,500.00
Bottle, perfume, 4¾"	1,200.00	1,500.00	1,800.00
Bottle, toilet, 7½"	1,200.00	1,500.00	1,800.00
Bowl, 3", almond	275.00	300.00	375.00
Bowl, 8", cupped	975.00	1,200.00	1,300.00
Bowl, 9", flared	950.00	1,200.00	1,300.00
Bowl, 12", oval	1,500.00	1,800.00	1,800.00
Bowl, bouillon	175.00	250.00	275.00
Bowl, finger	110.00	135.00	145.00
Box, cigarette, 3½" x 4¼"	850.00	1,250.00	1,500.00
Box, powder, 5", round	850.00	1,250.00	1,500.00
Candlestick, 2½" high, pr.	500.00	650.00	750.00
Celery, 10", 3 part	850.00	950.00	1,000.00
Comport, 7", wide	850.00	950.00	1,000.00
Creamer	200.00	250.00	300.00
Light, ceiling fixture, 10"		1,500.00	1,500.00
Light, ceiling fixture, 16"		2,500.00	2,500.00
Light, table light		1,200.00	1,200.00

	Smokey Topaz Jungle Green	Cased Colors	French Opal French Crystal Silver
Light, wall sconce		1,500.00	1,500.00
Pitcher, 8¼"	2,500.00	3,000.00	4,000.00
Plate, 7"	75.00	100.00	150.00
Plate, 8"	75.00	100.00	150.00
Plate, 10"	250.00	275.00	300.00
Plate, 15"	1,275.00	1,500.00	1,500.00
Relish, 2 part	350.00	450.00	500.00
Sugar	200.00	250.00	300.00
Sundae	100.00	135.00	150.00
Tray for decanter set	2,000.00	2,250.00	2,500.00
Tumbler, 2 oz., flat, 2¾"	110.00	135.00	160.00
Tumbler, 3 oz., ftd.	125.00	150.00	175.00
Tumbler, 9 oz., flat	125.00	175.00	200.00
Tumbler, 10 oz., ftd.	175.00	300.00	350.00
Tumbler, 12 oz., flat	175.00	300.00	350.00
Tumbler, 15 oz., ftd., 7"	350.00	450.00	500.00
Vase, 6"	850.00	1,000.00	1,500.00
Vase, 9½"	1,500.00	2,500.00	3,000.00
Vase, 16"	10,000.00	12,000.00	12,000.00

Colors: crystal, amber, pink, green, red, cobalt blue

Lancaster Colony continues to produce some Sandwich pieces in their lines today. Mostly the bright blue, green, or amberina color combinations were made by Indiana from Duncan moulds and were sold by Montgomery Ward in the early 1970s. I just saw a Sunset (amberina) bowl priced for $95.00, labeled rare Sandwich glass, at an antique market last weekend. The cobalt blue and true red pieces pictured here seem to excite a few Duncan collectors. Tiffin also made a few Sandwich pieces in milk glass and Chartreuse out of Duncan moulds before they were sold to Lancaster Colony.

I have eliminated the factory catalog pages of Sandwich from this book. If those interest you, an older copy of this book will have to be found in the secondary market.

An abundance of crystal Sandwich stemware makes it as inexpensive to buy as nearly all currently made imported stemware sold in department stores. If you enjoy this design, now would be a good time to start picking it up while you can still afford the gasoline to search for it.

	Crystal
Ashtray, 2½" x 3¾", rect.	10.00
Ashtray, 2¾", sq.	8.00
Basket, 6½", w/loop hdl.	135.00
Basket, 10", crimped, w/loop hdl.	225.00
Basket, 10", oval, w/loop hdl.	275.00
Basket, 11½", w/loop hdl.	250.00
Bonbon, 5", heart shape, w/ring hdl.	15.00
Bonbon, 5½", heart shape, hdld.	15.00
Bonbon, 6", heart shape, w/ring hdl.	20.00
Bonbon, 7½", ftd., w/cover	50.00
Bowl, 2½", salted almond	11.00
Bowl, 3½", nut	10.00
Bowl, 4", finger	12.50
Bowl, 5½", hdld.	15.00
Bowl, 5½", ftd., grapefruit, w/rim liner	17.50
Bowl, 5½", ftd., grapefruit, w/fruit cup liner	17.50
Bowl, 5", 2 pt., nappy	12.00
Bowl, 5", ftd., crimped ivy	40.00
Bowl, 5", fruit	10.00
Bowl, 5", nappy, w/ring hdl.	12.00
Bowl, 6", 2 pt., nappy	15.00
Bowl, 6", fruit salad	12.00
Bowl, 6", grapefruit, rimmed edge	17.50
Bowl, 6", nappy, w/ring hdl.	18.00
Bowl, 10", salad, deep	75.00
Bowl, 10", 3 pt., fruit	100.00
Bowl, 10", lily, vertical edge	52.50
Bowl, 11", cupped nut	55.00
Bowl, 11½", crimped flower	57.50
Bowl, 11½", gardenia	45.00
Bowl, 11½", ftd., crimped fruit	65.00
Bowl, 12", fruit, flared edge	45.00
Bowl, 12", shallow salad	40.00
Bowl, 12", oblong console	40.00

	Crystal
Bowl, 12", epergne, w/ctr. hole	100.00
Butter, w/cover, ¼ lb.	60.00
Cake stand, 11½", ftd., rolled edge	110.00
Cake stand, 12", ftd., rolled edge, plain pedestal	90.00
Cake stand, 13", ftd., plain pedestal	90.00
Candelabra, 10", 1-lite, w/bobeche & prisms	85.00
Candelabra, 10", 3-lite, w/bobeche & prisms	225.00
Candelabra, 16", 3-lite, w/bobeche & prisms	275.00
Candlestick, 4", 1-lite	15.00
Candlestick, 4", 1-lite, w/bobeche & stub. prisms	35.00
Candlestick, 5", 3-lite	50.00
Candlestick, 5", 3-lite, w/bobeche & stub. prisms	135.00
Candlestick, 5", 2-lite, w/bobeche & stub. prisms	110.00
Candlestick, 5", 2-lite	35.00
Candy, 6", sq.	395.00
Candy box, w/cover, 5", flat	60.00
Candy jar, w/cover, 8½", ftd.	85.00
Cheese, w/cover (cover 4¾", plate 8")	135.00
Cheese/cracker (3" compote, 13" plate)	55.00
Cigarette box, w/cover, 3½"	22.00
Cigarette holder, 3", ftd.	27.50
Coaster, 5"	12.00
Comport, 2¼"	15.00
Comport, 3¼", low ft., crimped candy	25.00

	Crystal
Comport, 3¼", low ft., flared candy	17.50
Comport, 4¼", ftd.	25.00
Comport, 5", low ft.	25.00
Comport, 5½", ftd., low crimped	30.00
Comport, 6", low ft., flared	27.50
Condiment set (2 cruets, 3¾" salt & pepper, 4 pt. tray)	125.00
Creamer, 4", 7 oz., ftd.	10.00
Cup, 6 oz., tea	10.00
Epergne, 9", garden	150.00
Epergne, 12", 3 pt., fruit or flower	275.00
Jelly, 3", indiv.	9.00
Mayonnaise set, 3 pc.: ladle, 5" bowl, 7" plate	32.00
Oil bottle, 5¾"	35.00
Pan, 6¾" x 10½", oblong, camelia	65.00
Pitcher, 13 oz., metal top	65.00
Pitcher, w/ice lip, 8", 64 oz.	145.00
Plate, 3", indiv. jelly	6.00
Plate, 6", bread/butter	7.00
Plate, 6½", finger bowl liner	9.00
Plate, 7", dessert	9.00
Plate, 8", mayonnaise liner, w/ring	10.00
Plate, 8", salad	10.00
Plate, 9½", dinner	40.00
Plate, 11½", hdld., service	40.00
Plate, 12", torte	45.00
Plate, 12", ice cream, rolled edge	60.00
Plate, 12", deviled egg	85.00
Plate, 13", salad dressing, w/ring	50.00
Plate, 13", service	45.00
Plate, 13", service, rolled edge	45.00
Plate, 13", cracker, w/ring	35.00
Plate, 16", lazy susan, w/turntable	115.00
Plate, 16", hostess	100.00
Relish, 5½", 2 pt., rnd., ring hdl.	18.00
Relish, 6", 2 pt., rnd., ring hdl.	20.00
Relish, 7", 2 pt., oval	22.00
Relish, 10", 4 pt., hdld.	30.00
Relish, 10", 3 pt., oblong	32.50
Relish, 10½", 3 pt., oblong	32.50
Relish, 12", 3 pt.	45.00
Salad dressing set: (2 ladles, 5" ftd. mayonnaise, 13" plate w/ring)	100.00

	Crystal
Salad dressing set: (2 ladles, 6" ftd. div. bowl, 8" plate w/ring)	85.00
Salt & pepper, 2½", w/glass tops, pr.	20.00
Salt & pepper, 2½", w/metal tops, pr.	20.00
Salt & pepper, 3¾", w/metal top (on 6" tray), 3 pc.	30.00
Saucer, 6", w/ring	4.00
Stem, 2½", 6 oz., ftd., fruit cup/jello	11.00
Stem, 2¾", 5 oz., ftd., oyster cocktail	15.00
Stem, 3½", 5 oz., sundae (flared rim)	12.00
Stem, 4¼", 3 oz., cocktail	15.00
Stem, 4¼", 5 oz., ice cream	12.50
Stem, 4¼", 3 oz., wine	22.50
Stem, 5¼", 4 oz., ftd., parfait	32.00
Stem, 5¼", 5 oz., champagne	20.00
Stem, 6", 9 oz., goblet	18.50
Sugar, 3¼", ftd., 9 oz.	9.00
Sugar, 5 oz.	8.00
Sugar (cheese) shaker, 13 oz., metal top	75.00
Tray, oval (for sugar/creamer)	10.00
Tray, 6" mint, rolled edge, w/ring hdl.	17.50
Tray, 7", oval, pickle	15.00
Tray, 7", mint, rolled edge, w/ring hdl.	22.00
Tray, 8", oval	18.00
Tray, 8", for oil/vinegar	22.00
Tray, 10", oval, celery	18.00
Tray, 12", fruit epergne	52.00
Tray, 12", ice cream, rolled edge	55.00
Tumbler, 3¾", 5 oz., ftd., juice	12.00
Tumbler, 4¾", 9 oz., ftd., water	16.00
Tumbler, 5¼", 13 oz., flat, iced tea	22.50
Tumbler, 5¼", 12 oz., ftd., iced tea	20.00
Urn, w/cover, 12", ftd.	195.00
Vase, 3", ftd., crimped	22.50
Vase, 3", ftd., flared rim	18.00
Vase, 4", hat shape	25.00
Vase, 4½", flat base, crimped	30.00
Vase, 5", ftd., flared rim	25.00
Vase, 5", ftd., crimped	45.00
Vase, 5", ftd., fan	45.00
Vase, 7½", epergne, threaded base	65.00
Vase, 10", ftd.	75.00

SATURN, Blank #1485, A.H. Heisey & Co., c. 1931

Colors: crystal, Zircon or Limelight green, Dawn

Limelight and Zircon are the same color. Zircon was originally made in 1937. In the 1950s, it was made again by Heisey, but called Limelight. Zircon prices are rising, especially all sizes of plates, both pitchers and shakers but the important word is rising. Some dealers price a piece of glass and carry it for years without selling it, even after thousands of miles of travel. I have seen one Zircon comport for over six years making long journeys. It would seem that a reduction in price might be a smart move in order to sell it.

Crystal Saturn prices are remaining steady.

	Crystal	Zircon Limelight
Ashtray	10.00	150.00
Bitters bottle, w/short tube, blown	75.00	
Bowl, baked apple	25.00	100.00
Bowl, finger	15.00	65.00
Bowl, rose, lg.	40.00	
Bowl, 4½", nappy	15.00	
Bowl, 5", nappy	15.00	90.00
Bowl, 5", whipped cream	15.00	150.00
Bowl, 7", pickle	35.00	
Bowl, 9", 3 part, relish	20.00	
Bowl, 10", celery	15.00	
Bowl, 11", salad	40.00	140.00
Bowl, 12", fruit, flared rim	35.00	100.00
Bowl, 13", floral, rolled edge	37.00	
Bowl, 13", floral	37.00	
Candelabrum, w/"e" ball drops, 2-lite	175.00	500.00
Candle block, 2-lite	95.00	350.00
Candlestick, 3", ftd., 1-lite	30.00	500.00
Comport, 7"	50.00	550.00
Creamer	25.00	180.00
Cup	10.00	160.00
Hostess Set, 8 pc. (low bowl w/ftd. ctr. bowl, 3 toothpick holders & clips)	65.00	300.00
Marmalade, w/cover	45.00	500.00
Mayonnaise	8.00	80.00
Mustard, w/cover and paddle	60.00	350.00*

*Zircon $800.00 at 1998 **auction.**

	Crystal	Zircon Limelight
Oil bottle, 3 oz.	55.00	650.00
Pitcher, 70 oz., w/ice lip, blown	65.00	550.00
Pitcher, juice	40.00	500.00
Plate, 6"	5.00	50.00
Plate, 7", bread	5.00	55.00
Plate, 8", luncheon	10.00	60.00
Plate, 13", torte	25.00	
Plate, 15", torte	30.00	
Salt & pepper, pr.	45.00	600.00
Saucer	5.00	40.00
Stem, 3 oz., cocktail	15.00	75.00
Stem, 4 oz., fruit cocktail or oyster cocktail, no ball in stem, ftd.	10.00	75.00
Stem, 4½ oz., sherbet	8.00	70.00
Stem, 5 oz., parfait	10.00	110.00
Stem, 6 oz., saucer champagne	10.00	95.00
Stem, 10 oz.	20.00	100.00
Sugar	25.00	180.00
Sugar shaker (pourer)	80.00	
Sugar, w/cover, no handles	25.00	
Tray, tidbit, 2 sides turned as fan	25.00	110.00
Tumbler, 5 oz., juice	8.00	80.00
Tumbler, 7 oz., old-fashion	10.00	
Tumbler, 8 oz., old-fashion	10.00	
Tumbler, 9 oz., luncheon	15.00	
Tumbler, 10 oz.	20.00	80.00
Tumbler, 12 oz., soda	20.00	85.00
Vase, violet	35.00	160.00
Vase, 8½", flared	55.00	225.00
Vase, 8½", straight	55.00	225.00
Vase, 10½"		260.00

Colors: amber, green

Seville continues to be the most neglected Fostoria pattern in this book. For some reason, it has never caught on with collectors in either green or amber. Take a good look at this. It is attractive, 70 plus years old, and Fostoria made — a winning combination; plus, Fostoria's no longer in business. Seville would be an inexpensive Elegant pattern to collect despite there not being huge displays at shows. You might have to ask for it if it is not out for sale. Green would be easier to obtain than amber as you may note by the lack of amber in my photos. The butter dish, pitcher, grapefruit and liner, and sugar lid are all troublesome to find, but oh, so gratifying when you do run across them. Those pieces are costly items, but not as dear as those same pieces in other Fostoria patterns such as June or Versailles.

	Amber	Green
Creamer, #2350½, ftd.	12.50	13.50
Cup, #2350, after dinner	25.00	30.00
Cup, #2350, flat	10.00	12.50
Cup, #2350½, ftd.	10.00	12.50
Egg cup, #2350	30.00	35.00
Grapefruit, #945½, blown	45.00	50.00
Grapefruit, #945½, liner, blown	35.00	40.00
Grapefruit, #2315, molded	25.00	32.00
Ice bucket, #2378	55.00	65.00
Pickle, #2350, 8"	13.50	15.00
Pitcher, #5084, ftd.	275.00	325.00
Plate, #2350, bread and butter, 6"	3.50	4.00
Plate, #2350, salad, 7½"	5.00	5.50
Plate, #2350, luncheon, 8½"	6.00	6.50
Plate, #2321, Maj Jongg (canape), 8¾"	35.00	40.00
Plate, #2350, sm. dinner, 9½"	12.00	13.50
Plate, #2350, dinner, 10½"	35.00	45.00
Plate, #2350, chop, 13¾"	30.00	35.00
Plate, #2350, round, 15"	45.00	50.00
Plate, #2350, cream soup liner	5.00	6.00
Platter, #2350, 10½"	30.00	35.00
Platter, #2350, 12"	40.00	50.00
Platter, #2350, 15"	85.00	110.00
Salt and pepper shaker, #5100, pr.	65.00	75.00
Sauce boat liner, #2350	25.00	30.00
Sauce boat, #2350	55.00	75.00
Saucer, #2350	3.00	3.00
Saucer, after dinner, #2350	5.00	5.00
Stem, #870, cocktail	15.00	16.00
Stem, #870, cordial	65.00	70.00
Stem, #870, high sherbet	18.00	18.00
Stem, #870, low sherbet	14.00	15.00
Stem, #870, oyster cocktail	16.50	17.50
Stem, #870, parfait	30.00	35.00
Stem, #870, water	22.00	24.00
Stem, #870, wine	25.00	28.00
Sugar cover, #2350½	80.00	110.00
Sugar, fat, ftd., #2315	13.50	14.50
Sugar, ftd., #2350½	12.50	13.50
Tray, 11", center hdld., #2287	27.50	30.00
Tumbler, #5084, ftd., 2 oz.	35.00	40.00
Tumbler, #5084, ftd., 5 oz.	13.50	15.00
Tumbler, #5084, ftd., 9 oz.	15.00	16.50
Tumbler, #5084, ftd., 12 oz.	18.00	20.00
Urn, small, #2324	85.00	120.00
Vase, #2292, 8"	75.00	95.00

	Amber	Green
Ashtray, #2350, 4"	17.50	22.50
Bowl, #2350, fruit, 5½"	10.00	12.00
Bowl, #2350, cereal, 6½"	18.00	25.00
Bowl, #2350, soup, 7¾"	20.00	35.00
Bowl, #2315, low foot, 7"	18.00	22.00
Bowl, #2350, vegetable	22.00	27.50
Bowl, #2350, nappy, 9"	30.00	37.50
Bowl, #2350, oval, baker, 9"	25.00	30.00
Bowl, #2315, flared, 10½", ftd.	25.00	30.00
Bowl, #2350, oval, baker, 10½"	35.00	40.00
Bowl, 10", ftd.	35.00	42.50
Bowl, #2350, salad, 10"	30.00	35.00
Bowl, #2329, rolled edge, console, 11"	27.50	40.00
Bowl, #2297, deep, flared, 12"	30.00	32.50
Bowl, #2371, oval, console, 13"	35.00	40.00
Bowl, #2329, rolled edge, console, 13"	32.00	40.00
Bowl, #2350, bouillon, flat	13.50	18.00
Bowl, #2350½, bouillon, ftd.	14.00	18.00
Bowl, #2350, cream soup, flat	14.50	20.00
Bowl, #2350½, cream soup, ftd.	15.50	20.00
Bowl, #869/2283, finger, w/6" liner	22.00	30.00
Butter, w/cover, #2350, round	210.00	295.00
Candlestick, #2324, 2"	18.00	22.00
Candlestick, #2324, 4"	16.00	22.00
Candlestick, #2324, 9"	45.00	50.00
Candy jar, w/cover, #2250, ½ lb., ftd.	110.00	150.00
Candy jar, w/cover, #2331, 3 pt., flat	75.00	100.00
Celery, #2350, 11"	15.00	17.50
Cheese and cracker, #2368 (11" plate)	40.00	45.00
Comport, #2327, 7½", (twisted stem)	20.00	25.00
Comport, #2350, 8"	27.50	35.00
Creamer, #2315½, flat, ftd.	13.50	15.00

193

Colors: amber, green, pink, crystal

"Spiral Flutes" is a Duncan & Miller pattern that is easily spotted by collector because it has the look of several well known Depression glass patterns. Numerous Duncan & Miller patterns have suffered due to limited enlightenment on that company's wares.

"Spiral Flutes" has pieces that are rarely seen. However, the three smaller plates, 5" and 6¾" bowls, and the seven ounce footed tumbler abound. After that, there is little easily found. Green can be assembled more quickly than any other color. Amber and crystal sets may be rounded up, but few collectors are presently attempting to collect those colors. I have seen few two-tone (amber/crystal) pieces like the comport in front of the picture on page 196. If you discover others, let me know.

	Amber Green Pink
Candle, 3½"	25.00
Candle, 7½"	65.00
Candle, 9½"	90.00
Candle, 11½"	135.00
Celery, 10¾" x 4¾"	17.50
* Chocolate jar, w/cover	295.00
Cigarette holder, 4"	35.00
Comport, 4⅜"	15.00
Comport, 6⅝"	17.50
Comport, 9", low ft., flared	55.00
Console stand, 1½" h. x 4⅝" w.	12.00
Creamer, oval	8.00
Cup	9.00
Cup, demi	25.00
* Fernery, 10" x 5½", 4 ftd., flower box	395.00
Grapefruit, ftd.	20.00
Ice tub, handled	95.00
Lamp, 10½", countess	295.00
Mug, 6½", 9 oz., handled	30.00
Mug, 7", 9 oz., handled	36.00
Oil, w/stopper, 6 oz.	225.00
Pickle, 8⅝"	12.00
Pitcher, ½ gal.	195.00
Plate, 6", pie	3.00
Plate, 7½", salad	4.00
Plate, 8⅜", luncheon	4.00
Plate, 10⅜", dinner	22.50
Plate, 13⅝", torte	27.50
Plate, w/star, 6" (fingerbowl item)	6.00
Platter, 11"	40.00
Platter, 13"	60.00

	Amber Green Pink
Bowl, 2", almond	13.00
Bowl, 3¾", bouillon	15.00
Bowl, 4⅜", finger	7.00
Bowl, 4¾", ftd., cream soup	15.00
Bowl, 4" w., mayonnaise	17.50
Bowl, 5", nappy	6.00
Bowl, 6½", cereal, sm. flange	35.00
Bowl, 6¾", grapefruit	7.50
Bowl, 6", hdld. nappy	22.00
Bowl, 6", hdld. nappy, w/cover	95.00
Bowl, 7", nappy	15.00
Bowl, 7½", flanged (baked apple)	22.50
Bowl, 8", nappy	17.50
Bowl, 8½", flanged (oyster plate)	22.50
Bowl, 9", nappy	27.50
Bowl, 10", oval, veg., two styles	45.00
Bowl, 10½", lily pond	40.00
Bowl, 11¾" w. x 3¾" t., console, flared	30.00
Bowl, 11", nappy	30.00
Bowl, 12", cupped console	30.00

*Crystal, $135.00

	Amber Green Pink		Amber Green Pink
Relish, 10" x 7⅜", oval, 3 pc. (2 inserts)	125.00	Tumbler, 3⅜", ftd., 2½ oz., cocktail (no stem)	7.00
Saucer	3.00	Tumbler, 4¼", 8 oz., flat	30.00
Saucer, demi	5.00	Tumbler, 4⅜", ftd., 5½ oz., juice (no stem)	14.00
Seafood sauce cup, 3" w. x 2½" h.	25.00	Tumbler, 4¾", 7 oz., flat, soda	35.00
Stem, 3¾", 3½ oz., wine	17.50	Tumbler, 5⅛", ftd., 7 oz., water (1 knob)	8.00
Stem, 3¾", 5 oz., low sherbet	8.00	Tumbler, 5⅛", ftd., 9 oz., water (no stem)	20.00
Stem, 4¾", 6 oz., tall sherbet	12.00	Tumbler, 5½", 11 oz., ginger ale	70.00
Stem, 5⅝", 4½ oz., parfait	17.50	Vase, 6½"	20.00
Stem, 6¼", 7 oz., water	17.50	Vase, 8½"	30.00
Sugar, oval	8.00	Vase, 10½"	40.00
Sweetmeat, w/cover, 7½"	125.00		

Colors: crystal, some blown stemware in Zircon

Heisey's Stanhope is another Deco pattern that more than Heisey collectors are seeking. Deco people seem to adore the red or black "T" knobs, which were inserted in all the round handles of Stanhope. "T" knobs, in the price listings, are insert handles (black or red, round, wooden knobs) which are like wooden dowel rods that act as horizontal handles. The insert handles are whimsical to some; but others think them magnificent. Although items are priced with or without the knobs, you can expect items to fetch 20% to 25 % less when they are missing. I had a devil of a time selling that rarely seen candy in the photo below since it was missing the insert.

Notice that prices have held their own except for the ever present stemware. Some people mistake the salad bowl shown at the bottom of page 198 for a punch bowl; it would not hold much punch, but enough salad for a small dinner party.

	Crystal
Ashtray, indiv.	25.00
Bottle, oil, 3 oz., w or w/o rd. knob	325.00
Bowl, 6", mint, 2 hdld., w or w/o rd. knobs	35.00
Bowl, 6", mint, 2 pt., 2 hdld., w or w/o rd. knobs	35.00
Bowl, 11", salad	90.00
Bowl, finger, #4080 (blown, plain)	10.00
Bowl, floral, 11", 2 hdld., w or w/o "T" knobs	80.00
Candelabra, 2-lite, w bobeche & prisms	180.00
Candy box & lid, rnd., w or w/o rd. knob	180.00
Cigarette box & lid, w or w/o rd. knob	65.00
Creamer, 2 hdld., w or w/o rd. knobs	45.00
Cup, w or w/o rd. knob.	25.00
Ice tub, 2 hdld., w or w/o "T" knobs	70.00
Jelly, 6", 1 hdld., w or w/o rd. knobs	25.00
Jelly, 6", 3 pt., 1 hdld., w or w/o rd. knobs	25.00
Nappy, 4½", 1 hdld., w or w/o rd. knob	25.00
Nut, indiv., 1 hdld., w or w/o rd. knob	40.00
Plate, 7"	20.00

	Crystal
Plate, 12", torte, 2 hdld., w or w/o "T" knobs	35.00
Plate, 15", torte, rnd. or salad liner	45.00
Relish, 11", triplex buffet, 2 hdld., w or w/o "T" knobs	35.00
Relish, 12", 4 pt., 2 hdld., w or w/o "T" knobs	55.00
Relish, 12", 5 pt., 2 hdld., w or w/o "T" knobs	55.00
Salt & pepper, #60 top	125.00
Saucer	10.00
Stem, 1 oz., cordial, #4083 (blown)	70.00
Stem, 2½ oz., pressed wine	35.00
Stem, 2½ oz., wine, #4083	25.00
Stem, 3½ oz., cocktail, #4083	20.00
Stem, 3½ oz., pressed cocktail	25.00
Stem, 4 oz., claret, #4083	25.00
Stem, 4 oz., oyster cocktail, #4083	10.00
Stem, 5½ oz., pressed saucer champagne	20.00
Stem, 5½ oz., saucer champagne, #4083	15.00
Stem, 9 oz., pressed goblet	45.00
Stem, 10 oz., goblet, #4083	22.50
Stem, 12 oz., pressed soda	45.00
Sugar, 2 hdld., w or w/o rd. knobs	45.00
Tray, 12" celery, 2 hdld., w or w/o "T" knobs	55.00
Tumbler, 5 oz., soda, #4083	20.00
Tumbler, 8 oz., soda, #4083	22.50
Tumbler, 12 oz., soda, #4083	25.00
Vase, 7", ball	100.00
Vase, 9", 2 hdld., w or w/o "T" knobs	85.00

Colors: crystal

This pattern was produced in crystal only. Some items may have a variant in the pattern consisting of punties (thumb prints) around the item just above the sunburst.

Bottle, molasses, 13 oz.	175.00
Bottle, oil, 2 oz.	70.00
Bottle, oil, 4 oz.	70.00
Bottle, oil, 6 oz.	70.00
Bottle, water	75.00
Bridge Set: Approx. 5" each.	
Club	45.00
Diamond	65.00
Heart	65.00
Spade	45.00
Bowl, 4", round, scalloped top	22.00
Bowl, 4½", round, scalloped top	22.00
Bowl, 5", round, scalloped top	25.00
Bowl, 5", finger,	25.00
Bowl, 5", hdld.	25.00
Bowl, 5", three corner, hdld.	30.00
Bowl, 6", round	30.00
Bowl, 7", round	35.00

Bowl, 7", oblong	35.00
Bowl, 8", round	40.00
Bowl, 8", round, ftd.	40.00
Bowl, 9", round	40.00
Bowl, 9", round, ftd.	65.00
Bowl, 9", oblong	45.00
Bowl, 10", round	50.00
Bowl, 10", round, ftd.	85.00
Bowl, 10", oblong	45.00
Bowl, 10", round punch, pegged bottom & stand	175.00
Bowl, 12", round, punch & stand	150.00
Bowl, 12", oblong	55.00
Bowl, 14", round, punch & stand	150.00
Bowl, 15", round, punch & stand	160.00
Butter and domed cover	125.00
Cake plate 9", ftd.	165.00
Cake plate, 10, ftd.	165.00

199

Celery tray, 12"	45.00
Comport, 5", ftd.	45.00
Comport, 6", ftd.	45.00
Creamer, lg.	45.00
Creamer, hotel	40.00
Creamer, individual	45.00
Cup, punch, two styles	15.00
Egg cup, ftd.	65.00
Goblet, water	165.00
Mayonnaise and underplate	55.00
Pickle jar and stopper	145.00
Pickle tray, 6"	35.00
Pitcher, 1 qt., upright	145.00
Pitcher, 1 qt., bulbous	145.00
Pitcher, 3 pt., upright	150.00
Pitcher, 3 pt., bulbous	150.00

Pitcher, ½ gal., upright	175.00
Pitcher, ½ gal., straight sided	175.00
Pitcher, ½ gal., bulbous	185.00
Pitcher, 3 qt. upright	225.00
Pitcher, 3 qt., bulbous	235.00
Plate, torte, 13"	35.00
Rose bowl, 3", footed	145.00
Salt & pepper, 3 styles	95.00
Spooner	90.00
Sugar, lg.	45.00
Sugar, hotel	40.00
Sugar, individual	45.00
Toothpick holder	135.00
Tumbler, 2 styles	40.00
Vase, orchid, 6"	90.00

Colors: crystal, red, blue, green, yellow

There are added price listings for Fostoria's Sun Ray included since several collectors have been kind enough to supply them. Pricing is still tricky due to the disparity of prices I am finding. I price crystal; but be aware of pieces that are found in red, blue, green, and yellow. I rarely see Sun Ray in colors; so, I doubt that you could assemble a set in color. A few colored pieces among your crystal would probably add to its appeal.

On page 202 the cream soup is tab handled (first item in row 4). By putting a lid on the cream soup (last item row 5), it becomes an onion soup according to Fostoria's catalogs. The condiment tray with cruets and mustards in row 5 is moulded like a cloverleaf similar to the one in Fostoria's American. It is evidently more unusual than the American one, but not as many collectors are seeking it.

The fourth item in row 4, page 202 is not Sun Ray although it may be difficult to determine from the angle it is pictured. This shows that there are similar patterns that could blend with Sun Ray or drive you to distraction if you are a purist. If you are a beginner, you might mistake this as Sun Ray as I once did when I first started buying this pattern. I leave it here as a lesson.

Notice the two tumblers on the left in row 1. One has frosted panels and the other is clear. Pieces with frosted panels were given a separate designation, Glacier, by Fostoria. Some Sun Ray enthusiasts are willing to mix the two, but, most gather one or the other. Both patterns sell in the same price range although Glacier is more limited in supply.

	Crystal		Crystal
Almond, ftd., ind.	12.00	Pitcher, 64 oz., ice lip	115.00
Ashtray, ind., 2510½	8.00	Plate, 6"	8.00
Ashtray, sq.	12.00	Plate, 7½"	10.00
Bonbon, hdld.	16.00	Plate, 8½"	14.00
Bonbon, 3 toed	17.50	Plate, 9½"	28.00
Bowl, 5", fruit	10.00	Plate, 11", torte	35.00
Bowl, 9½", flared	30.00	Plate, 12", sandwich	35.00
Bowl, 12", salad	35.00	Plate, 15", torte	65.00
Bowl, 13", rolled edge	42.50	Plate, 16"	70.00
Bowl, custard, 2¼", high	12.00	Relish, 2 part	18.00
Bowl, hdld.	35.00	Relish, 3 part	22.00
Butter, w/lid, ¼ lb.	35.00	Relish, 4 part	24.00
Candelabra, 2-lite	60.00	Salt dip	12.50
Candlestick, 3"	20.00	Saucer	3.00
Candlestick, 5½"	27.50	Shaker, 4", pr.	45.00
Candlestick, duo	40.00	Shaker, individual, 2¼", #2510½, pr.	40.00
Candy jar, w/cover	50.00	Stem, 3½", 5½ oz., sherbet, low	12.00
Celery, hdld.	25.00	Stem, 3¼", 3½ oz., fruit cocktail	12.00
Cigarette and cover	22.00	Stem, 3", 4 oz., cocktail, ftd.	12.00
Cigarette box, oblong	25.00	Stem, 4⅞", 4½ oz., claret	25.00
Coaster, 4"	8.00	Stem, 5¾", 9 oz., goblet	16.00
Comport	25.00	Sugar, ftd.	12.00
Cream soup	27.50	Sugar, individual	12.00
Cream soup liner	8.00	Sweetmeat, hdld., divided, 6"	30.00
Cream, ftd.	12.00	Tray, 6½", ind. sugar/cream	10.00
Cream, individual	12.00	Tray, 10½", oblong	40.00
Cup	12.00	Tray, 10", sq.	40.00
Decanter, w/stopper, 18 oz.	75.00	Tray, condiment, 8½", cloverleaf	45.00
Decanter, w/stopper, oblong, 26 oz.	95.00	Tray, oval hdld.	25.00
Ice bucket, no handle	55.00	Tumbler, 2¼", 2 oz., whiskey, #2510½	12.00
Ice bucket, w/handle	65.00	Tumbler, 3½", 5 oz., juice, #2510½	12.50
Jelly	16.00	Tumbler, 3½", 6 oz., old fashion, #2510½	14.00
Jelly, w/cover	45.00	Tumbler, 4⅛", 9 oz., table, #2510½	13.00
Mayonnaise, w/liner, ladle	45.00	Tumbler, 4¾", 9 oz., ftd., table	14.00
Mustard, w/cover, spoon	45.00	Tumbler, 4⅝", 5 oz., ftd., juice	15.00
Nappy, hdld., flared	13.00	Tumbler, 5¼", 13 oz., ftd., tea	18.00
Nappy, hdld., reg.	12.00	Tumbler, 5⅛", 13 oz., tea, #2510½	20.00
Nappy, hdld., sq.	14.00	Vase, 3½", rose bowl	25.00
Nappy, hdld., tri-corner	15.00	Vase, 5", rose bowl	32.50
Oil bottle, w/stopper, 3 oz.	35.00	Vase, 6", crimped	40.00
Onion soup, w/cover	45.00	Vase, 7"	50.00
Pickle, hdld.	22.00	Vase, 9", sq. ftd.	55.00
Pitcher, 16 oz., cereal	45.00	Vase, sweet pea	75.00
Pitcher, 64 oz.	75.00		

SUNRISE MEDALLION, "Dancing Girl," #758, Morgantown Glass Works,

late 1920s – early 1930s

Colors: pink, green, blue, crystal

Sunrise Medallion (Morgantown's etching #758) traditionally had been christened "Dancing Girl" by collectors. Newer collectors are more willing to use the correct Sunrise Medallion name.

Catalog measurements were regularly reported in ounces, not heights. Most measurements for height in this book come from physically measuring the item. Those twisted stem items (#7642½) are slightly taller than their plain stem counterparts (#7630, called "lady leg" stems). Measurements listed here are mainly from the #7630 line that I acquire more often than twisted one. Twisted blue and crystal champagnes, sherbets, and waters are the only #7642½ stems I have found. If you have others, I would appreciate having measurements.

Blue is the favored color of collectors, but that is true in almost all patterns. Pink and crystal turn up occasionally and are not as expensive. Green seems to be rare with only a few pieces surfacing. I have only owned a green sugar and 10" vase, but I have seen a picture of a creamer. It was not for sale. Speaking of creamer and sugars, they are the most difficult to find pieces. I had the blue creamer and sugar for over 15 years until a collector in California convinced me he wanted to own them more than I. For such a highly priced pitcher, the blue one turns up with regularity in the Northwest. There are two different styled oyster cocktails, which look more like a bar tumbler to me. I had six and they varied from a little over to a little under four ounces.

The cordials are regularly seen in crystal, but only a few blue ones have appeared. I have never found a twisted stem cordial.

	Crystal	Blue	Pink Green
Bowl, finger, ftd.		85.00	
Creamer		325.00	275.00
Cup	40.00	100.00	80.00
Parfait, 5 oz.	55.00	135.00	100.00
Pitcher		595.00	
Plate, 5⅞", sherbet	6.00	18.00	10.00
Plate, 7½", salad	15.00	30.00	25.00
Plate, 8⅜"	12.50	30.00	22.50
Saucer	15.00	22.50	17.50
Sherbet, cone	20.00		
Stem, 1½ oz., cordial	110.00	375.00	225.00
Stem, 2½ oz., wine	45.00	85.00	55.00
Stem, 6¼", 7 oz., champagne (twist stem, 6¾")	25.00	50.00	40.00
Stem, 6⅛", cocktail	30.00	55.00	40.00
Stem, 7¾", 9 oz., water (twist stem, 8¼")	35.00	75.00	55.00
Sugar		300.00	250.00
Tumbler, 2½", 4 oz., ftd.	25.00	150.00	
Tumbler, 3½", 4 oz., ftd.			35.00
Tumbler, 4¼", 5 oz., ftd.	45.00	65.00	50.00
Tumbler, 4¼", flat	20.00		
Tumbler, 4¾", 9 oz., ftd.	20.00	60.00	45.00
Tumbler, 5½", 11 oz., ftd.	35.00	85.00	65.00
Tumbler, 5½", flat	25.00		
Vase, 6" tall, 5" wide			395.00
Vase, 10", slender, bud	65.00	400.00	295.00
Vase, 10", bulbous bottom			350.00

Colors: amber, Carmen, crystal, Forest Green, Royal Blue

   Tally Ho is a massive Cambridge pattern in both production and the size of many of its pieces. It has been previously represented in this book in various patterns from Elaine to Valencia. For purposes of identification, the heavy pressed one-color stems are listed as goblets in the listing below and the blown, thin, tall crystal stems with colored bowls are listed as stems. Ice buckets seem to be plentiful in all colors and etched crystal ones are a prize catch. Crystal punch bowl sets can be found with cups and ladles with colored handles as well as all crystal. The ones with colored handles are preferred.

	Amber Crystal	Carmen Royal	Forest Green
Ashtray, 4"	12.50	22.50	18.00
Ashtray, 4" w/ctr. hdld.	17.50	27.50	25.00
Ash well, 2 pc., ctr. hdld.	20.00	35.00	30.00
Bowl, 4½", ftd., fruit/sherbet	12.50	22.50	20.00
Bowl, 5", frappe cocktail, 10 side rim	17.50	27.50	25.00
Bowl, 6", iced fruit, 10 side rim	25.00	40.00	35.00
Bowl, 6", 2 hdld.	17.50	27.50	25.00
Bowl, 6", 2 hdld. nappy	17.50	27.50	25.00
Bowl, 6½", grapefruit, flat rim	20.00	35.00	30.00
Bowl, 6½", 2 hdld.	20.00	35.00	30.00
Bowl, 7", fruit, 10 side rim	20.00	35.00	30.00
Bowl, 8"	25.00	40.00	35.00
Bowl, 8½", 3 comp.	45.00	70.00	65.00
Bowl, 9"	30.00	50.00	40.00
Bowl, 9", pan	30.00	50.00	40.00

	Amber Crystal	Carmen Royal	Forest Green
Bowl, 10", pan	30.00	50.00	45.00
Bowl, 10½", belled	35.00	60.00	50.00
Bowl, 10½", 2 comp. salad	30.00	55.00	45.00
Bowl, 10½", 2 hdld.	40.00	55.00	45.00
Bowl, 10½", 3 comp.	40.00	75.00	65.00
Bowl, 10½", low ft.	40.00	85.00	65.00
Bowl, 11", flat, flared	35.00	65.00	50.00
Bowl, 12", oval celery	25.00	40.00	35.00
Bowl, 12", pan	35.00	70.00	55.00
Bowl, 12½", flat rim	35.00	75.00	50.00
Bowl, 12½", belled	35.00	70.00	50.00
Bowl, 13", ftd., punch	195.00	350.00	250.00
Bowl, 13½", salad, flared	30.00	60.00	40.00
Bowl, 17", pan	35.00	65.00	45.00
Bowl, 2 comp., 2 ladle, salad dressing, flared	30.00	60.00	40.00

TALLY HO

	Amber Crystal	Carmen Royal	Forest Green
Bowl, 2 comp., 2 ladle, salad dressing, rnd.	30.00	60.00	40.00
Bowl, 2 ladle, spouted, salad dressing	30.00	60.00	40.00
Bowl, finger	17.50	27.50	25.00
Bowl, sauce boat	25.00	40.00	35.00
Candelabrum, 6½", w/bobeche & prism	50.00	100.00	65.00
Candlestick, 5"	25.00	40.00	35.00
Candlestick, 6"	30.00	45.00	40.00
Candlestick, 6½"	40.00	55.00	50.00
Cheese & cracker, 11½", 2 hdld	60.00	90.00	65.00
Cheese & cracker, 13½"	65.00	95.00	70.00
Cheese & cracker, 17½"	70.00	100.00	75.00
Cheese & cracker, 18"	75.00	105.00	80.00
Coaster, 4"	10.00	20.00	15.00
Cocktail shaker, 50 oz., ftd., chrome top	75.00	150.00	95.00
Cocktail shaker, hdld., ftd., chrome top	75.00	165.00	100.00
Comport, tall frappe cocktail, 10 side rim	35.00	60.00	45.00
Comport, 4½" tall	17.50	27.50	25.00
Comport, 6", tall ft., flat, mint	40.00	55.00	50.00
Comport, 6½", tall ft., raised edge	40.00	55.00	50.00
Comport, 7", low ft.	40.00	55.00	50.00
Comport, 8", low ft.	45.00	70.00	65.00
Comport, 9", low ft., raised edge	55.00	80.00	75.00
Comport, low ft., mint	17.50	27.50	25.00
Cookie jar w/lid, chrome hdld. (ice pail w/lid)	85.00	160.00	135.00
Creamer, ftd.	12.50	27.50	20.00
Cup, 2½ oz., hdld., whiskey	12.50	27.50	20.00
Cup, ftd.	10.00	20.00	17.50
Cup, punch, flat	10.00	25.00	17.50
Decanter, 34 oz.	50.00	90.00	65.00
Decanter, 34 oz., hdld.	60.00	100.00	75.00
Goblet, brandy inhaler	40.00	65.00	50.00
Goblet, claret	15.00	30.00	22.00
Goblet, cocktail	14.00	24.00	16.00
Goblet, cordial	30.00	50.00	40.00
Goblet, goblet	20.00	35.00	30.00
Goblet, low ft., brandy inhaler	40.00	65.00	50.00
Goblet, low sherbet	12.50	20.00	17.50
Goblet, oyster cocktail	14.00	22.00	18.00
Goblet, tall sherbet	15.00	25.00	20.00
Goblet, wine	18.00	30.00	24.00
Ice pail, chrome hdld.	65.00	95.00	75.00
Jug, 74 oz., tankard, flat bottom	125.00	225.00	195.00
Jug, 88 oz., rnd. bottom	145.00	295.00	235.00
Mug, 6 oz., punch	12.50	25.00	15.00
Mug, 12 oz., hdld. stein	25.00	40.00	35.00
Mug, 14 oz., hdld. stein, rnd. bottom	30.00	50.00	35.00
Plate, 6", bread & butter	10.00	15.00	12.50
Plate, 7", 2 hdld.	20.00	30.00	25.00
Plate, 7½", salad	12.50	20.00	17.50
Plate, 8", salad	15.00	20.00	18.00
Plate, 9½", lunch	35.00	55.00	40.00
Plate, 10½", dinner	45.00		
Plate, 11½", 2 hdld., sandwich	35.00	60.00	50.00
Plate, 13½", raised edge	35.00	60.00	50.00
Plate, 14", chop	35.00	60.00	50.00
Plate, 14", w/4" seat in center	40.00	65.00	55.00
Plate, 17½", Sunday night supper	40.00	75.00	60.00
Plate, 17½"	40.00	75.00	60.00
Plate, 18", w/4" seat in center	45.00	80.00	65.00
Plate, 18", buffet lunch	45.00	80.00	65.00
Plate, 18", ftd., weekend supper	50.00	85.00	70.00
Plate, finger bowl	10.00	15.00	12.50
Plate, salad dressing liner	12.50	20.00	17.50
Plate, sauce boat liner	12.50	20.00	17.50
Relish, 6", 2 comp., 2 hdld.	20.00	30.00	25.00
Relish, 8", 2 hdld., 3 comp.	25.00	35.00	30.00
Relish, 10", 4 comp.	25.00	40.00	30.00
Saucer	3.00	5.00	4.00
Shaker, w/glass top	25.00	50.00	35.00
Stem, 1 oz., "T" stem cordial	30.00	60.00	45.00
Stem, 2½ oz., high stem wine	20.00	40.00	30.00
Stem, 3 oz., ftd., tumbler	15.00	35.00	25.00
Stem, 3 oz., high stem cocktail	15.00	35.00	25.00
Stem, 4 oz., low stem cocktail	15.00	35.00	25.00
Stem, 4½ oz., low sherbet	12.50	20.00	17.50
Stem, 4½ oz., high stem claret	20.00	30.00	25.00
Stem, 5 oz., ftd., tumbler	12.50	20.00	17.50
Stem, 5 oz., low stem juice	12.50	20.00	18.00
Stem, 6 oz., high stem juice	15.00	25.00	20.00
Stem, 6½ oz., low stem sherbet	15.00	25.00	20.00
Stem, 7½ oz., high sherb.	18.00	30.00	25.00
Stem, 10 oz., high stem	20.00	32.50	25.00
Stem, 10 oz., low stem lunch	22.00	35.00	28.00
Stem, 12 oz., ftd. tumbler	20.00	35.00	28.00
Stem, 14 oz., high stem	20.00	45.00	30.00
Stem, 16 oz., ftd., tumbler	20.00	45.00	30.00
Stem, 18 oz., tall stem	25.00	50.00	35.00
Sugar, ftd.	12.50	27.50	20.00
Top hat, 10"	100.00	250.00	150.00
Tumbler, 2½ oz.	30.00	50.00	40.00
Tumbler, 5 oz.	25.00	40.00	35.00
Tumbler, 7 oz., old fashion	25.00	40.00	35.00
Tumbler, 10 oz., short	25.00	42.00	35.00
Tumbler, 10 oz., tall	25.00	45.00	35.00
Tumbler, 14 oz., rnd. bottom	17.50	32.50	27.50
Tumbler, 15 oz.	20.00	35.00	30.00
Vase, 12", ftd.	95.00	195.00	155.00

Colors: crystal, some yellow and cobalt blue

As with Duncan's Sandwich, Tear Drop stemware can be found and priced inexpensively enough that you could use it today without buying new expensive stems. Those who owned Tear Drop used it; so, mint condition dinner plates and additional serving pieces are not easily located. This is an excellent starting point for those looking for an easily found and reasonably priced Elegant pattern.

Colored pieces pictured may have been produced at Tiffin from Duncan moulds. Reprints of original Duncan catalogs showing stemware and tumblers can be found in earlier editions of this book. In order to have room for the newly listed patterns, I had to remove some catalog pages that I have previously shown.

	Crystal
Ashtray, 3", indiv.	7.00
Ashtray, 5"	8.00
Bonbon, 6", 4 hdld.	12.00
Bottle, w/stopper, 12", bar	155.00
Bowl, 4¼", finger	7.00
Bowl, 5", fruit nappy	8.00
Bowl, 5", 2 hdld., nappy	10.00
Bowl, 6", dessert, nappy	8.00
Bowl, 6", fruit, nappy	8.00
Bowl, 7", fruit, nappy	9.00
Bowl, 7", 2 hdld., nappy	10.00
Bowl, 8" x 12", oval, flower	50.00
Bowl, 9", salad	30.00
Bowl, 9", 2 hdld., nappy	25.00
Bowl, 10", crimped console, 2 hdld.	32.50
Bowl, 10", flared, fruit	30.00
Bowl, 11½", crimped, flower	35.00
Bowl, 11½", flared, flower	32.50
Bowl, 12", salad	40.00
Bowl, 12", crimped, low foot	40.00
Bowl, 12", ftd., flower	50.00
Bowl, 12", sq., 4 hdld.	45.00
Bowl, 13", gardenia	35.00
Bowl, 15½", 2½ gal., punch	110.00
Butter, w/cover, ¼ lb., 2 hdld.	25.00
Cake salver, 13", ftd.	55.00
Canape set (6" plate w/ring, 4 oz., ftd., cocktail)	30.00
Candlestick, 4"	12.50
Candlestick, 7", 2-lite, ball loop ctr.	30.00
Candlestick, 7", lg. ball ctr. w/bobeches, prisms	90.00
Candy basket, 5½" x 7½", 2 hdld., oval	85.00
Candy box, w/cover, 7", 2 pt., 2 hdld.	65.00
Candy box, w/cover, 8", 3 pt., 3 hdld.	70.00
Candy dish, 7½", heart shape	22.50
Celery, 11", 2 hdld.	20.00
Celery, 11", 2 pt., 2 hdld.	22.50
Celery, 12", 3 pt.	25.00
Cheese & cracker (3½" comport, 11" 2 hdld. plate)	45.00
Coaster/ashtray, 3", rolled edge	7.00
Comport, 4¾", ftd.	12.00
Comport, 6", low foot., hdld.	15.00

	Crystal
Condiment set, 5 pc. (salt/pepper, 2 3 oz. cruets, 9", 2 hdld. tray)	125.00
Creamer, 3 oz.	8.00
Creamer, 6 oz.	6.00
Creamer, 8 oz.	8.00
Cup, 2½ oz., demi	12.00
Cup, 6 oz., tea	6.00
Flower basket, 12", loop hdl.	100.00
Ice bucket, 5½"	85.00
Marmalade, w/cover, 4"	40.00
Mayonnaise, 4½" (2 hdld. bowl, ladle, 6" plate)	40.00
Mayonnaise set, 3 pc. (4½" bowl, ladle, 8" hdld. plate)	40.00
Mustard jar, w/cover, 4¼"	40.00
Nut dish, 6", 2 pt.	11.00
Oil bottle, 3 oz.	22.50
Olive dish, 4¼", 2 hdld., oval	15.00
Olive dish, 6", 2 pt.	15.00
Pickle dish, 6"	15.00
Pitcher, 5", 16 oz., milk	55.00
Pitcher, 8½", 64 oz., w/ice lip	120.00
Plate, 6", bread/butter	4.00
Plate, 6", canape	10.00
Plate, 7", 2 hdld., lemon	12.50
Plate, 7½", salad	5.00
Plate, 8½", luncheon	7.00
Plate, 10½", dinner	40.00
Plate, 11", 2 hdld.	27.50
Plate, 13", 4 hdld.	30.00
Plate, 13", salad liner, rolled edge	30.00
Plate, 13", torte, rolled edge	30.00
Plate, 14", torte	35.00
Plate, 14", torte, rolled edge	35.00
Plate, 16", torte, rolled edge	37.50
Plate, 18", lazy susan	75.00
Plate, 18", punch liner, rolled edge	60.00

	Crystal
Relish, 7", 2 pt., 2 hdld.	17.50
Relish, 7½", 2 pt., heart shape	22.50
Relish, 9", 3 pt., 3 hdld.	30.00
Relish, 11", 3 pt., 2 hdld.	32.50
Relish, 12", 3 pt.	35.00
Relish, 12", 5 pt., rnd.	35.00
Relish, 12", 6 pt., rnd.	40.00
Relish, 12", sq., 4 pt., 4 hdld.	40.00
Salad set, 6" (compote, 11", hdld. plate)	37.50
Salad set, 9" (2 pt. bowl, 13" rolled edge plate)	75.00
Salt & pepper, 5"	27.50
Saucer, 4½", demi	3.00
Saucer, 6"	1.50
Stem, 2½", 5 oz., ftd., sherbet	5.00
Stem, 2¾", 3½ oz., ftd., oyster cocktail	7.50
Stem, 3½", 5 oz., sherbet	6.00
Stem, 4", 1 oz., cordial	30.00
Stem, 4½", 1¾ oz., sherry	25.00
Stem, 4½", 3½ oz., cocktail	12.50
Stem, 4¾", 3 oz., wine	17.50
Stem, 5", 5 oz., champagne	10.00
Stem, 5½", 4 oz., claret	20.00
Stem, 5¾", 9 oz.	12.00
Stem, 6¼", 8 oz., ale	16.00
Stem, 7", 9 oz.	16.00
Sugar, 3 oz.	8.00
Sugar, 6 oz.	6.00

	Crystal
Sugar, 8 oz.	8.00
Sweetmeat, 5½", star shape, 2 hdld.	35.00
Sweetmeat, 6½", ctr. hdld.	30.00
Sweetmeat, 7", star shape, 2 hdld.	40.00
Tray, 5½", ctr. hdld. (for mustard jar)	12.00
Tray, 6", 2 hdld. (for salt/pepper)	12.00
Tray, 7¾", ctr. hdld. (for cruets)	12.50
Tray, 8", 2 hdld. (for oil/vinegar)	12.50
Tray, 8", 2 hdld. (for sugar/creamer)	12.00
Tray, 10", 2 hdld (for sugar/creamer)	12.00
Tumbler, 2¼", 2 oz., flat, whiskey	18.00
Tumbler, 2¼", 2 oz., ftd., whiskey	14.00
Tumbler, 3", 3 oz., ftd., whiskey	14.00
Tumbler, 3¼", 3½ oz., flat, juice	7.00
Tumbler, 3¼", 7 oz., flat, old-fashioned	12.00
Tumbler, 3½", 5 oz., flat, juice	8.00
Tumbler, 4", 4½ oz., ftd., juice	9.00
Tumbler, 4¼", 9 oz., flat	10.00
Tumbler, 4½", 8 oz., flat, split	10.00
Tumbler, 4½", 9 oz., ftd.	10.00
Tumbler, 4¾", 10 oz., flat, hi-ball	11.00
Tumbler, 5", 8 oz., ftd., party	10.00
Tumbler, 5¼", 12 oz., flat, iced tea	15.00
Tumbler, 5¾", 14 oz., flat, hi-ball	17.50
Tumbler, 6", 14 oz., iced tea	17.50
Urn, w/cover, 9", ftd.	135.00
Vase, 9", ftd., fan	30.00
Vase, 9", ftd., round	40.00

Color: crystal, amber, cobalt, red

Terrace is another Duncan pattern that has been pretty much ignored over the years by collectors outside the Pittsburgh area due to limited distribution and lack of information. I seem to be writing about a lot of Duncan patterns in this section of the book. It looks as if the people responsible for naming Duncan patterns only had the P, S, and T section of the dictionary when it came time to delegate names.

I have bought at least 90% of the items pictured within fifty miles of Washington, Pennsylvania, where it was produced. From what collectors have told me, I doubt if much of this pattern was ever sold west of the Mississippi. The majority of Terrace collectors seek red and cobalt blue. Little amber is available and most of that found has an etching on it, which is difficult to match. Those yearning for crystal usually look for First Love or some other etching rather than Terrace itself. Finding enough colored Terrace to photograph has been difficult; I have spent years buying a piece here and a piece there to accumulate what you see.

Note the crystal bowls with cobalt bases. They also are found with red bases. Learn to identify that base pattern so you do not pass one of these. I am sure food presented itself better in that crystal top than in blue or red.

	Crystal Amber	Cobalt Red		Crystal Amber	Cobalt Red
Ashtray, 3½", sq.	17.50	30.00	Plate, 11", hdld.	30.00	
Ashtray, 4¾", sq.	20.00	95.00	Plate, 11", hdld., cracker w/ring	30.00	110.00
Bowl, 4¼", finger, #5111½	30.00	75.00	Plate, 11", hdld., sandwich	30.00	
Bowl, 6¾" x 4¼", ftd., flared rim	30.00		Plate, 12", torte, rolled edge	32.50	
Bowl, 8" sq. x 2½", hdld.	55.00		* Plate, 13", cake, ftd.	75.00	210.00
Bowl, 9" x 4½", ftd.	42.00		Plate, 13", torte, flat edge	35.00	
Bowl, 9½" x 2½", hdld.	45.00		Plate, 13", torte, rolled edge	37.50	
Bowl, 10" x 3¾", ftd., flared rim	55.00		Plate, 13¼", torte	35.00	195.00
* Bowl, 10¼" x 4¾", ftd.	75.00	145.00	Relish, 6" x 1¾", hdld., 2 pt.	20.00	50.00
Bowl, 11" x 3¼", flared rim	32.50		Relish, 9", 4 pt.	35.00	100.00
Butter or cheese, 7" sq. x 1¼"	120.00		Relish, 10½" x 1½", hdld., 5 pt.	65.00	
Candle, 3", 1-lite	25.00	70.00	Relish, 12", 4 pt., hdld.	40.00	
Candle, 4", low	25.00		Relish, 12", 5 pt., hdld.	40.00	
Candlestick, 1-lite, bobeche & prisms	75.00		Relish, 12", 5 pt., w/lid	100.00	295.00
Candlestick 2-lite, 7" x 9¼", bobeche & prisms	100.00		Salad dressing bowl, 2 pt., 5½" x 4¼"	45.00	95.00
Candy urn, w/lid	135.00	425.00	Saucer, sq.	6.00	12.00
Cheese stand, 3" x 5¼"	25.00	40.00	Saucer, demi	5.00	
Cocktail shaker, metal lid	85.00	195.00	Stem, 3¾", 1 oz., cordial, #5111½	42.50	
Comport, w/lid, 8¾" x 5½"	150.00	425.00	Stem, 3¾", 4½ oz., oyster cocktail, #5111½	20.00	
Comport, 3½" x 4¾" w	30.00	80.00	Stem, 4", 5 oz., ice cream, #5111½	14.00	
Creamer, 3", 10 oz.	18.00	45.00	Stem, 4½", 3½ oz., cocktail, #5111½	22.50	
Cup	15.00	40.00	Stem, 5", 5 oz., saucer champagne, #5111½	15.00	50.00
Cup, demi	20.00		Stem, 5¼", 3 oz., wine, #5111½	32.50	
Mayonnaise, 5½" x 2½", ftd., hdld., #111	35.00		Stem, 5¼", 5 oz., ftd. juice, #5111½	20.00	
Mayonnaise, 5½" x 3½", crimped,	32.00		Stem, 5¾", 10 oz., low luncheon goblet, #5111½	22.00	
Mayonnaise, 5¾" x 3", w/dish hdld. tray	35.00	75.00	Stem, 6", 4½ oz., claret, #5111½	45.00	
Mayonnaise, w/7" tray, hdld	35.00		Stem, 6½", 12 oz., ftd. ice tea, #5111½	32.50	
Nappy, 5½" x 2", div., hdld.	18.00		Stem, 6¾", 10 oz., tall water goblet, #5111½	25.00	
Nappy, 6" x 1¾", hdld.	22.00	35.00	Stem, 6¾", 14 oz., ftd. ice tea, #5111½	32.50	
Pitcher	325.00	995.00	Sugar, 3", 10 oz.	15.00	45.00
Plate, 6"	12.00	25.00	Sugar lid	12.50	60.00
Plate, 6", hdld., lemon	14.00	30.00	Tumbler, 4", 9 oz., water	17.50	40.00
Plate, 6", sq.	14.00	30.00	Tray, 8" x 2", hdld., celery	17.50	
Plate, 7"	17.50	35.00	Urn, 4½" x 4½"	27.50	
Plate, 7½"	18.00	35.00	Urn, 10½" x 4½"	100.00	350.00
Plate, 7½", sq.	19.00	38.00			
Plate, 8½"	20.00	25.00			
Plate, 9", sq.	25.00	75.00			
Plate, 11"	30.00	90.00			

*Colored foot

Colors: Blue, green, and pink

Thistle Cut appears on two Fry dinnerware lines which are both illustrated in the photo. Line 3101 is shown by all the round pieces in the photo; and Line 3104 is the octagon shaped. The stems with the disc connectors (beehive shape) are usually found with the round line. You can find this cutting on pink (Rose), green (Emerald), or blue (Azure). Most collectors have referred to the blue as "Cornflower" over the years

I bought this set about 25 years ago because of the blue color, which I found interesting. It sat in storage unidentified until Cathy was researching the first *Pattern Identification* book. She was scrounging for patterns for the book and discovered this set which she was able to determine the maker. We took all the extra pieces to a show where a dealer quickly bought it. As with Duncan patterns, I rarely find Fry patterns outside a circle of one hundred miles of Pittsburgh.

About ten years ago, I visited the descendants of the Fry factory owners. They still have all the old glass formulas that Fry used and some wonderful Fry glass including a rare Fry insulator, which I had never seen before. In fact, I didn't even know they made insulators, but it was a beauty and I was told it was extremely rare. No doubt in my mind.

	All colors		All colors
Bowl, 9", round	65.00	Plate, 10", round, dinner	45.00
Candlestick	35.00	Saucer	5.00
Cup	30.00	Stem, high sherbet	25.00
Plate, 8", octagonal, luncheon	15.00	Stem, juice, ftd.	27.50
Plate, 8", round, luncheon	15.00	Stem, low sherbet	20.00
Plate, 10½", octagonal, dinner	45.00	Stem, water goblet	30.00

Colors: crystal and crystal w/pale burgundy, champagne (yellow), and green-blue lustre stain; more intense ruby color replaced pale burgundy later; black turtles in 1952

Westmoreland's Thousand Eye is probably that company's most recognized pattern and had one of the longest production runs of any pattern save English Hobnail. It was introduced in 1934 and discontinued, except for turtles, in 1956. The turtle cigarette box has been reproduced. Those decorated turtles pictured are an earlier production. Evidently these were one of the favorite retail pieces as there are so many seen today. Fairy lamps, both footed and flat versions, were a late 1970s production.

I continue to run into a 13" bowl on an 18" plate. They are usually crystal, but are seen in other colors as well. They are commonly attributed to Westmoreland's Thousand Eye line, but are actually Canton's Glass Line 100 (which probably came from Paden City). The colored pieces were evidently Paden City, but Canton did advertise they would make standard colors as well as special colors if the customer so wanted. They used many of Paden City's moulds after that company's demise.

Many Thousand Eye pieces are suggestive of earlier pattern glass items. This seems to be another of the patterns that collectors really love or cannot abide. Stemware abounds and like some of the Duncan patterns, you can buy these older pieces and use them less expensively than many of today's glassware lines sold in department stores. Thousand Eye is durable, but it was used rather extensively. You need to check plates and other flat pieces for scratches and wear. Mint condition flatware is harder to find than any of the stems or tumblers. That footed comport in the front is a mayonnaise. The heavy crimped piece on the left in the back would make a great paperweight, but I think it was meant to be a vase.

	Crystal
Ashtray (sm. turtle)	8.00
Basket, 8", hdld., oval	45.00
Bowl, 4½", nappy	8.00
Bowl, 5½", nappy	12.00
Bowl, 7½", hdld.	22.50
Bowl, 10", 2 hdld.	37.50
Bowl, 11", belled	35.00
Bowl, 11", crimped, oblong	45.00
Bowl, 11", triangular	45.00
Bowl, 11, round	40.00
Bowl, 12", 2 hdld., flared	45.00
Candelabra, 2 light	40.00
Cigarette box & cover (lg. turtle)	30.00
Comport, 5", high ft.	22.50
Creamer, high ft.	12.50
Creamer, low rim	10.00
Cup, ftd., bead hdld.	8.00
Fairy lamp, flat.	45.00
Fairy lamp, ftd.	50.00
Jug, ½ gal.	95.00
Mayonnaise, ftd., w/ladle	30.00
Plate, 6"	5.00
Plate, 7"	7.50
Plate, 8½"	10.00
Plate, 10", service	25.00
Plate, 16"	35.00
Plate, 18"	55.00
Relish, 10", rnd.	30.00
Saucer	3.00
Shaker, ftd., pr.	30.00
Stem, 1 oz., cordial	15.00
Stem, 2 oz., wine	12.00
Stem, 3 oz., sherry	12.50
Stem, 3½ oz., cocktail	10.00
Stem, 5 oz., claret	12.50

	Crystal
Stem, 8 oz.	10.00
Stem, high ft., sherbet	8.50
Stem, low ft., sherbet	7.50
Stem, parfait, ftd.	12.50
Sugar, high ft.	12.50
Sugar, low rim	10.00
Tumbler, 1½ oz., whiskey	10.00
Tumbler, 5 oz., flat ginger ale	8.00
Tumbler, 5 oz., ftd.	8.00
Tumbler, 6 oz., old fashion	10.00
Tumbler, 7 oz., ftd.	9.00
Tumbler, 8 oz., flat	9.00
Tumbler, 9 oz., ftd.	10.00
Tumbler, 12 oz., ftd., tea	12.50
Vase, crimped bowl	25.00
Vase, flair rim	25.00

Colors: azure, green

Around 25 years ago, there were eight champagnes and water goblets sitting at a flea market in Louisville, Kentucky. I looked at them for several months, but did not know what they were or who made them. Money was tight enough I couldn't afford them not knowing what I was buying. Finally, Cathy went to that market with me; and when she saw them, there went $400 with no discounts! We called the etch "Tinkerbell" for lack of a better name. The stem line itself is known as #7631 Jewel stem.

I talked to Jerry Gallagher at the Heisey show about ten years later and told him about "Tinkerbell" etched stems we had found. He said they sounded like Morgantown to him and "Tinkerbell" was what he was calling them, also! We took half of them to Heisey the next year and they sold like hot cakes. The next year we took a couple of each and they sold a little slower, and kept one of each. I have only seen these in blue and I was never able to find a cordial for my collection; but that is not the only one that has eluded me.

The green bud vase is 10" tall and was found in an antique mall near Columbus, Ohio. It remains the only piece of green "Tinkerbell" I have seen. A four piece water bottle set is one of the most interesting pieces in this pattern. Hopefully, I can show it to you in the future.

	Azure Green
Bowl, finger, ftd.	100.00
Night or medicine set bottle, 4 pc. (med. bottle w/stop, night glass, w/water bottle)	600.00
Plate, finger bowl liner	35.00
Stem, 1½ oz., cordial	175.00
Stem, 2½ oz., wine	135.00

	Azure Green
Stem, 3½ oz., cocktail	125.00
Stem, 5½ oz., saucer champagne	125.00
Stem, 5½ oz., sherbet	100.00
Stem, 9 oz., goblet	150.00
Vase, 10", plain top, ftd., #36 Uranus	350.00
Vase, 10", ruffled top, ftd., #36 Uranus	400.00

Colors: Rose pink, Topaz, yellow

Rose colored Trojan sells faster than Topaz for me, since the supply of this color seems to be less than the demand. Yellow also sells quite well, but Topaz has always been more prevalent in the market. A few years ago there was a surplus of Topaz being offered for sale due to the marketing of some large collections. Now collectors are once again having trouble finding serving pieces at prices they want to pay.

Soup and cereal bowl prices have increased more than all other Trojan pieces in the last few years. Soup bowls are rarely seen. If you find either one, be pleased and pull out the checkbook or credit card. There are limited chances to obtain these. Don't be kicking yourself five years later that you should've purchased them!

If you order or buy via ads, you need to know the following Fostoria facts: liner plates for cream soups and mayonnaise are the same piece; two-handled cake plates come with and without an indent in the center. The indented version also serves as a plate for one of two styles of cheese comports; bonbon, lemon dish, sweetmeat, and whipped cream bowls all come with loop or bow handles; and sugars come with a straight or ruffled edge. Strangely enough, it is the ruffled top sugar that takes a lid.

Trojan stemware can be found except for cordials and clarets in either color. Clarets are nearly impossible to find in most Fostoria patterns. If you need them, you had better buy them whenever you find them. The claret has the same shape as the wine, but holds four ounces as opposed to the three ounces of the wine. Yes, wine glasses in those days held 2 to 3½ ounces of liquid. This confuses today's collector who is used to wine goblets holding eight ounces or more. In those days, that volume was for water.

Both the quarter and half-pound candies are pictured on page 215. They sell in about the same price range, but I see fewer of the quarter pound in my travels. On that bottom row are two ice dishes with inserts. The ice dish has to have the Trojan pattern to be the correct one. I once bought a twelve- place setting of Trojan where the ice dishes were plain which made a very large difference in the price. The inserts themselves are always plain without the pattern. Pictured are the shrimp and tomato juice inserts. The first item in the top row is the grapefruit. It takes a liner with the pattern on it. The inserts are equally valuable in price. Do not pay big bucks for plain liners.

	Rose	Topaz
Ashtray, #2350, lg.	35.00	30.00
Ashtray, #2350, sm.	30.00	25.00
Bottle, salad dressing, #2983	595.00	395.00
Bowl, baker, #2375, 9"		75.00
Bowl, bonbon, #2375		22.50
Bowl, bouillon, #2375, ftd.		20.00
Bowl, cream soup, #2375, ftd.	40.00	35.00
Bowl, finger, #869/2283,		
w/6¼" liner	55.00	50.00
Bowl, lemon, #2375	24.00	20.00
Bowl, #2394, 3 ftd., 4½", mint	25.00	22.00
Bowl, #2375, fruit, 5"	25.00	22.00
Bowl, #2354, 3 ftd., 6"	50.00	45.00
Bowl, cereal, #2375, 6½"	60.00	45.00
Bowl, soup, #2375, 7"	125.00	110.00
Bowl, lg. dessert, #2375, 2 hdld.	85.00	75.00
Bowl, #2395, 10"	115.00	80.00
Bowl, #2395, scroll, 10"	100.00	90.00
Bowl, combination #2415,		
w/candleholder handles	250.00	195.00
Bowl, #2375, centerpiece, flared		
optic, 12"	70.00	65.00
Bowl, #2394, centerpiece, ftd., 12"	85.00	70.00
Bowl, #2375, centerpiece,		
mushroom, 12"	85.00	65.00

	Rose	Topaz
Candlestick, #2394, 2"	25.00	22.50
Candlestick, #2375, flared, 3"	30.00	25.00
Candlestick, #2395½, scroll, 5"	75.00	65.00
Candy, w/cover, #2394, ¼ lb.	295.00	260.00
Candy, w/cover, #2394, ½ lb.	225.00	200.00
Celery, #2375, 11½"	50.00	40.00
Cheese & cracker, set, #2375, #2368	85.00	75.00
Comport, #5299 or #2400, 6"	65.00	50.00
Comport, #2375, 7"	65.00	50.00
Creamer, #2375, ftd.	22.50	20.00
Creamer, tea, #2375½	60.00	50.00
Cup, after dinner, #2375	50.00	40.00
Cup, #2375½, ftd.	20.00	18.00
Decanter, #2439, 9"	1,395.00	995.00
Goblet, claret, #5099, 4 oz., 6"	125.00	80.00
Goblet, cocktail, #5099, 3 oz., 5¼"	32.50	30.00
Goblet, cordial, #5099, ¾ oz., 4"	110.00	75.00
Goblet, water, #5299, 10 oz., 8¼"	42.50	33.00
Goblet, wine, #5099, 3 oz., 5½"	60.00	45.00
Grapefruit, #5282½	60.00	50.00
Grapefruit liner, #945½	50.00	40.00
Ice bucket, #2375	100.00	90.00
Ice dish, #2451, #2455	55.00	45.00
Ice dish liner (tomato, crab, fruit),		
#2451	20.00	10.00

	Rose	Topaz
Mayonnaise ladle	30.00	30.00
Mayonnaise, w/liner, #2375	60.00	50.00
Oil, ftd., #2375	395.00	295.00
Oyster, cocktail, #5099, ftd.	30.00	27.50
Parfait, #5099	70.00	50.00
Pitcher, #5000	495.00	350.00
Plate, #2375, canape, 6¼"	35.00	25.00
Plate, #2375, bread/butter, 6"	8.00	7.00
Plate, #2375, salad, 7½"	12.00	10.00
Plate, 2375, cream soup or mayo liner, 7½"	15.00	12.00
Plate, #2375, luncheon, 8¾"	20.00	18.00
Plate, #2375, sm., dinner, 9½"	35.00	30.00
Plate, #2375, cake, handled, 10"	65.00	50.00
Plate, #2375, grill, rare, 10¼"	100.00	90.00
Plate, #2375, dinner, 10¼"	85.00	70.00
Plate, #2375, chop, 13"	80.00	70.00
Plate, #2375, round, 14"	80.00	75.00
Platter, #2375, 12"	90.00	75.00
Platter, #2375, 15"	175.00	150.00
Relish, #2375, 8½"		45.00
Relish, #2350, 3 pt., rnd., 8¾"	55.00	50.00
Sauce boat, #2375	150.00	105.00

	Rose	Topaz
Sauce plate, #2375	50.00	45.00
Saucer, #2375, after dinner	10.00	10.00
Saucer, #2375	8.00	6.00
Shaker, #2375, pr., ftd.	130.00	110.00
Sherbet, #5099, high, 6"	30.00	25.00
Sherbet, #5099, low, 4¼"	22.00	18.00
Sugar, #2375½, ftd.	22.50	20.00
Sugar cover, #2375½	150.00	125.00
Sugar pail, #2378	250.00	200.00
Sugar, tea, #2375½	55.00	45.00
Sweetmeat, #2375	25.00	22.00
Tray, 11", ctr. hdld, #2375	60.00	50.00
Tray, #2429, service & lemon insert		265.00
Tumbler, #5099, ftd., 2½ oz.	60.00	45.00
Tumbler, #5099, ftd., 5 oz., 4½"	35.00	30.00
Tumbler, #5099, ftd., 9 oz., 5¼"	25.00	20.00
Tumbler, #5099, ftd., 12 oz., 6"	50.00	40.00
Vase, #2417, 8"	200.00	150.00
Vase, #4105, 8"	275.00	200.00
Vase, #2369, 9"		250.00
Whipped cream bowl, #2375	37.50	30.00
Whipped cream pail, #2378	150.00	125.00

Colors: crystal, Flamingo pink, Moongleam green, Marigold amber/yellow, Sahara yellow, some Alexandrite (rare)

There has been some minor price increases in Twist recently. Most Twist pieces are marked with the H in diamond. Stemmed pieces are usually marked on the stem itself.

Few collectors have searched for crystal, but there is a growing force of new collectors being attracted to this Deco looking pattern. That amber/yellow colored ice bucket below is in the color, Marigold; and the pink/purple color is Alexandrite. Both are rare Heisey colors. Be aware that Marigold is difficult to find in mint condition because the applied color has a tendency to chip or peel. Items that are beginning to deteriorate will continue to do so. If you have a choice in owning a piece of this rarely seen color that has some problems, pass it unless it is very inexpensive. Nothing can be done to restore it and there have been many that have tried.

Oil bottles, large bowls, and the three-footed utility plates have seen upward price adjustments. The individual sugar and creamer have both disappeared into collections; grab one if you get a chance. The Moongleam cocktail shaker is missing from most collections. Cocktail shakers in the other colors have never surfaced.

	Crystal	Flamingo	Moongleam	Marigold	Alexandrite	Sahara
Baker, 9", oval	25.00	35.00	45.00	60.00		
Bonbon, individual	15.00	35.00	40.00	40.00		
Bonbon, 6", 2 hdld.	10.00	20.00	25.00	30.00		
Bottle, French dressing	50.00	90.00	110.00	135.00		
Bowl, cream soup/bouillon	15.00	25.00	32.00	50.00		
Bowl, ftd., almond/indiv. sugar	35.00	45.00	55.00	75.00		
Bowl, indiv. nut	10.00	25.00	40.00	45.00		
Bowl, 4", nappy	10.00	30.00	35.00	40.00		
Bowl, 6", 2 hdld.	7.00	20.00	20.00	25.00		
Bowl, 6", 2 hdld., jelly	10.00	20.00	28.00	30.00		
Bowl, 6", 2 hdld., mint	7.00	20.00	35.00	30.00		20.00
Bowl, 8", low ftd.		80.00	80.00	85.00		
Bowl, 8", nappy, ground bottom	20.00	50.00	55.00	60.00		
Bowl, 8", nasturtium, rnd.	45.00	70.00	90.00	80.00	450.00	80.00
Bowl, 8", nasturtium, oval	45.00	70.00	90.00	80.00		
Bowl, 9", floral	25.00	40.00	50.00	65.00		

	Crystal	Flamingo	Moongleam	Marigold	Alexandrite	Sahara
Bowl, 9", floral, rolled edge	30.00	40.00	45.00	65.00		
Bowl, 12", floral, oval, 4 ft.	45.00	100.00	110.00	90.00	550.00	85.00
Bowl, 12", floral, rnd., 4 ft.	30.00	40.00	50.00	65.00		
Candlestick, 2", 1-lite		40.00	50.00	85.00		
Cheese dish, 6", 2 hdld.	10.00	20.00	25.00	30.00		
Claret, 4 oz.	15.00	30.00	40.00	50.00		
Cocktail shaker, metal top			400.00			
Comport, 7", tall	40.00	90.00	120.00	150.00		
Creamer, hotel, oval	25.00	40.00	45.00	50.00		
Creamer, individual (unusual)	30.00	50.00	60.00	65.00		
Creamer, zigzag handles, ftd.	20.00	40.00	50.00	70.00		
Cup, zigzag handles	10.00	25.00	32.00	35.00		
Grapefruit, ftd.	15.00	25.00	35.00	60.00		
Ice tub	50.00	125.00	110.00	125.00		125.00
Ice bucket					425.00	
Pitcher, 3 pint	95.00	175.00	230.00			
Mayonnaise	35.00	65.00	80.00	80.00		
Mayonnaise, #1252½	20.00	35.00	45.00	50.00		
Mustard, w/cover, spoon	40.00	90.00	140.00	100.00		
Oil bottle, 2½ oz., w/#78 stopper	50.00	140.00	170.00	200.00		
Oil bottle, 4 oz., w/#78 stopper	50.00	110.00	120.00	120.00		90.00
Plate, cream soup liner	5.00	7.00	10.00	15.00		
Plate, 8", Kraft cheese	20.00	40.00	60.00	50.00		
Plate, 8", ground bottom	7.00	14.00	20.00	30.00		20.00
Plate, 10", utility, 3 ft.	40.00	70.00	70.00			
Plate, 12", 2 hdld., sandwich	30.00	60.00	90.00	80.00		
Plate, 12", muffin, 2 hdld., turned sides	40.00	80.00	90.00	80.00		
Plate, 13", 3 part, relish	10.00	17.00	22.00	35.00		
Platter, 12"	15.00	50.00	60.00	75.00		
Salt & pepper, ftd.	100.00	140.00	160.00	200.00		140.00
Saucer	3.00	5.00	7.00	10.00		
Stem, 2½ oz., wine, 2 block stem	30.00	50.00	50.00	60.00		
Stem, 3 oz., oyster cocktail, ftd.	10.00	30.00	40.00	50.00		
Stem, 3 oz., cocktail, 2 block stem	10.00	30.00	45.00	50.00		
Stem, 5 oz., saucer champagne, 2 block stem	10.00	35.00	25.00	30.00		
Stem, 5 oz., sherbet, 2 block stem	10.00	18.00	40.00	28.00		
Stem, 9 oz., luncheon (1 block in stem) *	40.00	60.00	70.00	70.00		
Sugar, ftd.	20.00	30.00	37.50	60.00		
Sugar, hotel, oval	25.00	45.00	50.00	50.00		
Sugar, individual (unusual)	30.00	50.00	60.00	65.00		
Sugar, w/cover, zigzag handles	25.00	40.00	60.00	80.00		
Tray, 7", pickle, ground bottom	7.00	35.00	35.00	45.00		
Tray, 10", celery	30.00	50.00	50.00	40.00		40.00
Tray, 13", celery	25.00	50.00	60.00	50.00		
Tumbler, 5 oz., soda, flat bottom	10.00	25.00	32.00	36.00		
Tumbler, 6 oz., ftd., soda	10.00	25.00	32.00	36.00		
Tumbler, 8 oz., flat, ground bottom	15.00	45.00	70.00	40.00		
Tumbler, 8 oz., soda, straight & flared	12.00	35.00	40.00	40.00		
Tumbler, 9 oz., ftd., soda	20.00	45.00	50.00	60.00		
Tumbler, 12 oz., iced tea, flat bottom	20.00	50.00	60.00	70.00		
Tumbler, 12 oz., ftd., iced tea	20.00	45.00	50.00	60.00		

*also made 2 block stem, 9 oz.

Colors: crystal, pink

Valencia is frequently mistaken with a similar Cambridge pattern, Minerva. Notice in the photo of Valencia that the lines in the pattern are perpendicular to each other (think of a volleyball net). On Minerva, the lines in the pattern meet on a diagonal forming diamonds instead of squares. I have explained that in every book, but have continually been amazed at the number of dealers who have handed me a piece and asked which one is it. Perhaps if you connect "Val" of Valencia to "vol" of volleyball net, you'll remember. Valencia had a limited distribution; dealers are not as familiar with it as with other Cambridge patterns.

Valencia has many pieces that would fetch large sums in other Cambridge patterns, where demand is great. With Valencia, there are so few collectors that rare pieces often are very underpriced. Most pieces shown are ardently desired in Rose Point, but are only just being noticed in Valencia. Valencia items are, without a doubt, rarer than the enormously popular Rose Point. However, rarity is only secondary in collecting, however; demand is the driving force!

Some of the more exceptional pieces pictured include the square, covered honey dish (row 3, #1), the Doulton pitcher, and that metal-handled piece in the top row. Cambridge called that handled item a sugar basket. This is similar to Fostoria's sugar pail, but closer in size to Fostoria's whipped cream pail. Terminology used by glass companies in those days sometimes confuses collectors today.

	Crystal		Crystal
Ashtray, #3500/124, 3¼", round	12.00	Relish, #1402/91, 8", 3 comp.	60.00
Ashtray, #3500/126, 4", round	16.00	Relish, #3500/64, 10", 3 comp.	60.00
Ashtray, #3500/128, 4½", round	20.00	Relish, #3500/65, 10", 4 comp.	65.00
Basket, #3500/55, 6", 2 hdld., ftd.	30.00	Relish, #3500/67, 12", 6 pc.	250.00
Bowl, #3500/49, 5", hdld.	18.00	Relish, #3500/112, 15", 3 pt., 2 hdld.	110.00
Bowl, #3500/37, 6", cereal	27.50	Relish, #3500/13, 15", 4 pt., 2 hdld.	110.00
Bowl, #1402/89, 6", 2 hdld.	18.00	Salt and pepper, #3400/18	65.00
Bowl, #1402/88, 6", 2 hdld., div.	20.00	Saucer, #3500/1	3.00
Bowl, #3500/115, 9½", 2 hdld., ftd.	40.00	Stem, #1402, cordial	75.00
Bowl, #1402/82, 10"	45.00	Stem, #1402, wine	40.00
Bowl, #1402/88, 11"	50.00	Stem, #1402, cocktail	25.00
Bowl, #1402/95, salad dressing, div.	45.00	Stem, #1402, claret	50.00
Bowl, #1402/100, finger, w/liner	45.00	Stem, #1402, oyster cocktail	20.00
Bowl, #3500, ftd., finger	35.00	Stem, #1402, low sherbet	16.00
Candy dish, w/cover, #3500/103	150.00	Stem, #1402, tall sherbet	20.00
Celery, #1402/94, 12"	32.00	Stem, #1402, goblet	28.00
Cigarette holder, #1066, ftd.	55.00	Stem, #3500, cordial	75.00
Comport, #3500/36, 6"	30.00	Stem, #3500, wine, 2½ oz.	40.00
Comport, #3500/37, 7"	45.00	Stem, #3500, cocktail, 3 oz.	22.00
Creamer, #3500/14	17.00	Stem, #3500, claret, 4½ oz.	50.00
Creamer, #3500/15, individual	20.00	Stem, #3500, oyster cocktail, 4½ oz.	20.00
Cup, #3500/1	20.00	Stem, #3500, low sherbet, 7 oz.	16.00
Decanter, #3400/92, 32 oz., ball	235.00	Stem, #3500, tall sherbet, 7 oz.	18.00
Decanter, #3400/119, 12 oz., ball	175.00	Stem, #3500, goblet, long bowl	28.00
Honey dish, w/cover, #3500/139	165.00	Stem, #3500, goblet, short bowl	28.00
Ice pail, #1402/52	100.00	Sugar, #3500/14	15.00
Mayonnaise, #3500/59, 3 pc.	45.00	Sugar, #3500/15, individual	20.00
Nut, #3400/71, 3", 4 ftd.	65.00	Sugar basket, #3500/13	155.00
Perfume, #3400/97, 2 oz., perfume	175.00	Tumbler, #3400/92, 2½ oz.	25.00
Plate, #3500/167, 7½", salad	12.00	Tumbler, #3400/100, 13 oz.	25.00
Plate, #3500/5, 8½", breakfast	14.00	Tumbler, #3400/115, 14 oz.	27.00
Plate, #1402, 11½", sandwich, hdld.	35.00	Tumbler, #3500, 2½ oz., ftd.	25.00
Plate, #3500/39, 12", ftd.	40.00	Tumbler, #3500, 3 oz., ftd.	18.00
Plate, #3500/67, 12"	40.00	Tumbler, #3500, 5 oz., ftd.	17.00
Plate, #3500/38, 13", torte	50.00	Tumbler, #3500, 10 oz., ftd.	20.00
Pitcher, 80 oz., Doulton, #3400/141	395.00	Tumbler, #3500, 12 oz., ftd.	25.00
Relish, #3500/68, 5½", 2 comp.	30.00	Tumbler, #3500, 13 oz., ftd.	25.00
Relish, #3500/69, 6½", 3 comp.	35.00	Tumbler, #3500, 16 oz., ftd.	30.00

Colors: blue, yellow, pink, green

Fostoria line numbers, which also apply to June and Fairfax listings, are cataloged for each piece of Versailles. All colors of Versailles are in demand and the increased prices indicate that the cadre of buyers is pushing up the price. Blue Versailles no longer stands at the top of the class since green has attracted hordes of new collectors especially on the West Coast. Perhaps those sun-blessed climes lend themselves to the cooling beauty of green. I bought some green cordials last fall and was quite surprised at the results when I ran them on an Internet auction. I used to avoid buying green Versailles, as it was difficult to sell. That is no longer true; I am having trouble keeping it.

All Fostoria soup and cereal bowls are quietly disappearing from the market. There is a cereal pictured in front in pink, you should know I have never found soups in any color of Versailles other than yellow.

Be sure to see page 87 for Fostoria stemware identification. Confusion reigns because stem heights are similar. Here, shapes and capacities are more important. Yellow Versailles is always found on stem line #5099 which has a cascading stem; all other Versailles is found on stem line #5098, which is illustrated, in both pictures.

	Pink Green	Blue	Yellow
Ashtray, #2350	30.00	35.00	25.00
Bottle, #2083, salad dressing, crystal glass top	600.00	950.00	500.00
Bottle, #2375, salad dressing, w/ sterling top or colored top	495.00	895.00	450.00
Bowl, #2375, baker, 9"	95.00	150.00	85.00
Bowl, #2375, bonbon	30.00	35.00	25.00
Bowl, #2375, bouillon, ftd.	25.00	40.00	25.00
Bowl, #2375, cream soup, ftd.	40.00	55.00	35.00
Bowl, #869/2283, finger, w/6" liner	50.00	85.00	50.00
Bowl, lemon	25.00	22.00	30.00
Bowl, 4½", mint, 3 ftd.	33.00	45.00	27.50
Bowl, #2375, fruit, 5"	30.00	45.00	30.00
Bowl, #2394, 3 ftd., 6"			40.00
Bowl, #2375, cereal, 6½"	55.00	85.00	45.00
Bowl, #2375, soup, 7"	110.00	160.00	90.00
Bowl, #2375, lg., dessert, 2 hdld.	100.00	135.00	90.00
Bowl, #2375, baker, 10"	95.00	135.00	85.00
Bowl, #2395, centerpiece, scroll, 10"	100.00	145.00	90.00
Bowl, #2375, centerpiece, flared top, 12"	85.00	110.00	75.00
Bowl, #2394, ftd., 12"	85.00	110.00	75.00
Bowl, #2375½, oval, centerpiece, 13"	65.00	135.00	
Candlestick, #2394, 2"	35.00	45.00	30.00
Candlestick, #2395½, 3"	40.00	60.00	35.00
Candlestick, #2395½, scroll, 5"	55.00	70.00	45.00
Candy, w/cover, #2331, 3 pt.	200.00	285.00	
Candy, w/cover, #2394, ¼ lb.			225.00
Candy, w/cover, #2394, ½ lb.			175.00
Celery, #2375, 11½"	85.00	125.00	75.00
Cheese & cracker, #2375 or #2368, set	85.00	135.00	85.00
Comport, #5098, 3"	35.00	50.00	30.00
Comport, #5099/2400, 6"	75.00	95.00	75.00
Comport, #2375, 7½"	50.00	95.00	
Comport, #2400, 8"	75.00	140.00	
Creamer, #2375½, ftd.	20.00	25.00	20.00
Creamer, #2375½, tea	45.00	75.00	45.00
Cup, #2375, after dinner	60.00	75.00	40.00
Cup, #2375½, ftd.	20.00	25.00	19.00
Decanter, #2439, 9"	1,200.00	2,000.00	895.00
Goblet, cordial, #5098 or #5099, ¾ oz., 4"	125.00	150.00	100.00
Goblet, #5098 or #5099, claret, 4 oz., 6"	110.00	165.00	100.00
Goblet, cocktail, #5098 or #5099, 3 oz., 5¼"	35.00	45.00	33.00
Goblet, water, #5098 or #5099, 10 oz., 8¼"	100.00	85.00	50.00
Goblet, wine, #5098 or #5099, 3 oz., 5½"	75.00	110.00	65.00
Grapefruit, #5082½	50.00	65.00	40.00

	Pink Green	Blue	Yellow
Grapefruit liner, #945½, etched	50.00	65.00	40.00
Ice bucket, #2375	90.00	125.00	80.00
Ice dish, #2451	45.00	65.00	40.00
Ice dish liner (tomato, crab, fruit), #2451	20.00	20.00	10.00
Mayonnaise, w/liner, #2375	70.00	85.00	60.00
Mayonnaise ladle	30.00	40.00	30.00
Oil, #2375, ftd.	395.00	595.00	350.00
Oyster cocktail, #5098 or #5099	30.00	40.00	28.00
Parfait, #5098 or #5099	70.00	95.00	55.00
Pitcher, #5000	450.00	595.00	395.00
Plate, #2375, bread/butter, 6"	9.00	12.00	8.00
Plate, #2375, canape, 6"	25.00	40.00	32.00
Plate, #2375, salad, 7½"	13.00	18.00	13.00
Plate, #2375, cream soup or mayo liner, 7½"	13.00	20.00	13.00
Plate, #2375, luncheon, 8¾"	15.00	25.00	15.00
Plate, #2375, sm., dinner, 9½"	40.00	50.00	35.00
Plate, #2375, cake, 2 hdld., 10"	50.00	65.00	40.00
Plate, #2375, dinner, 10¼"	100.00	120.00	75.00
Plate, #2375, chop, 13"	75.00	95.00	60.00
Platter, #2375, 12"	100.00	135.00	85.00
Platter, #2375, 15"	160.00	225.00	135.00
Relish, #2375, 8½"	33.00		38.00
Sauce boat, #2375	175.00	250.00	125.00
Sauce boat plate, #2375	35.00	60.00	25.00
Saucer, #2375, after dinner	10.00	25.00	10.00
Saucer, #2375	4.00	6.00	5.00
Shaker, #2375, pr., ftd.	125.00	175.00	110.00
Sherbet, #5098/5099, high, 6"	30.00	37.50	30.00
Sherbet, #5098/5099, low, 4¼"	25.00	32.50	25.00
Sugar, #2375½, ftd.	20.00	25.00	20.00
Sugar cover, #2375½	140.00	200.00	125.00
Sugar pail, #2378	200.00	295.00	165.00
Sugar, #2375½, tea	45.00	75.00	45.00
Sweetmeat, #2375	20.00	25.00	20.00
Tray, #2375, ctr. hdld., 11"	55.00	75.00	50.00
Tray, service & lemon	325.00	450.00	250.00
Tumbler, flat, old-fashioned (pink only)	125.00		
Tumbler, flat, tea (pink only)	135.00		
Tumbler, #5098 or #5099 2½ oz., ftd.	75.00	100.00	65.00
Tumbler, #5098 or #5099, 5 oz., ftd., 4½"	30.00	40.00	25.00
Tumbler, #5098 or #5099, 9 oz., ftd., 5¼"	35.00	45.00	30.00
Tumbler, #5098 or #5099 12 oz., ftd., 6"	45.00	65.00	40.00
Vase, #2417, 8"			225.00
Vase, #4100, 8"	250.00	350.00	
Vase, #2385, fan, ftd., 8½"	250.00	350.00	
Whipped cream bowl, #2375	30.00	35.00	25.00
Whipped cream pail, #2378	200.00	250.00	175.00

Note: See page 87 for stem identification.

Colors: amber, green; some Blue

Amber Vesper is the color most often found. Today, the popularity of amber wanes when compared to other colors. Obviously, from the abundance of amber glassware made in the late 1920s and 1930s, it was an exceedingly popular color then. There is little blue Vesper to be found on the market at a price collectors are willing to pay. The Fostoria name for the particular blue color of Vesper is simply Blue. Hardly original, I agree; but that does distinguish it from the lighter blue dubbed Azure by Fostoria. Hard to find, attractive, colored glassware often is priced out of the reach of the average collector. Blue Vesper has not reached that point yet, but it is rapidly rising in price. Green Vesper is more easily obtained than Blue, but has not attracted many collectors. That lack of collector appeal these 70 years later makes for more reasonable prices for green than for Blue or amber. Many amber Vesper items are easily found; others will take some patience and searching. There are some that confound their admirers. Difficult to acquire are the vanity set (combination perfume and powder jar), moulded and blown grapefruits, egg cup, butter dish, both styles of candy dishes, and the Maj Jongg (8¾" canapé) plate. It is the high sherbet that fits the ring on that plate. All of these have been pictured in earlier editions; but finding them, today, has also been a problem for me.

Vesper comes on stem line #5093 and tumbler line #5100. The shapes are slightly different from those Fostoria etches found on the Fairfax blank (page 87). Cordials, clarets, and parfaits are the most difficult stems to acquire while the footed, 12 ounce iced tea and 2 ounce footed bar are the most difficult tumblers.

Etched amber Fostoria patterns might possibly be the "sleepers" in this glass collecting field. I have seen gorgeous table settings made with amber glass with the appropriate accoutrements.

	Green	Amber	Blue
Ashtray, #2350, 4"	25.00	30.00	
Bowl, #2350, bouillon, ftd.	20.00	22.00	35.00
Bowl, #2350, cream soup, flat	25.00	30.00	
Bowl, #2350, cream soup, ftd.	22.00	25.00	35.00
Bowl, #2350, fruit, 5½"	12.00	18.00	30.00
Bowl, #2350, cereal, sq. or rnd., 6½"	30.00	35.00	50.00
Bowl, #2267, low, ftd., 7"	25.00	30.00	
Bowl, #2350, soup, shallow, 7¾"	30.00	45.00	55.00
Bowl, soup, deep, 8¼"		45.00	
Bowl, 8⅞"	32.00	40.00	
Bowl, #2350, baker, oval, 9"	65.00	75.00	100.00
Bowl, #2350, rd.	45.00	55.00	
Bowl, #2350, baker, oval, 10½"	75.00	90.00	145.00
Bowl, #2375, flared bowl, 10½"	50.00	55.00	
Bowl, #2350, ped., ftd., 10½"	55.00	65.00	
Bowl, #2329, console, rolled edge, 11"	37.50	40.00	
Bowl, #2375, 3 ftd., 12½"	50.00	55.00	125.00
Bowl, #2371, oval, 13"	55.00	60.00	
Bowl, #2329, rolled edge, 13"	50.00	55.00	
Bowl, #2329, rolled edge, 14"	55.00	60.00	
Butter dish, #2350	425.00	850.00	
Candlestick, #2324, 2"	22.00	28.00	
Candlestick, #2394, 3"	23.00	25.00	
Candlestick, #2324, 4"	24.00	25.00	50.00
Candlestick, #2394, 9"	85.00	100.00	100.00
Candy jar, w/cover, #2331, 3 pt.	135.00	125.00	295.00
Candy jar, w/cover, #2250, ftd., ½ lb.	295.00	250.00	
Celery, #2350	25.00	28.00	45.00
Cheese, #2368, ftd.	22.00	25.00	
Comport, 6"	26.00	30.00	50.00
Comport, #2327 (twisted stem), 7½"	35.00	40.00	75.00
Comport, 8"	55.00	60.00	85.00
Creamer, #2350½, ftd.	16.00	22.00	

	Green	Amber	Blue
Creamer, #2315½, fat, ftd.	20.00	25.00	35.00
Creamer, #2350½, flat		25.00	
Cup, #2350	15.00	16.00	40.00
Cup, #2350, after dinner	42.00	42.00	85.00
Cup, #2350½, ftd.	15.00	16.00	35.00
Egg cup, #2350		45.00	
Finger bowl and liner, #869/2283, 6"	32.00	35.00	65.00
Grapefruit, #5082½, blown	55.00	60.00	90.00
Grapefruit liner, #945½, blown	50.00	50.00	55.00
Grapefruit, #2315, molded	55.00	60.00	
Ice bucket, #2378	85.00	95.00	250.00
Oyster cocktail, #5100	25.00	30.00	40.00
Pickle, #2350	26.00	30.00	50.00
Pitcher, #5100, ftd.	335.00	395.00	595.00
Plate, #2350, bread/butter, 6"	7.00	8.00	12.00
Plate, #2350, salad, 7½"	10.00	12.00	18.00
Plate, #2350, luncheon, 8½"	14.00	18.00	25.00
Plate, #2321, Maj Jongg (canape), 8¾"		55.00	
Plate, #2350, sm., dinner, 9½"	25.00	30.00	40.00
Plate, dinner, 10½"	45.00	82.00	
Plate, #2287, ctr. hand., 11"	30.00	35.00	65.00
Plate, chop, 13¾"	40.00	45.00	85.00
Plate, #2350, server, 14"	55.00	65.00	110.00
Plate, w/indent for cheese, 11"	25.00	30.00	
Platter, #2350, 10½"	45.00	50.00	
Platter, #2350, 12"	65.00	75.00	150.00
Platter, #2350, 15",	110.00	125.00	225.00
Salt & pepper, #5100, pr.	75.00	90.00	
Sauce boat, w/liner, #2350	165.00	195.00	
Saucer, #2350, after dinner	12.00	12.00	25.00
Saucer, #2350	4.00	5.00	8.00
Stem, #5093, high sherbet	18.00	20.00	35.00
Stem, #5093, water goblet	28.00	32.00	55.00
Stem, #5093, low sherbet	16.00	18.00	30.00
Stem, #5093, parfait	40.00	45.00	70.00
Stem, #5093, cordial, ¾ oz.	70.00	75.00	150.00
Stem, #5093, wine, 2¾ oz.	37.50	40.00	65.00
Stem, #5093, cocktail, 3 oz.	28.00	30.00	50.00
Sugar, #2350½, flat		22.00	
Sugar, #2315, fat, ftd.	18.00	20.00	32.00
Sugar, #2350½, ftd.	14.00	16.00	
Sugar, lid	200.00	195.00	
Tumbler, #5100, ftd., 2 oz.	35.00	45.00	70.00
Tumbler, #5100, ftd., 5 oz.	18.00	22.00	45.00
Tumbler, #5100, ftd., 9 oz.	18.00	22.00	50.00
Tumbler, #5100, ftd., 12 oz.	30.00	40.00	65.00
Urn, #2324, small	100.00	110.00	
Urn, large	115.00	135.00	
Vase, #2292, 8"	100.00	110.00	210.00
Vanity set, combination cologne/ powder & stopper	265.00	310.00	425.00

Note: See stemware identification on page 87.

Colors: crystal, Sahara, Cobalt, rare in pale Zircon

Victorian has surfaced for sale more in the last few years than I have ever seen. At a show I attended there was a large set displayed for sale. All the rarely found items sold early. The rest of the set did not sell well, because I believe, it was offered above market price. Rare pieces sold to avid collectors who needed them and price be hanged. It may take some time to find a collector willing to pay wild prices on commonly found items. Notice the two tumblers used as a pattern shot. The taller one is Victorian while the similar one is Duncan's Block. Block is an older ware often confused with Victorian and you can understand why. Most Victorian pieces are marked with the Heisey H inside a diamond.

Heisey Victorian was only made in the colors listed. If you find pink, green, or amber Victorian in your travels, then you have Imperial's legacy to the pattern made in 1964 and 1965. These colors are usually also marked with the H in diamond trademark; they were made from Heisey moulds after Heisey was no longer in business. I just saw a set of amber offered rather reasonably last weekend. A sign proclaimed rare Heisey amber and only $4.00 each. Rare and $4.00 do not seem to belong in the same sentence. Amber Victorian is striking, but know that it is Imperial and not Heisey; and, right now collectors of older Heisey tend to spurn Imperial made wares.

Imperial also made about ten pieces in crystal but there is no magic way to separate that which Heisey made from Imperial. They are not as ignored by Heisey collectors as are the colored Victorian pieces. I rather believe that point of view may be erroneous, particularly since Imperial is now no longer in business. In the grand scheme of things, future collectors may someday covet those colored wares.

	Crystal
Bottle, 3 oz., oil	65.00
Bottle, 27 oz., rye	180.00
Bottle, French dressing	80.00
Bowl, 10½", floral	50.00
Bowl, finger	25.00
Bowl, punch	250.00
Bowl, rose	90.00
Bowl, triplex, w/flared or cupped rim	125.00
Butter dish, ¼ lb.	70.00
Candlestick, 2-lite	110.00
Cigarette box, 4"	80.00
Cigarette box, 6"	100.00
Cigarette holder & ashtray, ind.	30.00
Comport, 5"	60.00
Comport, 6", 3 ball stem	140.00
Compote, cheese (for center sandwich)	40.00
Creamer	30.00
Cup, punch, 5 oz.	10.00
Decanter and stopper, 32 oz.	70.00
Jug, 54 oz.	400.00
Nappy, 8"	40.00
Plate, 6", liner for finger bowl	10.00
Plate, 7"	20.00
Plate, 8"	35.00
Plate, 12", cracker	75.00
Plate, 13", sandwich	90.00

	Crystal
Plate, 21", buffet or punch bowl liner	200.00
Relish, 11", 3 pt.	50.00
Salt & pepper	65.00
Stem, 2½ oz., wine	30.00
Stem, 3 oz., claret	28.00
Stem, 5 oz., oyster cocktail	22.00
Stem, 5 oz., saucer champagne	20.00
Stem, 5 oz., sherbet	18.00
Stem, 9 oz., goblet (one ball)	26.00
Stem, 9 oz., high goblet (two ball)	30.00
Sugar	30.00
Tray, 12", celery	40.00
Tray, condiment (s/p & mustard)	150.00
Tumbler, 2 oz., bar	40.00
Tumbler, 5 oz., soda (straight or curved edge)	25.00
Tumbler, 8 oz., old fashion	35.00
Tumbler, 10 oz., w/rim foot	40.00
Tumbler, 12 oz., ftd. soda	30.00
Tumbler, 12 oz., soda (straight or curved edge)	28.00
Vase, 4"	50.00
Vase, 5½"	60.00
Vase, 6", ftd.	100.00
Vase, 9", ftd., w/flared rim	140.00

Colors: crystal; rare in amber

Waverly #1519 mould blank is better known for the Orchid and Rose etchings appearing on it than for itself, though it's a wonderful, graceful blank!

	Crystal
Bowl, 6", oval, lemon, w/cover	45.00
Bowl, 6½", 2 hdld., ice	60.00
Bowl, 7", 3 part, relish, oblong	30.00
Bowl, 7", salad	20.00
Bowl, 9", 4 part, relish, round	25.00
Bowl, 9", fruit	30.00
Bowl, 9", vegetable	35.00
Bowl, 10", crimped edge	25.00
Bowl, 10", gardenia	20.00
Bowl, 11", seahorse foot, floral	70.00
Bowl, 12", crimped edge	35.00
Bowl, 13", gardenia	30.00
Box, 5", chocolate, w/cover	80.00
Box, 5" tall, ftd., w/cover, seahorse hdl.	90.00
Box, 6", candy, w/bow tie knob	45.00
Box, trinket, lion cover (rare)	600.00
Butter dish, w/cover, 6", square	65.00
Candleholder, 1-lite, block (rare)	100.00
Candleholder, 2-lite	40.00
Candleholder, 2-lite, "flame" center	65.00
Candleholder, 3-lite	70.00
Candle epergnette, 5"	15.00
Candle epergnette, 6", deep	20.00
Candle epergnette, 6½"	15.00
Cheese dish, 5½", ftd.	20.00
Cigarette holder	60.00
Comport, 6", low ftd.	20.00

Comport, 6½", jelly	35.00
Comport, 7", low ftd., oval	50.00
Creamer, ftd.	25.00
Creamer & sugar, individual, w/tray	50.00
Cruet, 3 oz., w/#122 stopper	75.00
Cup	14.00
Honey dish, 6½", ftd.	50.00
Mayonnaise, w/liner & ladle, 5½"	50.00
Plate, 7", salad	9.00
Plate, 8", luncheon	10.00
Plate, 10½", dinner	50.00
Plate, 11", sandwich	20.00
Plate, 13½", ftd., cake salver	70.00
Plate, 14", center handle, sandwich	65.00
Plate, 14", sandwich	35.00
Salt & pepper, pr.	60.00
Saucer	4.00
Stem, #5019, 1 oz., cordial	60.00
Stem, #5019, 3 oz., wine, blown	20.00
Stem, #5019, 3½ oz., cocktail	15.00
Stem, #5019, 5½ oz., sherbet/champagne	9.00
Stem, #5019, 10 oz., blown	20.00
Sugar, ftd.	25.00
Tray, 12", celery	20.00
Tumbler, #5019, 5 oz., ftd., juice, blown	20.00
Tumbler, #5019, 13 oz., ftd., tea, blown	22.00
Vase, 3½", violet	60.00
Vase, 7", ftd.	35.00
Vase, 7", ftd., fan shape	45.00

Colors: amber, crystal, Ebony w/gold, Emerald green

Wildflower can be found etched on numerous Cambridge blanks, but mostly on #3121 stems. I have attempted to price a sample portion of the pattern, but (as with other Cambridge patterns shown in this book) there is a never-ending list. You can rationalize that, like Rose Point, almost any Cambridge blank may have been used to etch Wildflower. I have given you the rudiments. Price gold encrusted, crystal items up to 25% higher. Price colored items about 50% higher except for Ebony, gold encrusted which bring double or triple the prices listed. A majority of collectors are searching for crystal because that can be found. Wildflower may not be as popular as Rose Point, but it is steadily gaining on Rose Point.

	Crystal		Crystal
Basket, #3400/1182, 2 hdld., ftd., 6"	35.00	Plate, crescent salad	185.00
Bowl, #3400/1180, bonbon, 2 hdld., 5¼"	32.50	Plate, #3900/20, bread/butter, 6½"	14.00
Bowl, bonbon, 2 hdld., ftd., 6"	35.00	Plate, #3400/176, 7½"	10.00
Bowl, #3400/90, 2 pt., relish, 6"	30.00	Plate, #3900/161, 2 hdld., ftd., 8"	20.00
Bowl, #3500/61, 3 pt., relish, 6½"	50.00	Plate, #3900/22, salad, 8"	20.00
Bowl, #3900/123, relish, 7"	35.00	Plate, #3400/62, 8½"	18.00
Bowl, #3900/130, bonbon, 2 hdld., 7"	35.00	Plate, #3900/24, dinner, 10½"	95.00
Bowl, #3900/124, 2 pt., relish, 7"	35.00	Plate, #3900/26, service, 4 ftd., 12"	60.00
Bowl, #3400/91, 3 pt., relish, 3 hdld., 8"	37.50	Plate, #3900/35, cake, 2 hdld., 13½"	85.00
Bowl, #3900/125, 3 pt., celery & relish, 9"	40.00	Plate, #3900/167, torte, 14"	65.00
Bowl, #477, pickle (corn), ftd., 9½"	32.50	Plate, #3900/65, torte, 14"	65.00
Bowl, #3900/54, 4 ft., flared, 10"	55.00	Salt & pepper, #3400/77, pr.	50.00
Bowl, #3900/34, 2 hdld., 11"	67.50	Salt & pepper, #3900/1177	45.00
Bowl, #3900/28, w/tab hand., ftd., 11½"	72.50	Saucer, #3900/17 or #3400/54	3.50
Bowl, #3900/126, 3 pt., celery & relish, 12"	55.00	Set: 2 pc. Mayonnaise, #3900/19	
Bowl, #3400/4, 4 ft., flared, 12"	70.00	(ftd. sherbet w/ladle)	55.00
Bowl, #3400/1240, 4 ft., oval, "ears" hdld., 12"	85.00	Set: 3 pc. Mayonnaise, #3900/129 (bowl, liner, ladle)	60.00
Bowl, #3900/120, 5 pt., celery & relish, 12"	55.00	Set: 4 pc. Mayonnaise, #3900/111 (div. bowl, liner, 2 ladles)	62.00
Butter dish, #3900/52, ¼ lb.	225.00	Stem, #3121, cordial, 1 oz.	70.00
Butter dish, #3400/52, 5"	150.00	Stem, #3121, cocktail, 3 oz.	30.00
Candlestick, #3400/638, 3-lite, ea.	70.00	Stem, #3121, wine, 3½ oz.	55.00
Candlestick, #3400/646, 5"	45.00	Stem, #3121, claret, 4½ oz.	65.00
Candlestick, #3400/647, 2-lite, "fleur-de-lis," 6"	47.50	Stem, #3121, 4½ oz., low oyster cocktail	18.00
Candy box, w/cover, #3400/9, 4 ftd.	125.00	Stem, #3121, 5 oz., low parfait	45.00
Candy box, w/cover, #3900/165, rnd.	110.00	Stem, #3121, 6 oz., low sherbet	22.00
Cocktail icer, #968, 2 pc.	75.00	Stem, #3121, 6 oz., tall sherbet	32.50
Cocktail shaker, #3400/175	150.00	Stem, #3121, 10 oz., water	37.50
Comport, #3900/136, 5½"	50.00	Sugar, 3900/41	20.00
Comport, #3121, blown, 5⅜"	65.00	Sugar, indiv., 3900/40	25.00
Creamer, #3900/41	22.00	Tray, creamer & sugar, 3900/37	15.00
Creamer, #3900/40, individual	25.00	Tumbler, #3121, 5 oz., juice	30.00
Cup, #3900/17 or #3400/54	22.00	Tumbler, #3121, 10 oz., water	30.00
Hat, #1704, 5"	295.00	Tumbler, #3121, 12 oz., tea	37.50
Hat, #1703, 6"	395.00	Tumbler, #3900/115, 13 oz.	40.00
Hurricane lamp, #1617, candlestick base	225.00	Vase, #3400/102, globe, 5"	60.00
Hurricane lamp, #1603, keyhole base & prisms	225.00	Vase, #6004, flower, ftd., 6"	60.00
Ice bucket, w/chrome hand, #3900/671	135.00	Vase, #6004, flower, ftd., 8"	70.00
Oil, w/stopper, #3900/100, 6 oz.	125.00	Vase, #1237, keyhole ft., 9"	110.00
Pitcher, ball, #3400/38, 80 oz.	235.00	Vase, #1528, bud, 10"	110.00
Pitcher, #3900/115, 76 oz.	195.00	Vase, #278, flower, ftd., 11"	120.00
Pitcher, Doulton, #3400/141	350.00	Vase, #1299, ped. ft., 11"	150.00
		Vase, #1238, keyhole ft., 12"	125.00
		Vase, #279, ftd., flower, 13"	225.00

Note: See pages 236 – 237 for stem identification.

YEOMAN, Blank #1184, A.H. Heisey & Co., c. 1915

Colors: crystal, Flamingo pink, Sahara yellow, Moongleam green, Hawthorne orchid/pink, Marigold deep, amber/yellow; some cobalt, and Alexandrite

Hawthorne Yeoman is pictured on page 233. That color is the most sought in this pattern. Etched designs on Yeoman blank #1184 will bring 10% to 25% more than the prices listed below. Empress etch is the most commonly found pattern on Yeoman blanks and the most collectible. You will find many pieces with silver decorations, but these were not done at the Heisey factory. Yeoman has some very desirable pieces for item collectors such as cologne bottles, oil bottles, and sugar shakers. Most Yeoman pieces are marked with the familiar H in a diamond. One of the primary reasons this pattern is so collectible is due to the colors in which it was made. This is another pattern where you may discover Marigold items.

	Crystal	Flamingo	Sahara	Moongleam	Hawthorne	Marigold
Ashtray, 4", hdld. (bow tie)	10.00	20.00	22.00	25.00	30.00	35.00
Bowl, 2 hdld., cream soup	12.00	20.00	25.00	30.00	35.00	40.00
Bowl, finger	5.00	11.00	17.00	20.00	27.50	30.00
Bowl, ftd., banana split	7.00	23.00	30.00	35.00	40.00	45.00
Bowl, ftd., 2 hdld., bouillon	10.00	20.00	25.00	30.00	35.00	40.00
Bowl, 4½", nappy	4.00	7.50	10.00	12.50	15.00	17.00
Bowl, 5", low, ftd., jelly	12.00	20.00	25.00	27.00	30.00	40.00
Bowl, 5", oval, lemon and cover	30.00	60.00	65.00	75.00	90.00	90.00
Bowl, 5", rnd., lemon and cover	30.00	60.00	65.00	75.00	90.00	90.00
Bowl, 5", rnd., lemon, w/cover	15.00	20.00	25.00	30.00	40.00	50.00
Bowl, 6", oval, preserve	7.00	12.00	17.00	22.00	27.00	30.00
Bowl, 6", vegetable	5.00	10.00	14.00	16.00	20.00	24.00
Bowl, 6½", hdld., bonbon	5.00	10.00	14.00	16.00	20.00	24.00
Bowl, 8", rect., pickle/olive	12.00	15.00	20.00	25.00	30.00	35.00
Bowl, 8½", berry, 2 hdld.	14.00	22.00	25.00	30.00	35.00	50.00
Bowl, 9", 2 hdld., veg., w/cover	35.00	60.00	60.00	70.00	95.00	175.00
Bowl, 9", oval, fruit	20.00	25.00	35.00	45.00	55.00	55.00
Bowl, 9", baker	20.00	25.00	35.00	45.00	55.00	55.00
Bowl, 12", low, floral	15.00	25.00	35.00	45.00	60.00	55.00
Candle vase, single, w/short prisms & inserts	90.00			150.00		
Cigarette box (ashtray)	25.00	60.00	65.00	70.00	80.00	100.00
Cologne bottle, w/stopper	100.00	160.00	160.00	160.00	170.00	180.00
Comport, 5", high ftd., shallow	15.00	25.00	37.00	45.00	55.00	70.00
Comport, 6", low ftd., deep	20.00	30.00	34.00	40.00	42.00	48.00
Creamer	10.00	25.00	20.00	22.00	50.00	28.00
Cruet, 2 oz., oil	20.00	70.00	80.00	85.00	90.00	85.00
Cruet, 4 oz., oil	30.00	70.00	80.00	85.00		
Cup	5.00	20.00	20.00	25.00	50.00	
Cup, after dinner	20.00	40.00	40.00	45.00	50.00	60.00
Egg cup	20.00	35.00	40.00	45.00	60.00	60.00
Grapefruit, ftd.	10.00	17.00	24.00	31.00	38.00	45.00
Gravy (or dressing) boat, w/underliner	13.00	25.00	30.00	45.00	50.00	45.00
Marmalade jar, w/cover	25.00	35.00	40.00	45.00	55.00	65.00
Parfait, 5 oz.	10.00	15.00	20.00	25.00	30.00	35.00
Pitcher, quart	70.00	130.00	130.00	140.00	160.00	180.00
Plate, 2 hdld., cheese	5.00	10.00	13.00	15.00	17.00	25.00
Plate, cream soup underliner	5.00	7.00	9.00	12.00	14.00	16.00
Plate, finger bowl underliner	3.00	5.00	7.00	9.00	11.00	13.00
Plate, 4½", coaster	3.00	5.00	10.00	12.00		
Plate, 6"	3.00	6.00	8.00	10.00	13.00	15.00
Plate, 6", bouillon underliner	3.00	6.00	8.00	10.00	13.00	15.00

	Crystal	Flamingo	Sahara	Moongleam	Hawthorne	Marigold
Plate, 6½", grapefruit bowl	7.00	12.00	15.00	19.00	27.00	32.00
Plate, 7"	5.00	8.00	10.00	14.00	17.00	22.00
Plate, 8", oyster cocktail	9.00					
Plate, 8", soup	9.00					
Plate, 9", oyster cocktail	10.00					
Plate, 10½"	20.00	50.00		50.00	60.00	
Plate, 10½", ctr. hdld., oval, div.	15.00	26.00		32.00		
Plate, 11", 4 pt., relish	20.00	27.00		32.00		
Plate, 14"	20.00					
Platter, 12", oval	10.00	17.00	19.00	26.00	33.00	
Salt, ind. tub (cobalt: $30.00)	10.00	20.00		30.00		
Salver, 10", low ftd.	15.00	50.00		70.00		
Salver, 12", low ftd.	10.00	50.00		70.00		
Saucer	3.00	5.00	7.00	7.00	10.00	10.00
Saucer, after dinner	3.00	5.00	7.00	8.00	10.00	10.00
Stem, 2¾ oz., ftd., oyster cocktail	4.00	8.00	10.00	12.00	14.00	
Stem, 3 oz., cocktail	10.00	12.00	17.00	20.00		
Stem, 3½ oz., sherbet	5.00	8.00	11.00	12.00		
Stem, 4 oz., fruit cocktail	3.00	10.00	10.00	12.00		
Stem, 4½ oz., sherbet	3.00	10.00	10.00	12.00		
Stem, 5 oz., soda	9.00	8.00	30.00	20.00		
Stem, 5 oz., sherbet	5.00	5.00	7.00	9.00		
Stem, 6 oz., champagne	6.00	16.00	18.00	22.00		
Stem, 8 oz.	5.00	12.00	18.00	20.00		
Stem, 10 oz., goblet	10.00	15.00	45.00	25.00		
Sugar, w/cover	15.00	45.00	45.00	50.00	70.00	40.00
Sugar shaker, ftd.	50.00	95.00		110.00		
Syrup, 7 oz., saucer ftd.	30.00	75.00				
Tray, 7" x 10", rect.	26.00	30.00	40.00	35.00		
Tray, 9", celery	10.00	14.00	16.00	15.00		
Tray, 11", ctr. hand., 3 pt.	15.00	35.00	40.00			
Tray, 12", oblong	16.00	60.00	65.00			
Tray, 13", 3 pt., relish	20.00	27.00	32.00			
Tray, 13", celery	20.00	27.00	32.00			
Tray, 13", hors d'oeuvre, w/cov. ctr.	32.00	42.00	52.00	75.00		
Tray insert, 3½" x 4½"	4.00	6.00	7.00	8.00		
Tumbler, 2½ oz., whiskey	3.00	20.00	25.00	40.00		
Tumbler, 4½ oz., soda	4.00	6.00	10.00	15.00		
Tumbler, 8 oz.	4.00	15.00	20.00	20.00		
Tumbler, 10 oz., cupped rim	4.00	15.00	20.00	22.50		
Tumbler, 10 oz., straight side	5.00	15.00	20.00	22.50		
Tumbler, 12 oz., tea	5.00	20.00	25.00	30.00		
Tumbler cover (unusual)	35.00					

Diane
1066
11 oz. Goblet

Tally Ho
1402
Brandy Inhaler (Tall)

Appleblossom
3025
10 oz. Goblet

Gloria
3035
3 oz. Cocktail

Cleo
3077
6 oz. Tall Sherbet

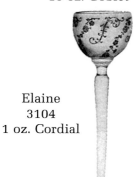

Elaine
3104
1 oz. Cordial

Diane
3106
9 oz. Goblet Tall Bowl

Cleo
3115
3½ oz. Cocktail

Gloria
3120
6 oz. Tall Sherbet

Wildflower
3121
10 oz. Goblet

Diane
3122
9 oz. Goblet

Portia
3124
3 oz. Wine

Portia
3126
11 oz. Tall Sherbet

Apple Blossom
3130
6 oz. Tall Sherbet

Gloria
3135
6 oz. Tall Sherbet

Apple Blossom
3400
11 oz. Lunch Goblet

Elaine
3500
10 oz. Goblet

Chantilly
3600
2½ oz. Wine

Chantilly
3775
4½ oz. Claret

Chantilly
3625
4½ oz. Claret

Chantilly
3779
1 oz. Cordial

OTHER BOOKS BY GENE FLORENCE

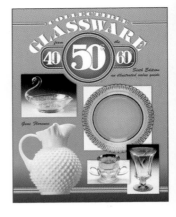

Collectible
GLASSWARE from the 40s, 50s & 60s, 6th Edition
Covering collectible glassware made after the Depression era, this is the only book available that deals exclusively with the mass-produced and handmade glassware from this period. It is completely updated, featuring many original company catalog pages and 14 new patterns — making a total of 102 patterns from Anniversary to Yorktown, with many of the most popular Fire-King patterns in between. Each pattern is alphabetically listed, all known pieces in each pattern are described and priced, and gorgeous color photographs showcase both common and very rare pieces. 2002 values.

Item #5897 • ISBN: 1-57432-236-2 • 8½ x 11 • 240 Pgs. • HB • $19.95

Collector's Encyclopedia of
DEPRESSION GLASS, 15th Edition
Since the first edition of *Collector's Encyclopedia of Depression Glass* was released in 1972, it has been America's #1 bestselling glass book. Glassware authority Gene Florence now presents this completely revised 15th edition, with the previous 116 popular patterns and 17 additional patterns, to make this the most complete reference to date. With the assistance of several nationally known dealers, this book illustrates and prices items in demand. Dealing primarily with the glass made from the 1920s through the end of the 1930s, this beautiful reference book contains stunning color photographs, vintage catalog pages, updated values, and a special section on reissues and fakes. 2002 values.

Item #5907 • ISBN: 1-57432-246-X • 8½ x 11
256 Pgs. • HB • $19.95

Anchor Hocking's
FIRE-KING & More, 2nd Edition
From the 1930s to the 1960s Anchor Hocking Glass Corp. of Lancaster, Ohio, produced an extensive line of glassware called Fire-King. Their lines included not only dinnerware but also a plethora of glass kitchen items — reamers, measuring cups, mixing bowls, mugs, and more. This is the essential collectors' reference to this massive line of glassware. Loaded with hundreds of new full-color photos, vintage catalog pages, company materials, facts, information, and values, this book has everything collectors expect from Gene Florence. 2002 values.

Item #5602 • ISBN: 1-57432-164-1 • 8½ x 11
224 Pgs. • HB • $24.95

Glass
CANDLESTICKS of the Depression Era
Florence has compiled this book to help identify the candlestick patterns made during the Depression era. More than 500 different candlesticks are shown in full-color photographs. Many famous glassmakers are represented, such as Heisey, Cambridge, Fostoria, and Tiffin. The descriptive text for each candleholder includes pattern, maker, color, height, and current collector value. 2000 values.

Item #5354 • ISBN: 1-57432-136-6 • 8½ x 11 • 176 Pgs. • HB • $24.95

KITCHEN GLASSWARE of the Depression Years, 6th Edition
This exciting new edition of our bestselling *Kitchen Glassware of the Depression Years* is undeniably the definitive reference on the subject. Many new photographs and new discoveries and information make this book indispensable to all glass collectors and dealers. More than 5,000 items are showcased in beautiful professional color photographs with descriptions and values. Many new finds and exceptionally rare pieces have been added. The highly collectible glass from the Depression era through the 1960s fills its pages, in addition to the ever-popular Fire-King and Pyrex glassware. This comprehensive encyclopedia provides an easy-to-use format, showing items by color, shapes, or patterns. The collector will enjoy the pages of glass, from colorful juice reamers, shakers, rare and unusual glass knives, to the mixing bowls and baking dishes we still find in our kitchen cupboards. 2001 values.

Item #5827 • ISBN: 1-57432-220-6 • 8½ x 11 • 272 Pgs. • HB • $24.95

Florence's Glassware
PATTERN IDENTIFICATION Guide

Florence's Glassware Pattern Identification Guides are great companions for his other glassware books. Volume I includes every pattern featured in his *Collector's Encyclopedia of Depression Glass, Collectible Glassware from the 40s, 50s, and 60s,* and *Collector's Encyclopedia of Elegant Glassware,* as well as many more — nearly 400 patterns in all. Volume II holds nearly 500 patterns, with no repeats from Volume I. Volume III contains nearly 500 patterns as well, with no repeats from the first two books. Carefully planned close-up photographs of representative pieces for every pattern show great detail to make identification easy. With every pattern, Florence provides the names, the companies which made the glass, dates of production, and even colors available. These guides are ideal references for novice and seasoned glass collectors and dealers, and great resources for years to come. No values.

> Vol. I • Item #5042 • ISBN: 1-57432-045-9 • 8½ x 11 • 176 Pgs. • PB • $18.95
> Vol. II • Item #5615 • ISBN: 1-57432-177-3 • 8½ x 11 • 208 Pgs. • PB • $19.95
> Vol. III • Item #6142 • ISBN: 1-57432-315-6 • 8½ x 11 • 224 Pgs. • PB • $19.95

Pocket Guide to
DEPRESSION GLASS & More, 13th Ed.

Gene Florence has completely revised his *Pocket Guide to Depression Glass.* Our new thirteenth edition is released at the great, low retail price of $12.95. This popular guide has been completely revised with over 4,000 values updated to reflect the ever-changing market. Many of the photographs have been reshot to improve the quality and add new finds. There are a total of 119 new photos for this edition, including 29 additional patterns that have not appeared in previous editions. These gorgeous photographs show great detail, and the listings of the patterns and their available pieces make identification simple. There is even a section on re-issues and the numerous fakes flooding the market. Many collectors have referred to this book as much more than just a "pocket guide," it's the perfect book to take with you on your searches through shops and flea markets. This is the ideal companion to Florence's comprehensive *Collector's Encyclopedia of Depression Glass.*

> Item #6136 • ISBN: 1-57432-309-1 • 5½ x 8½ • 224 Pgs. • PB • $12.95

VERY RARE GLASSWARE of the Depression Years

These popular books by Gene Florence will help the collector spot those rare and valuable pieces of Depression glass that may come around once in a lifetime. Florence is America's leading glassware authority, and these books are considered required reading. They are jam-packed with full-color photos and information featuring rare examples of Depression items, as well as elegant and kitchen items. There are absolutely no repeats in any of the books. All are "musts" for anyone interested in Depression glass — they are necessary tools to help spot those very rare pieces and let you know what they are actually worth.

> Third Series • Item #3326 • ISBN: 0-89145-510-8
> 8½ x 11 • 144 Pgs. • HB • 1995 values • $24.95
> Fifth Series • Item #4732 • ISBN: 0-89145-739-9
> 8½ x 11 • 192 Pgs. • HB • 1997 values • $24.95
> Sixth Series • Item #5170 • ISBN: 1-57432-095-5
> 8½ x 11 • 176 Pgs. • HB • 1999 values • $24.95

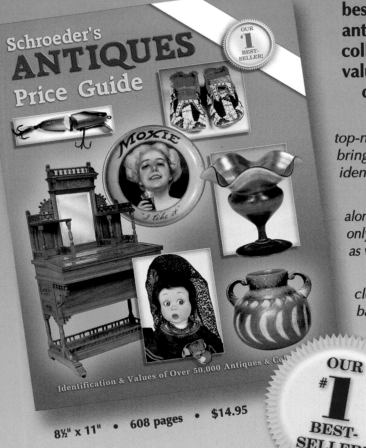